The Promise of Trinitarian Theology

The Promise of Trinitarian Theology

Theologians in Dialogue with T. F. Torrance

EDITED BY
ELMER M. COLYER

ROWMAN & LITTLEFIELD PUBLISHERS, INC.
Lanham • Boulder • New York • Oxford

ROWMAN & LITTLEFIELD PUBLISHERS, INC.

Published in the United States of America
by Rowman & Littlefield Publishers, Inc.
4720 Boston Way, Lanham, Maryland 20706
www.rowmanlittlefield.com

12 Hid's Copse Road
Cumnor Hill, Oxford OX2 9JJ, England

British Library Cataloguing in Publication Information Available

Library of Congress Cataloging-in-Publication Data

The promise of Trinitarian theology : theologians in dialogue with T.F. Torrance / [edited by] Elmer M. Colyer.
p. cm.
Includes bibliographical references and index.
ISBN 0-7425-1293-2 (alk. paper) — ISBN 0-7425-1294-0 (pbk. : alk. paper)
1. Torrance, Thomas Forsyth, 1913– 2. Theology, Doctrinal—History—20th century. 3. Trinity—History of doctrines—20th century. 4. Religion and science—History—20th century. I. Colyer, Elmer M., 1956–

BX4827.T67 P76 2001
230'.044'092—dc21

2001019881

Printed in the United States of America

™ The paper used in this publication meets the minimum requirements of American National Standard for Information Sciences—Permanence of Paper for Printed Library Materials, ANSI/NISO Z39.48-1992.

Dedicated to Thomas F. Torrance,
minister, churchman, and theologian

Contents

Preface

Thomas F. Torrance is widely acclaimed as one of the premier theologians of the twentieth century. One of the leading theologians in the dialogue between theology and philosophy of science, he was awarded the Templeton Foundation Prize for Progress in Religion in 1978. Torrance's important book *Theological Science* received the first "Collins Award" in Britain for the best work in theology, ethics, and sociology relevant to Christianity for 1967-1969. Torrance started the *Scottish Journal of Theology,* which he edited for over thirty years, founded the *Scottish Church Theology Society*, and served as moderator of the General Assembly of the Church of Scotland in 1976-1977.

In 1950 he became professor of church history at New College, the University of Edinburgh, and then two years later moved to the chair of Christian Dogmatics, which he held until his retirement in 1979. Torrance has written over thirty books and several hundred articles.

This monograph is a concerted effort on the part of a team of theologians to further conversation about the theology of T. F. Torrance. The chapters of this volume analyze and evaluate Torrance's career and theological oeuvre. The book is also designed to honor Tom Torrance and his immense contribution to the development of Trinitarian and scientific theology. The chapters were written during the year 2000, the fiftieth anniversary year of Torrance's appointment as a professor at New College.

The chapters that comprise this volume are written by noted theologians from North America and Europe. Some of the authors are former students of Torrance. All have worked extensively with his theology. One of the unique facets of the book is that Torrance contributes a chapter of his own in which he responds to all the other chapters.

The first chapter, written by Torrance's brother David, summarizes Tom's life and career. The second by Alasdair Heron locates Torrance within the Reformed tradition and assesses his contribution to that tradition. The rest of the chapters analyze pivotal themes in Torrance's theology and enter into critical dialogue with Torrance.

Chapters 3, 4, and 5 deal with the core content of Torrance's theology: his Christology, pneumatology, and doctrine of God. Andrew Purves's essay on Christology offers a comprehensive overview of this theme in Torrance's work. The chapter by Gary Deddo is virtually the only thing that has been published on Torrance's doctrine of the Spirit. Finally, Colin Gunton, a major British theologian who has written extensively on the doctrine of the Trinity, provides a significant analysis and evaluation of Torrance's views on the Trinity.

Chapters 6 and 7 discuss, respectively, Torrance's *theology of the sacraments* and Torrance as a *practical theologian.* George Hunsinger maintains that Torrance's work on the sacraments is arguably the most significant development in this area of theology within the Reformed tradition since John Calvin. Ray Anderson sees and develops what many students and readers miss: the intensely practical and pastoral dimension interwoven in all of Torrance's theology, despite its difficult and technical texture.

The final four chapters address the areas of Torrance's work for which he has become most well known: theological method and the dialogue between theology and natural science. Torrance's view of revelation and scripture is the subject of chapter 8 (by Kurt Richardson). Chapter 9 provides a comprehensive overview of Torrance's *scientific theological method* by locating his position within a narrative on modern epistemology from Descartes through Hume and Kant to Einstein and Michael Polanyi.

Chris Kaiser, a scientist and theologian himself, writes on Torrance's relationship to Albert Einstein. The chapter by Mark Achtemeier (chapter 11) outlines the contours of Torrance's vision for a positive and mutually beneficial relationship between Christian faith and natural science.

All of these chapters evaluate, as well as analyze, Torrance's contributions on the topics covered. This critical dimension is designed to help create a dialogue with Professor Torrance concerning his theology. Torrance enters the dialogue personally in the final chapter, responding to the chapters by his former students, colleagues, and friends.

Establishing a dialogue with Torrance about his theology seems a fitting way to honor this outstanding theologian by seriously engaging his thought and encouraging others to do the same as well. Yet because these essays are about one of the most important theologians living today, the book is much more than a tribute to Tom Torrance and his work. The volume serves multiple ends.

The book provides an introduction to Torrance and his theology and serves as a handbook for those researching his work. The selected bibliography, the bibliographic material in the notes, and the biographical chapter guide readers into Torrance's career, publications, and important secondary literature. Together the chapters constitute a comprehensive analysis and evaluation of Torrance's theology. Finally the book is itself theology in the best sense, for here some of the important theologians writing today engage in a comprehensive dialogue with one of the most important theologians of the past century.

This monograph on Torrance's thought can be used in multiple contexts. It can be a textbook in courses on Torrance's theology or a guide for research on his work. The book can stand alone as an introduction to Torrance's thought. It will be of interest to scientists and theologians concerned with the dialogue between theology and natural science. Historians or historical theologians concerned with Scottish, ecumenical, or Reformed theology in the twentieth century will also find the book useful as will scholars examining the appropriation of Karl Barth's theology in the English-speaking world.

I want to thank the contributors for their excellent chapters on Torrance's work and Rowman & Littlefield Publishers for their support in publishing the book. Everyone's cooperation has made my editorial duties a pleasure. I also wish to thank the Association of Theological Schools, Daniel O. Aleshire, executive director, and Lilly Endowments, Inc. for the Lilly Small Grant that I received in 2000-2001 which enabled me to devote the entire summer of 2000 to this writing project.

I also express my appreciation for the work of my most recent research assistant, Greg Schrimpf, a scholar in his own right, who gracefully completed the many mundane tasks associated with moving a volume to publication. I am grateful for the contributions of Luann LeConte, my secretary, and of James Dauer and Realff Ottesen, research assistants who participated in the project at an earlier stage. Most of all, I want to thank Tom Torrance. The book is dedicated to him in gratitude for his contributions which have enriched my life as a Christian, a pastor, and a theologian, and the lives of so many others as well.

Chapter 1

Thomas Forsyth Torrance:

Minister of the Gospel, Pastor, and Evangelical Theologian

by David W. Torrance

In August 1999, Professor Alister McGrath of Oxford University published his book, *T. F. Torrance, an Intellectual Biography*. When the invitation was extended to me to write a biography of my brother, I foresaw that my biography of Tom would be somewhat different and more personal than that of McGrath's. I have always enjoyed a warm affectionate relationship with Tom and wish to focus attention on some of the influences which have helped to shape his character, his Christian faith, and his missionary zeal as a minister of the Gospel. I will say something about his theological development and work and something about the opposition to his theological position, which has sometimes arisen. I gladly acknowledge my debt to McGrath.

Family Background

Tom was born on 30 August 1913 in Chengdu, in the province of Sichuan, West China. He is the second of six children born to the Rev. Thomas and Annie Torrance. The oldest, Mary Monlin, was born on 10 May 1912 in Shanghai. The others were each born in Chengdu: Grace Brownlee on 7 January 1915, Margaret Ramsay on 30 September 1917, James Bruce on 3 February 1923, and David Wishart on 22 June 1924.

To understand the circumstances of his birth in China and some of the influences which helped to shape and direct his life, it is necessary to say something about our father and mother. Ours was a very happy home. We were blessed with loving and godly parents.

Father was born in Scotland at Muirhead Farm, Harthill, in the parish of Shotts. Grandfather was a small dairy farmer. The family church where father was baptized and in which he grew up was the Kirk of Shotts. It is a church which has witnessed some of the greatest revivals in Scotland. As a young man, father came to a personal faith in the Lord through the ministry of a neighboring minister, the Rev. Shaw, for whom he had always a great affection. He declined however to leave his own church. Father felt the call to the ministry and to the mission-field, having been much impressed by the work of David Livingstone.

Grandfather was a deeply religious person and possessed his own theological library. He was willing to support his son financially if he entered the ministry of the Church of Scotland but declined to help him if he pursued a missionary calling. This meant that father was thrown back on his faith in God and on his own initiative. Although at that time the Free Church of Scotland was deeply involved in missionary work in Africa and India, my father in his faithful commitment to the Established Kirk, unlike several of his would-be missionary friends, declined to join in the foreign mission activity of the Free Church. Accordingly he had to look farther afield in order to pursue his calling. After studying at Hulme Cliff College, near Sheffield, and Livingstone College, London, father sailed for China in 1895 under the auspices of the China Inland Mission. He arrived in Shanghai on 1 January 1896.

After language study at which he excelled in the CIM language training center, he was stationed in Chengdu, West China. In those days, the journey up the river Yangtze from Shanghai to Chengdu by river steamer and sampan took nine weeks. Very quickly, he gained a remarkable mastery of the Chinese language. He threw himself into the work of evangelism, which continued to be his passion for the rest of his life.

At the same time he studied the history of China, translated some of the ancient Chinese classics, became interested in the topography of the land, was given permission to enter some of the ancient tombs, helped to found the West China University Museum, and became, among other things, a proficient ceramic scholar. He was made a fellow of the Royal Geographical Society in recognition of his explorations in Sichuan and publications in several learned journals. He brought back various items for the British Museum in London and the National Museum of Scotland in Edinburgh. Always his consuming concern, however, was to help the people of West China to faith in Christ.

In 1910, when back in Scotland, he attended the International Missionary Conference in New College, Edinburgh. This for him was a turning point. That same year he returned to China in order to take over the Sichuan agency of the American Bible Society, based in Chengdu, which he served for twenty-five years. He represented the British and Foreign as well as the American Bible Society, not only in Chengdu, but in Chungking as well, where he was able to give assistance to the agency of the National Bible Society of Scotland.

His transfer to the Bible Society from the China Inland Mission was a happy one. It gave him more scope for his considerable energy and missionary zeal. Although continuing his scholarly pursuits into Chinese history and archaeology, he took the Gospel not only to the peoples of western Sichuan, but to the tribespeople in the upper Min and To Valleys in the Min Shan Mountains that reach toward Tibet. In particular he took the Gospel to the Xiang (Ch'iang) peoples of the upper Min and To Valleys. They were of semitic origin, were there before the Han Chinese, and were the ones the Chinese authorities claim to be the oldest of the aboriginal "nationalities" in China.

In his final year alone father and his colporteurs distributed over a million Bibles, Testaments, and portions of Scripture in western Sichuan. Throughout his ministry he had the joy of seeing several Chinese and Xiang churches established. On his retirement in 1935 the churches said of him that no one had done more to take the Gospel to West China and gave him several inscribed and embroidered tributes.

On 1 August 1911 father married Annie Elizabeth Sharpe, an Anglican, who worked in Guan Xian about thirty miles northwest of Chengdu. Mother had come to personal faith in Christ through her cousin while working in London. She too felt and answered the call to serve the Lord in China. She sailed for China in 1907 under the auspices of the China Inland Mission. After language school she was stationed in the Province of Sichuan. The marriage was a very happy one.

Both father and mother had a deep faith, grounded on God's Word. Both were much given to prayer. With such parents no family could have been given a better spiritual start to life or been taught more of the Word of God. No one of us can remember a time when the family did not meet together each day for family worship. Father or mother read a portion of Scripture and, as the family knelt, led in prayer. This practice continued through school and university, as long as the family, or some of the family, remained at home.

Theirs was a living, dynamic faith centered not on a system of belief, but on the Person of Christ. They had a deep reverence for Scripture as the Word of God. We were never taught any particular doctrine about the Bible other than that it is God's Word. We were taught that if we approach Scripture in the right way in prayer, it is the place where we will meet and encounter God, hear him speak and discern his will for our lives. In addition to reading it together, we were each encouraged to read the Bible for ourselves and read it through every year. This is a custom which we have continued for many years, often reading through the Bible twice a year, as did father.

This emphasis on the Bible as the place of encounter between humanity and God and the fact that faith is not based on a system of belief but on the Person of the Living God meant that neither Tom nor any of the family ever experienced any tension between their personal evangelical faith and their studies of philosophy, science, or theology. For that we are grateful. This is an experience which is different from that of many others from an evangelical background where unhappily the emphasis was laid not so much on the Person of Christ as on a system of belief.

China was not an easy country in which to serve as a missionary. Father survived the Boxer Rising in 1900, escaping through South China to Hong Kong. The revolution of Sun Zhongstun (Sun Yat-Sen) brought a measure of relief. The period 1901-1914 is often regarded as "the high-water mark of Christian work in China." Much of the country, however, particularly in the north and west, remained unsettled. After the communist revolution in Russia in 1917, atheistic literature and military arms began pouring into China, falling into the hands of local warlords. Soon there were anti-Christian and antiforeign riots in Chengdu.

In 1927, because the country had become so unsettled, the British Consul ordered all British families to leave. Several missionaries had been killed near Chengdu, and a Canadian missionary friend of our mother had recently been beheaded in the street. Among the final memories of the family was our taking refuge in the armored bridge of a river steamer under a hail of fire from communist soldiers on the banks of the Yangtze River. Through it all, the faith of our parents shone through. There was the realization of the near Presence of God and of answered prayer, without which the family would not have survived. These experiences made a deep impression on Tom and the rest of the family and greatly strengthened his faith in God and his love.

Early Years

Despite the unrest, however, China was a good and exciting country in which to grow up. Where else could a boy go to school each day, as Tom did, with two sisters in a sedan chair and another riding with him on the back of a mule? Inevitably the horizons of the mind were widened. There was breathtaking scenery in the summer months when the family went up into the mountains. Tom later accompanied father on his evangelistic travels in the upper reaches of the Min and To Valleys to the mountain villages of the Xiang people. He saw both the need for the Gospel and the profound way that the Gospel changed peoples' lives.

From his early years he wanted himself to be a missionary to the peoples of West China and Tibet. This desire continued with him until almost the end of his university education, when his missionary enthusiasm was deepened and transformed into his desire to promote and teach Christ-centered theology. His interest in China, his love for the Chinese people, and his concern that they should receive the Gospel, however, continued throughout his life.

Tom was fourteen when the family returned to Scotland. Thereafter, Mother remained with the family in Scotland. Father, feeling that his work in China, particularly among the Xiang peoples, was not finished, returned to China for seven further years until his retirement. The decision for Mother to remain in Scotland was in order to give the family a home and to ensure that each of the family grew up to love and serve the Lord, which was the prayerful longing of both parents. Their faithfulness at this time, which was not easy for either parent, was rewarded. The three daughters each married ministers, one of whom was also a doctor, and two with their husbands served for some years in the mission-field in central Africa. The three sons entered the ministry of the Church of Scotland.

For a while the family resided in Bellshill in Lanarkshire before removing to Edinburgh. It was at Bellshill Academy that Tom began to display academic ability. Our sister Grace came first in Scotland in the Higher Latin examination. Prior to that, and at the Canadian Primary School in Chengdu, life was too full of other interests and fun for Tom to be overconcerned with lessons. Mother often quoted the occasion when Tom, still at primary school, one day played truant from school. His teacher came to the house and on meeting him asked him a simple arithmetical question. When Tom out of fun deliberately gave her a wrong answer, she stamped her foot and told Mother that Tom was stupid!

Books were always part of our home. Both Mother and Father read widely, particularly in theology. John Calvin was a household name. Books both from family and public libraries were much used. Tom always regarded mother as the theologian of the family. She encouraged us while still at school to read Luther's *Commentary on Galatians*, Robert Bruce on *The Sacraments*, and Rutherford's *Letters*, together with the great missionary classics. When Tom entered the Faculty of Divinity at New College, she gave him a copy of Karl Barth's *Credo*, and so was among those who helped to introduce Tom to the writings of the greatest Reformed theologian since the Reformation. Although they never put any pressure on us academically, being more concerned that we grew up as good men and women, with faith in God, than with our attaining academic distinctions, it was ever anticipated that each of the family would go on to university, which we did.

Education

After leaving school, Tom proceeded to Edinburgh University to study classics and philosophy under Norman Kemp Smith and A. E. Taylor. His interest extended to the philosophy of science. This was an exhilarating period of his life. Because father retired at that time and the family was short of money, Tom cut short his study of philosophy and in 1934 went on to New College where in 1937 he gained the D.B. degree with distinction in theology, the First Cunningham Fellowship as Dux of College, and the Aitken Fellowship for postgraduate study. Prior to that, in his second year he was awarded a Blackie Travel Scholarship for six months travel and study in the Middle East.

Throughout his studies both in the Faculty of Arts and that of Divinity, Tom took an active part in student evangelistic activities, both within the university and further afield in various towns and parishes in Scotland. Many came to faith in Christ through these activities. On one occasion after my speaking at a women's meeting in Aberdeen, a lady in her eighties spoke to me and asked me to say to my brother Tom that she and her husband both came to Christ forty years previously at a mission which Tom led in her parish. She and her husband had not revealed this at the time.

The two teachers in the Divinity Faculty who exercised the most positive and lasting influence on Tom, as on many others, were Hugh Ross Mackintosh and Daniel Lamont. Both in their own way were leading exponents of conservative evangelical theology. For Tom their teaching had an immense appeal. Mackintosh insisted that student sermons should be expository and evangelistic, "preaching for a verdict," as he would put it. The atoning love of God was to be given central place. To speak of Christianity without mentioning the atonement, he argued, was "as inept as a sentence without a verb." When he first met Karl Barth in Edinburgh the one question he asked him was about his doctrine of the atonement. For Mackintosh there must always be a close link between theology and mission and any theology which was not missionary and evangelistic in attitude was not worthy of the name.

Mackintosh's lectures and his books, particularly *The Doctrine of the Person of Christ* (1912) and *The Christian Experience of Forgiveness* (1927), which remained set texts for Edinburgh divinity students until the 1970s, emphasized the centrality of Christ, the atonement, and the missionary cause. This has remained central to all Tom's theology. Mackintosh's emphasis on the relation between theology and mission deeply influenced Tom in his evangelistic faith and desire to be a missionary. Mackintosh opened his eyes as he opened the eyes of others to the importance and relevance of Christian dogmatics for the whole of the Christian life. It also helped Tom to understand his own missionary calling and redirect it into the field of theological research and education.

In his second year at New College Tom organized a missionary conference to which he brought Robert Wilder, one of the founders of the Student Volunteer Missionary Movement. Years later a friend at that conference reported hearing Wilder say to Mackintosh, "Isn't it good that Tom Torrance is going to be a missionary?" Mackintosh responded: "One of these days he will succeed me in New College."

Daniel Lamont, who lectured in apologetic and pastoral theology, also exercised a deep influence on Tom. Lamont had previously been a mathematician and physicist and for a while assisted Lord Kelvin in Glasgow. He wrote, among other books, *Christ in the World of Thought*, where he endeavored to relate evangelical and christological truth to modern science. Lamont introduced Tom to the thought of Karl Heim of Tübingen. Tom was critical of Heim's Kantian presuppositions but years later became a member of the Karl Heim Gesellschaft. Under Daniel Lamont were laid the early foundations for much of Tom's later thinking in this important area.

John Baillie was at this time professor of divinity at New College. He had succeeded W. P. Paterson at Edinburgh in 1934. He and his brother Donald, who taught in the University of St. Andrews, are generally regarded as the most important Scottish theologians of the mid twentieth century. He has continued through his writings to influence the Church in Scotland. Tom always had a deep respect for him, particularly for his writings on prayer, and valued his friendship, but was critical of the ideas associated with him and his brother.

Although John Baillie felt that Barth's theology should be taken seriously, with his brother Donald he remained rather hostile to Barth's theology. Tom felt that their hostility was misplaced and if they had accepted the christological Trinitarian bases of Barth's theology they would not have been so troubled with the tension between their personal faith and theology or between their faith and the "philosophical reason" on which they laid such emphasis. The Baillies, particularly John, never resolved that tension.

In 1936 William A. Curtis, principal of New College, had asked Tom, on his receipt of a Blackie Travel Scholarship, to "shepherd" a small group of students as part of their studies in a visit to the Holy Land. Undoubtedly Tom's early experiences in China helped him to cope with the customs and peoples in the Middle East, in circumstances which others found rather difficult. It also encouraged him, not always wisely, to venture farther afield than the others in his travels, not only in the Holy Land, but through Syria, Jordan, and Iraq. He had many interesting and at times dangerous experiences.

On one occasion in Iraq he was mistaken for a Jewish spy, arrested, and sentenced to death by hanging! Mercifully he managed to persuade the authorities that he was not a spy, was sent back under guard to Baghdad, and deported to Damascus.

From Syria he visited Turkey where he joined an archaeological expedition engaged in uncovering Constantine's Palace and the Church of St. Mary. After several weeks there he sailed to Athens for a period of hard study in preparation for his D.B. examinations. It was there in Athens that he had his first encounters with the Greek Orthodox Church. On his way home he visited Rome and arrived back in Edinburgh in time for the examinations that summer.

When still in Syria, Tom had learned that H. R. Mackintosh, his much respected teacher, had died, and felt that the bottom had fallen out of his theological education. Tom, who planned to specialize in dogmatics, had hoped to spend his third year being taught almost exclusively by Mackintosh. That was not now to be.

In 1937 Tom was licensed by the Presbytery of Edinburgh as a probationer minister of the Church of Scotland. Ordination lay ahead but it would be three years before that came about.

Having been already introduced to Barth's theology, through H. R. Mackintosh, John McConnachie (1875-1948), at that time parish minister of St. John's Dundee, and others (including Mother), Tom arranged to study in Basel and stayed in the Theologisches Alumneum, an ancient theological student house at 17 Hebelstrasse. Prior to that Tom had spent the summer in Berlin studying German and then went on to Marburg to live with a German family for further study. It was not the easiest or best of times for a British national to be staying in Germany. The Nazification of German culture was oppressive. Tom disliked it and got himself into trouble on several occasions by criticizing it.

Barth's seminar for the academic year 1937-1938 consisted of some fifty students. Barth never thought that a student was truly theologically qualified unless he understood Latin and could read it proficiently. He set his new students a test in translating a Latin text and prescribed an essay to estimate their theological acumen and ability. From them he selected a smaller group to form a more intimate seminar (the *Sozietät*) which met in his own house once a week. Tom was selected as a member of the *Sozietät*. In a letter to his friend Eduard Thurneysen, Barth expressed his approval of "der Schottlander."

Barth without doubt was the greatest theologian since the Reformation and Tom was immensely impressed by his manner of teaching and by the biblical content, depth, and theological breadth of his lectures, together with his remarkable understanding of other theologians, Reformed, Lutheran, Anglican, and Roman Catholic.

Tom had hoped to write a dissertation on the scientific structure of Christian dogmatics, a subject the importance of which already had begun to fascinate him in Edinburgh. To Tom's disappointment, Barth felt he was too young to tackle this subject and encouraged him to write on "the doctrine of grace in the second-century Fathers." This Tom proceeded to do. However, because events took an unexpected turn, he was unable to complete this study until 1946.

A Year at Auburn

When Tom returned to Edinburgh in the summer of 1938, it was with the intention of returning to Basel in the autumn. He looked forward to continuing his research into the Apostolic Fathers and continuing to attend the lectures of Barth, which he found so exciting. Things turned out differently.

Professor John Baillie had recommended him to his friends at Auburn Theological Seminary, in New York, who were looking for someone to teach systematic theology. Baillie put pressure on Tom to accept an appointment there. Tom was surprised and at first disconcerted. John Baillie had himself taught theology in Auburn Seminary from 1919 to 1927, before moving to Canada to take up the chair of systematic theology in Toronto, and then to teach at Union Theological Seminary in New York, before moving in 1934 to the chair of divinity in Edinburgh. Throughout the years, Baillie had kept in touch with his friends at Auburn where he had been very happy. Auburn at that time was passing through a difficult period when Professor John Bennet, Baillie's successor there, suddenly left for California. Baillie differed from Tom theologically. Nonetheless he had considerable regard for him as a theologian and as a person. So Tom agreed and was very happy there. However, because of international circumstances and the imminence of war, he stayed there only one year.

In some ways the appointment of Tom to lecture in Auburn was unusual. From its start in 1837, and increasingly so, Auburn had become associated with and representative of the more liberal tradition emerging within American Presbyterianism. It advocated liberty in thought and in teaching. It had grown to expect its staff, theologically, to stand at some distance from the traditional teaching of the Reformation. It was regarded as a bulwark against fundamentalism. Although Tom was never a fundamentalist, he stood firmly within the Reformation position. He accepted the teaching of the Word of God, was evangelical, and had been deeply influenced by such conservative scholars as H. R. Mackintosh and Karl Barth. His appointment therefore was interesting and surprising. It did, however, prove acceptable.

At the age of twenty-five and having completed only one year of post- graduate studies in theology, Tom had to work extremely hard in order to produce lectures covering the whole range of systematic theology. He concentrated on the doctrine of Christ, the doctrine of the Triune God, and the doctrine of Revelation. He gave courses on theology and philosophy, theology and science, and theology and art. And in so doing he laid the foundation for his research into and teaching of systematic theology at a later period.

It was characteristic of his teaching then and ever since that we can understand the teaching of Christ only as we understand it together with his work and Person. Christian theology and preaching are centered on the Person of Christ in union with his saving work and teaching. At times in Auburn, and later at New College, this central emphasis on the saving life and Person of Christ, and of the Christian's union with Christ, created tension among some of his students. It was difficult for them to learn the lesson that only as we personally yield to Christ in faith and obedience and prayer can we really understand him. They felt confronted by God and challenged in their lives. Under Tom's teaching, some students in Auburn, and not a few later on in New College, were led by the Holy Spirit to commit their lives to Christ, and attained peace with

God.

Tom's lectures caused considerable interest not only in Auburn but also far beyond. In the spring and summer of 1939 invitations to teach came first from McCormick Theological Seminary in Chicago and then from Princeton University in New Jersey. The invitation to McCormick Seminary came after Tom lectured for an hour on the doctrine of Grace. President Stone recommended to the board of directors that Tom be appointed in the first instance for one year and if that turned out to be acceptable to all parties, that he be appointed assistant professor to be followed by promotion to full professor within two years. Tom was grateful for the offer. Knowing, however, that other interesting possibilities were opening up, he declined the offer.

Princeton University, not the Princeton Theological Seminary, had recently created a new chair, in order to start teaching theology along with the liberal arts on an "objective basis" and in a "dispassionate, non-proselytizing way." Tom was invited to an interview and met with three professors from Princeton University. They explained their proposal that theology should be taught not on a confessional or church basis but as one of the liberal arts. Tom's response was that he would be happy to teach theology *as a science.*

When he was asked to explain that, he replied in terms which he has since developed at length. "In a rigorous science, we think not as we choose to think, but as we are compelled to think in accordance with the nature of the object, and thus in ways which are governed by the objective grounds on which the science rests. The rigorous nature of scientific questioning could be applied equally well to Christian Theology." Tom pointed out, however, that if he were to teach theology in an objective or "dispassionate way," he could not guarantee that in his teaching of theology in this scientific way students would not be converted. Two other candidates in addition to Tom were interviewed. Somewhat to his surprise he was offered the chair the next day.

The War Period

International events, however, were moving fast. Increasingly it appeared that war between Britain and Germany was inevitable and imminent. Tom did not want to be out of his own country when it was at war. Very reluctantly he declined the invitation. He found this to be one of the most difficult decisions of his life. It certainly proved to be far reaching. His future, after the war, was to be in his own country of Scotland.

Tom returned to the U.K. in the summer of 1939. On Sunday, 3

September, war was declared between Britain and Germany. On his return, with war being imminent but not yet declared, Tom offered to be a chaplain in the army. To his surprise his offer was not accepted. Although he had been licensed to preach by the Church of Scotland, he had not served in a parish and was not yet ordained as a minister of Word and Sacrament. The circumstances in which ordination would be conferred would alter, but at that time he was informed that it would be at least two years before an offer for chaplaincy work in the armed forces would be accepted.

Disappointed over the rejection of his offer for army chaplaincy, Tom turned to the issue of his unfinished dissertation. With the country at war, a return to Basel was out of the question, yet he was anxious to continue work on the project. Accordingly, the autumn saw him registered as a postgraduate student at Oriel College, Oxford.

Intellectually and academically Tom found it a very stimulating period of his life. Despite wartime restrictions, which were beginning to affect the life and teaching of the university, Tom was able to participate in philosophical and theological discussions with a number of well-known Oxford personnel such as Austin Farrer, Raymond Klibansky, Eric L. Mascall, and the Scottish philosopher who later became his friend, Donald MacKinnon.

During this period he worshipped in St. Columba's Presbyterian Church, close to Oriel College, where both the provost of Oriel College, W. D. Ross, and the vice-provost, Markus N. Tod, also worshipped. His evangelical, missionary zeal led him to participate very fully in student Christian activities. He played a significant part in the mission organized by the Oxford Inter-Collegiate Christian Union (OICCU). Very soon he was invited by the leaders of the Christian Union to preach the Gospel in place of another who had been unable to come. At the same time he had also become involved in the work of the rival Student Christian Movement (SCM).

The InterVarsity Fellowship (IVF), the parent body of OICCU, always felt uneasy when someone endeavored to support both movements, believing that support for SCM detracted from the witness of IVF, which endeavored to adhere more strictly to Scripture and was more evangelical. Furthermore, at that time, and right up to the sixties or early seventies, the leaders of IVF were very critical of the teaching of Karl Barth. It was known that Tom had studied in Basel and theologically had been influenced by Barth. Sadly, therefore, the IVF brought pressure on OICCU during the latter part of the mission to withdraw their support for Tom. After the war, although Tom was frequently invited to speak to the Edinburgh Christian Union, before it was disaffiliated from IVF, and to other Scottish IVF student meetings, he was never asked to speak at a national IVF conference outside of Scotland.

Throughout his life Tom has leaned heavily on Scripture, adhering to it as God's dynamic living Word. His discussions at Oxford then and for a number years,on this subject and on the Doctrines of Revelation and Grace have troubled many evangelicals. Some are still troubled.

For Tom theology must be tested and born out in the Christian life. With his evangelical missionary zeal for the furtherance of Christ's Kingdom and the building up of his Church, he was anxious to experience the work of the parish ministry. For him this desire had become even more urgent with the country now at war. Many ministers had gone off as chaplains in the armed forces, so that there was a growing shortage of ministers at home. He felt that it was inappropriate for him at present to continue in further academic study. Accordingly, he wrote to the secretary of the Church and Ministry Department of the Church of Scotland stating his desire to seek a parish.

Tom was ordained and inducted to Alyth Barony Parish Church on Wednesday, 20 March 1940. Alyth is a lovely town, near the foot of Glen Isla, on the north side of Strathmore, in Perthshire. At that time it had approximately 2,500 inhabitants. It was situated in the midst of a large farming community.

Because of the constant threat of enemy air raids, many children from Britain, for the sake of their safety, were evacuated from the cities to the country. I was the youngest of our family and over ten years younger than Tom. My parents, who had retired to Edinburgh, decided that I should leave Edinburgh, and so I stayed with Tom in Perthsire for some eighteen months. I travelled eleven miles each day, generally by bicycle, to high school in Blairgowrie. A housekeeper came in each day to cook meals for the two of us and to tidy the house. These were very happy days. I enjoyed Tom's company and believe that he enjoyed mine.

In Tom's leisure time, which was not too frequent, we played chess, walked, or fished the Alyth burn or the river Isla. On one occasion we were invited to accompany a gamekeeper of the Airlie estates, a man with the interesting name of Alexander (known locally as Sandy Eck), deer shooting. One incident will long be remembered. In the summer of 1940 my two brothers, Tom and James, with three farmers' sons camped for ten days at the head of Glen Isla in the Canness Glen. We lived chiefly on trout, which were in abundant supply, and on rabbits, which were numerous.

Toward the end of our holiday we were asked to move our campsite lower down the Glen because of the start of deer shooting. At the end of a long and glorious day climbing over the slopes of Tom Buidhe and watching the deer on the steep slopes of Glen Doll, in the late evening we packed our tents and walked down four miles to the foot of Glen Brichty. We were tired when just before midnight, with the tents pitched, the tea made but not drunk, we sat around a roaring fire. In the mountains we had for a few days forgotten about the war and regulations concerning the blackout.

Suddenly we heard the distinctive noise of a German plane coming up the glen. Clearly it had spotted our fire. Hurriedly our precious tea was thrown on the fire and we sat holding a blanket over the glowing embers. The plane passed overhead and some moments later we heard six explosions as it dropped its bombs. They landed on the other side of the hill from us and no harm was done apart from scarring the mountainside and scaring a few deer. We were afraid to relight the fire and remembered the need for the blackout. It was the kind of incident that Tom would all too frequently experience in Italy, later in the war.

Tom threw himself with great energy into the work of the parish. During this period as a minister, he visited all the members of his congregation in their homes again and again. He visited the sick in hospital and cared for the lapsed. He worked hard at his sermon preparation and also led a series of Bible classes. He was diligent in the preparation of new communicants. A friend of mine was converted to Christ in one of his communicant classes, entered the ministry, and has recently retired.

Always his desire was to present Christ to his people. To that end he regularly read a portion of Scripture in each home and prayed. Christ was central to all his preaching. In keeping with his much loved mentor, H. R. Mackintosh, he preached for a verdict, challenging his congregation to come to terms with the grace of God and the fruits of Christ's atonement. His stress was upon the unconditional grace of the Lord Jesus Christ. They were called by God freely to accept as a gift his loving offer of salvation without which we are lost. Undoubtedly, this disturbed many of the congregation, as it disturbed many in his next congregation of Beechgrove in Aberdeen and many of his future students. It is often hard for good hardworking Kirk folk to accept that what *they* do does not avail for salvation. As Tom preached through Romans, Corinthians, and other passages of Scripture, he had the joy of seeing several come for the first time to a joyful faith in the Lord. His congregation came to love him and were sad when he left them in November 1947 to become minister of Beechgrove Aberdeen.

During this period and despite being busy in parish work, Tom was encouraged by Dr. John McConnachie, minister of St. John's Church, Dundee, and well known through his writings on Barth, to join the Angus Theological Club. Tom attended their meetings in Dundee as often as he could, finding them stimulating, and at the same time wrote various articles and reviews. He published eight pieces during his period in Alyth.

Army Chaplain

After three years in the parish ministry Tom felt certain that he must serve in the British army. This time he did not offer his services to the Royal Army Chaplain's Department, on the ground that if he did he might be required to continue to serve as a chaplain for some time after the war ended. Under the circumstances, he offered his services to the Church of Scotland "Committee on Huts and Canteen Work for H.M. Forces." They provided through their chaplains both pastoral care and practical assistance to Scottish soldiers on wartime service. His offer was gladly accepted and arrangements were made for our brother-in-law, the Rev. Kenneth MacKenzie, who was married to our sister Margaret and later became a missionary in Central Africa, to look after the parish until another arrangement could be made by the presbytery.

A few weeks later, Tom was sent to North Africa and the Middle East and sailed on a ship laden with troops to reinforce the 51st Highland Division and other units preparing for the invasion of Sicily. The original plan was that Tom would work in Cairo and then Jerusalem. In fact, his first major mission involved driving over 1,500 miles of desert in a mobile canteen to deliver Turkish delight to Scottish troops in Tobruk and Tripoli. It took him and his driver Jock Patterson, a Black Watch soldier from Dundee, three-and-a-half days. Preparations at that time were being made for the invasion of Italy.

His first assignment as chaplain was to the 41st Light Anti-Aircraft Regiment. They formed part of a combined assault force planning to invade the Dodecanese Islands in the Aegean, with a view to an invasion of northern Greece. These plans took Tom north to Haifa. The Germans, however, learned of the proposed invasion. Some four or five thousand men were lost in the initial attack and the whole project was scrapped.

During the subsequent period of inaction Tom wrote to every home in his congregation in Alyth in order to keep them informed about his own activities. He also enjoyed a short period of leave in which with others he explored the Sinai Peninsula, climbed Mount Sinai, and returned to St. Catherine's Monastery in the Sinai Peninsula, which he had first visited as a student in 1935.

There was a serious shortage of army chaplains and Tom was keen to play his full part and be ready for action. Major General Denys Reid, noted for his distinguished service in a series of long-range desert patrols across North Africa, was in command of the 10th Indian Division, which was preparing to go to Italy. Reid, the son of a Church of Scotland minister in Inverness, invited Tom to come as chaplain in his division. Tom readily agreed. Indian divisions were made up of British and Indian troops in roughly equal numbers. Equipped with his mobile canteen truck and driver, Tom embarked a few weeks later on a small ship laden with tanks for the port of Taranto. From there he made his way to the battle line at Ortona.

Italy witnessed some of the toughest fighting of the war. After the battle of Cassino and after the fall of Rome, the Tenth Indian Division, which was trained for mountain warfare, was deployed to fight its way north through the mountains that form the central spine of Italy. The last real battle was fought on the Argenta-Idice line when the Germans were routed. Soon after the German army caved in all along the Po River. In the village of Malabergo, near the Renoi, the Tenth Indian Division heard the cease-fire.

Through his mobile canteen and the successive trucks assigned to him, as one after another was shot up, Tom was able to help the troops in a practical way, offering hot tea and buns. Other work kept him busy. Whenever possible Tom joined the most forward troops, with whom he found the best pastoral openings. In battle he sometimes acted as a stretcher-bearer, ministered to the wounded, and helped to bury the dead of both sides, British and German, together with Italian civilians. He made a point of joining with and praying with soldiers in their forward positions. Whenever possible he joined with other chaplains in taking services of worship and celebrating Holy Communion. These were generally and of necessity short.

He found that spiritually his most valuable work was in individual personal conversations, when soldiers would open up their hearts in their concern for loved ones at home. It was often then that many a soldier gave his heart to the Lord. He was always ready to speak of the Lord Jesus Christ, his mercy, forgiveness, and salvation, and the need to commit one's life to him. The Cross and Resurrection were always central to his message. Many were glad to listen and ask questions, although naturally some were indifferent. Throughout those two years in the army in the Middle East and in Italy he had the joy of seeing men being converted to Christ and growing in faith.

His insistence, wherever possible, of being with the frontline troops, meant that he was constantly in danger. Time and again he escaped miraculously. On one occasion with a forward patrol they crossed through the German line and entered a farmhouse that was occupied by German soldiers. They were spotted and came under fire. Managing to shelter behind a small wall, he and another were the only ones to return.

On another occasion when being shelled they lay in a ditch. His head touched the feet of the man in front while his feet touched the head of the man behind. Both the man in front and the man behind were killed. Miraculously he was not even wounded. It was in situations of danger that there grew a close bond between the padre and the men, and Tom felt that it was then that he was often able to fulfill his proper ministry in the Gospel. He was awarded the MBE for bravery.

His experiences as a padre, his personal conversations with men facing danger and death, crystallized with greater intensity in his mind the necessity for a Christian faith that related to real life, a faith that could stand all the stresses and strains of life, and bring comfort and deliverance in Christ to the living and the dying. These experiences reinforced the need for complete harmony between theology, preaching, and daily life. In his future teaching Tom often talked of a "paper theology," by which he meant a formal theology that was not really biblical or evangelical, that did not relate to the whole of life, that could not bring comfort to the dying or the living, and that was simply of human construction.

Throughout his hectic army service, Tom managed to listen to classical music on a small portable gramophone belonging to an army friend in command of divisional ordinance. He preferred Bach or Mozart before a battle but Beethoven afterwards. His great joy was his Greek New Testament which he always kept with him. In addition, when occasion offered, he discussed theology with other chaplains. Shortly before the end of the war he was invited to give some lectures to Church of Scotland chaplains in Assisi. Understandably he entitled those lectures "Theology and Action."

The war in Europe ended in May 1945. A day or two later, he wrote to me in India, where I was serving as a soldier in the 14th Indian Division. In that letter Tom expressed many of his thoughts and feelings. He was overwhelmed with the fact that he was still alive, and even uninjured, in light of all that he had experienced. He believed that again and again God had given him courage and sustained him in the face of death and destruction. Like many others he felt ashamed that he was preserved while others were not. He recognized in ways that words cannot express that God had chosen to spare him for a purpose. His first desire, as he said in his letter, was in prayer to rededicate his life unreservedly to God and seek his will. Two months later in London he made his way to St. Martin-in-the-Fields in order, again in thankfulness for his survival, to commit his life unreservedly to God and ask what God wanted him to do.

Postwar Years

Although encouraged to return to Oxford and minister in St. Columba's, Tom felt that his future lay in Scotland and so he returned in the late summer of 1945 to resume ministry in Alyth.

With his pastoral concern, his first task was to resume the systematic visitation of the congregation. Of particular concern for him were the families which had been bereaved as a result of the war. These weighed heavily on him.

At the same time he worked hard to complete work on his doctoral dissertation held up by the war and have it printed, so that he could submit it. After a few months he sent it to the University of Basel. He travelled in May 1946 to Basel for his *Rigorosum*, which he took, along with Barth's younger son Christoph, under Karl Ludwig Schmidt, Oscar Cullmann, and Fritz Lieb. He was awarded his doctorate magna cum laude. His thesis, entitled *The Doctrine of Grace in the Apostolic Fathers*, was published by Oliver and Boyd, in paperback form in 1946, and later in 1948 in a hardbound edition.

Between 1941 and 1946 he published twelve reviews and articles in addition to his thesis. Up to and including the year 1950 when he was appointed to a University Chair in Edinburgh, in addition to the re-publication of his thesis, he added another twenty-three publications.

Concerned for the revival of Scottish theology, on a biblical and evangelical basis, in 1945 Tom founded the Scottish Church Theology Society. In 1947, with his desire to interpret the relevance of the Reformed Tradition for today, particularly in relation to John Calvin and Athanasius, he published, through the Lutterworth Press, *Calvin's Doctrine of Man*. In 1948 he launched the *Scottish Journal of Theology*. And in 1952 he jointly founded the Society for the Study of Theology. Tom had long reflected on the need for the development of these projects prior to their launch, and had discussions about them with J. K. S. Reid, a paratrooping padre friend of his in Italy, who was later to join him in editing the *SJT*. Those plans had occupied much of his thinking during his period of war service. He believed their launch was necessary to help consolidate evangelical theological thinking.

In October 1946 Tom married Margaret Edith Spear, a nurse from Bath who during the war had served as a nurse in St.Thomas's Hospital, the most-bombed hospital in London, where she had a harrowing time. Thirteen times bombs meant for the House of Commons across the river landed on St. Thomas's Hospital. Since her student days in Edinburgh Margaret had been a friend of our sister Margaret, who with her husband the Rev. Kenneth MacKenzie was that summer and autumn on missionary furlough from Africa.

It was a very happy marriage. Margaret has been of immense help to Tom and helped to provide a very happy home. They have two sons and a daughter. Thomas, born in 1947, is an elder in the Church and senior lecture in economics in Heriot-Watt University; Iain, born in 1949, is a minister of the Church of Scotland and professor of theology in Aberdeen; and Alison, born in 1951, is a medical doctor in general practice in Edinburgh. She also is actively involved in the Church.

Margaret and Tom have always shared the same spiritual and evangelical outlook. When the family was young they together continued the practice of our parents in having daily family worship. Margaret and the family have been, and are, very supportive of Tom. They are a loving united family.

Early in 1947 Sir Hector Hetherington, principal of Glasgow University, wrote asking Tom to apply for the chair of divinity there. In the circumstances Prof. John G. Riddell who, from 1934 to 1947, had occupied the church chair of systematic theology at Trinity College in Glasgow, was appointed. Tom was then invited to apply for that chair but declined.

In 1947 shortly after the birth of Thomas, Tom was invited to be minister of Beechgrove Church Aberdeen, where at one time both Professors H. R. Mackintosh and J. S. Stewart had been ministers. Tom accepted and on 13 November was inducted to his new charge. Beechgrove was a rather larger and busier parish than Alyth. Tom became immersed in preaching and pastoral work and in his short ministry there made a profound impact on the congregation who gave him their respect and affection.

At the same time articles and reviews continued to flow. A number of books were published then or at a later period, including *When Christ Comes and Comes Again* and *The Apocalypse Today* (a series of sermons first preached at Alyth during the war on the book of Revelation).

Professor in Edinburgh

By this time it was apparent to others that Tom was destined to teach theology, which he regarded as a continuance of his evangelical and missionary calling. Tom always regarded as a valuable and necessary preparation for his theological teaching his ten years in practical pastoral ministry, which includes his two years in military service. His great regret has always been that many engaged in theological teaching and in the preparation of others for the ministry have not themselves had pastoral experience prior to their teaching appointments. Our brother James served for seven years in the parish ministry before being appointed to teach theology first as a lecturer in Edinburgh then as professor in Aberdeen. Prior to his entering the ministry he served during the war in the RAF, which he believes gave him practical experience of people that was vital to the ministry.

In 1950, with the retirement of Professor Hugh Watt, who that year became moderator of the General Assembly of the Church of Scotland, there was a vacancy in the chair of church history in New College. To his surprise Tom was offered the chair. Although not altogether ideal from his perspective, he accepted the offer and his appointment was confirmed by the General Assembly in May of that year. Thereafter ensued twenty-nine years of teaching in Edinburgh University, in New College.

As professor of church history, it would be true to say that he taught "historical theology" rather more than "church history" in the strict sense. I myself as a student at New College during that period attended many of his lectures. As was customary at that time, he always opened and closed his lectures with prayer. This was a practice which he continued until he retired. For the students of church history his lectures helped to open up the theology of the Early Church and of the Reformation. Such was the impression that he made that two years later when he transferred to the chair of Christian dogmatics, there was a determined move to appoint another theologian rather than historian to teach church history, and his friend James S. McEwen was appointed.

His engagement with church history deepened his understanding of theology and helped him to be even more aware of his own theological roots which went deep into the Scottish theological tradition. In 1958 he translated and edited the book much loved by our mother, *The Mystery of the Lord's Supper: Sermons on the Sacrament Preached in the Kirk of Edinburgh in A.D.1589* by Robert Bruce. Many years later, in 1996, he published *Scottish Theology from John Knox to John McLeod Campbell.*

In 1952, on the retirement of Professor G. T. Thomson, who when in Aberdeen had translated the first volume of Karl Barth's *Church Dogmatics*, Tom was appointed to the chair of Christian dogmatics in Edinburgh that had been held by his former teacher and mentor H. R. Mackintosh.

The appointment was not without difficulties. For years, since 1934 when he was appointed to New College, John Baillie, together with his brother Donald at St. Andrews, theologically dominated the Scottish scene. Although somewhat affected by Barth, neither approved of Barth and were cautious, even critical, of those sympathetically approving of

Barth's theology. John Baillie was due to retire in 1956 and would not be in a position to control the course which the college would thereafter take theologically. Tom's appointment to the chair of Christian dogmatics at the age of thirty-nine years would give him a lengthy period of teaching and would inevitably mean a change in the theological direction of the college. Baillie believed that Tom had proved that he was well qualified and good as a teacher and researcher in the history of doctrine. He wanted Tom to remain in the chair of church history. He felt that it was for the good of the college. Despite his objections, however, Tom was appointed.

There were two chairs in theology. John Baillie occupied the chair of divinity, sometimes called the chair of philosophical theology or more simply, philosophy and religion. Tom now occupied the chair of Christian dogmatics which covered the field of systematic theology.

Tom lectured for the most part on Christology and soteriology, and conducted seminars on patristic theology using as texts works of Athanasius, Basil, and Hilary. He also lectured on church, ministry, and sacraments." John Baillie, however, surprisingly decided to offer lectures on Christology and the sacraments, using as textbooks his brother Donald's works, *God Was in Christ* and *The Theology of the Sacraments*. Maybe, as students thought, Baillie wished to correct Tom's theology! I myself as a student attended the lectures of both professors on these subjects.

Tom's curriculum of theological teaching was, to his great disappointment, limited insofar as he was not to lecture on the Doctrine of God, including the Doctrine of the Trinity. These subjects were deemed to fall within the field of Divinity and therefore assigned to Baillie, and after Baillie to his successor, John McIntyre. It was after his retirement from New College that Tom published several of his major works on Christian theology, including the doctrine of God, namely, *The Trinitarian Faith* (1988), *Trinitarian Perspectives* (1994), and *The Christian Doctrine of God, One Being Three Persons* (1996).

In lecturing to postgraduate students undertaking theological research, Tom was unrestricted. This allowed him to lecture on themes close to his heart.

In the fifties, sixties, and seventies, through its academic staff, the reputation of New College grew and became famous worldwide. Students came from Europe, U.S.A., Africa, Asia, and Australasia. Increasingly, members of the staff, often through the influence or invitations from former overseas students, were invited to lecture in universities abroad. Tom was one who gained a worldwide reputation and invitations have continued to come to lecture abroad, perhaps more so since his retirement from the chair of Christian dogmatics.

Of the subjects close to his heart, Tom was concerned in lecturing and publishing to show the relevance for today of Calvin and the Reformers, and also the relevance for today of the great Alexandrian theologians of the Early Church. Mention has already been made that in 1949 he published *Calvin's Doctrine of Man.* In 1958 he wrote an introduction and historical notes to a republication of *Tracts and Treatises on the Reformation* by John Calvin. In 1959 he translated and edited with an introduction *the School of Faith: The Catechisms of the Reformed Church.* Tom arranged for a new translation from Latin to English of the twelve volumes of Calvin's *Commentaries on the New Testament,* which he and I coedited between the years 1961 and 1968.

His interest in Calvin and the Reformation led him to become deeply involved in ecumenical activity. When home from China in 1910 our father had attended the great International Missionary Conference which was held in Edinburgh that year and gave rise to the International Missionary Council. The vision of a world won for Christ demanded for its accomplishment a united Christian witness on the part of the Churches, which echoes our Lord's Prayer in John 17.

Ecumenical Involvement

Tom had grown up within this context but felt the need to recover Church unity on a sound theological basis. He felt that Calvin's theology was particularly relevant within the ongoing ecumenical debate. Along with his friend and colleague, J. K. S. Reid, now professor of theology in Aberdeen, Tom wrote extensively on the two volumes of preparatory studies for the World Council of Churches meeting in Amsterdam in 1948, and the issues raised by the Third World Conference on Faith and Order which met at Lund in August 1952, which he attended as a representative of the Church of Scotland.

As a representative of the Church of Scotland in dialogue with the Church of England, he wrote in 1955 *Royal Priesthood* in which he endeavored to address some of the main issues confronting union between Reformed and Episcopal Churches. In it he developed the idea, discussed in the Reformation, of "bishop in presbytery" as a possible way forward.

Tom believed firmly in the need for rigorous biblical and theological study on the part of participants in dialogue. He believed that union, whether of individuals or churches, could only take place "in Christ" and on the basis of Christ's atonement. Only as churches shared together in Christ's death could they be raised together as one in Christ. Not all delegates were willing to engage in such rigorous theological study. At times Tom felt that he was somewhat of a lone voice and therefore chose to retire from some, but not all, active ecumenical engagement and endeavored to make his contribution through writing, focusing attention on the doctrines of the church, ministry, and sacraments.

A major contribution in this connection was his appointment, within the Church of Scotland, as convener of a special commission on baptism. Under his leadership the commission surveyed the Church's understanding of baptism from the New Testament to the present day. The final reports were presented to the General Assemblies of 1961 and 1962.

Tom served on the Faith and Order Commission of the World Council of Churches from 1952 to 1962. In 1974 he took part in the Reformed-Roman Catholic Study Commission on the Eucharist, which met in the Netherlands. This preceded three important publications by the British Council of Churches Study Commission on Trinitarian Doctrine, cochaired by our brother, the Rev. Professor James Torrance, and the Orthodox theologian Costa Carras.

Probably Tom's greatest ecumenical contribution followed his visit to the ecumenical patriarch and other leaders of the Greek Orthodox Church on behalf of the World Alliance of Reformed Churches. He had already been in conversation with the Greek Orthodox Church, which had welcomed his theological involvement. Tom proposed that the Churches should enter into dialogue, seeking theological consensus on the doctrine of the Trinity, for agreement there would cut behind all other disagreements. The ecumenical patriarch and other patriarchs of the Greek Orthodox Church responded very favorably. By 1983 all fourteen Orthodox Churches became involved. After extended discussions between 1986 and 1990, an "Agreed Statement on the Doctrine of the Holy Trinity" was reached at Geneva on 13 March 1991. This was a major achievement on the part of the Churches and Tom's contribution was recognized.

Earlier in 1954 he had called for discussions within the Orthodox Communion between Chalcedonian and non-Chalcedonian or "monophysite" theologians. Agreement between them was eventually reached early in 1973. Tom was then invited to Addis Ababa by Methodios the Greek Orthodox archbishop of Axum, the see in Ethiopia founded by Athanasius, to join in commemorating the death of Athanasius in 373, and in celebrating the theological agreement Tom had initiated. There he was consecrated by Methodios as a presbyter of the Greek Orthodox Church, and given the honorary title of protopresbyter. Earlier in 1970, at a session of the General Assembly in Edinburgh, the patriarch of Alexandria had conferred on him the Cross of St. Mark, which was followed in 1977 by Tom's being given the Cross of

Thyateira by the Greek Orthodox archbishop in London.

Scholar and Churchman

Tom was deeply interested in the theology of Karl Barth, on which he lectured both to undergraduate and more particularly to postgraduate students. Along with Professor Geoffrey Bromiley of Fuller Theological Seminary, U.S.A., he coedited the translation of all thirteen volumes of Barth's *Church Dogmatics* in addition to the index volume. The project was begun in 1952 and completed in 1972. He is presently involved in the reediting of them for transposal onto a CD for use through a computer.

In 1962 he published, *Karl Barth: An Introduction to His Early Theology, 1910-1931,* and in 1990, *Karl Barth: Biblical and Evangelical Theologian.* Tom much appreciated Barth's emphasis on the centrality of the Person and atonement of Jesus Christ, and his doctrine of the Trinity. He responded warmly to the way Barth endeavored to develop in the most rigorous way a theology that was faithful to the Word of God. He has never followed Barth slavishly. At times he has differed from Barth, for example in revising Barth's account of so-called natural theology.

Tom also developed areas of biblical theology, which are in harmony with Barth's theology yet not stressed, such as the vicarious nature of Christ's humanity and the Christian life as a "living union with Christ." Barth responded favorably to Tom's suggestions in this area. Tom also developed theological science in relation to other scientific disciplines, to which Barth had not given his attention, but to which he gave his blessing.

Considerable debate has arisen over the years about the interpretation of Barth's theology. Some people have challenged Tom's understanding of Barth's theology. Prior to the publication of his book, *Karl Barth: An Introduction to His Early Theology, 1910-1931,* Tom personally discussed with Barth the development of his theology. Barth wrote to him to say that of all his students and readers Tom was the one who understood him best. With Barth's instigation, and that of Oscar Cullmann, Tom was urged to accept an invitation to the chair of dogmatics in Basel. Barth looked on Tom as his most natural successor. Although tempted, for he and Margaret loved Switzerland, Tom declined to leave Scotland.

An interest particularly close to his heart and one on which he lectured to postgraduate students was theology and science. He has pioneered work, and written and published many books, on the relations of theology and science. In 1969 he published *Theological Science*, which was hailed by Michael Polanyi, and soon translated into French as *déjà classique*. To Tom's joy it is also being translated into Chinese. This was followed later on by *Reality and Evangelical Theology* and *Reality and Scientific Theology*, and *Transformation and Convergence in the Frame of Knowledge*. In 1969 he published *Space, Time, and Incarnation* and in 1976 *Space, Time, and Resurrection.*

The disciplines of natural science and theology are qualitatively different in the types of knowledge offered. Both have an objective base in reality. Both must be pursued rigorously and faithfully along the lines determined by the object of study. Theology has as its objective center of study the revelation of the Person and Work of Christ and the doctrine of the Holy Trinity. Yet, theology and science belong together in the unified order of God's creation, and require to learn from one another and are dependent on one another. Theological studies should be regarded together with the scientific approach to the investigation of the world as facets of one comprehensive and coherent theological method, rather as isolated episodes within an essentially fragmented discipline.

In his moderatorial address to the General Assembly of the Church on 26 May 1977, Tom declared: "I do not believe that the Christian Church has anything to fear from the advance of science. Indeed the more truly scientific inquiry discloses the structures of thc created world, the more at home we Christians ought to be in it, for this is the creation which came into being through the Word of God and in which that Word has been made flesh in Jesus Christ our Lord. The more I engage in dialogue with scientists and understand the implications of their startling discoveries, the more I find that, far from contradicting the fundamental beliefs, they open up the whole field for a deeper grasp of the Christian doctrines of creation, incarnation, reconciliation, resurrection and not least the doctrine of the Holy Spirit."

Tom's research into and writing about theology and science brought him many invitations abroad. In 1969 he became a member, and from 1972 to 1981 president, of the Académie Internationale des Sciences Religieuses. In 1973 he was a founder member, and from 1976 to 1977 president, of the Institute of Religion and Theology of Great Britain and Ireland, and in 1976 a member of the Académie Internationale de Philosophie des Sciences. Since 1979 he has been a fellow of the Royal Society of Edinburgh and since 1982 a fellow of the British Academy in London. In 1970 he was awarded a Litt.D. degree on submission of five published works on theological method. In 1978 he was awarded the prestigious Templeton Prize for Progress in Religion on the basis of his writings on the interaction of science and theology. In 1983, he was honored by Heriot-Watt University, Edinburgh, with an honorary doctor of science for his work into the study of scientific method in the relation of science and theology.

His twenty-nine years of teaching in New College were often eventful and sometimes controversial. He had for sixteen years (from 1960-1976) as a colleague our brother James. James was appointed to lecture on the history of Christian thought. He lectured in both the Department of Divinity, on the philosophy of religion, and also in the Department of Systematic Theology. James lectured and researched widely on Calvin, church and state, Scottish theology, Puritanism and federal theology, on grace, law and rabbinic Judaism, covenant and contract, the theology of worship, contemporary continental theology, etc. His research carried him in a different direction from Tom.

Nonetheless they were always in theological agreement. They shared the same passion for Christ and the same evangelical outlook. James had earlier led several student missions. It was an encouragement to have him as a colleague until he was appointed, commencing 1 January 1977, to the chair of theology in Aberdeen. Professors William Manson and James S. Stewart, who had been very good friends, had by this time both retired.

On Tom's retirement in 1979, surprisingly, the Roman Catholic theologian James Mackie was appointed to succeed him in the chair of theology. His appointment seems to have been a reaction to the theology for which Tom stood and greatly troubled the General Assembly that year.

That and other appointments took New College in a different theological direction. The result was that for some years the majority of Church of Scotland candidates for the ministry made Aberdeen their first preference and many of the postgraduate theological students gravitated to Aberdeen, to study under James, helping to make the Postgraduate School of Theology in that university rather large.

Those who tended to be liberal in theology were always troubled by Tom and James. Interestingly, the opposition which they both encountered most frequently, and still do, was from would-be evangelicals. It has generally centered on their understanding of Christ's atoning death and resurrection, and of the unconditional nature of Grace, as expounded, for example, in Tom's Didsbury lectures, *The Mediation of Christ*.

Basic to all Tom's theology and to James's, and in this they follow Calvin and Athanasius, is that our salvation is dependent on the "vicarious humanity and sole priesthood of Christ." As Athanasius had taught, Christ the incarnated Son of God ministers the things of God to us and of us to God. They believe that this is the teaching of Scripture, yet many theologians and many evangelicals fail to give proper attention to the humanity of Christ and its relation to our salvation.

Such theologians and evangelicals strongly resist a doctrine of redemption through the whole vicarious life of Christ from his birth of the Virgin Mary to his crucifixion, resurrection, ascension, and heavenly intercession. They favor a severely judicial notion of atonement as a transaction which took place on the Cross. Atonement for them is in terms of external relations between Christ and sinful people.

Tom and James believe that redemption is not to be regarded simply as a matter of an external transaction between God and the sinner, dependent on Christ's atoning death, and in such a way that Christ's work is separate from his Person. It is not, as James likes to say (following Calvin), a "legal contract." This Tom has developed in his book, *Theology in Reconciliation* (1965), and James in his book, *Worship, Community, and the Triune God of Grace* (1996).

When God took our humanity in Jesus Christ, Jesus lived out a perfect human life in redemptive obedience to the Father. He took on himself our sinful humanity, without sinning himself, died bearing his own divine judgment on our sin, rose in body with power from the dead, ascended as man on our behalf, and ever lives to make intercession for us. To use Calvin's words, "in a wondrous exchange" he invites us to take his place before the Father and imparts to us his own human life of righteousness. His life of faith, of prayer, of service to the Father, all become ours in Christ, in union with him, through the Holy Spirit. A favorite verse of Tom's (and our mother's) and one frequently mistranslated is Galatians 2:20: "The life I live in the body, I live by the faith *of* the Son of God, who loved me and gave himself for me."

Following this failure to understand the "vicarious humanity and sole priesthood of Christ," in Tom's and James's view many evangelicals, and liberals, have an inadequate doctrine of Grace. In preaching that "*If* we repent God will forgive us," they are holding to a notion of "conditional grace." Both Tom and James argue that they are detracting from the free Grace of God and are unscriptural. In Christ, God has redeemed the world. His offer of love and forgiveness is unconditional. His forgiveness of us precedes our repentance, and for us today precedes our birth. His unconditional offer of Grace is that through which the Holy Spirit brings us to repentance and salvation. If we reject his offer then we are lost. Tom has written on this subject in his article "The Atonement: The Singularity of Christ and the Finality of the Cross: the Atonement and the Moral Order." On this issue of "unconditional grace," where both have been so criticized by evangelicals in the U.K. and in the U.S.A., they have frequently seen conversions to Christ, both through their lecturing and their writing.

Tom has always taken a very active interest in the life of the Church.

For the year 1976-1977, he was elected moderator of the General Assembly of the Church of Scotland. Although there are considerable restrictions imposed upon a moderator in what he may say during his year of office, throughout Tom made clear his abiding concern for renewal in the Church through more serious biblical, theological teaching and preaching. He wanted the Bible to be preached in the churches so that Sunday by Sunday people might hear for themselves "the living and dynamic Word of God." In his book *Preaching Christ Today: The Gospel and Scientific Thinking* (1994), he says, "It was James Denney who used to say that our theologians should be evangelists and our evangelists theologians. This is something, I believe, we must learn again in our calling to preach Christ today." On Tuesday, 17 May 1977, at the National Service of Thanksgiving in Scotland on the occasion of the Silver Jubilee of her Majesty the Queen, in his sermon as moderator, he preached from 2 Corinthians 5:18: "All things are of God who has reconciled us to himself through Christ, and has given to us the ministry of reconciliation."

His deep concerns for the Church were incorporated in a document which he wrote and was signed by a number of others in addition to himself. It was entitled *Urgent Call to the Kirk* and was in 1983 sent to every minister of the Church of Scotland. The document says:

> We believe that the Church of Scotland is in deep spiritual crisis. . . . Erosion of fundamental belief has sapped its inner confidence, discarding of great Christian convictions has bereft it of vision and curtailed its mission, detachment of preaching from the control of biblical revelation has undermined its authority as the Church of Christ, neglect in teaching the truth of the Gospel has allowed the general membership to become seriously ignorant of the Christian Faith. With this loss of evangelical substance the Kirk fails to be taken seriously. . . .This calls for our repentance. The hungry sheep look up and are not fed. . . . We call upon the Kirk to commit itself afresh to Jesus Christ and his Gospel and to carry out an evangelical rebuilding of its faith, life and mission. Jesus Christ must be brought back into the centre of the Church and all its life, thought and activity, for He is the sole source of God's incarnate self-revelation, the unique way to God the Father, the only ground of salvation and the one foundation and norm of the Church. The Spirit of Jesus Christ alone can quicken and renew the Church and make it one body with Christ. . . . Mission and evangelism must be given priority.

In that document, Tom clearly revealed his commitment to the spiritual renewal of the Church and his passion for Christ. To that end he had dedicated his life, his ministry, his teaching, and all his biblical, theological, and scientific research.

In his concern for evangelism and the renewal of the Kirk in Scotland Tom drew up a letter, signed by other former moderators of the Church of Scotland inviting the evangelist Dr. Billy Graham to Scotland. This led to the all-Scotland mission led by Billy Graham in 1990.

Tom has never lost his love for China and missionary zeal that China's millions should come to faith in Christ. He has three times returned to China, in 1984, in 1986, and again eight years later in 1994, visiting the places where our father worked and he was born. He had the joy of meeting some who had come to faith in Christ through father's ministry.

On his second visit, he was able to hand over funds which he had raised toward the rebuilding of churches that were destroyed through the cultural revolution in China (1964-1979). On his return from China in 1984, he wrote a letter to over thirty Church leaders throughout the world to say that what China desperately needed was Bibles and pastors, and called for the funding and establishing of a printing press.

To his great joy this appeal was taken up by several Bible societies: the American Bible Society, the British and Foreign, and the Scottish Bible Societies, and by Dr. Chan Young Choi of the United Bible Societies in Kowloon, who won the agreement of Bishop K. H. Ting of Nanjing, and particularly by Dr. John Erickson of the United Bible Societies centered in New York. More than seven million dollars was raised, and an eight-acre plot of ground was purchased near Nanjing on which The Amity Printing Press was established in March 1985. Since then over twenty million Bibles have been printed and distributed throughout China. Tom felt in this that he was helping to carry out in a new way the Bible Society work of his father.

Tom has continued to write and lecture. Despite his age, he has remained intellectually and spiritually as alert as ever. Alister McGrath has said, "Torrance's list of published works contain roughly 320 works which originated during his twenty-nine year period as a professor at Edinburgh. Since retiring from that position in 1979, he has added a further 260 items, including some of his most significant works."[1] Last summer (1999), *Passion for Christ* was published. In it the three of us as brothers have endeavored to share our vision of the Gospel.

He had been awarded two doctorates for work submitted and has since received eight honorary doctorates from different universities. He has received a remarkable number of other honors, distinctions, and appointments. Through it all he remains a servant of the Gospel with a passion for Christ and the furtherance of his Kingdom. Both to his own and to his extended family and friends he continues to be a source of help, strength, and inspiration. They enjoy his love and appreciate his continuing kindness and generosity and his willingness to forgive even when wrongly criticized or attacked theologically. They share his joy that his siblings and many of his extended family are witnesses to the Gospel.

I close with extracts from two of his prayers offered in the General Assembly of the Church of Scotland, May 1977. They reveal his own spiritual pilgrimage and quest, and also his prayerful concern for the Church.

> Heavenly Father . . . we thank Thee for our incarnate Saviour, his life on earth and his death on the Cross; we bless Thee that he interceded for us in his life and prayed for us in his death, making his soul an offering for our sin, and that he ever lives as our Mediator at thy right hand. Continue to pour out upon us, O Lord . . . the Spirit of thy Son, that joined to him in the life he prayed and the death which he offered on our behalf we may learn daily to pray as he prayed and live as he lived: that all we do . . . may please Thee.
>
> May the heavenly intercession of thy Beloved Son so prevail on behalf of thy Church that constrained by divine love it may proclaim the Gospel to all the world until every nation becomes his inheritance and the uttermost parts of the earth are the possession of his Kingdom. Bless with the mighty aid of thy Holy Spirit those who work to the glory of thy Name in distant lands. Give them wisdom and courage in all their difficulties, and the great joy of gathering men and women and children into the one fold of the Saviour of mankind.

Note

1. Alister E. McGrath, *T. F. Torrance: An Intellectual Biography* (Edinburgh: T&T Clark, 1999), 107.

Chapter 2

T. F. Torrance in Relation to Reformed Theology

by Alasdair Heron

This chapter attempts to map the place of T. F. Torrance in the tradition of Reformed theology, a somewhat tricky undertaking for at least two reasons. First of all, the very term "Reformed," as in "Reformed Church" or "Reformed theology," is more than a little slippery, depending on where it is being used and by whom. Second, while it is clear enough in a broad way that Torrance is rightly seen as a major representative of that tradition, and while he also understands himself as standing within it, it is equally clear that as an area of historical and constructive systematic theology it is indeed *one* of his wide-ranging interests, but only one of several, and not perhaps the most prominent or most extensively treated by him.

1. The associations and overtones of the adjective "Reformed" tend to be rather different in different contexts. In Germany it designates a non-Lutheran minority within the German Protestant Churches, and the "non-Lutheran" aspect tends to be in the forefront of awareness both inside and outside the Reformed communities. By contrast, in countries where the majority Protestant party at the time of the consolidation of the Reformation was more colored by the example of Zwingli's Zürich or Calvin's Geneva (Switzerland, France, the Netherlands, or Scotland for example), there is generally, except among historians and theologians, little sense of any difference between "Reformed" and "Protestant." Or to stay for a moment with Scotland: there is indeed practically no difference in the public mind between "Protestant," "Reformed," and "Presbyterian," so dominant did the Presbyterian polity become in Scotland once the Episcopalian challenge was finally defeated in the wake of what it is

probably no longer politically correct to call the Glorious Revolution.

In England, by contrast, to say nothing of North America, it is more obvious that "Reformed" and "Presbyterian" are not synonymous and that Presbyterianism is only one wing of the Reformed family, which also includes on the one hand descendants of other historic European forms of synodal Church polity, and on the other hand the Congregationalist heirs of English Puritan independentism. Nor does the diversity end there, for it was also this English Reformed theological and ecclesiastical matrix that in the early seventeenth century brought forth a new family of Baptist Churches distinct from the Mennonite and other communities descending from the radical Reformation.

2. This breadth and variety can be illustrated in a number of ways. One illuminating example might be the sheer diversity and number of Reformed confessions of faith[1] by contrast with the closed Autheran canon[2] (or the even more narrowly defined Anglican articles). Another might be the range of membership of the World Alliance of Reformed Churches[3] (a considerably less homogeneous body than its Anglican or Lutheran equivalents) as well as the great variety of theological and political interests reflected in its study and action programs over, say, the last twenty years.[4] Or one might point to the spectrum reflected in the sterling efforts of Donald McKim in recent years to document the width of historical and theological aspects of the Reformed tradition.[5] Yet another example is the volume of papers recently edited by David Willis and Michael Welker, *Toward the Future of Reformed Theology,*[6] to which T. F. Torrance himself was one of the contributors.

3. In view of this internal variety (to say nothing of a good number of hotly disputed or at least controversial issues within the Reformed theological tradition) it seems unlikely that any theologian could today successfully attempt to repeat the endeavor of Heinrich Heppe a century and a half ago to sum up and present the entire Reformed tradition in a broadly unified way and to do so by appeal to the foundational epoch represented by Bullinger and Calvin and the Reformed theology of the next three or four generations after them.[7]

By the same token, even the most committed of Reformed theologians can hardly represent the whole tradition unless he is possessed of the rare capacity to play chess against himself, and the logically impossible ability to win simultaneously with both black and white. Torrance himself makes it abundantly clear that he is far from affirming everything that passes or has passed for Reformed theology. With him as with any other Reformed theologian one must look more closely to find which aspects of the Reformed tradition have influenced him, which he has accepted or rejected, which he has sought to modify, and what success he has had in the process.

4. Torrance's published work, from his doctoral dissertation on the doctrine of Grace in the apostolic fathers to his most recent books, together with the recently published reprints of several others, does include a good deal of substantial treatment, historically and theologically, of aspects of the Reformed tradition.[8] That, however, is far from being the only focus of his interest, which ranges considerably more widely than that of most representatives of the discipline of systematic theology. (It would be instructive, if not perhaps entirely kind to some of those others, to undertake a quantitative and qualitative comparison of Torrance's published work with that of certain of his contemporaries in chairs of systematic theology in Scotland during the decades of his tenure in Edinburgh.)[9] Four main fields stand out in his bibliography: patristics; Calvin and later Reformed theology; ecumenical theology; method in theology and in natural science. In each of these his work has been substantial. But what is the connecting thread, and can it lead us to a clearer picture of his *Reformed* connection, apart from the mere fact that aspects of Reformed theology have constituted *one* of his specialist interests?

Finding the Thread

I believe such a thread can be detected and would like first of all to trace it in Torrance's own contribution to the Willis/Welker collection, a republication of an article first published in 1983, "The Substance of Faith."[10] The immediate background to this article was a renewal of debate in the Church of Scotland about the terms of subscription to the *Westminster Confession*, on which the Church's Panel on Doctrine had published a volume of articles.[11] T. F. Torrance was not a member of the panel's working group, though his brother James had contributed a substantial paper, inter alia criticizing some aspects of the scheme of federal theology which plays a large part in framing the perspective of the *Confession*.[12] Other contributions had dealt with the background history and the teaching of the *Confession*, with recent debate, and with the current legal position within the Church, with similar discussions and developments in other Presbyterian Churches in various parts of the world and with a range of personal views on the way forward.

The term "substance of faith" which Torrance addressed in this article is used in the formula of subscription to the *Westminster Confession* in the Church of Scotland. This requires of those being ordained recognition of the *Confession* as the principal subordinate standard of the Church but at the same time admits liberty of opinion in such matters as do not enter into the substance of the faith. This formulation had been devised following major nineteenth-century debates and controversies as an attempt to preserve the official status of the *Confession* without insisting on the rigidity of subscription that had led to the expulsion of such distinguished men as John McLeod Campbell, Edward Irving, and Alexander Scott from the ministry of the pre-Disruption national Church.[13] Like all such compromise formulae, it was not without a measure of inbuilt ambiguity as it (perhaps deliberately?) avoided actually defining what was in fact of the substance of the faith and what could safely be regarded as a matter of theological opinion, but not as authoritatively binding.

My interest here is not primarily in exploring that issue per se, but rather in observing how Torrance set about clarifying and deepening the question. That can reveal a good deal about his own perspective and method, and also about how he characteristically views the relation between issues in Reformed theology and his other main fields of interest.

Essentially, his handling of the matter proceeds in three stages: First he surveys the history of the question and the issues in nineteenth-century discussion among Presbyterians on both sides of the Atlantic in order to draw out more precisely what was meant by "the substance of the faith" and by the implicit contrast between such substance and matters less central or less definitive. Second, this survey leads to the identification of the central emphases of the *Catholic* faith as expressed in the *Nicene Creed* as constituting what is intended by "the substance of the faith." This material takes up the greater part of the article and shows what is in Torrance's work a regular, indeed, a characteristic, move from issues in *Reformed* theology to the more fundamental stratum of the *Church fathers*.

Third, however, come three brief references with methodological implications, all designed to tease out the implications of the distinction Basil of Caesarea drew in the fourth century between *kerygma* and *dogma*, coupled with Torrance's own distinctive insistence that *kerygma* refers not only to the *act of proclamation* but to the *self-communication of the one proclaimed.* The references are to Irenaeus, Clerk Maxwell,[14] and Einstein, but let him speak for himself:

It was in just this way that we find the substance or the deposit of faith being understood by Irenaeus. He referred to it as the objective and dynamic core of the *kerygma* which constantly gives substance to faith and renews the life of the Church, the deposit of faith which ever remains the same, identical with itself, and which rejuvenates the faith of the Church. Regarded in this light, the distinction between the substance of the faith and dogmatic expressions of it has to do, not merely with the fact that dogmatic expressions of the faith do not encapsulate the truth but refer to it objectively beyond themselves, but with the fact that the truth is embodied in the incarnate person and acts of God the Son in Jesus Christ . . . .

Let me use an analogy from modern science to illustrate the basic point that must be grasped here. I refer to Clerk Maxwell's emphasis upon "embodied mathematics" or to Einstein's insistence that geometry and experience interpenetrate one another, in view of which both claimed that, taken by themselves, mathematical propositions may be certain but they are not true; they are true only if they are embodied in empirical reality. That is to say, we have to reckon with the fact that empirical and theoretical factors inhere in one another at all levels, in reality and in our knowledge of it. This means that the mathematical formulations of features of reality are true only if they point beyond themselves to structures in which physical and intelligible elements belong inseparably together. The mathematical structures of our scientific theories cannot be identified with ontic structures in nature itself, for they are no more than conceptual means through which we apprehend those structures in nature independent of our theories . . . .

Mutatis mutandis, that is precisely what we are concerned with in distinguishing the substance of the faith from our explicit formulations of it. Empirical and theoretical, historical and theological elements coinhere inseparably together in the substance of the faith, so that we are unable to reduce it to explicit formulations in doctrinal statements or formulations. The formulations which we are compelled to make in obedience to the self-manifestation of the truth point away from themselves to the truth . . . all the Church's formulations of the fundamental doctrines or truths of the faith must be subordinated to the living reality of Jesus Christ, himself the incarnate Word and Truth of God.[15]

With these brief references and this highly concentrated summary of his own theological epistemology Torrance turns what might have been a somewhat specialized and purely historical enquiry (whether into nineteenth-century Presbyterianism or into the Early Church and the fourth-century Arian crisis) into reflection on what actually enables and drives Christian faith and Christian theology. His aim is to bring back into contemporary discussion of what might appear to be simply issues of ecclesiastical authority and juridical definition the critical edge supplied by reflection on the realities involved and on the means by which we seek to understand and express them. That at the same time can explain and justify the fact that in the process the very term "substance of faith" is brought to mean something rather different from what was probably in the minds of those who originally drew up the formula of subscription.

The Case of Scottish Theology

There *in nuce* we have T. F. Torrance's understanding of an appropriate method of theological enquiry. I do not say *the* method, for Torrance would rightly resist such a simplistic reduction of a complex field offering multifarious possibilities of creative investigation, and not only because he ranks with justice as one of the profoundest interpreters of Michael Polanyi, whose *Personal Knowledge* is a monument to the complexity in simplicity and simplicity in complexity of fundamental issues of epistemology and scientific method.[16] It is, however, *a* method, a method which selects and follows through identifiable steps, chosen not arbitrarily or by accident, but in the deliberate expectation that they will prove fruitful.[17]

Thus a question or theme is identified and sketched as it arises or arose in a particular context. The analysis is deepened by going back to a treatment or controversy of particular seminal relevance as opening a view of the abiding theological heart of the matter. The issue is then made contemporary for theology and Church in a fresh way with the help of relevant insights offered from other fields of enquiry, these being employed not to offer diversion from the originally theological topic, but to enable its treatment with renewed seriousness in the hope of a clearer grasp of what it really involves.

How far, however, can this type of method be seen, described, or claimed as distinctively *Reformed?* The particular *problem* addressed certainly arose in a specific Reformed tradition, that of Westminster Presbyterianism, but a similar procedure, once learnt, could equally be applied to issues arising elsewhere. The *conceptual and hermeneutical instruments* employed seem in fact to owe more on the one hand to Torrance's study and interpretation of patristic hermeneutics and on the other to his engagement with the epistemology and methodology of the natural sciences, in particular of physics, in the light of the revolution that discipline has experienced in the last hundred years.

It is also hard to suppress the impression when surveying Torrance's bibliography that in the last thirty years study of the specifically Reformed tradition has somewhat receded into the background, while the patristic and methodological fields have been largely dominant. The books on Calvin's hermeneutics (1988) and on Scottish theology (1996) are, I think, only apparently an exception: the first represents a working up of material originally gathered many years earlier but not at the time published, while the second documents a return to an earlier field of interest. Indeed Torrance's own preface to *Scottish Theology* tends to confirm the impression made by his bibliography; it also casts an endearingly honest light on the sometimes highly fortuitous circumstances leading to a book's seeing the light of day at all:

> For many years I have collected old Scottish books in the hope that one day I might be able to write a history of Scottish Theology from 1560 to 1850, if only to supplement those that have already appeared: James Walker, *The Theology and Theologians of Scotland, chiefly those of the Seventeenth and Eighteenth Centuries* (Edinburgh 1888), and John Macleod, *Scottish Theology in Relation to Church History Since the Reformation* (Edinburgh, 1943). Hitherto that has not proved possible as I have been heavily engaged with Christian dogmatics, Patristic theology, and with the relation between Christian theology and science. Then after I had completed what I thought to be my last book, *The Christian Doctrine of God, One Being Three Persons*,[18] my old purpose was renewed. I had been asked to prepare a chapter on Scottish theology from the Reformation to the Disruption for the volume being published in commemoration of the 150th anniversary of New College, Edinburgh.[19] When I agreed to do this I turned back to my collection of old Scottish theology, and read and studied again books I had not read for many years, and some I had not read at all. I found that in order to write the short chapter asked of me, I had to reinform myself very fully. In order to get a proper grip on it all I had to write much more than was needed for New College. In this way I became caught up in preparing a small volume for publication, but when I worked over it again and again, it grew under my hand, and I found myself producing this book.[20]

A late return to home ground, as it were, but one initially at least more suggested from without than deliberately steered towards from within. Yet if one is looking for a convenient concentration of substantial material reflecting Torrance's engagement with Reformed theology subsequent to Calvin and prior to Karl Barth and his own venerated teacher Hugh Ross Mackintosh,[21] this is probably the best place to look for it. Here too at the latest, if by any chance we had failed to notice it before, we hear an undertone which ever and again makes itself audible in his theology[22] and which he shares with his brother James: a pronounced distaste for certain aspects of Puritan Calvinism combined with the conviction that a radical and destructive shift occurred in theological and pastoral perspective between Calvin and the Calvinists. His diagnosis is succinct and devastating:

> Following upon the teaching of the great Reformers there developed what is known as "federal theology," in which the place John Calvin gave to the biblical conception of the covenant was radically altered through being schematized to a framework of law and grace governed by a severely contractual notion of covenant, with a stress upon a primitive "covenant of works," resulting in a change in the Reformed understanding of the "covenant of grace." This was what Protestant scholastics called "a two-winged," and not "a one-winged" covenant, which my brother James has called a bilateral and a unilateral conception of the Covenant. The former carries with it legal stipulations which have to be fulfilled in order for it to take effect, while the latter derives from the infinite love of God, and is freely proclaimed to all mankind in the grace of the Lord Jesus Christ. It was the imposition of a rigidly logicalized federal system of thought upon Reformed theology that gave rise to many of the problems which have afflicted Scottish theology, and thereby made central doctrines of predestination, the limited or unlimited range of the atoning death of Christ, the problem of assurance and the nature of what was called "the Gospel offer" to sinners. This meant that relatively little attention after the middle of the seventeenth century was given to the doctrine of the Holy Trinity and to a trinitarian understanding of redemption and worship. Basic to this change was the conception of the nature and character of God. It is in relation to that issue that one must understand the divisions which have kept troubling the Kirk after its hard-line commitment to the so-called "orthodox Calvinism" of the Westminster standards, and the damaging effect that had upon the understanding of the Word of God and the message of the Gospel. It must be added that a study of the vicissitudes of

> the Kirk reveals that commitment to the National Covenant and the Solemn League and Covenant had the effect of politicizing theology in a rather misleading and unhelpful way— this is a matter from which the Church of Scotland and the Free Churches of Scotland still suffer.[23]

Clearly Torrance sees the history of Reformed theology, at least in this particular Scottish tradition, as anything but a seamless robe. The dominant line of the tradition through the centuries is chiefly subjected to highly critical examination and called to judgment for far-reaching theological and pastoral defects. The theologians positively regarded and warmly recommended are rather those outside or in conflict with the mainstream, the tradition among others of the Erskines and the other Marrowmen (and of what came to be known as the Original Secession) in the eighteenth century, of Thomas Erskine of Linlathen, Edward Irving, and above all John McLeod Campbell in the first half of the nineteenth. This is a very different perspective, for example, from that offered in the second of the works to which Torrance refers in his preface, John Macleod's *Scottish Theology in Relation to Church History,* and not only in that Macleod offers a fuller survey covering, albeit synoptically, many more figures and issues in a much more comprehensive way.[24]

It is above all the theology of the nineteenth century and the case of McLeod Campbell that John Macleod, representing as he did the Free Church tradition, sees very differently from Torrance. There, however, it must be said that the line pursued by Torrance corresponds to the majority tendency in Scottish ecclesiastical and theological historiography since the latter part of the nineteenth century, and corresponds to what he learned from Mackintosh, as well, no doubt, as to the theology and piety he absorbed from childhood from his missionary parents.[25]

If we add to this observation another, we can perhaps specify Torrance's relation to the Reformed tradition yet more precisely. His work on Reformed theological history after the sixteenth century concentrates very largely on the Scottish, only marginally on the English Puritan, and scarcely at all on the European continental or North American strands (apart on occasion from B. B. Warfield and the Princeton theology of the late nineteenth and early twentieth century). He does not, for example attempt in dogmatics to repeat what Karl Barth undertook, namely a massive critical reworking of the main themes of classical Reformed (and Lutheran) dogmatics from the age of Protestant orthodoxy, though that might have appeared a possible program for one interested in historical theology as a field of academic endeavor and aware of how much even Barth had not covered.

One has the impression, however, that that task never really attracted him, perhaps because he felt it had already been adequately done by Barth, perhaps because of his dislike of so much of what he found or sensed in the world of Reformed scholasticism, perhaps because that program would easily have run out into purely antiquarian theological history rather than vital and constructive dogmatic theology.[26] By contrast the Church fathers on the one side and the epistemological and methodological fascination of the sciences on the other seem to have presented themselves quite simply as more challenging and more rewarding, more exciting intellectually and theologically, more promising as setting the agenda for a theology oriented to the future as well as to the past.

What Is Reformed?

Confirmation of this general assessment is offered by one of Torrance's own statements of his view of Reformed theology: the 1988 Donnell Lecture delivered at Dubuque Theological Seminary on "The Distinctive Character of the Reformed Tradition" and published in the collection of essays honoring his former doctoral student Ray Anderson.[27] Much of what is summarized in that very compact address can perhaps be better understood and appreciated against the background I have tried to outline in the preceding pages. Without attempting to repeat again all that Torrance concentrates into it, let me nevertheless highlight the main emphases.

He begins by stressing that it is in its *doctrine of God* that a theological tradition, and in particular "the whole Reformed tradition from John Calvin to Karl Barth" reveals its real character. Typical of the theologians of the Reformed Church is that they emphasized "the sovereign majesty of the mighty, living, acting, speaking God" as opposed to "Latin patristic and medieval notions of the immutability and impassibility of God, often construed in Aristotelian terms of the Unmoved Mover."[28]

One can even speak here of a paradigmatic shift at the Reformation "from dialectical to dialogic discourse, from abstract questions about essence to concrete questions about event, and thus from mainly static to dynamic modes of thought," as illustrated by "Calvin's reversal of the stereotyped medieval questions: *quid sit, an sit, quale sit.*" Protestant orthodoxy, however, both Reformed and

Lutheran, soon "lapsed back into rather static patterns of thought," although "the urgent concern of the Reformation with doctrines of redeeming and saving event have [*sic*] ever since characterized the whole Protestant tradition." This makes the Reformation the second point in its long history when "the Church has had to struggle for the central truth of the Gospel."[29]

A further step, however was required, and for this the Reformed tradition had some time to wait:

> If the Nicene Fathers had to lay their main emphasis upon the *being* of God in his acts, the Reformers had to lay their main emphasis upon the *acts* of God in his being. It is to Karl Barth's great merit that he has brought these two emphases together in a doctrine of the dynamic being of God, particularly evident in his identification of the electing and revealing act of the eternal God with the incarnation of his beloved Son in space and time.[30]

"The whole Reformed tradition from John Calvin to Karl Barth" seems at points at least to mean rather "the Reformed tradition initiated by Calvin, subsequently distorted almost beyond recognition by the Calvinists, but then recovered and deepened—particularly by Barth." It is in this perspective that Torrance goes on to itemize the four thematic complexes that he presents as characteristic of the Reformed tradition thus identified.

First of all *Predestination and Providence* are summarized, and interpreted in a way that seems to owe rather more to Barth's treatment in *Church Dogmatics* II.2 than to Calvin's in *The Eternal Predestination of God* or *Institutio* III.21-24. One might, incidentally, also hazard the thought that the criticisms here directed against "a split in people's understanding between predestination and the saving activity of Christ in space and time . . . a tendency towards a Nestorian view of Christ that keeps cropping up in Calvinist theology"[31] could with some justification be directed against Calvin himself. Calvin is certainly not responsible for everything that went wrong in subsequent Reformed theology, but it is hard to let him entirely off the hook at this point.[32]

Second comes *the doctrine of the Trinity*, here expounded as turning on a relational concept of the person associated especially with Calvin (in the wake of Richard of St. Victor and Duns Scotus) and described as having

> very far reaching implications in the whole course of the Reformed tradition—not least in respect of the doctrines of the

> knowledge of God and of justification by grace through personal union with Christ, together with the cognate doctrines of Eucharistic Communion and of the Church as the body of Christ. But it also had a wider application to the social structure of humanity and even a startling relevance to physical science in generating insight into the fact that relations of things to one another may belong to what things really are in themselves.[33]

In the exposition of these ideas the situation is reversed as compared with the previous section. What is described here as characterizing the Reformed tradition in fact owes very little to Barth, except for hints at analogies in his thought. It has much greater affinity with Calvin (though the case for a special theological and historical influence of his concept of "person" may be overstated), with the tradition of Scottish Reformed theology that came to the fore in the second half of the nineteenth century and was continued among others by Milligan,[34] Wotherspoon, and Mackintosh, and with Torrance's own methodological interests.

The focus on Calvin is if anything even more apparent in the two remaining sections, which both have to do with issues of epistemology and theological method.[35] Under *Reformed Conceptuality,* Torrance emphasises the "profound epistemological shift from optical to acoustic modes of knowing and thinking" associated with the Reformation and identifies three "main ingredients" of "the particular mode of conceptuality to which Calvin's emphasis on the inseparable relation of Word and Spirit gave rise in the Reformed tradition":

> (1) God's Word is "not some Word detached from God but is consubstantial with him."
> (2) Authentic knowledge of God is never non-conceptual and depends on the *testimonium internum* of the Spirit *as internal to God.*
> (3) Knowledge of God by his Word and Spirit "eschews intelligible as well as sensible images."[36]

Under *Reformed Hermeneutics* the priority given by Calvin to the question *qualis sit* is seen as changing the character of the questions themselves. "They were no longer dialectical questions designed to clarify the logical structure of a set of propositions, but open, *interrogative questions* designed to bring to light the distinctive nature of the realities under investigation." Torrance traces an association in Calvin between this *activa interrogatio* and the principles of the *analogia fidei*, of justification by faith and of the impropriety of all human speech about God such that all our knowledge of God is born of obedience "through such a cognitive indwelling of theologians in the Holy Scriptures that the objective truths of divine revelation become steadily imprinted upon their minds." He then ends his survey by drawing attention to similarities between Calvin and Francis Bacon on the question of interrogative questioning and James Clerk Maxwell and the Scottish Reformed tradition in the onto-relational understanding of persons in theology and particles in dynamic field theory, and concludes "that Reformed theology may still have a very important part to play in our understanding of the kingdom of nature as well as the kingdom of God."[37]

Taking this article as a whole, it would be fair to say that the scenario developed in it is largely dominated by Calvin (except on the matter of predestination, where Barth is brought in to help, as also for a tendency sometimes to interpret Calvin's ideas on theological method in the light of questions formulated in ways belonging more to the realm of post-Enlightenment theological and philosophical debate) and by issues in theological and scientific epistemology, with more than a hint that Reformed theology has been and could yet again become of assistance in the exploration and understanding of the kingdom of nature, themes which of course are developed more fully in Torrance's work on theological science.

To repeat what by now must have become sufficiently clear: it is not really the historical tradition of Reformed theology per se that interests Torrance or to which he feels himself committed. It is rather *the tradition of Reformed theology at those points where it has been or can again become creative in terms of theological enquiry or in terms of its constructive interaction with other fields of investigation, especially in the natural sciences*. Hence in particular his high appreciation of Barth, even though Barth, as is well known, held back from any too close contact between Christian dogmatics and natural science, insisting rather on the need to draw a clear boundary between them, in spite of the similarities Torrance and others saw between the methodological implications of his theology and trends in physics in particular.[38]

Torrance and Barth

This last point can serve to highlight the distinctiveness of Torrance's contribution to Reformed theology from yet another angle. Not only does he opt decidedly for Calvin against later Calvinism of the Puritan, and hyper-Calvinist varieties, and then for Barth over against other, more conservative tendencies in recent Reformed thought. He also shows independence over against Barth in two ways. First, in a "higher" understanding of the priesthoood of Christ, and with it order, ministry, sacraments, and liturgy, here reflecting the revived Scottish Reformed heritage of the nineteenth-century over against the "low Church," antiliturgical and antisacramental, virtually congregationalist ecclesiology to which Barth subscribed, here reflecting widespread (though not, it must be said, universal) tendencies among the Swiss and German Reformed Churches.[39] Second, in pursung energetically the dialogue with the sciences, and while accepting Barth's criticisms of a certain style of *natural theology,* the search for a fresh *theology of nature* in which scientific research and discovery can be seen as part of the calling of humanity as "priest of creation."[40]

It is probably the case that his outlook and sensibilities in both these areas were already molded before he came into direct contact with Barth. It should of course be remembered here that in spite of his early reputation as a, indeed *the* British Barthian and in spite of all his enormous efforts to make Barth's theology known, he was never in fact a Barthian in the sense of the "Barthian school." He studied with Barth only briefly as a postgraduate student, and as a teacher he did not set out to propagate "Barthian theology" as a program, as I can testify both as a former student and junior colleague.[41] He was (and to this day is) much too original, independent, and plain interested in the subjects of his own theological studies to act and sound merely like an echo of Barth.

So even if one were inclined to define modern Reformed theology by reference to Barth (as some would do), one would have to recognize in that perspective too that T. F. Torrance is no mere follower. But that, in the end of the day, actually fits perfectly with his understanding of what theology, including Reformed theology, ought to be: not the slavish following of any teacher or tradition, however brilliant or venerable, but the bringing of the mind into grateful subjection to the glorious revelation of the truth and reality of God in the light of him who for us and for our salvation came down . . . and was made man.

Notes

1. E. F. Karl Müller, *Die Bekenntnisschriften der reformierten Kirche* (1903; reprint, Zürich: Theologische Buchhandlung, 1987); W. Niesel, ed., *Bekenntnisschriften und Kirchenordnungen der nach Gottes Wort reformierten Kirch* (Zürich: Evangelischer Verlag Zollikon, 1938); L. Vischer, ed., *Reformed Witness Today: A Collection of Confessions and Statements of Faith Issued by Reformed Churches* (Bern: Evangelische Arbeitsstelle Ökumene Schweiz, 1982).

2. *Die Bekenntnisschriften der evangelisch-lutherischen Kirche, herausgegeben im Gedenkjahr der augsburgischen Konfession 1930* and frequently reprinted since (most recently, Göttingen: Vandenhoek & Ruprecht, 1998), contains the classic Lutheran canon: the three creeds of the ancient Church; the Augsburg Confession with Melanchthon's Apology and De Potestate et Primatu Papae; Luther's Catechisms and Schmalcald Articles; the Formula of Concord.

3. World Alliance of Reformed Churches, *List of Member Churches*, Geneva, April 2000: "The World Alliance of Reformed Churches, founded in 1875, links 75 million Christians in 215 Congregational, Presbyterian, Reformed and United Churches in 106 countries around the world."

4. Documented in the series *Studies from the WARC* and in the journals *Reformed World* and *Update* (all published by WARC, Geneva). See also K. B. Gerschwiler, *Ökumenische Theologie in den Herausfor-derungen der Gegenwart. Lukas Vischer zum 65. Geburtstag* (Göttingen: Vandenhoek & Ruprecht, 1991); A. P. F. Sell, *A Reformed, Evangelical, Catholic Theology* (Grand Rapids, Mich.: Eerdmans, 1991); M. Opocensky, "Reformierter Weltbund," *TRE* 28 (1997): 419-23.

5. D. K. McKim, ed., *Encyclopedia of the Reformed Faith* (Louisville, Ky.: Westminster/John Knox Press & Edinburgh: T&T Clark, 1992); *Major Themes in the Reformed Tradition* (Grand Rapids, Mich.: Eerdmans, 1992).

6. D. Willis and M. Welker, eds., *Toward the Future of Reformed Theology: Tasks, Topics, Traditions* (Grand Rapids, Mich.: Eerdmans, 1999). A similar thematic breadth is well reflected, for example, in H. Deuser u.a., Hg., *Gottes Zukunft - Zukunft der Welt: FS für Jürgen Moltmann zum 60. Geburtstag* (Munich: Kaiser, 1986); H. A. Oberman, *Reformiertes Erbe: FS für Gottfried W. Locher zu seinem 80. Geburtstag (= Zwingliana* XIX/1-2) (Zürich: Theologischer Verlag, 1992/1993).

7. H. Heppe's *Die Dogmatik der evangelisch-reformierten Kirche dargestellt und aus den Quellen belegt* was originally published in 1861. Ernst Bizer's revised edition appeared in 1934 (Neukirchen: Neukirchener

Verlag, 1958); Eng. trans. by G. T. Thomson, *Reformed Dogmatics Set Out and Illustrated from the Sources* (London: George Allen & Unwin, 1950).

8. The most comprehensive bibliography is to be found in Alister E. McGrath, *T. F. Torrance: An Intellectual Biography* (Edinburgh: T&T Clark, 1999), 249-96. Torrance's main books on specifically *Reformed* topics are *Calvin's Doctrine of Man* (London: Lutterworth Press, 1949); *Kingdom and Church: A Study in the Theology of the Reformation* (Edinburgh: Oliver and Boyd, 1956) (admittedly including Luther as well as Calvin and Bucer!); *Karl Barth: An Introduction to His Early Theology, 1910-1931* (New York: Harper, 1972); *The Hermeneutics of John Calvin* (Edinburgh: Scottish Academic Press, 1988); *Karl Barth: Biblical and Evangelical Theologian* (Edinburgh: T&T Clark, 1990); *Scottish Theology from John Knox to John McLeod Campbell* (Edinburgh: T&T Clark, 1996). The articles in the same field are too numerous to list here, but several of the most significant are contained in *Theology in Reconstruction* (London: SCM; Grand Rapids, Mich.: Eerdmans, 1965): "The Influence of Reformed Theology on the Development of Scientific Method," 62-75; "Knowledge of God and Speech about Him according to John Calvin," 76-98; "The Word of God and the Nature of Man," 99-116; "Justification: Its Radical Nature and Place in Reformed Doctrine and Life," 150-68; "The Roman Doctrine of Grace from the Point of View of Reformed Theology," 169-92; "A New Reformation?" 259-83. Two other collections from a few years later, *God and Rationality* (London: Oxford University Press, 1971) and *Theology in Reconciliation: Essays towards Evangelical and Catholic Unity in East and West* (London: Geoffrey Chapman, 1975) lean respectively more heavily towards questions of method and patristic studies with ecumenical implications. Mention should also be made of the translations and editions of *The Mystery of the Lord's Supper: Sermons on the Sacrament Preached in the Kirk of Edinburgh in A.D. 1589 by Robert Bruce* (London: James Clark, 1958) and *The School of Faith: The Catechisms of the Reformed Church* (London: James Clark, 1959), as well as of his coediting of the revision of Wotherspoon and Kirkpatrick, *A Manual of Church Doctrine according to the Church of Scotland* (London: Oxford University Press, 1965), of Calvin's *New Testament Commentaries* and of the English edition of Barth's *Church Dogmatics.*

9. The two members of the same generation who come closest (leaving aside James Torrance) are doubtless J. K. S. Reid and John McIntyre, but both in range of serious academic interests and volume of publications they come very far behind. Other significant Scottish contributions to theology were made by Donald MacKinnon and John Macquarrie, but mostly outside of Scotland and in Anglican ecclesiastical domicile.

10. T. F. Torrance, "The Substance of Faith," in Willis and Welker, *Reformed Theology,* 167-77; originally in *Scottish Journal of Theology* 36, no. 3 (1983): 327-38. Cf. also the rather longer article by Torrance, "The Deposit of Faith," *Scottish Journal of Theology* 36, no. 1 (1983): 1-28.

11. A. I. C. Heron, ed., *The Westminster Confession in the Church Today,* (Edinburgh: St. Andrew Press, 1982).

12. J. B. Torrance, "Strengths and Weaknesses of the Westminster Theology," in Heron, ed., *Westminster Confession*, 40-54. This article was subsequently fiercely criticized as misrepresenting federal theology (C. S. McCoy and J. Wayne Baker, *Fountainhead of Federalism: Heinrich Bullinger and the Covenantal Tradition* [Louisville, Ky.: Westminster/John Knox Press, 1991], 8), but the criticism rather misses the point though it is right to insist that federal theology should not *only* be seen through Westminster spectacles.

13. See the relevant material in Torrance's *Scottish Theology,* especially chapters 8 and 9, 257-317.

14. Unfortunately misspelled in Willis and Welker, *Reformed Theology,* as *Clark* Maxwell.

15. Willis and Welker, *Reformed Theology*, 176-77.

16. Michael Polanyi, *Personal Knowledge. Towards a Postcritical Philosophy,* (London: Routledge, 1958). Cf. T. F. Torrance, ed., *Belief in Science and in Christian Life: The Relevance of Michael Polanyi's Thought for Christian Faith and Life* (Edinburgh: Handsel Press, 1980).

17. It is also, it may be added, the kind of method Torrance was concerned to inculcate in students of systematic theology. In retrospect some of us can confirm how successful he was, but also how difficult it could be for those of us trained in this way to get attuned to the same wave-length as the products of other schools (and vice versa)!

18. T. F. Torrance, *The Christian Doctrine of God: One Being Three Persons* (Edinburgh: T&T Clark, 1996). Like two other of Torrance's major later publications, *The Trinitarian Faith: The Evangelical Theology of the Ancient Catholic Church* (Edinburgh: T&T Clark, 1988), and *Divine Meaning: Studies in Greek Patristic Hermeneutics* (Edinburgh: T&T Clark, 1992), this is essentially a study in dogmatic theology by way of the Church fathers.

19. T. F. Torrance, "From John Knox to John McLeod Campbell," in *Disruption to Diversity: Edinburgh Divinity, 1846-1996,* ed. D. F. Wright and G. D. Babcock (Edinburgh: T&T Clark, 1996), 1-28.

20. T. F. Torrance, *Scottish Theology*, ix.

21. On Mackintosh see R. Redman, *Reformulating Reformed Theology: Jesus Christ in the Theology of Hugh Ross Mackintosh*, (Lanham, Md.: University Press of America, 1997).

22. One of many examples that could be mentioned is Torrance's warm and generous reminiscence, "John Baillie at Prayer," in *Christ, Church, and Society: Essays on John Baillie and Donald Baillie,* ed. D. Fergusson (Edinburgh: T&T Clark, 1993), 253-61.

23. Fergusson, *Church and Society*, x-xi.

24. This is not, it should be said, intended as a criticism of Torrance's *Scottish Theology.* He himself states in the preface, "This book is not really a history, but comprises brief soundings," ix. The dominant perspective is

nonetheless clearly apparent. An impression of how much a really comprehensive history would have to cover in the light of the sources and secondary materials available today can be gleaned from the *Dictionary of Scottish Church History and Theology,* ed. N. M. deS. Cameron et al. (Edinburgh: T&T Clark, 1993).

25. If I may add a parallel here from my own family history. My father, John Heron (1913-1987), who was for many years closely associated with T. F. Torrance in theological work for the Church of Scotland, in particular as secretary of the Special Commission on Baptism which Torrance convened, might not unfairly be described, like Torrance himself, as a Catholic Barthian, the Catholic element being represented in his case too by a great sympathy for Eastern Orthodoxy, long-standing ecumenical engagement, a profound sense of liturgy in the tradition of the Church Service Society, and a staunch refusal to follow Barth in his deconstruction of sacramental baptismal theology. Like Torrance, too, he came from an ecclesiastical and theological background which was more "evangelical" than "Calvinist" or "Catholic." His father, William Heron (1881-1961), worked after leaving school first in the mines, then as an evangelist with the Lanarkshire Christian Union. When already more than thirty years old, he made the decision to study divinity at Trinity College and subsequently became a minister of the United Free Church in Bainsford, Falkirk, then after the Union of 1929 of the reunited Church of Scotland in Springburn, Glasgow. His mother, Jessie Findlater (1889-1978), grew up in the Original Secession congregation in Carluke and acted as secretary to its distinguished minister Dr. Alexander Smellie, author among other works of *Men of the Covenant* (London: Andrew Melrose, 1903; 1908). Her brother, Robert Findlater, was the last clerk of the Synod of the Original Secession Church, leading it back into union with the Church of Scotland in the 1950s. In these last two generations I therefore seem to detect a similar development in my own family to that in the Torrances with the difference that they form a much larger theological dynasty!

26. Another personal reminiscence to illustrate the point. Some years ago when teaching in Pittsburgh Theological Seminary I was visited there by David Harned, himself much influenced by Torrance and author of a series of lively and engaging contemporary theological books, including *Images for Self-Recognition: The Christian as Player, Sufferer, and Vandal* (New York: Seabury, 1977) and *Creed and Personal Identity* (Philadelphia: Fortress Press, 1981). When he saw that I was engaged in reading and taking notes on some book on Reformed orthodoxy (I think it was probably Keith Sprunger's *The Learned Dr. William Ames* [Urbana, Ill.: University of Illinois Press, 1972]) his reaction was a puzzled enquiry why on earth I was wasting my time on that! I can also remember Torrance's own amusement on hearing that even in lectures in Erlangen I use the good old acronym "TULIP" to fix the five points of classical Calvinism in the bemused minds of my mainly Lutheran students!

27. T. F. Torrance, "The Distinctive Character of the Reformed Tradition," in *Incarnational Ministry: Essays in Honor of Ray S. Anderson,* ed. C. H. Kettler and T. H. Speidell (Colorado Springs, Colo.: Helmers and Howard, 1990), 2-15.

28. Cf. T. F. Torrance, "Karl Barth and the Latin Heresy," *Scottish Journal of Theology* 39, no. 3 (1986): 289-308.

29. Torrance, "Reformed Tradition," 2-3.

30. Torrance, "Reformed Tradition," 3.

31. Torrance, "Reformed Traditiom," 4-5.

32. My friendly disagreement with Torrance on this matter is of more than thirty years standing, so probably neither of us is likely to change his mind now. But it would be disingenuous of me not to advert to it.

33. Torrance, "Reformed Tradition," 5.

34. W. Milligan, *The Resurrection of Our Lord* (London: Macmillan, 1890); *The Ascension and Heavenly Priesthood of Our Lord* (London: Macmillan, 1892).

35. Observant readers will notice the thematic overlap in these pages with the articles on Reformed theology reprinted in Torrance, *Reconstruction* and listed above (n. 8).

36. Torrance, "Reformed Tradition," 9-11.

37. Torrance, "Reformed Tradition," 11-15.

38. Cf. Karl Barth, *Church Dogmatics* I.1, §1 and the introduction to *Church Dogmatics* III.1; G. Howe, "Parallelen zwischen der Theologie Karl Barths und der heutigen Physik"; E. Wolf et al., *Antwort: Karl Barth zum 70. Geburtstag* (Zürich: Evangelischer Verlag, 1956), 409-22; A. M. Finke, *Karl Barth in Grossbritannien: Rezeption und Wirkungsgeschichte* (Neukirchen: Neukirchener Verlag, 1995).

39. See for example the perceptive and revealing comments of Reinhold Niebuhr after a conversation with Barth in 1947 in Ursula M. Niebuhr, ed., *Remembering Reinhold Niebuhr* (San Francisco: Harper, 1991), 236-40.

40. What still appear to me to be the key emphases are summarized in my *A Century of Protestant Theology* (London: Lutterworth; Philadelphia: Westminster, 1980), 209-14.

41. A little more on this is to be found in my paper "Karl Barth: A Personal Engagement," in J. Webster, ed., *The Cambridge Companion to Karl Barth* (Cambridge: Cambridge University Press, 2000), 296-306.

Chapter 3

The Christology of Thomas F. Torrance

by Andrew Purves

The theology of Thomas F. Torrance is a theology of the knowledge of God in and through Jesus Christ. Although there are books and essays where Torrance interprets the history of Christology and presents a positive position, there is no one source where Christology is fully and systematically expounded. The interpreter has to draw upon and systematize a huge range of published material in which Torrance returns to basic themes as he reworks them in an attempt to express ever more correspondingly and coherently his understanding of the person and work of Jesus Christ.[1]

Christology is the study of *God* comc among us revealingly and savingly in Jesus Christ. This means who and what God is toward us in Jesus Christ God is antecedently and eternally in himself.[2] "Everything hinges upon the reality of God's *self*-communication to us in Jesus Christ . . . so that for us to know God in Jesus Christ is really to know him as he is in himself."[3] For Torrance, then, Christology is worked out on the basis of a realist and unitary outlook upon God and the universe in which Jesus Christ is known from the knowledge he gives us of himself in his own inner relation to God the Father, and in his incarnate Person as mediator.[4] In this way Jesus Christ is known a posteriori in terms of the actual relations and reality that constitute him as the Logos of God. Thus the relation between Christ and God, and the relation between the message and work of Jesus and his Person, remain attached.

This exposition is organized around three central themes in Torrance's Christology: (1) the homoousial relationship between Christ and the Father as this is brought to expression in the face of the cosmological dualism he insists is inherent in Western thought; (2) the relationship between the incarnation and the atonement; and (3) the significance of the twofold ministry of Jesus Christ. Characterizations of and critical reflections on Torrance's Christology will close the discussion.

The *Homoousion* in the Context of Dualism

Torrance insists that the Early Church was faced (and the Church continues to be faced) with a cosmological and epistemological dualism of immense proportion that threatens the Gospel. The theological development of the Christian doctrine of the incarnation occurred over and against the philosophical notion of a fundamental disjunction or separation (*chorismos)* between the "real" world of the intelligible and the phenomenological or less "real" or shadowy world of the sensible.[5] This disjunction is found in one form or another in ancient times in the middle dialogues of Plato, in Aristotle, Clement, and Origen, and in Augustine, and in modern times in Descartes, Newton, and Kant. "The Church found itself struggling with two powerful ideas that threatened to destroy its existence: (*a*) the idea that God himself does not intervene in the actual life of men in time and space for he is immutable and changeless, and (*b*) that the Word of God revealed in Christ is not grounded in the eternal Being of God but is detached and separated from him and therefore mutable and changeable."[6] If this disjunction holds, Christianity falls apart. It drives a wedge between God as creator and God in redemption in such a way that it cuts into the unity of the incarnation by separating Christ's divinity from his humanity, thereby also destroying the atonement and rendering impossible the Christian doctrine of God. "This created a real problem for the Church's understanding of the Incarnation as a real *egeneto sarx* on the part of the Logos, for it inhibited a serious consideration of a real *becoming* of the intelligible in the sensible, or of the eternal in the contingent."[7]

The effect is to shut God out of the world. It means that God has not really come among us in Jesus Christ. Incarnation, in which case, is apparent but not real, for God only seemed to become a man, which is docetic. Or Jesus is considered to be only a godly man, even the most godly, but not God, which is ebionite.[8] In either case, the world of God and the world of the creature remain separated. The consequence is the collapse of redemption into mythology and the language of symbol. Salvation has then no historical or empirical dimension; and Jesus is not ontologically grounded in God. This leads to the loss of meaning in christological speech because it has no objective reference in God corresponding to it.

This absolute separation between God and the world has come into modern thought in a most damaging way through Immanuel Kant. Kant argued for an axiomatic distinction between unknowable things in themselves and what is scientifically knowable, namely, things as they appear to us. Kant limited knowledge to what we can make out of these appearances, insisting on a bifurcation between the realm of hypothetical entities and ideas from the realm of phenomenal objects and events. According to Torrance,

> this implied a deep split in human experience: between the experience of man as a being in the world of phenomena, where he has no freedom, and the experience of man as a subject of the supersensual, or noumenal, world, where his only freedom belongs. . . . Kant severed the connection between science and faith, depriving faith of any objective or ontological reference and emptying it of any real cognitive content. . . . The whole history of nineteenth- and twentieth-century theology demonstrates that so long as people operate with an axiomatic disjunction between a noumenal realm of ideas and a phenomenal realm of events, nothing more than a merely moral or poetic or symbolic or mythological meaning can be given to the biblical account of the saving interaction of God with us in the world of space and time.[9]

For Torrance, the assumption of this cosmological dualism into Christology drives a wedge between Jesus' divinity and humanity, destroying the basic faith of the Church by cutting Christ into two aspects.[10] The false question that arises for Christology is: on which side of the dichotomy are we to think of Jesus Christ? In response, it had already become clear to the Greek theologians of the fourth century especially that a very different, unitary approach to the doctrine of Christ was needed, one in which they understood him right from the start in his wholeness and integrity as one person who is both God and human being.[11]

In view of the dualism between God and creation (which is not to be confused with the distinction between the creator and his creation) Torrance argues that we must start off on a different foot altogether. In order to know Christ aright it is necessary to know him as he discloses himself to us on his own terms, in the light of his being as the Logos of God and the Son of the Father. Knowing Jesus Christ on his own ground as he reveals that to us, our knowledge is reconciled to the truth of who he is in the unity of his incarnate personhood. In this way he is known according to his nature (*kata physin)* within the objective frame of meaning that he has created for the Church, through the apostolic testimony to him. Such knowledge proceeds to understand Jesus Christ in the light of internal relations within God, as far as we can apprehend that, and within the matrix of interrelations out of which he came as a son of Israel and Son of Man. This, according to Torrance, is to know him as he is in his own being, according to his own nature.

For Torrance, the historical answer to "this menace" of dualism was, and for him still is, the *homoousion* of the Nicene Creed, the doctrine that Jesus Christ, the Word of God, belongs to the divine side of reality, and is very God come into our world to redeem us.[12] In this way, the primary heuristic theological instrument by which a realist, unitary knowledge of Jesus Christ was developed is the doctrine of the *homoousion* through which the Church rejected the pagan disjunction between creation and redemption, and showed the nature of the incarnation and atonement for our salvation.

What is the nature of the relation between Jesus Christ and God the Father? This, according to Torrance, was the decisive issue set before the Church in the fourth century, as it still is. It was in answer to this question that the Nicene Fathers formulated their response, ratified by the Council of Constantinople, that we believe in God the Father, "And in the one Lord Jesus Christ, the Son of God, begotten from his Father, only-begotten, that is, from the being of the Father, God from God, Light from Light, true God from true God, begotten not made, of one being with the Father, through whom all things were made."[13] The central concept here is "of one being with the Father" (*homoousios to Patri).* It intends to express the oneness in being between the Father and the Son, making explicit also the identification of the Son with the Creator through the reference "through whom all things were made."[14] In this way, says Torrance, the Council "decided to cut away all ambiguity and remove any possibility for misunderstanding by inserting the crucial expression 'of one being with the Father'. . . which meant that the Son and the Father are equally God within the one being of God."[15] Although the *homoousion* is a nonbiblical term, it is a purely theological, i.e., scientific, construct or instrument[16] by which the Church has been able to apprehend and henceforth to protect the central evangelical truth of the gospel. In sum: (1), "it is the self-same God who is revealed to us as the Son and the Father."[17] And (2), "if the Son is eternally begotten of the Father *within* the being of the Godhead, then as well as expressing the oneness between the Son and the Father, *homoousios* expresses the distinction between them that obtains within that oneness."[18]

Interpreting this, Torrance says that "the *homoousios to Patri* was revolutionary and decisive: it expressed the fact that what God is 'toward us' and 'in the midst of us' in and through the Word made flesh, he really is *in himself*; that he is in the *internal relations* of his transcendent being the very same Father, Son and Holy Spirit that he is in his revealing and saving activity in time and space toward mankind."[19] The *homoousion* crystallizes the view that while the incarnation falls within the structures of our humanity, it also falls within the life and being of God.[20] This is the important point. In this way, Torrance understands that the *homoousion* protected the integrity of the gospel, being the hinge upon which the Creed turned and remaining still the cardinal concept to which the Church has returned again and again in the understanding and proclamation of the Gospel.

Two points may be noted. Firstly, there is the epistemological significance of the *homoousion.*[21] According to Torrance, without the *homoousion*, if Jesus Christ were not wholly God (*totus Deus* but not *totum Dei*), being only external to God, God would remain utterly unknowable for there is then no access for humankind to the Father through the Son and in the Holy Spirit.[22] This means we would have to think of Jesus Christ as having a transient symbolic relation to God.[23] But confessed as central to the Creed, the *homoousion* means "the Son of God in his incarnate Person is the place where we may know the Father as he is in himself, and know him accurately and truly in accordance with his own divine nature. The *homoousion* asserts that God *is* eternally in himself what he *is* in Jesus Christ, and, therefore, that there is no dark unknown God behind the back of Jesus Christ, but only he who is made known to us in Jesus Christ."[24]

There is, secondly, a soteriological significance to the *homoousion.*[25] When Jesus Christ is detached from God his word of forgiveness is the word only of one creature to another.[26] According to Torrance, "it is quite a difference when the face of Jesus is identical with the face of God, when his forgiveness of sin is forgiveness indeed for its promise is made good through the atoning sacrifice of God in Jesus Christ."[27] The point is: "*only God can save, but he saves precisely as man.*"[28] For Torrance, "the incarnation is to be understood, then, as a real becoming on the part of God, in which God comes *as man* and acts *as man*, all for our sake—from beginning to end God the Son acts among us in a human way."[29] In this case, "the work of atoning salvation does *not* take place *outside* of Christ, as something external to him, but takes place *within* him, *within* the incarnate constitution of his Person as Mediator."[30]

In view of the dualist outlook in religion and thought that

pervaded the ancient world, and that is extant still in theological liberalism, the Church must commit itself again to the Gospel of the incarnation of the Son of God, in which God in Christ has really come among us for our salvation. It must not be thought that in Torrance's mind, however, the term *homoousios* is sacrosanct and beyond reconsideration. All theological terms and concepts fall short of the realities they intend and are open to further modification in the light of it. It is important to register this methodological humility before the objectivity of God lest Torrance be wrongly accused of constructing a closed, rationalistic system of theology based deductively upon fourth-century Greek theology. Nevertheless, he argues that "the formulation of the *homoousion* proved to be of astonishing generative and heuristic power, for it was so well rooted in the source of the Church's faith that it was pregnant with intimations of still profounder aspects of divine reality in Jesus Christ pressing for realisation within the mind of the Church."[31] The formation of the *homoousion* was a turning point of far-reaching significance in which "it was recognised as uniquely constitutive for all subsequent theological and conciliar activity."[32] That is to say, the *homoousion* "took on the role of an interpretative instrument of thought through which the Church's general understanding of the evangelical and apostolic deposit of the Faith was given more exact guidance in its mission to guard, defend, and transmit the Faith in its essential truth and integrity."[33] In Torrance's assessment it became the all-important hinge upon which turned not only the Creed itself, but the development of the Christian doctrine of God and the assurance of the salvation of humankind.

The Incarnation and the Atonement[34]

According to Torrance, "the incarnation means that He by whom all things are comprehended and contained by assuming a body made room for Himself in our physical existence, yet without being contained, confined or circumscribed in place as in a vessel. He was wholly present in the body and yet wholly present everywhere, for He became man without ceasing to be God."[35] Such a statement depends for its coherence upon a notion of space according to which the relation between God and space is not itself a spatial relation.[36] God, the creator of space, stands in a nonspatial relation to creation, yet God has entered into space in such a way that all his relations with us occur within spatial (and temporal) reality. "The only knowledge (of God) possible for us is that which he mediates to us in and through this world. We do not and cannot know God in disjunction from his relation to this world, as if this world were not his creation or the sphere of his activity toward us."[37] When consideration is made of our Lord's resurrection, ascension, and *parousia*, the assumption of our spatial and temporal existence must also be maintained without reserve.[38]

Here Torrance is again battling against forms of the ancient dualist understanding of reality given with the bifurcation between what is real and changeless and what is unreal and evanescent by refusing to operate with an absolute separation between them. The problem the Early Church faced in order to develop a full understanding of the incarnation was the Greek view of a receptacle or container notion of space, which in its Aristotelian form held to the notion of space as delimited place defined as a containing vessel.[39] Because anything beyond space was held to be unthinkable and unintelligible, this implied that if God is intelligible, God must be finite, or if infinite, then unintelligible. Such a view threatened the substance of Christian faith. It denied God's transcendence as both creator of the physical universe and as the ground of all rationality, and it denied the possibility of the incarnation except in symbolic or metaphorical terms. In the thought of the Nicene Fathers, the two worlds of the creator and the creation, while distinct, came not to be seen as absolutely separated, or as only tangentially touching, but as actually intersecting in Jesus Christ.[40]

According to Torrance's analysis, "the essential key was found in the relation of the *homoousion* to the *creation*, that is, in the fact that the Lord Jesus Christ, who shares with us our creaturely existence in this world and is of one substance with the Father, is He through whom all things, including space and time, came to be."[41] Because Jesus Christ is truly and fully historical, while remaining what he ever was, "space is here a predicate of the Occupant, is determined by His agency, and is to be understood in accordance with His nature."[42] When the Son, who ever lives with the Father in the Father's "place," became incarnate, he becomes the "place" where God is really found in human history. A container view of space is now seen to be an inadequate conceptual model, for it is developed independently of the incarnation and outside of the unitary interaction between God and creation in Jesus Christ.

God did not just participate in the life of the man, Jesus, for incarnation is God really become human in Jesus Christ.

> The incarnation is to be understood, then, as a real becoming on the part of God, in which God comes *as man* and acts *as man*, all

> for our sake—from beginning to end God the Son acts among us in a human way (*anthropinos*) . . . . This understanding of Jesus Christ, as, not God *in man*, but God *as man*, implies a rejection of the idea that the humanity of Christ was merely instrumental in the hands of God, but it also implies, therefore, that the human life and activity of Christ must be understood from beginning to end in a thoroughly personal and *vicarious* way.[43]

Torrance rejects any view that suggests the incarnation was apparent but not real, or that Christ was only a godly man. Torrance goes on from the *homoousion*, then, to speak explicitly of Christ as the one in whom divine and human natures are united in his one person. This is the doctrine of the hypostatic union, about which, he believes, Christian theology has not given enough thought since the early centuries,[44] and which has tended to be developed in abstraction from the historical life and work of Jesus Christ.[45]

The hypostatic union is not to be thought of as a doctrine that expresses only the mystery of the person of Christ. In this doctrine, Jesus Christ and his incarnation are understood also soteriologically as falling within the life of God in such a way that he is the personal bridge between God and humankind that is grounded in the being of God and anchored in the being of humankind. Thus the *homoousion* is to "be taken along with a cognate conception about the indissoluble union of God and man in the one Person of Christ,"[46] for the *homoousion* and the hypostatic union together are two fundamental doctrines for understanding the church's faith in Jesus Christ.[47] Reconciliation is not something that is added to the hypostatic union; it is the hypostatic union at work in expiation and atonement.

In this way the incarnation and the atonement constitute both the ontological and the epistemological center of our knowledge of God. Jesus Christ is of God and humankind, being in the union of his person both Word of God and word of humankind in union with whom through the Holy Spirit we have communion with and knowledge of God. But Jesus Christ is also thereby the "place" where we come to a knowledge of ourselves, for as truly human, "the secret of every man, whether he believes it or not, is bound up with Jesus for it is in him that human contingent existence has been grounded and secured."[48] According to Torrance, then, "perhaps the most fundamental truth which we have to learn in the Christian Church . . . is that the Incarnation was the coming of God to save us in the heart of our *fallen* and *depraved* humanity, where humanity is at its wickedest in its enmity and violence against the reconciling love of God."[49] Thus, the whole of our humanity has to be assumed by Christ in the personal union of his two natures, not only our corrupted physical nature, but also our spiritual nature in which we have become alienated from God in our minds.

Torrance has developed the hypostatic union considered as an act of grace in terms of the complementary Patristic doctrines of anhypostasis and enhypostasis.[50] The hypostatic union is the personal union that takes place when the one person of the Son assumes human nature into himself, and thus into his divine nature. The union of divine and human natures is entirely the act of God in becoming a man. The result is that the Son of God exists as the man, Jesus, son of Mary, in the integrity of his human agency. Apart from this act of God in becoming human, however, Jesus would not have existed. In which case, the fully human life of Jesus must be regarded as grounded in the act of the Word of God becoming flesh. The doctrine of the anhypostasis asserts that Christ's human nature has its reality only in union with God, having no independent existence apart from the incarnation.

The doctrine of enhypostasis asserts that Christ's human nature was nevertheless a real and specific existence in which Jesus had a fully human mind, will, and body. This means we must think of the incarnation in terms not of God in humankind, but in terms of God as a man, yet without ceasing to be God. Jesus Christ the Word of God was really human, a man, at once the one and the many.[51] Thus we must not speak of the incarnation and the atonement as two actions, one of God, the other of the man, Jesus. We must speak rather of the one action of the "God-man," maintaining the unity of his Person, in which grace is understood in terms of Christ's human as well as his divine nature.[52] This means that the hypostatic union is to be understood not just in terms of incarnation, but also soteriologically in terms of the reconciliation between God and humankind, while reconciliation is to be understood not just in terms of the cross, but also in terms of the incarnation.

With this understanding of the incarnation it is possible to expound Torrance's teaching on the atonement. As noted, according to Torrance there is no proper knowledge of the incarnation that is not soteriological, and there is no basis for the atonement that is not incarnational. Because Christ's person and work are one, for in the New Testament he is redemption, he is righteousness, he is eternal life, the atonement must be understood in terms of the internal relations established by the doctrines of the *homoousion* and the hypostatic union.[53] The atonement is not an act established externally to Jesus Christ, taking place outside of him, as it were, in an instrumental way. When this happens, the atonement is understood only in terms of the moral order that is not yet redeemed or of a legal order that must be restored.[54] For Torrance, rather, the atonement takes place within Jesus Christ, in the ontological depths of his incarnate life in such a way that the incarnation itself is essentially redemptive.[55] "Thus the redemptive work of Christ was fully representative and truly universal in its range. Its vicarious efficacy has its force through the union of his divine Person as Creator and Lord with us in our creaturely being, whereby he lays hold of us in himself and acts for us from out of the inner depths of his coexistence with us and our existence with him, delivering us from the sentence of death upon us, and from the corruption and perdition that have overtaken us."[56] This does not imply that the incarnation by itself or as such is atonement. But it is important to recall that as the Incarnate One, Christ acts *personally* on our behalf in such a way that the personal and the ontological are held very closely together.[57]

On this ground Torrance develops his theology of the atonement as a substitutionary act of God in Christ for us, making our sin and death his own that we might partake of his righteousness and life. Torrance cites Athanasius, that "the whole Christ became a curse for us," taking upon himself our Adamic humanity, but triumphing over the forces of evil embedded within our existence, bringing his own holiness and obedience to bear in such a way as to condemn sin and deliver us from its power.[58] Again following Athanasius, Torrance is at pains to emphasize Christ's assumption and healing of our human mind. "It is the inner man, in his rational human soul, that man has fallen and become enslaved to sin. It is in the mind, not just the flesh . . . that sin is entrenched."[59] This means that redemption is necessarily closely linked to revelation in which the teaching of Jesus is to be regarded as an essential part of his saving work. Christ's life, from cradle to grave, in which he took on our whole humanity, and not just his death, is to be considered part of the atoning reconciliation.

We come now to consider the nature of the vicarious activity of Christ within the personal union of divine and human natures in the incarnate Son of God. Torrance asserts that "no one can provide for himself or for another a means of salvation which will be accepted in exchange for his life or soul. But this is precisely what Jesus claims to do: to give his *life* as a sacrificial propitiation or ransom (*lutron*), thereby giving an interpretation of his life and death in terms both of cultic atonement and of the suffering servant."[60] Thus, according to Torrance, two key verses form the basis for the doctrine of atonement and redemption: "For the Son of Man came not to be served but to serve, and to give his life a ransom for many" (Mark 10:45); and "This is my blood of the covenant, which is poured out for many"

(Mark 14:24). The means of redemption and the mode of the atonement are located in the shedding of the blood of Christ as a ransom. What does this mean?

The New Testament conception of redemption, and the price of this redemption or ransom, are deeply indebted to three Hebrew terms that are used to refer to different but interrelated aspects of divine redemption: *pdh, kpr,* and *g'l. Pdh* refers to the nature of the act of redemption, *kpr* refers to the atoning expiation as a sacrifice, and *g'l* refers to the nature or person of the redeemer.[61] These overlapping concepts are used to speak of the divine redemption of Israel out of Egypt, and, in Deutero-Isaiah, in association with the promise of a new Israel when God will redeem his people through an anointed servant.[62] In Torrance's view the New Testament writers gathered up the conception of redemption in the Old Testament, and reinterpreted it, though nowhere systematically, in terms of what God had become and done in Jesus Christ. This is found especially in the biblical concept of *apolytrosis* (redemption, deliverance) in which the main ingredients of the Hebrew usage are apparent though not schematized. Redemption by God's grace through the coming of Jesus Christ (e.g., Luke 21:28), redemption by expiation through the blood of Jesus Christ (Ephesians 1:7), and redemption in the Beloved (Ephesians 1:6) are apparent in New Testament usage.[63] *Apolytrosis*, in other words, is understood precisely in relation to the person and work of Jesus Christ.

One final aspect of Torrance's teaching on the atonement should be presented, namely, what is known as the "wonderful exchange," (*katallage*/reconciliation) in which Christ took our place that we might have his place.[64] It is "upon this concept of atoning exchange as its inner hinge that the whole doctrine of incarnational redemption through the descent (*katabasis*) and ascent (*anabasis*), the death and resurrection, the humiliation and exaltation, of the Son of God rests."[65] This has its biblical basis in the Pauline doctrine expressed at 2 Corinthians 8:9 (see also 5:21). Commenting on this text Torrance writes of "the great soteriological principle of sacrificial atoning exchange (*antallagma*), *the unassumed is the unredeemed*."[66] It embraces the entirety of the relationship between Christ and us. For Torrance the whole sweep of redemption is covered in this notion. Human nature is now anchored in God as Christ Jesus himself, crucified and risen. For this reason, theological anthropology begins first here, with the atonement.[67]

Further, it is in view of the atoning exchange that Torrance believes we must approach the question of impassibility and the issue of the redemption of suffering. The sufferings of Christ are not external to the person of Christ. "We must be quite definite about the fact that in the Lord Jesus Christ *God himself* has penetrated into our suffering, our hurt, our violence, our sinful alienated humanity, our guilty condition under divine judgment, and even into our dereliction."[68] God in Christ has done this in a thoroughly vicarious way in that in his pathos with and for us he has brought his divine *apatheia* or serenity to bear redemptively upon our passion. "It is an essential aspect of the atoning exchange in Jesus Christ that through his sharing in our passion (*pathos*) he makes us share in his own imperturbability (*apatheia*)."[69] Thus we have to think in such a way (dynamically and soteriologically on the ground of what actually took place) that in Christ God, through the passion of Christ, makes us to share in his own peace.[70]

In this way we see that redemption through the atoning exchange covers not only our sin, but also our plight as suffering men and women. This is not accomplished by divine *fiat,* or by some transaction conducted above our heads, as it were, but by a real incarnation into the heart of our creatureliness, to save us from within and from below by an astonishing act of love and grace.

The Twofold Ministry of Jesus Christ

As Torrance frequently indicates, he is deeply indebted to Athanasius in many ways. This indebtedness is found, for example, in his development of what the latter spoke of as Christ exercising a twofold ministry[71] in which he "*ministered not only the things of God to man but ministered the things of man to God*."[72] This is a vigorously developed theme in Torrance's Christology. It is especially important to explain how Torrance understands the role of Jesus Christ as the true human in his response to God on our behalf. When this is thought through in relation to the doctrine of union with Christ, Torrance introduces directly his understanding of our specific forms of response that are called forth by the Gospel.

Following Athanasius, Torrance asserts that in the depth of the vicarious humanity of Christ in the incarnation there is both a humanward and a Godward direction, in which Christ mediates God to us and us to God in the unity of his incarnate personhood. This is the direct correlate of the hypostatic union. Thus Torrance refers to the "double fact that in Jesus Christ the Word of God has become man, has assumed a human form, in order as such to be God's language to man, and that in Jesus Christ there is gathered up and embodied, in obedient response to God, man's true word to God and his true speech about God. Jesus Christ is at once the complete revelation of God to man and the correspondence on man's part to that revelation required by it for the fulfilment of its own revealing movement."[73] Hitherto we emphasized how Torrance has developed the ministry of the incarnate Son toward humankind. Now the stress falls upon the way he develops the response of the incarnate Son toward the Father, and, briefly, upon our participation in that response.

Torrance insists that because the Word of God has been addressed to us, and, as such, has actually reached us because it has been addressed to us in Jesus Christ, we have the Word that has found a response in our hearing and understanding. We do not begin with God alone or with humankind alone,

> but with God and man as they are posited together in a movement of creative self-communication by the Word of God. . . . A profound reciprocity is created in which God addresses His Word to man by giving it human form without any diminishment of its divine reality as God Himself speaks it, and in which He enables man to hear His Word and respond to it without any cancellation of his human mode of being. . . . Thus the Word of God communicated to man includes within itself meeting between man and God as well as meeting between God and man, for in assuming the form of human speech the Word of God spoken to man becomes at the same time the word of man in answer to God.[74]

Torrance identifies the foundation for the christological development of the incarnate reciprocity between God and humankind in the nature of the covenant partnership between God and Israel.[75] The pattern for covenanted reciprocity is found, for example, in the covenant established between God and Israel at Mt. Sinai. God knew that Israel would not be able to be faithful as God required. Thus, God, within the covenant established and maintained unilaterally by God, freely and graciously gave a covenanted way of responding so that the covenant might be fulfilled on their behalf. Israel was given ordinances of worship designed to testify that God alone can expiate guilt, forgive sin, and establish communion. This was not just a formal rite to guarantee propitiation between God and Israel, however. By its very nature, the covenanted way of response was to be worked into the flesh and blood of Israel's existence in such a way that Israel was called to pattern her whole life after it. Later, in the prophecies of the Isaiah tradition especially, the notions of guilt-bearer and sacrifice for sin were conflated to give the interpretative clue for the vicarious role of the servant of the Lord.

It would take the incarnation actually to bring that to pass, however, for Jesus Christ was recognized and presented in the New Testament both as the Servant of the Lord and as the divine Redeemer, not now only of Israel, but of all people.

> As the incarnate Son of the Father Jesus Christ has been sent to fulfill all righteousness both as priest and as victim, who through his one self-offering in atonement for sin has mediated a new covenant of universal range in which he presents us to his Father as those whom he has redeemed, sanctified and perfected for ever in himself. In other words, Jesus Christ constitutes in his own self-consecrated humanity the fulfilment of the vicarious way of human response to God promised under the old covenant, but now on the ground of his atoning self-sacrifice once for all offered this is a vicarious way of response which is available for all mankind.[76]

That is, Jesus Christ has fulfilled the covenant from both sides, from God's side, and from our side. In the incarnate unity of his person he is the divine-human Word "spoken to man from the highest and heard by him in the depths, and spoken to God out of the depths and heard by Him in the highest."[77] "Expressed otherwise, in the hypostatic union between God and man in Jesus Christ there is included a union between the Word of God and the word of man."[78] In which case, the Gospel is not to be understood as the Word of God coming to us, inviting our response, but as including "the all-significant middle term, the divinely provided response in the vicarious humanity of Jesus Christ."[79]

It is in terms of the vicarious humanity of God in Christ that the full meaning of the obedience of Christ and the cross may be understood. To this end Torrance is fond of citing Hebrews 3:1-6, where reference is made to Christ as the Apostle and High Priest of our confession. "Here we have described Christ's twofold function in priestly mediation. He is the Apostle or *Saliah* of God, and He is also our High Priest made in all points as we are, but without sin."[80] As High Priest, Jesus is contrasted with Moses, who was faithful in all his house as a servant (Numbers 12:7 and Hebrews 3:5), while Jesus is Son over his own house (Hebrews 3:6).

> In this particular passage the work of Christ as Apostle and High Priest, both in the sense of 'the Son over the House,' is described in terms of confession, *homologia*, a word which occurs in three

> other passages (3:1; 4.:4; 10:23). In each case it sets forth primarily the confession made by the High Priest as he enters within the veil. It is the confession of our sin before God and the confession of God's righteous judgement upon our sin. As Apostle Christ bears witness for God, that He is Holy. As High Priest He acknowledges that witness and says Amen to it. Again as Apostle of God He confesses the mercy and grace of God, His will to pardon and reconcile. As High Priest He intercedes for men, and confesses them before the face of God.[81]

This confession of Christ as Apostle and High Priest is not in word only, but includes the actual judgment of God at the cross and the actual submission of Christ in full and perfect obedience. But this obedience of Christ to the judgment of God must not be limited to his passive obedience only in which he was "made under the Law" to bear its condemnation in our name and on our behalf. For he lived also to bend back the will of humankind into a perfect submission to the will of God through a life lived in active filial obedience to his heavenly Father. Torrance understands, therefore, that the humanity of Christ was not external to the atonement, and that the atonement cannot be limited only to his passive obedience. Rather, Jesus Christ "*is* our human response to God"[82] in such a way that both his passive *and* active obedience are imputed to us,[83] for he not only suffered the judgment of God on the cross for us, but fulfilled the will of God in an obedient life of filial love. In view of this development of the vicarious humanity of Christ it is clear why Torrance insists that incarnation and atonement must be thought together, and why revelation and reconciliation are inseparable.

One final point remains to be discussed, namely, Torrance's doctrine of union with Christ, for it is only through this union that we partake of the blessings of his holy and obedient life.[84] Writing on the doctrine of deification through grace he notes that

> Reformed theology interprets participation in the divine nature as the union and communion we are given to have with Christ in his human nature, as participation in his Incarnate Sonship, and therefore as sharing in him in the divine Life and Love. That is to say, it interprets "deification" precisely in the same way as Athanasius in the *Contra Arianos*. It is only through *real and substantial union* (Calvin's expression) with him in his human nature that we partake of all his benefits, such as justification and sanctification and regeneration, but because in him human nature is hypostatically united to divine nature so that the Godhead dwells in him "bodily," in him we really are made partakers of

the eternal Life of God himself.[85]

Torrance has observed in a number of places that Scottish theology at the Reformation gave a place of centrality to the union of God and humankind in Christ, and to the understanding of the Christian life therefore as an offering to God only "by the hand of Christ" (Knox).[86] Thus, "it is in and through our union with him, that all that is his becomes ours."[87] And again: "It is only through union with Christ that we partake of the blessings of Christ, that is through union with him in his holy and obedient life . . . . Through union with him we share in his faith, in his obedience, in his trust and his appropriation of the Father's blessing."[88] In this way through union with Christ, Torrance's Christology moves seamlessly to his exposition of the Christian life. Union with Christ is given to us through the gift of the Holy Spirit, and as such is the ground of the church. "The Christian Church is what it is because of its indissoluble union with Christ through the Spirit, for in him is concentrated the Church and all ministry . . . . [Thus], there is only one ministry, that of Christ in his Body."[89] It is the case, then, that the Holy Spirit constitutes the church in union with its Head, joining us to Christ to share in his communion with the Father, and to bear faithful witness to him in the life of the world.

Torrance directs his readers to Galatians 2:20, and especially to the words *I yet not I but Christ.*[90] The message of the vicarious humanity of Christ is the Gospel on which we rely. The whole of the Christian life in all regards is included in the *I yet not I but Christ*, for in Jesus Christ all human responses "are laid hold of, sanctified and informed by his vicarious life of obedience and response to the Father. They are in fact so indissolubly united to the life of Jesus Christ which he lived out among us and which he has offered to the Father, as arising out of our human being and nature, that they are *our responses* toward the love of the Father poured out upon us through the mediation of the Son and in the unity of his Holy Spirit."[91]

Before we refer to our own faith, faith must be understood first of all in terms of "Jesus stepping into the relation between the faithfulness of God and the actual unfaithfulness of human beings, actualising the faithfulness of God and restoring the faithfulness of human beings by grounding it in the incarnate medium of his own faithfulness so that it answers perfectly to the divine faithfulness."[92] Jesus acts in our place from within our unfaithfulness, giving us a faithfulness in which we may share. He is both the truth of God and human being keeping faith and truth with God in the unity of God revealing himself and human being hearing, believing, obeying, and speaking his Word.[93] In this way our faith is grounded objectively yet personally in the One who believes for us; our faith depends upon the faithfulness of God in Christ for us. "Thus the very faith which we confess is the faith of Jesus Christ who loved us and gave himself for us in a life and death of utter trust and belief in God the Father. Our faith is altogether grounded in him who is 'author and finisher,' on whom faith depends from start to finish."[94] Indeed we are summoned to believe, but in such a way "in which our faith is laid hold of, enveloped, and upheld by his unswerving faithfulness."[95] We do not rely upon our own believing, "but wholly upon (Christ's) vicarious response of faithfulness toward God."[96]

Likewise with regard to worship, Torrance insists that Jesus Christ has embodied for us the response to God in such a way that henceforth all worship and prayer is grounded in him. "Jesus Christ in his own self-oblation to the Father *is* our worship and prayer in an acutely personalised form, so that it is only through him and with him and in him that we may draw near to God with the hands of our faith filled with no other offering but that which he has made on our behalf and in our place once and for all."[97] All approach to God is in the name and significance of Jesus Christ, "for worship and prayer are not ways in which we express ourselves but ways in which we hold up before the Father his beloved Son, take refuge in his atoning sacrifice, and make that our only plea."[98] Christ has united himself to us in such a way that he gathers up our faltering worship into himself, so that in presenting himself to the Father he presents also the worship of all creation to share in his own communion with the Father. Christ takes our place, and we trust solely in his vicarious self-offering to the Father.

The essential nature of the church, as of individual Christians, is participation in the humanity of Jesus Christ. That is, "the Church is Church as it participates in the active operation of the divine love."[99] As the Son is sent from the Father, so the being of the Church in love involves a sharing also in the mission of Jesus Christ. In this way, ministry is grounded upon a christological pattern (*hupodeigma*). Thus, "as the Body of which he is the Head the Church participates in His ministry by serving Him in history where it is sent by Him in fulfilment of His ministry of reconciliation."[100] The ministry of the Church is not another ministry, different from the ministry of Christ or separate from it, but takes its essential form and content from the servant-existence and mission of Jesus. The mission of the Church is not an extension of the mission of Jesus, but is a sharing in the mission of Jesus. "Thus Jesus Christ constitutes in Himself, in His own vicarious human life and service, the creative source and norm and pattern of all true Christian service."[101]

Formal Characterizations and Critical Reflections

Formal Characterizations

1. Torrance's Christology is expressed as an ongoing conversation between the critical interpretation of the history of Christian theology, with special focus on the fourth century Greek Fathers and the Reformers, and the positive position he advances.[102] This is illustrated in his presentation of the *homoousion* in the context of the radical separation between the sensible and intelligible worlds. The understanding of the *homoousion* in its historical setting in the fourth century as the way in which the church shook itself free from alien habits of mind and false presuppositions provides for Torrance the clue for the development of Christology today.

> Now I believe that the real problems which the Church has to face today are not those created by science and the changes in cosmological theory, but in the recrudescence of the old pagan disjunction between God and the world, in which redemption is divorced from creation and the mighty acts of God are removed from actual history. . . . Once this radical dichotomy is posited, then . . . the basic affirmation of the Christian faith, namely that in Jesus Christ we have none other than the Being of God himself in our human existence in space and time, is called in question as a rational statement in its own right and must be "re-edited" or "reinterpreted' as a correlate to human being or man's attitude to existence. . . . What is at stake here then is in a modern form the same problem that the Church faced when it battled with Gnostics and Arians in the early centuries. The great dividing line is once again the doctrine of the *Incarnation*, or if you will, the *homoousion.*[103]

Theology, accordingly, must engage in a critical revision of its own theoretical framework. Where theology today has inherited from the past and received from the present intellectual climate modes of thought that are not faithful to the divine realities as they declare themselves to us, then these pseudotheological factors must be removed and theology rebuilt upon its proper foundations. The classical theology of the faith is interpreted in the light of constructive proposals, and constructive proposals are constrained and reviewed in the light of the basic conceptions and prior formulations by which the church apprehended the basic content of the faith.

2. Torrance's Christology is characterized by a realist epistemology.[104] By such a realist method, Torrance argues that our "primary concepts arise in a situation where thought is already and immediately engaged with reality which is the ontological basis and rational source of their development, and they function as the hermeneutic media through which reality is disclosed to us in its inner relations and we on our part are enabled to grasp it in accordance with its objective structure and interpret it to others."[105] In a later book, and showing perhaps the influence of the personal and informal integrative process found in Michael Polanyi's teaching on the logic of discovery,[106] Torrance states that "disclosure of that divine order takes place only as we live in personal union and communion with Christ and find our minds under the impact of his Spirit becoming at home, as it were, in the field of God's self-revelation and self-communication. It is as we tune in to God's eternal purpose of love and grace embodied in the humanity of the Lord Jesus Christ that under the enlightenment of the Holy Spirit we are given the anticipatory insights or basic clues we need in developing formal cognition of that divine order, and so apprehend something of the trinitarian structure of God's self-revelation and self-communication to mankind."[107]

Knowledge is grounded in the subject of disclosure.[108] This is a very important point. In theology, knowledge is grounded in God, in and through Jesus Christ. As such, we come to know God *kata phusin*, according to God's nature, in such a way that the means of our knowing corresponds to what is known. Epistemology follows ontology.[109] Equally, rationality is not only the possession of the knowing subject, grounded antecedently in ourselves, but is present supremely in the Subject of God and which is known by us as God gives himself to be known through our participation in Christ, the Logos of God, through the Holy Spirit acting in our lives.[110]

3. Torrance's Christology is characterized by the integration of empirical and theoretical factors. Torrance finds a basis for the general epistemological axiom that all knowledge involves such integration in his study of the philosophy of science. But he finds it also already in the development of the theology of the ancient church where it fought for the unbroken relation in being and act between Jesus Christ and God the Father that was given expression in the doctrine of the *homoousios to Patri*.

With regard to empirical factors in theology, "the theologian is concerned with God as he reveals himself to us within space and time through historical Israel and in the incarnation of his Word in Jesus

Christ, so that we cannot divorce what God reveals to humankind from the medium of space-temporal structures which he uses in addressing his Word to human beings. Empirical correlates therefore have an ineradicable place in theology, as in natural science."[111] Further, because "we cannot cut off knowledge of God either from the world of which he is Creator or from ourselves who are creatures of this world . . . spatial and temporal, physical and historical coefficients are the *sine qua non* of any realist theological understanding and formulation."[112] Theology, therefore, operates within the God/humankind/world relation. The empirical correlate in theology means we understand that God has really entered our world so that the life of God has fallen within *the life of humankind.* The empirical correlate in theology leads further to a theology in which God, who has really entered our world so that *the life of God* has fallen within *the life of humankind*, can really be known *as God.*

By "the theoretical factor," Torrance means the conceptual frame, objectively grounded in reality itself, in terms of which empirical data make sense.[113] The problem that theologians face is deeply embedded in the modernist approach derived from phenomenalism in post-Kantian philosophy, whereby "a huge gap opened up between the phenomenal and the noumenal, or things as they appear to our human observation and things as they are alleged to be in themselves."[114] Knowledge is restricted to what appears to the senses and is demonstrable from observation or by deduction from observed data. Where there is no intrinsic relation between empirical and theoretical factors our knowledge is only the "convenient or operationally effective arrangements of our observational data."[115] The loss of the theoretical factor in biblical studies, for example, reduces the discipline either to positivistic historiography or anti-realist mythological construction. Thus we must "learn the importance of a genuinely *theological* approach to our source material. . . . So far as biblical texts are concerned, this calls for an unashamed theological exegesis and interpretation of them."[116] With regard to Christology, it means that the relation between God and Jesus Christ must be maintained. This is why the *homoousion* is so important. If that relation is severed, revelation is emptied of ultimate truth or reality, leaving only a symbolic or mythological way of thinking about Jesus Christ. Torrance's insistent reclamation of the *homoousion* and the hypostatic union is indicative of his attempt to understand the historicity of Jesus Christ in the light of his eternal reality and truth.

Critical Reflections

Torrance is frequently labeled a "Barthian."[117] The implication is that he more or less uncritically follows Karl Barth in method and content. However, as Daniel W. Hardy points out, he is attracted to Barth (and to Calvin) because his theology exemplifies a scientific theology.[118] This is an important insight because it establishes the ground of Torrance's theology in the attempt to think of God in a manner appropriate to, and corresponding to, God, which he finds in Calvin and Barth, but which he develops in his own way. Torrance continues the tradition, which he traces back beyond Barth and Calvin to Athanasius, of seeking to ground theology on its own subject matter, and to think out the doctrine of Jesus Christ in particular in the light of the incarnation understood in terms of the being and act of God.

Torrance argues for a realist approach in which knowledge involves the knower participating in Christ's own knowledge of God. That is, Torrance believes we must get past the distortions of mind in order to apprehend the reality of God independently of received language and culture so that our minds are changed by what we know in our knowing of God. Knowledge is discovery that transforms our mental constructs accordingly. We might here refer to the sanctification of the mind and language as they are brought more and more into conformity with the reality of God in Christ. Theological realism in Christology implies, therefore, that we do apprehend the ascended Lord Jesus Christ, and through him, God, not merely ideas about him, and that there is no external, independent court of appeal by which such claims to knowledge could be adjudicated. Knowledge of God in and through Jesus Christ is inevitably a profoundly personal knowledge, the result of the Trinitarian pattern of God's self-revelation becoming stamped on our minds. This is the sine qua non for knowledge of God in which experience and apprehension lead to a real knowing. Torrance speaks of "cognitive contact with the truths of divine revelation,"[119] which leads to the development of appropriate instruments by which to express the truths of the gospel of God's revealing and saving acts. It is this process that led to the *homoousios to Patri*, and the discernment of the immanent relations within God himself.[120]

Both Hardy and Patterson make the observation that Torrance verges on an appeal to a privileged knowledge unsullied by cultural contamination.[121] The critics identify three problems. First, there is the tendency to discount any role for constructing reality in our knowing of it, the option, perhaps, of a "soft" realism. Second, because all human experience is historically and contextually shaped, is it not the case we can never achieve a pure expression of our intuition of reality? To some extent, therefore, all speech, including theological speech, is political, economic, and so on. And third, there is the concern for the relation of theology to other branches of knowledge and Torrance's refusal to engage an independent epistemological justification.

These questions of theological method raise specifically christological questions. For Torrance there can be no independent appeal regarding knowledge claims concerning God because of the singularity of Jesus Christ, in whom alone God dwelt bodily (Colossians 2.9). That is, we cannot take utterly seriously the central Christian claim concerning Jesus Christ, both the incarnation and the atonement, and ask at the same time how that could be bracketed out in search of a general epistemological foundation.

The singularity of Jesus Christ, both in knowledge of God and as the one alone through whom we have communion with, the Father, is still a greatly contested issue. Torrance insists that God is known in and through Jesus Christ, with the result that Jesus Christ is the only "place" where God and humankind are united, and where "in Christ" knowledge of God is actual and not speculative or mythological. Because there is no independent tribunal to which one can make a public appeal, and because one must hold to the singularity of Jesus Christ, does that mean knowledge of God in Christ remains in an epistemological ghetto? There is a kind of scientific theological fideism operating here that is the result of the nature of God's revealing and saving act in Jesus Christ. We can only know God because we have faith in Jesus Christ, and thereby participate in his own knowledge of God, even though our faith is not perfect and we continue to see as in a glass darkly.

It is inaccurate to attribute a kind of theological language purity to Torrance. He aspires to a faithful knowledge of God in Christ, but recognizes that our statements about Jesus Christ, while actually faithful, remain always less than the reality to which they refer. Theological language is iconic, closed at one end yet open to transcendent reality at the other. It is a mistake to infer that he operates with a naive realism that allows language to mirror reality. God in Christ is not reducible to theological constructs, yet theological constructs can refer faithfully of God insofar as through our union with Christ we participate in the Son's knowledge of the Father. Our language remains always our language, not a heavenly language. It may depict reality, but it is never free from its historical and cultural context. Thus Torrance is aware that theology is ever open to revision and reformulation. But, even though it remains our language, with all of its limitations, we can and do apprehend the reality of God by moving through language to refer imagelessly to God,[122] for divine realities cannot be reduced to words. Words must be understood to point beyond to what is unimaginable though knowable. "That is to say, images in our thought and speech do not have a mimetic but only a signitive relation to divine Truth, and that somehow as they direct us to look at God or rather listen to him, we allow the divine Truth to break through to us apart from images."[123] God has come among us revealingly and savingly in Jesus Christ in such a way that we can speak truthfully of him in language as a transparent medium through which the reality of God shows through. Torrance does not confuse reality and language; neither does he allow the context of language to prevent knowledge of God.

Torrance certainly argues for a form of theological realism in Christology that demands theological construction as we seek to bring the Gospel to expression. His primary christological "tools" are theological constructions—the *homoousion* and the hypostatic union. The better christological question is to ask: Are these the best tools to employ to speak faithfully of Jesus Christ? Torrance argues that the Church has developed these theological tools and maintained them in use because they have proven to be immensely fruitful in keeping the Church faithful to the Gospel while opening up the mind of the Church to a deeper apprehension of God. The *homoousion* and the hypostatic union are uniquely the Church's tools, the former especially being of decisive importance as the central organizing truth at the level of understanding economic Trinitarian relations. These are neither arbitrary nor really disposable in Torrance's mind, even as they remain theological constructs.

The remarkable feature of Torrance's use of the *homoousion* and the hypostatic union is not the use as such, for they are common theological currency, but the rigor with which he developed them and pushed through them, as it were, to apprehend in some regard what or who God is ontically in himself.[124] His contribution lies in the identification of the epistemological and soteriological significance of the *homoousion* and the hypostatic union, and his profound confidence in this significance. We know God through our union with Christ, sharing in his knowledge of and communion with the Father. But, while Christ is one Person, this is a sharing in his human life with and knowledge of the Father, and only as such is it a sharing in his divine life and knowledge. There is a christological constraint to our knowledge of God for we have communion only with Christ in his human nature. Torrance knows this. His genius is that he has investigated the possibilities of a christologically mediated knowledge of and relationship with God as far as he has. This is not a privileged access, but a God-given christological access to be taken with seriousness and faithfulness. The scientific theological goal is clear as he moves from the *homoousion* to *perichoresis,* from the economic to the ontological Trinity "whereby we seek to formulate in forms of thought and speech the hypostatic, homoousial and perichoretic relations in the eternal dynamic Communion in loving and being loved of the three Divine Persons which God is."[125]

The question to put to Torrance's is this: Has he elevated critical realism above Christology and thereby pushed beyond the reverential limits of knowledge of God? The critics who so argue fail to realize that Torrance's constructive project rests on christological convictions and constraints, which have content entirely in and as Jesus Christ who is himself the One who compels and yet is also the limit of theological knowledge. These Torrance is unwilling to give up, for in his mind the truth of the Gospel is at stake, notwithstanding that at times the power of his language and the rigor of his dogmatic construction might suggest an alternative construal.

Notes

1. McGrath lists 633 published works, from 1941 to 1999, in Alister E. McGrath, *T. F. Torrance: An Intellectual Biography* (Edinburgh: T&T Clark, 1999). Very little secondary literature is as yet available on Torrance upon which one might build. The ALTA Religion Database 2000 lists only 140 references, although this is not a full bibliography of secondary sources. Perhaps it is the sheer volume of production, allied to the density of his writing, that has proved forbidding.

2. Thomas F. Torrance, *Theology in Reconstruction* (London: SCM; Grand Rapids, Mich.: Eerdmans, 1965), 36. Thus, "what God the Father has revealed of himself in Jesus Christ his Son, he is in himself; and what he is in himself as God the Father he reveals in Jesus Christ his Son. The Father and the Son are One, one in Being and one in Agency. Thus in Jesus Christ the Mediation of divine Revelation and the Person of the Mediator perfectly coincide. In Jesus Christ God has given us a Revelation which is identical with himself. Jesus Christ *is* the revelation of God." Thomas F. Torrance, *The Mediation of Christ* (Grand Rapids, Mich.: Eerdmans, 1983), 33. Torrance often makes reference to an illustration of this point in a story from his years as a military chaplain during the Second World War,

when a dying soldier asked him if God was really like Jesus—see, for example, Torrance, *Mediation*, 70, and Thomas F. Torrance, *Preaching Christ Today: The Gospel and Scientific Thinking* (Grand Rapids, Mich.: Eerdmans, 1994), 55. For an account and its interpretation see McGrath, *Intellectual Biography*, 74, where he cites the story at length from Torrance's unpublished war memoir.

3. Thomas F. Torrance, *Reality and Evangelical Theology* (Philadelphia: Westminster Press, 1982, The 1981 Payton Lectures), 23.

4. Torrance, *Mediation*, 60.

5. This is the distinction between the *kosmos noetos* and the *kosmos aisthetos*, the *mundus intelligibilis* and the *mundus sensibilis*. See Torrance, *Reconstruction*, 34, 175, 211; Thomas F. Torrance, *Space, Time, and Incarnation* (Oxford: Oxford University Press, 1978), 15, 43; Thomas F. Torrance, *The Ground and Grammar of Theology* (Charlottesville, Va.: University of Virginia Press, 1980), 21; Torrance, *Evangelical Theology*, 28, 55; Thomas F. Torrance, *The Trinitarian Faith: The Evangelical Theology of the Ancient Catholic Church* (Edinburgh: T&T Clark, 1988), 47, and 275 for the impact of this on the doctrine of the Church. With regard to Athanasius, see Thomas F. Torrance, *Theology in Reconciliation: Essays towards Evangelical and Catholic Unity in East and West* (London: Geoffrey Chapman, 1975), 224.

6. Torrance, *Reconstruction*, 261.

7. Torrance, *Reconstruction*, 175.

8. Torrance, *Trinitarian Faith*, 112-13.

9. Torrance, *Ground and Grammar*, 26-27. That this is the basis also for the distinction between *Geschichte* and *Historie*, found in much mid-twentieth-century Protestant theology, see Torrance, *Incarnation*, 63.

10. Torrance, *Mediation*, 63.

11. Torrance, *Mediation*, 63.

12. Torrance, *Reconstruction*, 261. Thomas F. Torrance, *The Christian Doctrine of God, One Being Three Persons* (Edinburgh: T&T Clark, 1996), 21.

13. Torrance, *Trinitarian Faith*, 116.

14. Torrance, *Trinitarian Faith*, 117.

15. Torrance, *Trinitarian Faith*, 122. See also Torrance, *Mediation*, 64.

16. Torrance, *Christian Doctrine*, 80.

17. Torrance, *Trinitarian Faith*, 124.

18. Torrance, *Trinitarian Faith*, 125.

19. Torrance, *Trinitarian Faith*, 130.

20. Torrance, *Ground and Grammar*, 160.

21. Torrance, *Reconstruction*, 34.

22. Torrance, *Trinitarian Faith*, 133.

23. Torrance, *Mediation*, 69.

24. Torrance, *Trinitarian Faith*, 135. See Torrance, *Mediation*, 70.

25. For the relation of the *homoousion* to grace, see Torrance, *Reconstruction*, 182f.

26. Torrance, *Mediation*, 68.

27. Torrance, *Mediation*, 70.

28. Torrance, *Trinitarian Faith*, 149.

29. Torrance, *Trinitarian Faith*, 150.

30. Torrance, *Trinitarian Faith*, 155

31. Torrance, *Christian Doctrine*, x.

32. Torrance, *Christian Doctrine*, xi.

33. Torrance, *Christian Doctrine*, 80.

34. As former students of Professor Torrance will no doubt remember, it was his custom at New College, in Dogmatics II, to assign the second term essay on the topic "The Interrelationship between the Incarnation and the Atonement." The idea, of course, was that they were so interlinked that they could not be properly thought of apart from each other without abstraction, thereby doing serious damage to our understanding of the Incarnation and the Atonement.

35. Torrance, *Incarnation*, 13.

36. Torrance, *Incarnation*, 2.

37. Torrance, *Evangelical Theology*, 24.

38. Torrance, *Incarnation*, 4, and also 61. In more general terms, "theological science cannot be pursued scientifically without being committed to a fundamental attitude to the world, for theological concepts without empirical correlates in our world of space and time would be empty and irrelevant for us." Torrance, *Ground and Grammar*, 45. See also Torrance, *Evangelical Theology*, 27.

39. Torrance, *Incarnation*, 7, and Thomas F. Torrance, *God and Rationality* (London: Oxford University Press, 1971), 123.

40. Torrance, *Incarnation*, 15.

41. Torrance, *Incarnation*, 14.

42. Torrance, *Incarnation*, 15.

43. Torrance, *Trinitarian Faith*, 150-51.

44. Torrance, *Preaching Christ*, 57.

45. Thomas F. Torrance, "Atonement and the Oneness of the Church," *Scottish Journal of Theology* 7, no. 3 (1954): 246, published also in Thomas F. Torrance, *Conflict and Agreement in the Church*, vol. 1, *Order and Disorder* (London: Lutterworth Press, 1959), 238-62.

46. Torrance, *Christian Doctrine*, 94. See also Torrance, *Ground and Grammar*, 165, and Torrance, *Preaching Christ*, 57.

47. Torrance is clear that in the development of the hypostatic union we respect the mystery and ineffability of the Incarnate One. This is exactly what he finds in the Chalcedonian development of the doctrine where the attempt was made to go no further than the carefully worked adverbs allowed.

48. Torrance, *Trinitarian Faith*, 183.

49. Torrance, *Mediation*, 48.

50. Torrance, *Christian Doctrine*, 160; Torrance, *Reconstruction*, 131 and 183; and Torrance, "Atonement and Oneness," 249ff. I have been assisted in what follows also by an unpublished and undated class handout from Professor Torrance, "Outline of the Doctrine of Christ."

51. Torrance, "Atonement and Oneness," 249. In conventional language, he was both man and a man, representing all humanity in the singularity of his specific, individuated manhood.

52. Torrance, *Reconstruction*, 183.

53. Torrance, *Preaching Christ*, 58.

54. For indeed the moral order is restored in the atonement, and set on a new basis. See Torrance, *Trinitarian Faith*, 160.

55. Torrance, *Preaching Christ*, 59. The influence of Athanasius becomes very clear at this point in Torrance's exposition of the doctrine of the atonement. The "atonement is not an act of God done *ab extra* upon man, but an act of God become man, done *ab intra*, in his stead and on his behalf; it is an act of God as man, translated into human actuality and made to issue out of the depths of man's being and life toward God." Torrance, *Trinitarian Faith*, 158-59.

56. Torrance, *Trinitarian Faith*, 155-56.

57. Torrance, *Trinitarian Faith*, 156-57.

58. Torrance, *Trinitarian Faith*, 161. Torrance cites from the *Theological Orations* Gregory of Nazianzus approvingly: "As long, therefore, as I am disobedient and rebellious by the denial of God and by my passions, Christ also is called disobedient on my account. But when all things have been subjected to him, then he himself will have fulfilled his subjection bringing me whom he has saved to God." Torrance, *Trinitarian Faith*, 162-63.

59. Torrance, *Trinitarian Faith*, 164.

60. Torrance, *Trinitarian Faith*, 169. For what follows, see also an unpublished class handout, "The Understanding of Redemption in the Early Church."

61. *Pdh* refers to a mighty act of God redeeming from unlawful thraldom, as in the bringing of Israel out of Egypt by the hand of God and with the substitutionary sacrifice of the Passover. It carries overtones of grace. The emphasis is upon the cost and nature of the redeeming act, and not upon the redeemer. *Kpr* means to blot out or to cover sin and guilt. It is primarily a cultic conception of redemption in which God is the subject, never the object, who makes atonement. It carries the notions of both judgment upon wrong through a life for a life and restoration to favor. *G'l* refers to redemption out of bondage undertaken by a kinsperson. The focus here is upon the redeemer, the person of the *go'el* who stands in for the person enslaved and who cannot redeem him- or herself.

62. Torrance, *Trinitarian Faith*, 171.

63. Only later did the concept of redemption come to an explicit systematic formulation. Thus Torrance finds in the Greek Fathers, for example, especially in Irenaeus, Athanasius, and Gregory of Nazianzus, the

development of the doctrine of the atonement in such a way that the dramatic, the priestly, and the ontological aspects of redemption were never separated, but held together: see Torrance, *Trinitarian Faith*, 172f.

64. For what follows see Torrance, *Trinitarian Faith*, 179-90; Torrance, *Christian Doctrine*, 250. See also Torrance, *Mediation*, 50. See also especially John Calvin, *Institutes of the Christian Religion*, IV.17.2.

65. Torrance, *Trinitarian Faith*, 180.

66. Torrance, *Christian Doctrine*, 250.

67. "It is precisely in Jesus . . . that we are to think of the whole human race, and indeed of the whole creation, as in a profound sense already redeemed, resurrected, and consecrated for the glory and worship of God," Torrance, *Trinitarian Faith*, 183.

68. Torrance, *Christian Doctrine*, 251.

69. Torrance, *Trinitarian Faith*, 186.

70. Torrance, *Christian Doctrine*, 251. This must not be interpreted to mean that he suffered in his humanity but not in his divinity, for he exists in unbroken unity with both God and humankind. For a discussion see also 252.

71. Torrance, *Mediation*, 83. References to Athanasius include *Contra Arianos*, I.41, 50; II.7, 12, 50, 65, 74; III.30, 38; IV.6.

72. Thomas F. Torrance, "Athanasius: A Study in the Foundations of Classical Theology," in Torrance, *Reconciliation*, 228.

73. Thomas F. Torrance, "The Place of Christology in Biblical and Dogmatic Theology," in Torrance, *Reconstruction*, 129.

74. Thomas F. Torrance, "The Word of God and the Response of Man," in Torrance, *Rationality*, 137-38.

75. For the following, see Torrance, *Mediation*, 83-86.

76. Torrance, *Mediation*, 86.

77. Torrance, *Rationality*, 138.

78. Torrance, *Rationality*, 142.

79. Torrance, *Rationality*, 145.

80. Thomas F. Torrance, *Royal Priesthood: A Theology of Ordained Ministry*, 2d ed. (Edinburgh: T&T Clark, 1993), 11.

81. Torrance, *Royal Priesthood*, 12.

82. Torrance, *Mediation*, 90.

83. Reformed theology argues that grace is imputed, not inferred or infused.

84. Thomas F. Torrance, "Justification: Its Radical Nature and Place in Reformed Doctrine and Life," in Torrance, *Reconstruction*, 158.

85. Thomas F. Torrance, "The Roman Doctrine of Grace from the Point of View of Reformed Theology," in Torrance, *Reconstruction*, 184.

86. See Thomas F. Torrance, *Scottish Theology from John Knox to John McLeod Campbell* (Edinburgh: T&T Clark, 1996), 42, and "Justification: Its Radical Nature and Place in Reformed Doctrine and Life," in Torrance, *Reconstruction*, 151.

87. Torrance, *Reconstruction*, 151.

88. Torrance, *Reconstruction*, 158-59.

89. Thomas F. Torrance, "The Foundation of the Church: Union with Christ through the Spirit," in Torrance, *Reconstruction*, 208.

90. Torrance, *Mediation*, 107. See also Torrance, *Preaching Christ*, 31.

91. Torrance, *Mediation*, 108.

92. Torrance, *Mediation*, 92.

93. Torrance, *Rationality*, 154.

94. Torrance, *Mediation*, 94.

95. Torrance, *Preaching Christ*, 31.

96. Torrance, *Rationality*, 154.

97. Torrance, *Mediation*, 97. See also Torrance, *Rationality*, 158.

98. Torrance, *Mediation*, 97-98.

99. Torrance, *Royal Priesthood*, 30.

100. Torrance, *Royal Priesthood*, 35.

101. Torrance, *Rationality*, 162.

102. See Daniel W. Hardy, "Thomas F. Torrance," in *The Modern Theologians: An Introduction to Christian Theology in the Twentieth Century*, vol. 1, David F. Ford, ed.(Oxford: Basil Blackwell Ltd, 1989), 73. For a highly critical interpretation of Torrance's interpretation of the history of theology, see Richard A. Muller, "The Barth Legacy: New Athanasius or Origen Redivivus? A Response to T. F. Torrance," *Thomist* 54 (1990): 673-704.

103. Thomas F. Torrance, "A New Reformation?" in Torrance, *Reconstruction*, 263. See also Thomas F. Torrance, "Theological Rationality," in Torrance, *Rationality*, 3-6; Thomas F. Torrance, "The Eclipse of God," in Torrance, *Rationality*, 29f; and Torrance, *Preaching Christ*, 43.

104. "Contemporary theological realists tend to operate with what might be termed a linguistic-window-on-reality model, however much the view from that window is acknowledged to be partial, theory-laden and in need of progressive revision. . . . It is governed by its object." Sue Patterson, *Realist Christian Theology in a Postmodern Age* (Cambridge: Cambridge University Press, 1999), 1. According to Janet Martin Soskice, theological realists are "those who, while aware of the inability of any theological formulation to catch the divine realities, none the less accept that there *are* divine realities that theologians, however ham-fistedly, are trying to catch." J. M. Sockice, "Theological Realism," in *The Rationality of Religious Belief* , W. J. Abraham and S. W. Holtzer, eds. (Oxford: Clarendon Press, 1987), 108, cited by Patterson, *Realist Christian Theology*, 12.

105. Torrance, *Rationality*, 17.

106. Hardy, "Torrance," 78.

107. Torrance, *Christian Doctrine*, 90.

108. Torrance, *Preaching Christ*, 45.

109. Hardy, "Torrance," 72.

110. Richard Muller calls Torrance's method a "principial" christocentricism, meaning a use of Christ as the *principium cognoscendi theologiae.* For Muller, this undercuts both natural revelation, with its proper role for the Logos distinct from incarnation, and the role of scripture. In fact, Muller quite misunderstands Torrance here, for above all else Christ is not a *principium,* not a fundamental principle, but the Person of the Word incarnate in our flesh, God with us as the man Jesus. For Torrance this is precisely the point, for Jesus Christ is the singular place as person where God has really come among us, not only in salvation, but also to make himself known as he really is. Theological realism, in Torrance's development of it, recognizes this personal singularity and seeks at all points to be faithful to it. See Muller, "The Barth Legacy," 690.

111. Torrance, *Preaching Christ*, 48.

112. Torrance, *Evangelical Theology*, 35-36.

113. For an extended discussion of the stratified structure of theological thinking from the evangelical and doxological to the theological to the higher theological level, see Torrance, *Christian Doctrine*, 88f.

114. Torrance, *Evangelical Theology*, 39.

115. Torrance, *Evangelical Theology*, 40.

116. Torrance, *Evangelical Theology*, 41-42.

117. Donald S. Klinefelter, "God and Rationality: A Critique of the Theology of Thomas F. Torrance," *Journal of Religion* 53 (1973): 117; also Muller, "The Barth Legacy"; and William J. Abraham, *Canon and Criterion in Christian Theology: From the Fathers to Feminism* (Oxford: Clarendon Press, 1998), 386.

118. Hardy, "Torrance," 74.

119. Torrance, *Christian Doctrine*, 91.

120. For an extended discussion see Torrance, *Christian Doctrine*, chapter 4.

121. Hardy, "Torrance," 88, and Patterson, *Realist Christian Theology*, 17.

122. Torrance, *Evangelical Theology*, 63.

123. Thomas F. Torrance, "Knowledge of God and Speech about Him according to John Calvin," in Torrance, *Reconstruction*, 91.

124. Torrance, *Christian Doctrine*, 98f.

125. Torrance, *Christian Doctrine*, 109.

Chapter 4

The Holy Spirit in T. F. Torrance's Theology

by Gary W. Deddo

In the theology of Thomas Torrance, the doctrine of the Holy Spirit represents the culmination of reflection on the doctrine of God as the Father and the Son, that is, the Life internal *(ad intra)* to the Trinity. It marks out, also, the point of departure for the completion of reflection on all of God's works external (*ad extra*) to the Triune life.

Introduction

The challenge to understanding Torrance's theology at this point is much the same as at all other points, but perhaps intensified. The reader is tempted to think that Torrance's work essentially involves the fine-tuned redefinition of terms within the historically orthodox Christian faith. However, the significance of Torrance's contribution can only be fully grasped when one realizes that his theological formulations call for the cultivation of new habits of mind, new ways of thinking, not just new thoughts.

Methodologically, Torrance approaches the doctrine of the Holy Spirit in a way consistent with every other part of his work. Knowledge of God is not an independent human possibility. Without the self-revealing action of God, which also must secure its effective reception, there could be no regulative knowledge of God. God can be apprehended only if, when, and where God has acted decisively to reveal himself. This is nowhere more emphatically the case than when giving consideration to God the Holy Spirit.

Definite knowledge of God as Holy Spirit is given through Jesus Christ the Son of God incarnate because this is the apex of revelation, the appointed meeting place of the whole God with humanity. There in the person, activity, and communication of Jesus we are led to the Father and to the Spirit. In that meeting God makes possible and actual knowledge of our creaturely relations with the Father, Son, and Spirit (*ad extra*), but also the internal and eternal relations of the Father, Son, and Spirit (*ad intra*). Thus Torrance's pneumatology, in conformity with the actuality of revelation, is Christocentric and incarnational in a way that comes to fruition in an onto-relational and Trinitarian formulation. What all this means we intend to unpack in terms of the Holy Spirit.

One more thing must be said before we can begin our exposition. The God revealed in Jesus Christ cannot be approached neutrally because in Jesus Christ God has not approached us neutrally. Revelation and reconciliation are inextricably related in the knowledge of this God. Thus, for Torrance, how we come to know the true identity of the Spirit is necessarily conditioned by Who the Holy Spirit is. Essentially for Torrance the Holy Spirit is rightly identified as the Spirit of Jesus Christ the Son of God and the Spirit of God the Father. The Spirit can only be personally recognized and identified in relation to Jesus Christ because the Spirit is the Spirit of Jesus and Jesus is the place where God the Father and God the Son have provided access to the knowledge of themselves. The place where the knowledge, faith, and worship of the people of God arise then is in and through Jesus Christ. In answer as to how God can be known, Torrance answers, the people of God come to know, trust, and worship the Father through the Son and in the Spirit.

From the focal point of God's self-revelation in Jesus we come to know God in relation to ourselves, in the meeting. Out of that meeting which calls for doxology and communion (*koinonia*) arises a deeper level of understanding. We come to grasp the nature of God's relationship to us as Father, Son, and Spirit, the relations and interactions of God with that which is not God, *ad extra*. Furthermore, out of that knowledge has grown, by the grace of God, an actual knowledge of the internal and eternal relations between the Father, Son, and Holy Spirit. Torrance along with the Early Church affirms that the truth of God in action towards us corresponds to the identity of God in the inner Triune life. That is, in Jesus Christ God the Father through the power of the Spirit is able to accomplish an astounding self-revelation so that we in the end can and do have an actual knowledge of God which is congruent with God's own self-knowledge as Father, Son, and Spirit.[1]

Following this pattern of God's self-revelation we will attempt to articulate some of the main insights Torrance has about the Holy

Spirit. We will, then, begin with the knowledge of the Spirit as made known in Jesus Christ.

The Holy Spirit and the Incarnate Son

For Torrance the disclosure of the Holy Spirit reached its fullness in Jesus Christ. Consequently, the Church came to know the Spirit through the incarnate Son. There was no independent revelation of the Spirit since the Spirit has no autonomous identity. The Spirit is the Spirit of the Father and of the Son.[2] In Jesus Christ the Church came to discover in the deepest way that the Holy Spirit is God and God is the Holy Spirit.[3] And furthermore it realized that the fulfillment of the direct working of God among his creatures through immediate relations with them is entirely dependent upon the Holy Spirit.[4]

In the presence of Jesus Christ the Church recognized that it was dealing in an intensely personal way with God the Father. Similarly it knew and came to articulate more and more explicitly that it was dealing in a profoundly immediate way with God the Spirit.[5] The roots of this revelation were grounded in the very life and activity of Jesus Christ. In fact Jesus' entire saving life-purpose could be summed up in saying that he came to take us to the Father and send us his Spirit.[6]

But most profoundly the deep connection between Jesus and the Spirit was recognized in the central act of his ministry at the Cross where the reality of his union with the Holy Spirit of God was most profoundly active and manifest. In the supreme obedience of hope, faith, and love, Jesus offered himself up by handing over his Spirit to the Father. Thus both the Apostle Paul and the author of the book of Hebrews explicitly propound the atoning work as one co-involving the Father, Son, and Holy Spirit.[7]

Torrance points out that this unity of presence and action led the Church in its declarations of faith to say that as the Son was one in being (*homoousios*) with the Father, so the Spirit was one in being (*homoousios*) with the Father and Son.[8] That is to say the Spirit sent by Jesus was to be regarded as divine and not as a creature. Thus, Torrance notes, the Early Church worshiped, sang, and offered prayer to the Father through the Son and in the Spirit.[9] It declared the Holy Spirit the Lord, the Giver of Life.[10]

This unity of Jesus and the Spirit was understood in terms of a unity of being and activity of the whole Triune God. Thus Athanasius spoke of the Father doing all things through the Word and in the Holy Spirit and said that the Spirit is the activity of the Son "who is not outside of him but in him as he is in the Father . . . [so that] we discern that there is only one godhead, in the Father who is above all things, in the Son who pervades all things, and in the Spirit who is active in all things through the Word."[11] In Torrance's words there is one operation of God in the world, but this takes form as a twofold activity in Jesus Christ and in the Spirit.[12] "There is not a separate activity of the Holy Spirit in revelation or salvation in addition to or independent of the activity of Christ, for what he does is to empower and actualise the words and works of Christ in our midst as the words and works of the Father."[13]

It follows then that in the self-giving and self-revelation of the Son we have the self-giving and self-revelation of the Father and of the Spirit.[14] That is we have the self-giving and self-revelation of the whole Triune God.[15] The astounding conclusion then is that God has made possible, and actual in Jesus, a true human knowledge of himself, not just as God is towards us, but in some real measure as God knows himself, as Father, Son, and Holy Spirit, from all eternity.[16]

For Torrance, a proper Christocentrism makes pneumatology no less central.[17] The doctrine of the Spirit develops from the doctrine of the Son.[18] In and through the incarnation of the Son of God the being and action of the Holy Spirit is revealed in two dimensions. Thus the Church in its own worship and doctrine traced out the two dimensions in terms of two relations: the relation of the Holy Spirit with the Triune life and also in relation to the creation. So, on the basis of the Person and Work of Jesus Christ, Torrance considers the Person and Work of the Holy Spirit in these two relations. We will take up Torrance's insights on the intra-Trinitarian relation first.

The Holy Spirit in Relation *ad intra*

The first thing that should be said about the Spirit is that the Spirit is God, is divine. This was uncontroversial in the Church until the fourth century when it was challenged. As noted above, Torrance traces out how the divinity of the Holy Spirit was subsequently defended and firmly established on the basis of the Incarnation of the Son of God and the apostolic deposit of faith given to the Church in its Scripture. The Spirit is the Lord, the Giver of Life, and is rightly to be regarded as one in being and act (*homoousios*) with the Father and Son.[19] The Holy Spirit is not a creature, even a supreme creature, but is to be acknowledged as the Eternal Creator Spirit (*Spiritus Creator*).[20]

The Holy Spirit Is Personal

The second thing prominent in Torrance's exposition of the Church's faith is that the Holy Spirit is personal. Following Gregory Nyssen, Torrance notes that the Holy Spirit exists personally with his own distinctive existence and acts with his own freedom to "choose, move and act as he wills with the power to carry out every purpose."[21] In the New Testament we find the Holy Spirit "speaking, witnessing, crying, grieving, interceding, intervening, creating, rebuking, judging, etc."[22] Jesus referred to the Spirit as "he" and as "the Paraclete," another Comforter who would be with us forever.[23] The Holy Spirit cannot be regarded as an impersonal emanation or a cosmological force or even as an energy of God.[24] For the being and the working (*energia*) of the Spirit can never be separated without calling into question the unity of the Trinity in being and activity.[25] The Holy Spirit is the intensely active presence of God himself among us through Jesus Christ.[26] In the Spirit we are confronted with God in his own irreducible transcendence and his own self-judgment and salvation.[27]

Speaking of Athanasius's understanding, Torrance says that since

> there is no separation between the Activity and the Being of God in the Trinity or in the Incarnation or in the work of the Spirit, that carries theology consistently forward from "the economic Trinity" into "the ontological Trinity," for what God is in the economy of his saving operations towards us in Jesus Christ he is antecedently and inherently and eternally in himself as the Triune God.[28]

God personally, really, and actually interacts with what he has made. The answer as to how this is possible for the holy, transcendent being of God to do this is through the Son and in the Spirit.

According to Torrance, the Early Church had to radically reconceptualize the nature of being itself, beginning with God's own being as made known in the incarnate Son. Then, all that was discovered and articulated about the Son was seen to follow in its own proper way for the Holy Spirit also.

This can be seen in the gradual but inexorable transformation in the mind of the Church of the Greek concept of *hypostasis*. This word was usually understood to be synonymous with *ousia*. However in the Church it became more and more associated with the words *proposon* (face, person) and *onoma* (name), terms which were decidedly unrelated to the notion of essential being. Under the impact of the recognition that the Son and the Spirit were *homoousios*, the notion of *hypostasis* (Person) was personalized.

Consequently, the Holy Spirit came to be regarded as having a real personal and objective subsistence in God and yet exercising the divine functions in his own Person.[29] Epiphanius saw a connection, on the one hand, between the "I am" of God's self-identification in Hebraic thought and *ousia*, and on the other, the notions of name, face, and *hypostasis*. Torrance sees Epiphanius bringing the Nicene belief in the Holy Spirit to a climactic conclusion. Thus Epiphanius could write,[30] "We call the Father God, the Son God, and the Holy Spirit God . . . . When you pronounce the *homoousion*, you declare that the Son is God of God, and the Holy Spirit is God of the same Godhead."[31]

A further explication given by Epiphanius of the nature of the divine persons (*hypostaseis*) indicates a profound intensification of the personal aspect. Rather than speaking of the different Persons as 'modes of existence,' as the Cappadocian Fathers did, Epiphanius preferred to speak of them more concretely as *enhypostatic* in God. That is, the living individuality and reality of the divine Persons is substantiated by coinhering together in the one being of God. Thus there are not three gods or three parts to God, but one Tripersonal God.[32] The Spirit, then, must belong to and flow from the inner being and light of the Holy Trinity.

For Torrance several other key elements are important for grasping the Church's understanding of its faith in God the Holy Spirit. Being *enhypostatic* in the Godhead the Holy Spirit came to be regarded uniquely as being "between" the Father and the Son.[33] Thus the Spirit was identified by a number of different theologians as being "in the midst of the Father and the Son," or being "the bond of the Trinity." The Spirit was also regarded as the "intermediate" between the Father and the Son and the "fellowship" or "communion" (*koinonia*) of the Father and the Son.[34] Augustine incorporated this insight when he expounded the doctrine of the Holy Spirit as "the consubstantial communion of the Father and the Son" and as "the mutual love where with the Father and the Son reciprocally love one another."[35]

Immediate Personal Activity of God

Against their Greek dualistic background, the most essential transformation in the Church's frame of mind was to regard divine being as being inherently personal and relational. In wrestling with the incarnate presence (*ensarkos parousia*) of God in Jesus and in light of the Old Testament revelation of the Face and Word of God, the Nicene theologians came to declare that "whatever is said and done by God is said and done exclusively *from the Person* (*ek prosopou*) of Christ" because "to see and hear the Lord Jesus Christ is to see and hear God the Father himself face to face."[36] In Jesus Christ God came in person. Furthermore, the recognition of the very presence of the Holy Spirit in the person and work of the Son only intensified and personalized the Church's grasp of the personal nature of the being of God. For the Spirit is the presence and immediate personal activity of the Creator "in the sheer reality of his own transcendent being" as Torrance puts it.[37] Like the Son, the Spirit is in God and of God, that is, from the very being of God.[38]

But not only was the conception of the being of God radically qualified by the incorporation of personal concepts. The notion of personhood itself was reciprocally transfigured. In the Church's consideration of the mutual presence and action of the Son and the Spirit *homoousios* with the Father, it was forced to clarify the nature of the differentiation of the Persons (*hypostaseis*). For the Father, Son, and Spirit must be understood as united in being while they remain personally and eternally distinguishable. If they are not distinguishable in terms of deity, eternality, being, act, and powers (or any other attribute appropriate to God), then in what does the difference consist?

All we can do here is point to the essential conclusion, as Torrance understands it, to which the Church through its teachers came. In short, the answer was that the being of God was constituted by personal relations internal to God. The being of God came to be regarded as inherently and eternally personal and relational.[39] The relations of the Persons belong to what the Persons of the Trinity are such that if the Spirit was not the Spirit of the Son, or if the Son was not the Son of the Father or the Father the Father of the Son, they would not be who they are. Torrance coins a term to represent this. He says that "person" becomes an "onto-relational" concept.[40] The Father could not be the Father without the Son and the Spirit, nor the Son be the Son, nor the Spirit be the Spirit. The interrelations between the three divine Persons Torrance says are "substantive relations or 'onto-relations.'"[41]

Following the lead of the New Testament itself in its indication of the relations among the divine Persons, each relation became associated with a distinct term. The Fatherhood of God was identified with paternity (begetting or unbegotten), the Son with filiation (being begotten), and the Spirit with spiration or procession.[42] The differentiation of the divine Persons is grounded in their differing relations which do not mitigate against their unity but rather established the oneness of the Triune being.[43] Thus, the only difference between the Persons is the difference of their "subsistent relations" (as they came to be called).[44]

The Church in the exposition of its faith could not easily find an existing term to properly refer to the essential and absolutely unique quality and reality of these subsistent onto-relations. Consequently, taking its lead from the apostolic witness, especially the Gospel of John where Jesus says "I am in the Father and the Father is in me," it is possible that it may have coined a term for that purpose. Torrance explains that based on the word *chorein* (from the root *choreo*, but not *choreuo*=to dance) meaning 'to make room, to contain, or to go,' the noun *perichoresis* (the prefix *peri-* indicating a circle) came to be used to point to the absolutely unique relations of the Triune Persons in terms of the mutual indwelling or reciprocal containing of one another.[45]

In the framework of this perichoretic apprehension of the Triune being-in-relation of God, the Holy Spirit was seen to uniquely proceed out of the coinherent communion of the Father and Son. In fact the Spirit himself was seen to be "the enhypostatic Love and Communion of Love in the perichoretic relations between the Father and the Son."[46] In this way the Church articulated the profound truth that God is Being in Loving Communion since the Spirit is the Union and Communion of love between the Father and the Son.

Procession of the Spirit

It was inevitable that the question of the procession of the Holy Spirit would arise. What exactly is meant by this subsisting relation in differentiation from the Father's paternity and the Son's filiation? Many of the teachers of the Church resisted attempts to probe any further than to affirm only what this relation is not: procession is not paternity or filiation but a unique relation appropriate to the Spirit in contrast to the two others.

However, representatives of the Western Church later went on to make one clarification regarding the procession of the Holy Spirit;

one which was sufficient to contribute to a schism between it and the Eastern branch of the Church. The West, in order to protect the divinity of the Son, altered the ecumenical Niceno-Constantinopolitan Creed by expanding the clause which said the Spirit proceeds from the Father by adding the word "and the Son" (*filioque*). The Eastern Church claimed this "double procession" threw the unity of the Godhead into disarray for now it seemed that there were two sources or founts for the spiration of the Holy Spirit.

Torrance invested a significant amount of his life in pursuit of a reconciliation between Eastern Orthodox and Western branches of the Church. His efforts along with those of others have indeed born fruit (or at least first fruits) in resolving the theological rift regarding the procession of the Spirit. We cannot even survey the history much less the story of the resolution of that dispute. We can only point out key elements which led to an official reconciling statement of agreement.

The newly agreed upon language that the Spirit proceeds "from the Father *through* the Son," as significant as it is, cannot convey the richness and theological depth of the understanding achieved which made it possible. Only consideration of the theological reflection that lies behind it can indicate its true meaning and value.[47] A brief summary must suffice.

The key to resolution was found in a renewed apprehension of the significance the teachings of Athanasius, Epiphanius, Didymus the Blind, Cyril of Alexandria, and Hilary over against what now seems the more ambiguous formulations of the Cappadocians. While making every qualification to avoid any subordinationism of the Son to the Father, the Cappadocians nevertheless tended to locate the unity of the Godhead in the mon-arche (*monarchia*) of the Father, at times speaking of the person of the Father as the cause and source of the being of the Son and Spirit.[48] In this frame it was more appropriate to speak of both the Son and the Spirit being from the Father, each in their own way. However, this way of putting it seemed to suggest that the divinity of the Son and the Spirit was derived.

On the basis of Athanasius's line of thinking, however, this problem could be avoided. On the basis of (1) a clear and profound understanding of the *homoousios* applying to the Trinity as a whole, (2) the *hypostaseis* considered as being *enhypostatic*, (3) the unity of action (*energia*) of the one God considered *enousious*, (4) the personal subsisting relations grasped in such a way that the perichoretic quality of them applies to the whole God (5) such that the Holy Spirit is seen to be the union and communion of the Father and the Son, and that (6) the relations then must not be construed in terms of causation but in terms of that perichoretic communion of the

Spirit, it should then be concluded that (7) the unity of Trinity must not be located in the person of the Father, but in the perichoretic Triunity of the being of God. The being of the Spirit does not proceed from the person of the Father, but rather the person of the Spirit proceeds from the person of the Father who, in his being, is in communion with the Son, i.e., in the communion that the Spirit is. In this frame, the deity of all the Persons is clearly underived. All the persons have their being by being perichoretically and enhypostatically Triune. Thus the Unity in being of God is none other than a Triunity.[49]

Perhaps the most succinct way of formulating this understanding is captured by Torrance's summary of Athanasius's doctrine of God as "Trinity in Unity and Unity in Trinity."[50] In this way the unity of the Godhead is secured without inadvertently being open to the charge of subordinationism or a hierarchy within the Godhead while the divinity of the Son is secure without inadvertently leaving the unity of the Godhead vulnerable to conceptual deterioration. It was in this way that agreement was reached between the two branches of the Church on the procession of the Spirit.

In concluding this section, I want to point our a few more things about the identity of the Holy Spirit within the relations internal to the Triune Life as Torrance understands it.

God Is Spirit

The Holy Spirit is to be regarded as one of the *hypostaseis* of the Triune God. However, it is proper, as is obvious in Holy Scripture, to speak of the whole of God as Spirit. Spirit can refer to God in an absolute way without referring to the distinction of persons. Spirit then is equally applicable to the Father, Son, and Holy Spirit. God as Spirit designates the divine nature of God and so of all the Persons. To say that God is Spirit designates his "infinite, transcendent, invisible, immaterial, immutable nature" and "characterizes what God is in himself, in the boundless perfection of his holy being."

But, Torrance goes on to say it also "characterizes what God is in his limitless freedom toward every thing that is not God."[51] Because God is Spirit and the Holy Spirit is God, "through the ineffability of his own personal mode of being, the Holy Spirit confronts us with the sheer ineffability of God, for in him we are in immediate touch with the ultimate being and acts of the All-Holy and Almighty before whom all our forms of thought and speech break off in wonder and adoration."[52]

By the Holy Spirit we are confronted by God the Spirit, God in his transcendent freedom to act according to his own divine Being and the "total sovereignty and power of His Presence."[53] As Spirit, God is imageless. God remains beyond human knowing in the unfathomable depth of his own infinite transcendent being and self-knowledge. The sheer otherness of God, incomprehensible by mere creatures, is manifest through the Holy Spirit. So Torrance says the Holy Spirit "guards the ultimate mystery and ineffability of God in virtue of the fact that while it is in the Spirit that we are confronted with the ultimate being and presence of God, he is not approachable in thought or knowable in himself. The Holy Spirit is *Spirit*. . . . He is 'Spirit of Spirit for God is Spirit.'"[54]

But there is another side to the freedom of God the Holy Spirit. In God's unlimited freedom God is also free to actually "impart" himself while nevertheless remaining infinitely and transcendently Lord over our creaturely existence. The freedom of God to be present to the creature means that in the Spirit God is free to bring to completion God's purposes for the creature by not only moving toward the creature but by acting in the creature to establish "an enduring ontological relation" with God.[55]

One final but important theme for Torrance on the doctrine of the Spirit is that by the Spirit God is to be regarded as intrinsically alive with activity both within and without the Triune life. "God is who he is in his activity towards us through the Son and in the Spirit . . . so it belongs to the essential nature of his eternal Being to move and energise and act."[56] This was a radically different apprehension of ultimate and transcendent reality as understood in a Greek frame of mind. Torrance notes that Aristotle's conception of God can be characterized as the activity of immobility and as one who moves the world only by being an object of its desire.[57]

The movement of the Spirit of God is spiritual and so unique. Its movement is therefore incomparable to creaturely movement. The power of God to act and the act of his power cannot be identified with human acts, accomplishments and power, or the working of nature.

All God's works *ad extra*, then, will share in the same spirituality of action. The act of God is a unified movement of Being and Act. God acts according to who he is and who he is generates what he does.[58] More particularly, the movement of God in all his ways "can be expressed in the Patristic formulation: *From the Father, through the Son, and in the Spirit* and *in the Spirit, through the Son, and to the Father*."[59] That is, God's works are all shaped by his Triune nature.

In creation and reconciliation/re-creation, the two greatest movements of God, we see the astounding freedom of God to act in the power and communion of his Spirit so that we can rightly say that by them God becomes something other than what he was. God has the freedom to be affected by something new, something not God.[60] For in creation God became something that he was not: a Creator. And in bringing about our reconciliation, the Son of God became incarnate, something that the Son of God was not.[61]

The Holy Spirit in Relation *ad extra*

We are now in a position to consider Torrance's understanding of the doctrine of the Holy Spirit in terms of the Spirit's relation to creation. Again we will only be able to provide the briefest survey of the most salient points.

Grounded in the Incarnation

At one point Torrance poignantly notes that

> Everything depends in the last analysis upon whether we believe in *a God who really acts* or not . . . interact[ing] with what he has made in such a way that he creates genuine reciprocity between us and himself within the space-time structures of existence in which he has placed us.[62]

The incarnation of the Son of God demonstrated that the God who was over all creation was free to become personally present and active within his creation. But in Jesus the activity of the Son was identified with the activity, presence, and power of the very Spirit of God.[63] Thus, in Jesus God was more particularly and profoundly at work *within* humanity as God the Holy Spirit. In light of this Torrance says, "the eternal relations within the Triune God have assumed an economic form within human history, while remaining immanent in the Godhead, thus opening out history to the transcendence of God while actualising the self-giving of God within it."[64] The Holy Spirit, who is the bond of the Trinity, by his mediation of the Son of God through the incarnation is also the bond between the inner life of God and the life of God in relation to creation external to God. That is, the Holy Spirit is "the divinely forged bond between the economic Trinity and the ontological Trinity."[65]

But the incarnation is not the revelation of a hidden general truth about the Spirit. It is an event, an accomplishment, the actual establishment of a new and renewed relationship of God with creation. In the double movement of God towards creation through the Son and in the Spirit, the relationship of all creation was put on an entirely new foundation. In particular, the Son of God incarnate received the Holy Spirit in his assumed humanity not for himself (already having the Spirit from all eternity for himself), but for us. He has the Holy Spirit for us, and so he promises to send it to us.[66] He lives in the power of the Spirit so that we might share with him in the life he has for us in the Spirit.[67] And as noted above, the Spirit is the communion of the Father and the Son. So for us to have the Spirit is for us to share in the Son's union and communion with the Father. Thus salvation consists in being drawn up in the Son into the very Triune life by the power of the Spirit.

For Torrance the Holy Spirit is the ontological connection between the Father and Son in their Trinitarian life, between the Son and his human nature in the incarnation, and between us and the incarnate Son. These relations each in their proper way are all onto-relations, that is, they are all being constituting relations.[68] Thus the atoning exchange which took place in Jesus renewed the very being of human nature.[69]

Torrance provides a profoundly ontological and so real, actual, personal, and relational grasp of the work of the Spirit. Torrance's realistic and ontological interpretation makes intelligible the reality and actuality of our relationship to God which demands a real and actual response of praise and worship.

Through consideration of a number of ever more comprehensive themes Torrance further discovers the intensely personal nature of the relationship established with humanity in Christ. Union with Christ, understood in an onto-relational way, encapsulates his grasp of the reality of relationship.[70] For Torrance salvation is the perfection and completion of our union and communion with the Father through the Son and in the Spirit.[71] That union with God actualizes a reconciling exchange[72] which affects us at the very core of our being, so that we become in relationship to God other than what we were on our own. For in that exchange we receive not some divine stuff or something external to us, but are united in person to Christ by the indwelling of the Holy Spirit, the same Spirit which was in Christ.[73]

To receive the Spirit is to receive God himself, because in the Spirit the Gift and the Giver are one. Through this communion with the Spirit we don't become divine but we are nevertheless united to God while remaining a (radically transfigured) creature.[74] This,

Torrance contends is the proper understanding of the Eastern Orthodox doctrine of *theosis*.

Torrance also likes to explain the indwelling of the Spirit as "interiorizing" because we are redeemed from our "in-turned and in-grown existence" through his possession of our subjectivities by actualizing God's own knowledge of himself in us and so turning our spirits "outward and upward to God."[75]

But most comprehensively and with an obvious Scriptural point of departure Torrance likes to explicate our union with Christ in terms of our having access to the Father through the Spirit. Jesus Christ is the One "through whom and with whom we have access to the Father in the Spirit, and through whom the Spirit lifts us up to have communion with the Father."[76]

The Radical Objectivity of Spirit

For Torrance the reality of union with Christ and the self-giving of God by the Holy Spirit mounts a radical critique of subjectivist, instrumentalist, legal, or institutionalized understandings. These approaches represent two dangers in connection with the doctrine of the Spirit: a false objectivity and a false subjectivity.

Regarding a false objectivity, Torrance points out that the Spirit cannot be identified through an analysis of its supposed effects, manifestations, or operations in creation, for this puts a deistic distance between the person of the Spirit and the works of the Spirit, the being of the Spirit and the Act of the Spirit.[77] The Spirit has also been wrongly identified with immanent principles of creation, often providing a base for a natural theology.[78] Within Catholicism the mistake made most often is the identification of the Church and its ministrations with the Spirit. The error in Protestantism is its identification of the Spirit with the human heart, religious affections, states of consciousness, moral rectitude (personal or social), or even with aesthetic sensitivity or experience.[79] These habits of mind confuse the Holy Spirit with the fallen, creaturely human spirit and subordinate and domesticate it to ourselves, our institutions, or creation.

Torrance is also concerned to warn against falsely objectifying the work of Christ and the Spirit by giving an improper emphasis to the legal or forensic dimensions of Christ's atoning work. Torrance's warning should not be regarded as a rejection of the judicial aspects of the atonement. Rather he places it in the much larger and deeper context of the unity of the Incarnate Person and Work of Christ, the unity of the Son and the Spirit, and the onto-relational nature of our union and communion with Christ.

He does this in order to keep the atoning work from being regarded in a mechanical, external, impersonal, and deistic fashion thereby bearing an unfaithful witness to the Scriptural account of the Persons of the Trinity and to the ontological depths of what was accomplished for us in the reconciliation and renewal of our human being in Christ communicated to us in the Spirit. So Torrance states that "the forensic element in justification reposes for its substance and meaning upon union with Christ."[80] He goes on to warn that when judicial justification and justifying faith are made the basis for a subsequent union with Christ both the meaning of justification and faith are altered and the Communion of the Spirit is displaced by inadequate judicial and cognitive notions of relation with God.[81]

But there is an opposite danger as well. In the West, Torrance suggests, there has been a growing tendency to identify the Spirit with the human spirit and creativity.[82] He insists that the Holy Spirit can in no way be identified with the human spirit or its experiences. The Spirit, although united to human subjectivity, can never be confused with it. The Spirit retains its sovereign lordship over and independent personhood within humanity. So while the Spirit may indeed indwell our subjectivity, the Spirit cannot be identified with our subjectivity.

Torrance often characterizes the real presence of the Spirit in us by saying that it constitutes a profound "objective inwardness" which can never be reduced to a psychological or even a sacramental inwardness.[83] The Holy Spirit always belongs to God and not to us. We may be possessed by the Spirit but the Spirit is never in our possession.[84]

It might seem that this view jeopardizes the integrity of humanity. But if humanity is constituted by its relation with its Creator and Redeemer, such that there is no such thing as human autonomy, then, for Torrance such union and communion in the Holy Spirit is no threat to humanity but is its fulfillment. For the Spirit is mediated to us in and through the perfected humanity of Jesus Christ. The only thing threatened is a claim to human autonomy which leads to alienation from God and death. In the Spirit God does not overwhelm us. Rather than a loss of self the Spirit provides its completion (*theosis*, *theopoiesis*, *teleiosis*).[85] The Spirit perfects our humanity in our humanity on the basis of the humanity of Jesus Christ.[86]

In fact, God gives his Spirit in order to emancipate us from "imprisonment in ourselves to be lifted up to partake of the living presence and saving acts of God the Creator and Redeemer."[87] And in order for this to happen the Holy Spirit must resist our spirits with "the implacable objectivity of His divine Being, objecting to our objectifying modes of thought and imparting himself to us in accordance with the modes of His own self-revealing through the Word."[88] The working of the Spirit "turn[s] us inside out" so that "our relations with the objective reality of God are brought to their telos."[89]

To highlight this aspect of the work of the Spirit, Torrance employs another unique term. Our relationship to the Spirit and the Word, he says, can only result in our "personalization" since only God is truly personal. We can speak of our selves as persons only in a derivative way. Torrance identifies both the Word and Spirit as a "personalizing Person" and humanity as "personalized persons."[90] The action of God by the Spirit in the humanity of the Son perfects/sanctifies our personhood, for by the Spirit we are given a share in the Son's perfected and so personalized human nature.[91] "Far from crushing our creaturely nature or damaging our personal existence, the indwelling presence of God through Jesus Christ and in the Holy Spirit has the effect of healing and restoring and deepening human personal being."[92] For Torrance our communion with Christ through the Spirit can rightly be understood as our humanization.[93]

In fact the ministry of the Spirit not only renews our relations with God, but as the "inner principle of *koinonia*," also renews relationships in society.[94] The living presence of God who confronts us as "personalizing Spirit" rehabilitates us in the context of the social structures of life.[95]

Actualizing, Participating, Responding in the Spirit

Torrance often speaks of the essential work of the Holy Spirit as actualizing subjectively in us what was accomplished for us objectively in Christ.[96] The Holy Spirit does not accomplish something distinct from what was accomplished in Christ in the power of the same Spirit. The Holy Spirit who unites Father and Son, the Son and our humanity, also shares with us all that was accomplished for us in Jesus Christ, our adoption, sanctification, and regeneration.[97]

For Torrance, this double mediation of Jesus by the Spirit and the Spirit by Jesus is also a two-way movement: from the Father to the Son in the Spirit and in the Spirit through the Son to the Father. The mediation of the Spirit involves a God-humanward movement and a human-Godward movement. There is also a vicarious aspect to both sides of that mediation. For the Spirit not only brings to us the objective effects worked out in the vicarious life of Jesus Christ, but also the subjective effects worked out in his humanity. That is, the Spirit enables us to share in Jesus' own faithful response to the Father. In the Spirit, God has the freedom "to actualize his relation with us and the freedom . . . to actualise our relation with himself."[98] Torrance notes, "Man's reception of the Holy Spirit is itself a creative work of God."[99]

This freedom of the Spirit can be seen quintessentially in the Apostle Paul's teaching that the Spirit is the Spirit of Sonship which leads us to cry out "Abba Father."[100] The Holy Spirit as our Paraclete, Advocate, exercises along with the Son a high priestly ministry on our behalf.[101]

The New Testament and Early Church had a profound understanding of the entire Christian life as a participation (sharing/communion/*koinonia*) in union with Christ by the power of the Holy Spirit. United in one Spirit with Christ we do nothing on our own, but by the Spirit share in all of Christ's response worked out for us throughout his whole vicarious life. This can especially be seen in our prayer. We do not know how to pray, but as our Advocate and Intercessor the Spirit empowers us to "participate in ways beyond our understanding in the prayer and worship of the glorified Christ."[102]

In our worship "the Holy Spirit comes forth from God, uniting us to the response and obedience and faith and prayer of Jesus, and returns to God, raising us up in Jesus to participate in the worship of heaven and in the eternal communion of the Holy Trinity."[103] In the Spirit we never worship or pray alone.

In fact our whole lives in every part are constituted a participation: a dynamic life of union and communion with God. For the only regeneration we have is a share (*koinonia*) in his.[104] The only holiness or sanctification we have is his already accomplished for us in him.[105] The only repentance, faith, obedience, love we have is his actualized in us by the Holy Spirit. The only baptism we undergo and eucharistic self-consecration we offer[106] is that which was made in the flesh and blood of Jesus Christ in the power of the same Spirit who makes us participate, share, be united to Jesus Christ. The only glory we give is the result of the mission of the Spirit.[107]

For Torrance participation in Christ by the Spirit is what is meant in the Epistle of 2 Peter by our being "partakers (*koinonoi* = sharers) of the divine (*theias*) nature." Torrance sums up his grasp of our participation with Christ in his explication of the doctrine of *theosis* usually associated with Eastern Orthodox teaching. He laments that this word is misleadingly translated "deification" since it has "nothing to do with the divination of man any more than the Incarnation has to do with the humanization of God." *Theosis* means that by grace we are raised up to find the true centers of our existence not in ourselves but in God according to his absolutely divine saving acts of election, adoption, regeneration, and sanctification in which we are made to share in that which God has accomplished for us.[108]

The Holy Spirit and Church

The work of Jesus Christ and the Spirit should not be taken in an individualistic way. For the Spirit unites us to Christ by incorporating us into the Body of Christ, the renewed people of God. The Spirit that comes from the depths of the Triune life creates and re-creates communion among people. The Spirit's personalizing and incorporating ministry makes us members of his Body and creates a "community of reciprocity" among them which "reflects the trinitarian relations in God himself."[109]

Individuals have their being by being in communion with others engrafted into Christ. The unifying Spirit creates community and so overcomes all divisions. The mission of the Church is "to bring all nations and races the message of hope in the darkness and dangers of our times . . . that the love of God in Jesus Christ may be poured out upon them by the Spirit, breaking down all barriers, healing all divisions and gathering them together as one universal flock."[110] The Spirit then makes a "new undivided race" sharing equally in the life and love of God.[111] The Church embraces all races and nations in a new covenant of the Spirit and in one universal people of God.[112]

In Torrance's view, there is and can be only one people of God and one covenant since there is only one God united in one Spirit who through one Mediator establishes one Body for one purpose. Following the teaching of the New Testament he holds that in the economy of God there are two forms of the one covenant and two phases or forms of the life of the people of God.[113] There is one covenant of grace with all creation. In the Old Testament God worked uniquely with Israel as his chosen people. The Spirit of God was indeed with them.[114] But at that point in God's economy Israel related to God in a relatively external way. For true indwelling of the Spirit could only occur subsequent to the reconciling atonement accomplished in the human flesh of Jesus Christ the one true high priest.

Israel had to wait in anticipation of the promise that it would enjoy a much more deeply and intensely personal knowledge of and communion with God.[115] Israel was the womb of preparation for the coming of the Word of God in the womb of Mary. That promise was fulfilled in Jesus Christ. For in him Jew and Gentile both have profound access to the Father through the Spirit, one which reconciles and heals all humanity.[116]

The pattern of God's covenantal purpose was to choose one people to be a channel of blessing to all humanity. The people of God have always had a mission to others. Ultimately that mission was to be fulfilled by Jesus Christ himself, the Chosen One. On behalf of the inclusion of all humanity the renewed people of God are incorporated in him first of all. The Church is such a Communion in the Spirit that it must transcend itself and reach out toward all those for whom Christ became Incarnate, lived, and died that they might be included in the life of God as well.[117]

The Church, then, is the immediate sphere of the Spirit's operation, but the world is nevertheless the mediate sphere.[118] The Church is the community where reconciliation is intensively actualized through the Spirit. But this is done "in order that it may be fulfilled extensively in all mankind and creation." The Church is "the new humanity within the world, the provisional manifestation of the new creation within the old."[119]

Those outside the Church are to be regarded in the sphere where this reconciliation has not yet been subjectively actualized but is nevertheless objectively accomplished for them in Jesus Christ.[120] In Torrance's view "no one has being apart from Christ" for "that is the decisive, final thing about the whole Incarnation including the death of Christ, that it affects all men, indeed the whole of creation, for the whole of creation is now put on a new basis with God, the basis of a Love that does not withhold itself but only overflows in pure unending Love."[121] Torrance notes that "we have to take seriously the fact that the Spirit was poured out on 'all flesh' and operates on 'all flesh.'"[122]

The Church is pressed into the service of the Spirit as it works out God's universal intention. Torrance exhorts the Church to keep its boundaries open to all and not limit the "range of the Communion of the Spirit." Rather, God intends to "catholicize" or "universalize" the Church thereby consummating "the fulness of Him who is all in all."[123] In this way the people of God have their existence in a way correlative to Jesus Christ, the One for the Many, the Many in the One and the One in the Many.

For Torrance, this does not mean that the Church will not live in tension with the world or that the Spirit will not have to resist the world. The Church in the power of the Spirit "calls the world into question, judges the will of the world to isolate itself from the love of God." The world will resist the Spirit. Torrance comments on the mystery of evil and the possibility of unbelief:

> All this is not to say that a man may not suffer damnation, for he may in spite of all reject Christ and refuse God's grace. How that is possible, we simply cannot understand; that a sinner face to face with the infinite love of God should rebel against it and choose to take his own way, isolating himself from that love—that is the bottomless mystery of evil before which we can only stand aghast, at the surd which we cannot rationalise, the enigma of Judas.

It may somehow be possible for the sinner to break off their engrafting in Christ. But "it is their own fault that they are rendered utter strangers to Him."[124] Consequently, "His being in hell is not the result of God's decision to damn him, but the result of his own decision to choose himself against the love of God and therefore of the negative decision of God's love to oppose his refusal of God's love just by being Love."[125]

When grasped in terms of the Person and Work of the Spirit the origin of the Church now comes into perspective. God has had a people from the very beginning. So Torrance writes, "It is important to remember that this Church was already in existence as Church when Christ died and rose again. The Church was not founded with Pentecost; nor indeed was it first founded with the Incarnation. It was founded with creation."[126]

Thus the Church is not the special independent creation of the Spirit.[127] As Torrance puts it, there is no Kingdom of the Spirit, but only a Kingdom of Christ in and by the Spirit. There is no Body of the Spirit, but only the Body of Christ.[128]

Pentecost then, is not an independent work of the Spirit added to the atonement.[129] The Church did not come into being with the Resurrection or with the pouring out of the Spirit at Pentecost.[130] Pentecost was the rebirth of God's missionary people.[131] By this work of the Spirit the one people of God, Israel, was opened up to the engrafting of all the peoples of the world.[132]

The Holy Spirit and the Knowledge of God

For Torrance the doctrine of the Spirit makes it clear that the relation between our knowledge of God and the Spirit is absolutely essential. For there could be no real knowledge of God without the Spirit, even within God! Consequently, this essential connection between pneumatology and epistemology also has significant implications for the doctrine of Scripture.

For Torrance, knowledge of God does not have its ontological origin in Scripture. First, knowledge of God is entirely at the disposal of God. It requires the deliberate personal decision and act of God since God is Spirit and we are not. The knowledge of God then is a matter of the grace of God. God, precisely as Spirit, can only be known where he has acted to reveal himself. "That is, the activity of the Spirit is the epistemological ground of our knowledge, for in Him we meet God's Being in His Act and His Act in His Being."[133] Our knowing of him cannot be determined by us (either positively by way of our confidence in our capacities or theoretical methodologies or negatively by our skepticism).[134] It must correspond to that act, decision, and "location" which God has appointed.[135]

Second the Spirit mediates the Incarnate Son in time and space: conceiving, anointing, indwelling, empowering, sanctifying, raising, and glorifying. The Spirit is the life, act, and energy of the Son. But also, the Spirit mediates a human knowledge of the transcendent God in Jesus.

Third, the Spirit makes possible, that is mediates, human openness to God.[136] First in the apostles by way of inspiration and then in all those who receive their word spoken and enscripturated.[137] The Spirit creates human capacity for receptivity.[138] And all this is possible because the Spirit puts us in actual, immediate, intuitive,[139] nonformal,[140] even empirical touch with the actual reality and presence of God himself as the Word, not just externally, but internally present to our very spirits.[141]

The end result of this revelatory activity of the Word and the Spirit is that in the light of the Spirit the Face of the Father is illuminated in the Son of God incarnate.[142] In this Trinitarian and incarnational way we come to have not just inductive or deductive knowledge about God but "we come to know him in some real measure as he is in himself since the Son and the Spirit are proper to the Being of God and dwell within his Being; and it is in the Spirit that our knowing of God really is knowing, since through participating in his Spirit . . . we are made partakers of God."[143]

Astoundingly, although all creaturely knowledge of God comes to us in some creaturely form, the revelatory action of the Spirit through the Word enables the forms to be transcended and prevents us from reducing that personal and actual knowledge to those creaturely forms. The Spirit communicates through the creaturely forms but not as creaturely forms. The knowledge of God in the Spirit is transformal. So Torrance writes that God relates the human forms to himself in such a way that they become "diacoustic" and "diaphanous" media. Without the work of the Holy Spirit all the forms of revelation would "remain dark and opaque but in and through His presence they become translucent and transparent."[144] The effect of this work is that our response to revelation "does not terminate on the media but on the Being of God Himself."[145]

God is Holy Spirit in Person and so must be known in accordance with his very nature, that is in a holy, godly, and personal way. This means that God cannot be approached neutrally in a disinterested, much less hostile, or autonomous manner. In fact, given the rebellious and enslaved nature of humanity, a radically reconciling work must accompany all revelatory work, for no cognitive union and communion can occur within an alienated relationship.[146]

The knowledge of God involves direct confrontation with the Spirit to question and convict us so that "by the Spirit we are carried beyond ourselves to genuine knowledge of Him."[147] At Pentecost, Torrance notes, the Spirit rescued us from our "sinful creativity," our religious propensity to mythologize and project ourselves onto God.[148]

The provision of Scripture, the deposit of faith, for the Church in no way obviates the gracious and powerful working of the Spirit. If there is to be any real reconciling knowledge of God, the Spirit is essential to the inspiration, preservation, and illumination of the Bible. The words are the instruments of the Spirit, as Torrance puts it. "The meaning of the words written is not found in the letters as such but in the divine actions which they express, and the written words are the instrument of the Spirit who writes them in our minds and lives if we receive them in accordance with his power and nature."[149]

Torrance follows Irenaeus's line of thought when he wrote that Scripture came from the Word and Spirit of God and so must be interpreted in terms of that Word and Spirit, thus ruling out all independent and private interpretations.[150] God did not speak once and then become mute, but by the same Spirit and Word continues to speak in and through the Scripture and its human forms of thought and speech so that "the Holy Scriptures point far beyond themselves to the sheer reality and glory of God who alone can bear witness to himself and create in us, beyond any capacity of our own, genuine knowledge of God."[151]

That is why anyone who would interpret Scripture "must pray to be enlightened by the same Spirit."[152] For interpretation of Holy Scripture is not merely a matter of definitions, grammar, and historical background, but a matter of real living union and communion, actual relationship with God. Scripture must be interpreted according to the creative and renewing power of the Spirit if we are to have God's word inscribed on our hearts and have our minds renewed after the likeness of Christ.[153] God the Father through his Word and Spirit is "eloquent Being."[154]

The revelation of the Triune God means God graciously extends himself in self-giving and self-revelation, acting and speaking in Person by His Word through the Holy Spirit. Without the presence of the Spirit there would be no break through to us of the transcendent God "in His reality as Being and thus in His distinction from our thought and speech of Him."[155]

Critique of Torrance's Doctrine of the Holy Spirit

Although Thomas Torrance has written only a few chapter-length treatments specifically devoted to pneumatology, his theological reflections are saturated in every part with reference to the Holy Spirit. In his view, in fact, nothing complete can be said about any topic in theology without some vital reference to the Holy Spirit.

When these references are taken together it is clear that Torrance has a very well developed and integrated theology of the Holy Spirit. Moreover, his writings on the topic make a fairly unique and powerful contribution to Christian theology. Indeed, he sounds a prophetic note in countering the tendency of much modern theology to reduce pneumatology to one or another aspect of anthropology.

From another angle, one could also regard Torrance's theology of the Holy Spirit as delivering a fatal blow to Harnack's thesis that the Greek fathers essentially Hellenized the Christian faith with ontological abstractions. Torrance shows how the Early Church fathers waged a diligent and largely successful battle against such uncritical adaptation of Greek dualistic ways of thinking. On the basis of their most faithful contributions Torrance has set forth a realist pneumatology which understands the Spirit in a most immediate, concrete, personal, and relational way.

It is true that often the person and work of the Spirit remains implicit in Torrance's treatment of other topics. However, I believe this approach actually corresponds to the nature of the subject matter, the Holy Spirit. It reflects the ineffable and self-effacing nature of the

Spirit whose ministry is to shed light on everything else rather than to be in the spotlight. Consequently, the working of the Spirit cannot and need not always be explicitly referenced. The form of Torrance's theology is shaped by the form of the revelation concerning the Holy Spirit.

Some may still find this lack of symmetrical treatment between the Father, Son, and Spirit a fault. Karl Barth has been critiqued in this very way, having been charged with a subordinationism of the Spirit. However, I submit that this brief survey of Torrance's pneumatology demonstrates that he has indeed securely laid a solid foundation for a doctrine of the Holy Spirit, even if he has not completed the entire superstructure which might be built upon it.

What Torrance has given us is a profoundly Trinitarian, incarnational, and onto-relational approach to the doctrine of the Spirit integrated intimately with the essential and core matters of the Christian faith. One could say that here in this doctrine, the realism of the Gospel itself reaches its climax and so the call to a living vital faith shines through it. For in the doctrine of the Spirit the transcendent majesty of God focuses on Who the Triune God is and on all that God has done for us and in us. The personal transcendence, immanence, and indwelling of God all find their proper place in the doctrine of the Spirit.

Torrance's pneumatology highlights the immediacy and efficacy of God which would remain obscure and at a deistic distance if left out of any presentation of the doctrines of the Father and the Son. The doctrine of the Spirit is radical and absolutely determinative of the shape of Torrance's theology. To take it as seriously, personally, and ineffably as Torrance has presented it calls for a decisive reorientation not just of our thought but of our lives. It does not leave much room for neutrality towards the subject matter. Torrance has provided the Church an astounding and reorienting presentation which in the end can only lead us to doxology.

This does not mean Torrance's theology is beyond question or is inimical to further development. However, strong opposition to Torrance's pneumatology will mostly come about at the level of profoundly divergent presuppositions regarding the Holy Spirit rather than over secondary matters. This will usually be the case because the essence of Torrance's work addresses very directly the most foundational issues regarding our faith in and understanding of the Holy Spirit.

Indicative of this is the fact that his pneumatology stands in radical contrast to any objectivizing, subjectivizing, institutionalizing, or other anthropomorphic renderings of the doctrine. Those who would resist his radical critique of these modern tendencies would be questioning the very foundation upon which Torrance builds his case. At this level, the argument would be over which spirit is the Holy Spirit.

Consequently, Torrance's pneumatology will draw some predictable critiques. As mentioned above, some will say it fails to give the Spirit equal time and development compared to the other Persons of the Trinity and so gives the impression of a subordinationism of the Spirit. However, if I understand Torrance's pneumatology correctly, the ineffable and self-effacing nature of the Spirit means that we should not expect an equally explicit treatment of the Spirit.

Some will complain that Torrance's view of the works of the Spirit does not show a proper independence from the other Trinitarian Persons and so fails to exhibit the equality of deity. However, once again, if Torrance is right about the co-inherent nature of the working of the Triune God, then one should not expect the Spirit to have some kind of autonomous working. Indeed, in Torrance's view the Father and Son's own actions *ad extra* have all too often been rendered far too independent from each other, thus distorting the proper communion of God in Act and Being in the Holy Spirit.

Torrance's challenge to those who make such foundational criticisms is for them to offer a more "balanced" presentation of the Spirit which will not in actuality reduce pneumatology to anthropology or a mythology of the human spirit. Such alternatives would most likely turn out to be incommensurable with Torrance's most foundational understandings of the person and work of the Spirit. With Torrance it seems that there is a foundationally decisive fork in the pneumatological road and one must choose one path or another. I would welcome his response to this characterization.

However, concerning the matter of greater development of his pneumatology, there are two very different reasons to hope for more of a superstructure to be built on Torrance's foundation. First, such hope could arise out of the awareness that much more could be drawn out of it because of its sheer coherence and profound integration with all other aspects of Christian faith. It was built for a superstructure.

A second reason for wanting more development might be the drive towards gaining more practical "how" explanations of the Spirit's working or more practical advice on what the Church should say or do. Torrance does not offer a lot which would directly satisfy this second concern for pragmatics. In part, this is due to the fact that asking a general "how" question of the working of the Holy Spirit (How does the Spirit unite the natures in Jesus?) is in his view incoherent. For the Holy Spirit itself is the answer to the ultimate "how" questions we might ask. How was Jesus conceived in the womb of Mary? By the Holy Spirit!

Referring to the agency of the Holy Spirit as the ultimate answer goes against the grain of modern Western habits of mind which seeks impersonal, causal, or instrumental means as explanation. For the most part agency has been eliminated from the category of being essential to explanation. But for Torrance the Triune agency in perichoretic communion is the ultimate explanation. Torrance's theology of the Spirit reestablishes the centrality of agency for theological description.

If my understanding of Torrance is correct, and I hope he will respond to this point, his pneumatology is a radical critique of the search for explanation in terms of impersonal, causal, or instrumental means, at least as it pertains to Christian theology. Agency, and ultimately the agency of the Holy Spirit, is the answer to the "how" questions which might be raised concerning God and God's people.

Torrance's pneumatology makes clear that we can never master the Holy Spirit, we cannot take control. The Holy Spirit cannot be faithfully compared to, say, electricity which is "always in the wires so you just have to get plugged in." Any attempt to corral the Holy Spirit, even for the purposes of God, could only constitute a repeat of Simon Magus's error when he tried to purchase the power of the Holy Spirit from the Apostles. To the degree that we want to go behind the back of the Holy Spirit and find out how God "really" did something, or even how we might do something "for God" is not to build on Torrance's foundation, but to attempt to raise a structure on an entirely different one. I suspect Torrance intends to give us no satisfaction in this direction.

However, if our concern is to seek out the implications of the doctrine of the Spirit for the work and ministry of the Church as Torrance has laid it out for us, I think it is clear that much can be written on that foundation. For the ministry of the Spirit is to enable us to participate in all the things that God has done, is doing, and will do for us and our salvation.

Torrance's pneumatology certainly is capable of providing a profound orientation and critique of all human participation in the things of God. The most thorough development in his thought in direct connection with his pneumatology involves matters of epistemology, revelation, theological method, and implications for our handling of Scripture. What he says illuminates the tremendous practical implications of the Holy Spirit in the areas of philosophy, theology, and biblical studies. Unfortunately, these issues are not of immediate concern to most pastors and laypersons who are often looking for very straightforward help in the mundane matters of Church work today.

The area of greatest investment laden with practical implications, however, is his contribution to the doctrine of the Trinity as it applies to the controversy over the *filioque*. Here we see united a theological and practical concern for the unity of the Body of Christ. His labor for more than fourteen years came to fruition in the historic document of 13 March 1991, "Joint Statement of the Official Dialogue between the Orthodox Church and the World Alliance of Reformed Churches," which included the announcement of an "Agreed Statement on the Holy Trinity." Incredible as it may seem, in principle the 1,000-year-old schism over the *filioque* has been resolved. This matter should no longer be an obstacle in the relations between the Eastern and Western branches of the one Body of Christ. Of course, the outworking of this agreement among all concerned parties will take some time. Nevertheless, this theological work on the Holy Spirit will stand as perhaps Torrance's greatest contribution to the life of the Church.

There are many other issues about which Torrance makes suggestive comments, e.g., on the Pentecostal/Charismatic movement. However, these remain largely undeveloped. I wonder how Torrance would respond to some of the controversies within the Charismatic movement such as the nature of the gifts. Would his understanding of the humanizing and personalizing nature of the Spirit provide for faithful discernment and exercise of the gifts of the Spirit? Torrance's theology is deliberately open ended and invites exploration of the "practical" implications of his work. The test of his contribution in these areas will be the adequacy of the foundation laid for others as they attempt to work out such developments.

There are a couple of matters somewhat closer to the foundational aims of Torrance's pneumatology that possibly could have benefitted from greater development. Anyone reading Torrance who is familiar with Scripture might wonder how Torrance himself would incorporate a variety of biblical passages which come to mind while reading his work, passages he neither references nor exegetes. While Torrance is rightly wary of anything that comes close to a proof texting approach to theology, the authority he explicitly grants to the apostolic witness and the references he makes to key passages along the way signal that his pneumatology is profoundly rooted in Scripture, so much so that one can only have confidence that his incorporation of more in-depth comments on particular texts and reference to additional passages would have been illuminating. While his handling of Scripture for doing theology is exemplary, at times one could wish for more discussion as to how he understands certain relevant biblical material to contribute to his theological thinking.

In particular, more extensive treatment of the Spirit in terms of the Old Testament would have been welcome. As it is, there is plenty to go on, but more explicit development of this could have enhanced his presentation. Other matters which might have been developed more thoroughly pertain to questions regarding resisting the Holy Spirit and even more particularly the blasphemy of the Holy Spirit. Of course Torrance briefly comments on these matters, and they are quite suggestive. But the question remains how he might approach these concerns especially in connection with Reformed notions of the irresistibility of Grace. A more in-depth treatment of the doctrine of sin in connection with the Spirit would have been illuminating as well. I would welcome any comments he might make in response to this.

There are a few practical concerns related to methodology which we might also mention. Torrance's explicit dialogue partners in his writings on the Holy Spirit are for the most part not living. Mainly he engages with a considerable selection of ante- and post-Nicene fathers and Calvin. Karl Barth is of course the most often mentioned contemporary. He also interacts at some length with Karl Rahner. One familiar with the contemporary discussions on Trinitarian theology, the development of the Charismatic movement, debates on cosmology, and matters involving the worship and mission of the Church in our pluralistic social and ideological context naturally will wish that Torrance might have interacted more directly with those presently teaching and writing on these topics. Such dialogue would not be for the purpose of staking out territory, but for locating, fine-tuning, and grasping more securely Torrance's own teaching. It could also contribute to an improved ability to critique various contemporary proposals (including Torrance's).

In my view much of what Torrance has said does indeed bear directly and critically on contemporary theologies of the Spirit. Torrance's whole pneumatology resists pantheistic and panentheistic tendencies as well as subjectivizing and mystical approaches to the Spirit. However, having Torrance directly address Pannenberg, Moltmann, Gunton, Jenson, or say John Zizioulas could be illuminating and helpful for observers of the discussion who must work through alternatives. Perhaps Torrance might comment on why he has not engaged in a thoroughgoing way contemporary theologies of the Spirit.

Of course, this is not to say that Torrance should have been preoccupied with every contemporary debate surrounding the Holy

Spirit. He selected his main task, the reconciliation of the Eastern and Western Church. The wealth of the riches he has mined from the Early Church fathers is invaluable. It has also provided a solid foundation for further faithful ecumenical engagement and progress in a way that participation in an exclusively contemporary debate never could. So, while we might have benefitted from Torrance's comments on other contemporary debates, we are nevertheless left a legacy which can inform debates and discussions for every time, including our own.[156]

Notes

1. Thomas F. Torrance, *Theology in Reconciliation: Essays towards Evangelical and Catholic Unity in East and West* (London: Geoffrey Chapman, 1975), 238. Cf. Thomas F. Torrance, *Divine Meaning: Studies in Greek Patristic Hermeneutics* (Edinburgh: T&T Clark, 1995), 201.

2. Torrance, *Divine Meaning*, 382.

3. Thomas F. Torrance, *Theology in Reconstruction* (London: SCM; Grand Rapids, Mich.: Eerdmans, 1965), 191, and Thomas F. Torrance, *The Trinitarian Faith: The Evangelical Theology of the Ancient Catholic Church* (Edinburgh: T&T Clark, 1988), 205ff.

4. Torrance, *Reconciliation*, 290-91. Cf. Torrance, *Trinitarian Faith*, 191.

5. Thomas F. Torrance, *The Christian Doctrine of God, One Being Three Persons* (Edinburgh: T&T Clark, 1996), 63.

6. Torrance, *Christian Doctrine*, 62-63, Torrance, *Reconstruction*, 200. Torrance, *Reconciliation*, 85-86. Torrance, *Divine Meaning*, 384.

7. Torrance, *Reconciliation*, 292. Torrance, *Divine Meaning*, 64, 199. See Eph. 2:18, Gal. 4:4-6, 1 Cor. 12:4-6, and Heb. 9:14. These passages are often cited or alluded to by Torrance.

8. Torrance, *Trinitarian Faith*, 199-202. Torrance, *Christian Doctrine*, 147.

9. Torrance, *Reconciliation*, 114.

10. Torrance, *Reconstruction*, 242. Torrance, *Divine Meaning*, 385.

11. Torrance, *Trinitarian Faith*, 202. Torrance, *Divine Meaning*, 200.

12. Torrance, *Reconciliation*, 101. Torrance, *Trinitarian Faith*, 202. Torrance, *Divine Meaning*, 195.

13. Torrance, *Christian Doctrine*, 196.

14. Torrance, *Christian Doctrine*, 64.

15. Torrance, *Trinitarian Faith*, 198. Torrance, *Divine Meaning*, 412.

16. Torrance, *Reconciliation*, 238. Torrance, *Divine Meaning*, 201.

17. Torrance, *Divine Meaning*, 216. A proper Christocentrism does not devolve into a Christomonism but leads to a true Trinitarianism. See also Torrance, *Reconciliation*, 253. Torrance finds this to be patently true in both Irenaeus and Athanasius. See Torrance, *Divine Meaning*, 60-62.

18. Torrance, *Trinitarian Faith*, 200.

19. Torrance, *Trinitarian Faith*, 195. Torrance, *Christian Doctrine*, 158.

20. Torrance, *Reconstruction*, 220ff. Torrance, *Trinitarian Faith*, 101.

21. Torrance, *Trinitarian Faith*, 192, 220.

22. Torrance, *Christian Doctrine*, 63.

23. Torrance, *Christian Doctrine*, 65. Torrance, *Trinitarian Faith*, 249.

24. Torrance, *Trinitarian Faith*, 192, 218, 226.

25. Torrance, *Divine Meaning*, 199-200. Torrance, *Trinitarian Faith*, 236. Torrance, *Reconciliation*, 252.

26. Torrance, *Divine Meaning*, 200.

27. Torrance, *Trinitarian Faith*, 192.

28. Torrance, *Divine Meaning*, 216.

29. Torrance, *Trinitarian Faith*, 218-19.

30. Torrance, *Trinitarian Faith*, 220.

31. Quoted in Torrance, *Trinitarian Faith*, 221, from Epiphanius, *Haer.* 69.72.

32. Torrance, *Trinitarian Faith*, 222. So also Didymus of Alexandria and Cyril of Jerusalem. See Torrance, *Trinitarian Faith*, 223, 247.

33. Torrance, *Trinitarian Faith*, 222.

34. Torrance, *Trinitarian Faith*, 234. Also see Torrance, *Christian Doctrine*, 167.

35. Quoted in Torrance, *Trinitarian Faith*, 234.

36. Torrance, *Trinitarian Faith*, 65.

37. Torrance, *Trinitarian Faith*, 210.

38. Torrance, *Trinitarian Faith*, 235.

39. Torrance, *Trinitarian Faith*, 233.

40. Torrance, *Christian Doctrine*, 157.

41. Torrance, *Christian Doctrine*, 156-57.

42. Torrance, *Trinitarian Faith*, 237.

43. "Their differentiating qualities instead of separating them actually serves their oneness with each other," Torrance, *Christian Doctrine*, 171.

44. Torrance, *Trinitarian Faith*, 233, 234, 239.

45. Torrance, *Christian Doctrine*, 170, n. 8 and 170-74.

46. Torrance, *Christian Doctrine*, 166, 171. Cf. 192.

47. The statement can be found in Thomas F. Torrance, ed., *Theological Dialogue between Orthodox and Reformed Churches*, vol. 2 (Edinburgh: Scottish Academic Press, 1993).

48. Most if not all of Torrance's writing on the Trinity bears upon this issue. For key parts of his understanding see especially Torrance, *Doctrine of God*, 180-94, Torrance, *Trinitarian Faith*, chs. 6 and 8, Torrance, *Reconciliation*, ch. 5, and most comprehensively, Thomas F. Torrance,

Trinitarian Perspectives: Toward Doctrinal Agreement (Edinburgh: T&T Clark, 1994).

49. Torrance regards, for example, Didymus the Blind's theology as being more successful at avoiding the ambiguities in the theologies of others which opened the door to the controversy over the procession of the Spirit. Torrance, *Trinitarian Faith*, 243-44.

50. Torrance, *Trinitarian Faith*, 302-30. This language is also reflected in the so-called Athanasian Creed (Quinquque Vult).

51. Torrance, *Trinitarian Faith*, 205.

52. Torrance, *Trinitarian Faith*, 213.

53. Thomas F. Torrance, *God and Rationality* (London: Oxford University Press, 1971), 171.

54. Torrance, *Trinitarian Faith*, 211, quoting Epiphanius.

55. Torrance, *Christian Doctrine*, 152.

56. Torrance, *Reconciliation*, 236-37. Torrance, *Divine Meaning*, 200.

57. Torrance, *Trinitarian Faith*, 73.

58. Torrance, *Reconciliation*, 235-36.

59. Torrance, *Reconciliation*, 290. Torrance, *Trinitarian Faith*, 233-34.

60. Torrance, *Christian Doctrine*, 217.

61. Torrance, *Reconciliation*, 237.

62. Torrance, *Reconciliation*, 100.

63. Torrance, *Reconciliation*, 236.

64. Torrance, *Reconciliation*, 102.

65. Torrance, *Christian Doctrine*, 154.

66. Torrance, *Reconciliation*, 235.

67. Torrance, *Reconstruction*, 246, 247.

68. Of course within the Trinity they are coinherently and consubtantially mutual. In the relations established with humanity first in Jesus Christ and then through him in us, they are radically asymmetrical for the creature is entirely dependent upon the initiative and objective accomplishment of the absolutely new mode of relationship by God.

69. Torrance, *Reconciliation*, 246.

70. Torrance, *Reconciliation*, 111-12, 230.

71. Torrance, *Reconciliation*, 110.

72. Torrance, *Reconciliation*, 110,111, 119. Torrance, *Rationality*, 174.

73. Torrance, *Trinitarian Faith*, 209. Torrance, *Reconciliation*, 140. Torrance, *Christian Doctrine*, 154. See also Torrance, *Reconciliation*, 103. On Irenaeus's understanding see Torrance, *Divine Meaning*, 73.

74. Torrance, *Christian Doctrine*, 63.

75. Torrance, *Rationality*, 173.

76. Torrance, *Reconciliation*, 292.

77. Torrance, *Trinitarian Faith*, 208.

78. Torrance, *Reconstruction*, 230.

79. Torrance, *Reconstruction*, 227-28, 242-43.

80. Thomas F. Torrance, trans. and ed., *The School of Faith: The Catechisms of the Reformed Church* (London: James Clarke, 1959), cx.

81. Torrance, *School of Faith*, cxi.

82. Torrance, *Reconstruction*, 268.

83. Torrance, *Divine Meaning*, 197-98. Torrance, *Reconciliation*, 234. Torrance, *Trinitarian Faith*, 208.

84. Torrance, *Divine Meaning*, 197-98. Torrance, *Reconciliation*, 234.

85. Torrance, *Reconciliation*, 134, 238-40. Torrance, *Divine Meaning*, 198, 202. Torrance, *Trinitarian Faith*, 198, 228.

86. Torrance, *Reconstruction*, 221.

87. Torrance, *Reconstruction*, 243.

88. Torrance, *Rationality*, 174.

89. Torrance, *Rationality*, 173, 174.

90. Torrance, *Trinitarian Faith*, 230, 231. Torrance, *Rationality*, 188-89, Thomas F. Torrance, *The Mediation of Christ* (Colorado Springs, Colo.: Helmers & Howard, 1992), 67-69. Torrance, *Christian Doctrine*,160-61.

91. Torrance, *Christian Doctrine*, 160, 220. Torrance, *Rationality*, 188-89. Torrance, *Trinitarian Faith*, 230-31.

92. Torrance, *Trinitarian Faith*, 230. Cf. 227, 229.

93. Torrance, *Christian Doctrine*, 161. Torrance, *Mediation*, 69.

94. Torrance, *Reconciliation*, 62.

95. Torrance, *Rationality*, 188.

96. Torrance, *School of Faith*, cvi.

97. Torrance, *Reconciliation*, 89 .

98. Torrance, *Christian Doctrine*, 152. Cf. 150.

99. Torrance, *Reconciliation*, 243.

100. Torrance, *Christian Doctrine*, 154. See also Torrance, *Reconciliation*, 114, and Torrance, *Divine Meaning*, 70.

101. Torrance, *Trinitarian Faith*, 249, 250 picking up the phraseology of Hyppolytus. See also Torrance, *Reconstruction*, 250, and Torrance, *Christian Doctrine*, 63.

102. Torrance, *Reconciliation*, 183-84. Cf. 209 and 186 on Origen.

103. Torrance, *Reconstruction*, 250. Cf. 249, 251. See also Torrance, *Reconciliation*, 211, 213.

104. Torrance, *Reconciliation*, 105.

105. Torrance, *Reconstruction*, 250, 251.

106. Torrance, *Reconciliation*, 118, 134.

107. Torrance, *Christian Doctrine*, 65.

108. Torrance, *Reconstruction*, 243.

109. Torrance, *Trinitarian Faith*, 250-51.

110. Torrance, *Reconstruction*, 193. Cf. Torrance, *Reconciliation*, 22.

111. Torrance, *Reconstruction*, 193.

112. Torrance, *Reconstruction*, 195.

113. Torrance, *School of Faith*, cxx, cxxxiv. Cf. Torrance, *Reconstruction*, 193.

114. Torrance, *Christian Doctrine*, 67ff. Torrance, *Trinitarian Faith*, 66, 192-93.

115. Torrance, *Christian Doctrine*, 67.

116. Torrance, *Christian Doctrine*, 70.
117. Torrance, *School of Faith*, cxxiv.
118. Torrance, *Reconstruction*, 204.
119. Torrance, *School of Faith*, cxxi.
120. Torrance, *School of Faith*, cxvii.
121. Torrance, *School of Faith*, cxii.
122. Torrance, *School of Faith*, cxvii.
123. Torrance, *School of Faith*, cxxiv. See also Torrance, *Reconciliation*, 21, and Torrance, *School of Faith*, cxxi.
124. Torrance, *School of Faith*, cxvii.
125. Torrance, *School of Faith*, cxv. Torrance also discusses a proper understanding of the irresistibility of grace and its distorting reformulation, building on Augustine, in terms of efficient causality and created grace. See Torrance, *Reconciliation*, 98. This understanding of the work of the Spirit also has implications for our view of hell. See Torrance, *School of Faith*, cxv.
126. Torrance, *School of Faith*, cxix, cxx.
127. Torrance, *Reconstruction*, 204.
128. Torrance, *Reconstruction*, 204-5.
129. Torrance, *Trinitarian Faith*, 190.
130. Torrance, *Reconstruction*, 204.
131. Torrance, *Reconstruction*, 195. See also Thomas F. Torrance, *Space, Time, and Resurrection* (Edinburgh: The Handsel Press, 1976), 121.
132. Torrance, *Reconciliation*, 24, 61. Torrance, *Christian Doctrine*, 64.
133. Torrance, *Rationality*, 255.
134. Torrance, *Rationality*, 165.
135. Torrance, *Reconstruction*, 233. Torrance, *Reconciliation*, 239.
136. Torrance, *Reconstruction*, 245ff.
137. Torrance, *Reconstruction*, 206. See also Torrance, *Divine Meaning*, 116, 274-5. Torrance, *Rationality*, 184.
138. Torrance, *Reconstruction*, 226, 252. Torrance, *Reconciliation*, 100.
139. Torrance, *Rationality*, 184.
140. Torrance, *Rationality*, 165.
141. Torrance, *Rationality*, 165, 166, 176.
142. Torrance, *Rationality*, 167. See also Torrance, *Trinitarian Faith*, 211-15.
143. Torrance, *Reconciliation*, 238.
144. Torrance, *Rationality*, 185.
145. Torrance, *Rationality*, 183-84.
146. Torrance, *Rationality*, 179.
147. Torrance, *Rationality*, 178. Cf. Torrance, *Christian Doctrine*, 150.
148. Torrance, *Reconstruction*, 255.
149. Torrance, *Divine Meaning*, 232.
150. Torrance, *Divine Meaning*, 129.

151. Torrance, *Divine Meaning*, 375.

152. Torrance, *Divine Meaning*, 275.

153. Torrance, *Divine Meaning*, 232. Cf. Torrance, *Rationality*, 186.

154. Torrance, *Rationality*, 179.

155. Torrance, *Rationality*, 175.

156. The results of these discussions are contained in the two volumes edited by Thomas F. Torrance, *Theological Dialogue between Orthodox and Reformed Churches*, vols. 1 and 2 (Edinburgh: Scottish Academic Press, 1985, 1993).

Chapter 5

Being and Person:

T. F. Torrance's Doctrine of God

by Colin Gunton

Something on the Sources

My first memory of Tom Torrance comes from a large student gathering in Bristol in 1963, when he shared the platform with, among others, Lesslie Newbigin. The congress was up-to-date for those days, with science and politics among the concerns, and our subject's address was, as might be expected, concerned with the former. But not in itself. The emphasis was on the necessity for scientist and theologian alike to obeise themselves before the reality which they served.

That introduces a theme central to Torrance's doctrine of God: that God's objective truth confronts us all with a demand which our subjective rationality may seek to encompass according to both God's and its limits, but which must never stray over those strict limits. The truth is prior to our appropriation of it. And a later memory is also definitive of the kind of theologian that Torrance is. It was a conference ordered around Rahner's book on the Trinity,[1] and an anecdote will illustrate the whole.

One evening, towards the end of the conference, some of us, clever, no doubt, but inexperienced, were discussing our profound disquiet with some of Rahner's theology. We took it to Tom, who placed the whole thing in somewhat wider context, before spending the night writing a response to the conference which summed its proceedings up magisterially, in a rounded paper which was later published, no doubt with minimal need for revision, as "Towards an Ecumenical Consensus on the Trinity."[2]

Many streams flow together into Torrance's doctrine of God, and to name them is to begin to understand something of its shape. Without doubt, the demand to obeise ourselves before the reality of God is something that comes from the Calvinist inheritance, but it is a Calvinism modified in both a Scottish and a modern way. A number of nineteenth-century Scots, among them Edward Irving and John McLeod Campbell, reacted against what they believed to be the rigidities of the piety formed under the aegis of the Westminster Confession and produced a theology designed to mitigate the effects of classic dual predestinarianism.

McLeod Campbell is particularly important for Torrance. His pastoral motivation drove him to stress Christ's identification with the human condition and to push towards a theology of his universal significance. The incarnation is as significant for him as Jesus' death, which is understood truly as God's self-giving. This remains throughout Torrance's career at the very center of his doctrine of God, and indeed of everything else.

The concern to ensure that God is truly given in Christ recurs in Torrance's early and continuing engagement with Karl Barth. For him, Barth is comparable only with Athanasius as the theologian in whom God's being and act are truly integrated. Barth's incarnational theology and attack on natural theology alike drive him, as Torrance understands him, not only to engage with the weaknesses of Calvin's tendency to posit a God hidden beyond Christ (a scholarly commonplace that Torrance accepts only with qualifications), but also with a much more deep-seated Western tendency.

From at least the time of Augustine onwards the modalist temptation to posit a God lying behind his acts has been one of the perennial pitfalls of our tradition, Catholic and Evangelical alike. (It is there that is to be seen the appeal to Torrance of Rahner's influential book, with its critique of his own Catholic tradition's tendency to open a breach between the one God and the Triune God.) Crucial for Torrance here is the figure of Athanasius, who can be said in some way or other to appear as a real presence in all of his thought. Part of his importance is to serve as the patristic forerunner of what Barth is in the modern age, although, as we shall see, that is only a part of a wide-ranging appeal.

Athanasius served Torrance as a theologian of God's being as Barth served as a theologian of his act (though the greatness of both is that they integrated the two) and it would be difficult to exaggerate the importance for him, in all aspects of his work, of the principle of the *homoousion.* "[T]he *homoousion* helps us to discern and makes us regard the Incarnation as falling within the Life of God himself and as thus providing the real ontological ground on which we think inseparably together the doctrine of the one God and the doctrine of the triune God."[3] However, that is to leap ahead.

Before we come to the One and the Three, we must pause to examine something of the basis and method of the doctrine of God which is so central to this theologian's work. The basis of the doctrine of God is to be found in the Gospel of Jesus Christ and the worship of the Church which responds to it and lives by it. If we may suspect that a touch of intellectualism is sometimes near the surface of this theology, that impression is always qualified by the firm evangelical and missionary orientation of Torrance's thought. In that sense, his missionary origins have never left him, for all his writing about God breathes a concern that the truth and rationality of the Gospel be communicated in and to the world.

Theology's task is to essay a rational account of the creed of the Church while remaining deeply entrenched in the Gospel. It is at this epistemological level that the thought of Michael Polanyi has exercised a deep influence. The scientist-philosopher, along with Einstein, is central to Torrance's attack on dualism, another recurring theme of his writing. Dualism is that which distorts the Christian knowledge of God and, indeed, has seriously incapacitated all the thought of the West. Two aspects of what is a broad-based syndrome are at the heart of Torrance's concern.

The first is the division between the world of sense and the world of intellect. Against this, Polanyi's teaching that human agents indwell the world of their experience, an insight which Torrance sees to derive from the teaching of the Fourth Gospel, is crucial. Modern intellectual life is vitiated because it is dualistically deprived of its basis in material being. A philosophy of the necessity of the human mind's continuity with the material world not only has Christian origins, but also is essential for the integration of thought and experience without which neither natural nor theological science can operate.

In line with this insight, and alongside Torrance's insistence on the rationality of both God and the theology of the Trinity, is a concern to integrate the empirical (a word which appears often in his writings) and the conceptual. We might say that it generates a realist parallel with Kant's essentially idealist epistemology. Theological concepts must have a corresponding empirical purchase if they are not to fly dualistically off into a theology which is not rooted in the Gospel.

The second dualism is parallel with that between mind and matter, and is between the being and act of God. Certain forms of the

"Latin Heresy"[4] have entrenched in the tradition the breach we have already met between the act of God (what he does) and his being (what he is). It is not too much of an exaggeration to say that Torrance's Trinitarian theology is a sustained attempt to overcome that dualism. And at the center of the enterprise of overcoming that dualism is the Nicene doctrine of the *homoousion*. A word count of Torrance's theology would almost certainly place the *homoousion* at the head of the major theological concepts which he employs, so that it is accordingly that much more difficult to give succinct expression to the wide-ranging use to which the concept is put. One could almost say that where Barth's theology of the Trinity is centered essentially on a theology of revelation, Torrance's is centered on the *homoousion*.

That is not to suggest that his is not also a theology of revelation, nor that there are not major methodological parallels with Barth. The level we have already mentioned, the level of the experience of the Gospel, is indeed the level of revelation. But where Barth places the threefold shape of the divine self-revelation, indeed christologically grounded, Torrance places a more firmly christological and incarnational center.

This is where the patristic influence is the strongest, and it takes form in a more definite use than is to be found in Barth of the concept of the divine economy, which Torrance defines as "the orderly movement in which God actively makes himself known to us in his incarnate condescension and his redemptive activity within the structures of space and time."[5] The allusion to space and time reminds us of the apologetic, perhaps better missionary, thrust of Torrance's theology, for as long ago as his definitive study of the incarnational relation of God to space and time he argued that God's movement into time in the Gospel both (historically) created the conditions for modern science and demonstrates (in the present) the scientific and theological falsity of a dualistic view of God and the world.[6] Crucial here to Torrance's reading of theological history is the view that under the impact of revelation Athanasius and the Greek fathers developed conceptions of the relation of God to time and space which transformed the whole of culture, crippled though the developments were in early modernity by the dualistic mechanism of the Newtonian tradition.[7] Again and again we are reminded: the Gospel of the economy shapes not only the Christian world but the world of culture as a whole.

The Triune Economy

To explain the epistemological and ontological function of the *homoousion* we must understand that Torrance goes beyond his modern teacher in drawing a firm parallel between natural and theological science. According to him, the former is based on everyday experience, and represents a development of the rationality already inherent in it. The first, experiential, level is thus already incipiently scientific. "At the ground or primary level of daily life, our experiences and cognitions are naturally and inseparably combined together."[8] The second or scientific level is that wherein conceptual integration is made of the first level. Essential for Torrance's general epistemology is that the second arise out of the first: "their function is to enable us to grasp and to understand common experience from the intelligible relations *intrinsic to it*, but which are not themselves directly experienced."[9] The third level is the metascientific (or second scientific) at which "we seek to deepen and simplify the organisation of basic concepts and relations developed at the scientific level."[10]

In theology there is a movement that is parallel, but not identical, to these three levels: from, we might say, the experienced Gospel to a rational account of the truth of the Gospel's God. The *homoousion* operates at all three levels, and in fact is crucial for their integration. At the first level is "the ground level of religious experience and worship" (and we may notice that Torrance is less reluctant than Barth to speak of experience in such a way) which is experience of "the Lord Jesus Christ clothed with his gospel," Trinitarianly construed. This is "*incipient theology*."[11]

The second level is concerned with the "appropriate intellectual instruments" with which to give a primary theological account of the experienced Gospel.[12] This is the level of the economy, and it is here that the *homoousion* is the hinge. It enabled, we might say, rational sense to be made of the God who made himself known in Jesus Christ. "That is to say, the *homoousios* was harnessed to the Gospel of salvation proclaimed in the New Testament and linked . . . to their belief 'in one God the Father Almighty, Maker of heaven and earth.'"[13] The rational achievement is that "The *homoousion* crystallises the conviction that while the incarnation falls within the structures of our spatio-temporal humanity in this world, it also falls within the Life and Being of God," and so is "the ontological and epistemological linchpin of Christian theology."[14]

Accordingly, the historic and enduring significance of the

Council of Nicaea consists in the fact that it entrenched in the Church the christological orthodoxy, which was established beyond all peradventure by Athanasius, that the Son of God is equal in godhead with the eternal Father. Arianism is correspondingly the most dangerous heresy, because it calls in question the reality of revelation at both divine and human levels.[15]

All this makes clear that the *homoousion* of the Son with the Father is crucial in the development of Torrance's theology. It represents God's contingent historical freedom to be fully present to the world in Christ and it drives the whole development. Yet it is not enough for a doctrine of the Trinity unless the *homoousion* of the Holy Spirit is also established.

Two aspects of Torrance's pneumatological thesis must here be mentioned. The first is that, although the divinity of the Spirit belonged to the tradition of the Church's faith, it was not until half a century after Nicaea that the conceptual development and elaboration, parallel to that of Christology, took place, momentum already having been provided by Athanasius and Gregory of Nazianzus in particular.

Second, the epistemological role of the Spirit's *homoousion* is essential for the development of the doctrine of the immanent Trinity. Positively, it enables a move to be made from God's economic action to his eternal being; negatively, it prevents us from reading up into God the kind of causal connections that are characteristic of the created world; our knowledge of God must remain spiritual.[16]

Before coming to the third level, let us pause to consider Torrance's theology of the economy, for that is what we are concerned with here. The function of the *homoousion* in this development is to obviate any hint of subordinationism in the relation of the persons of the Trinity. This has losses and gains. On the debit side is the fact that it downplays what came to be called the monarchy of the Father. We shall come later to Torrance's relation to the Cappadocian Fathers, and concentrate here on how this affects his interpretation of some of the earlier theologians.

In introduction, we must say that there is clearly an element of *economic* subordination (to be strictly distinguished from *ontological* subordination*ism*) in the Scriptures. The Son obeys the Father, does the Father's work and will hand over the kingdom to the Father, and so on (to combine elements of the Fourth Gospel's Christology with that of 1 Corinthians 15: 24-8). The concept of monarchy denotes the fact that the Son and the Spirit are mediators of the Father's work and rule. This is clearly expressed in Irenaeus's conception of the Son and the Spirit as the "two hands" of God, but it is not that which Torrance tends to draw upon, but rather the bishop's (equally real, but less prominent) insistence on the true divinity of the hands. Rightly or wrongly, the authority of Athanasius is played against the view that the Son and the Spirit mediate the Father's kingly rule: "the formula 'one Being, three Persons' . . . carried with it a doctrine of the *Monarchia* . . . as identical with the one indivisible being of the Holy Trinity."[17] We shall return to this question of whether the monarchy is that of the Father or of the whole Trinity, which is a central one for all Trinitarian theology.

On the credit side of Torrance's development is that what we can call, with due qualification, a homogeneous view of the persons in the economy (homogeneous in the sense that even at the economic level there is no doubt at all about their full and equal deity) ensures that the move between economy and immanent or eternal Trinity is made less problematic than it is in some accounts. If the Son and the Spirit are economically equal to the Father, there is no difficulty in the anti-Arian task of attributing to them full and eternal divine status. Even here, however, there is a complication, as an illuminating comparison with Barth will indicate.

In Barth, there is an element of subordination in the economy, in the sense that the Father commands and the Son obeys. However, this economic subordination is then, so to speak, read up into the eternal Trinity, where the economic subordination becomes, without being taken away, also and at once an immanent equality of being. So it is that Barth can say, on the basis of Christology, that it is as godlike to be humble as to be exalted: that there are within the being of God elements of commanding and obeying, of superordination and subordination.[18] This will serve as a useful way of understanding the ways in which Torrance is like and different from his great teacher, because what we can call the *homoousian* drive of his thought operates to minimize such elements and to stress the complete equality of the action and divinity alike of the three persons.

The "homogeneity" of the persons of the economic Trinity is expressed in a stress on the co-givenness of all three persons in God's reconciling and revelatory activity. Torrance argues that although there is not a doctrine of the Trinity as such in the New Testament, the whole Triune God is given in Jesus Christ. "It is the mutual relation between the incarnate Son and the Father that provides us with the ground on which we are given access to knowledge of the one God in his inner relations as Father, Son and Holy Spirit."[19] The point is stressed strongly: "in the New Testament this revelation of the mystery of God toward us is revelation of God as Father, Son and Holy Spirit in his *wholeness*."[20] To put the matter in the terms we have been using, the *homoousion* enables us to understand that in

Jesus Christ clothed with his Gospel we have access to the whole God, Father, Son, and Holy Spirit, all coequally divine. The economic Trinity gives access to the eternal God as he is in himself.

The Eternal Trinity

Discussion of the immanent Trinity is so complex and controverted a matter that we shall need at the outset to specify the main questions to be asked. The first concerns the basis of the move from economy to theology. By what right does thought move from history to eternity, from action in time to being in eternity?

The second concerns the function which the doctrine performs. A number of recent Trinitarian theologies have denied, or virtually denied, the need for a distinction between economic and immanent Trinity (between God's historical act and eternal being), perhaps most influentially Catherine Mowry LaCugna. For her, ontology is the enemy. "There is neither an economic nor an immanent Trinity; there is only the *oikonomia* that is the concrete realization of the mystery of *theologia* in time, space, history and personality."[21] Why, we must ask, does our theologian insist on the necessity of a proper and rigorous doctrine of the God's being, in distinction, but also inseparable, from his act?

The third question concerns the meaning and relation of the two central concepts, being and person. It is here that modalism is always the threat, especially in the West. Torrance is one of those theologians whose relation to Augustine is relatively critical (he likes to quote Barth's characterization of the great Western theologian as "sweet poison") and clearly wants his own Western inheritance to be deeply transformed by the thought of the Eastern Fathers.

The fourth question concerns the place of the particular persons within the being of the Trinity, and that brings us to the heart of the difference between the East and the West. What, in particular, are we to make of the Western addition to the creed that the Spirit proceeds from the Father *and the Son*, the *Filioque*? Karl Barth accepted and defended this doctrine by appeal to the economy of revelation among other factors.[22] What does Torrance make of the judgment of his teacher in this regard? We shall approach the four questions one by one.

1. *On what basis and with what justification do we move from the second, economic level, to the third?* Torrance's answer is that thought is *compelled* to go further because of the nature of what is

given at the second level, and again the *homoousion* is the reason: "for it enables us to deepen and refine our grasp of the self-revealing and self communicating of God to us as Father, Son and Holy Spirit, in such a way that our thought has to move from the secondary level in which we have to do with the economic Trinity to the tertiary or higher theological level where we have to do with the ontological Trinity."[23] The necessity so to move is, it must be stressed, rational rather than mechanical. If the theologian is to be true to what is presented in experience, then certain conclusions cannot be evaded without falsifying the empirical and conceptual implications of our Christian experience.

Here, without doubt, Torrance is following the method, though not in every respect the content, of Barth's great treatise on the Trinity. If revelation is truly God present to the world, then it is *God* present to the world, and what is given in time *is* the saving presence of the eternal God. Because it is the truthful God with whom we have to do, we know that he is giving us himself and not an external manifestation whose internal structuring may be different. The whole of Torrance's strategy is thus to strengthen and elaborate in terms of his patristic concept the insights that he had received, clothed in rather more nineteenth-century language, from Karl Barth.

2. *The function of the distinction between economy and theology*. It was the achievement of Athanasius in particular to have distinguished between the being and the will of God. God is always the Triune God, but not always creator, because while the Son comes from his being, the world is, *ex nihilo*, the product of his will. Athanasius's linking of creation and incarnation as both equally works of the divine will demonstrate the freedom of God. "They tell us that he is free to do what he had never done before, and free to be other than he was eternally."[24] The matter at stake becomes especially clear in Torrance's discussion of Rahner's so-called rule that "The 'Economic' Trinity is the 'Immanent' Trinity and the 'Immanent' Trinity is the 'Economic' Trinity."[25] He justifiably accuses Rahner of abstraction, an abstraction which takes the form in this case of the classic idealist mistake of confusing the order of knowing with the order of being, so that

> there is being confused a movement of logical thought from one doctrine of the Trinity to another, and a movement of understanding and devotion from God in his economic self-revelation to us in space and time to God as he eternally is in his inner divine life. The confusion between the two movements seems to be apparent when Rahner states that the "Immanent" Trinity is "the necessary

> condition of the possibility of God's free self-communication." Does this not involve a confusion between a necessary movement of thought (a logical necessity) and the kind of "necessity" arising from the fact that God has freely and irreversibly communicated himself to us?[26]

Against this, Torrance's more nuanced expression is that of Barth, albeit in this instance expressed in Rahnerian terms. There is an identity of outer and inner, because the self-communication in the Son and the Spirit is the self-communication of God; and yet it is because God is Triune in himself, "that he is free to communicate himself as Triune in the economy of salvation."[27]

3. *Being and person.* It is often said, oversimplification that it is, that in the East discussion of the Trinity moves from the three to the one, whereas in the West the reverse is the case. The real difference, however, tends not to be in the starting point but in the way in which the oneness and threeness of God are weighted in relation to one another, and whether, as often happens in the West, the oneness outweighs the threeness and makes the persons functionally indistinguishable to all intents and purposes. (That is, of course, another version of Rahner's complaint about the divorce of the doctrine of the one God from that of the Triune God that we have met above.)

In the case of our subject, the one and the three are interrelated from the very beginning, because the use made of the *homoousion* ensures that both are co-given from the outset. Indeed, the move from economy to theology has the effect of ensuring that God's threefold revelation shapes the treatment of his eternal being. It is in this light that we must approach our third question.

Torrance begins his definitive treatment of Trinitarian theology with the being of God. Once again, Athanasius is the dominant authority. He had already been drawn upon in the earlier *Trinitarian Faith* for his contrast between static and impersonal Aristotelian being and dynamic Trinitarian being. The Triune God is a philanthropic God, a borrowing from Athanasius which Torrance uses from time to time.[28] This God is "intrinsically and intensely personal," the ever-living God,[29] "*personal, dynamic and relational Being.*"[30]

Much, however, hangs on how this relationality is construed, and the key is to be found in the concept of perichoresis, which supplements that which can be obtained with the help of the *homoousion*. Where the latter stresses the utter reality of the presence of God in and to time and space, the former enables us to see that the whole God is given in the economy. *Perichoresis* refers to the mutual indwelling and coinherence of the persons of the Trinity, and "serves to hold powerfully together . . . the identity of the divine Being and the intrinsic unity of the three divine Persons."

Interestingly and unusually (for the concept normally performs the function of showing how three distinct persons can yet constitute one God) Torrance moves from perichoresis to person and not the other way around, arguing that *by virtue of* the concept of perichoresis there developed a new concept of the person in which "the relations between persons belong to what persons are."[31] Because *perichoresis* characterizes the historical revelation of the one God, its meaning is derived primarily from the economy, rather than in reflection on the relation of the eternal persons. It is the reason that we can speak of God being personal in his eternal being, and here reference is made to the claim of Hilary of Poitiers that God is not solitary.[32]

For his construing of the meaning of one being in three persons, in general, Torrance prefers Gregory of Nazianzus to Basil of Caesarea and Gregory of Nyssa because of the apparent traces of Origenist subordinationism in the latter two Cappadocians. As is well known, Basil did not speak explicitly of the *homoousion* of the Spirit, either for tactical reasons deriving from the nature of the dispute in which he was involved or because he was still infected with the Origenist disease, as Torrance tends to suspect. He is therefore rather ambivalent about Basil's achievement, often crediting him with a crucial defense of the Spirit's divinity, while criticizing him for failing to make the final step to an explicit affirmation of the Spirit's *homoousion*. What does he then see to be so important in the later Gregory's position? Here a brief review of the use he makes of two theologians whose contributions are almost as important for him as Athanasius's, Gregory of Nazianzus and John Calvin, will profit our enquiry.

The achievement of Gregory of Nazianzus is, for Torrance, twofold. First, he rejected any element of Origenist ontological hierarchy in the being of God. He numbers Gregory among those who understand God and his work "in the light of his undivided activity as Father, Son and Holy Spirit," and he cites in this context his saying, "When I say God, I mean Father, Son and Holy Spirit."[33] Second, Gregory had a more adequate conception of the person than Basil, rejecting as he did the latter's notion of the person as "*tropos hyparxeos* (mode of being or mode of existence)."[34]

The importance of this question is so great that we must pause to examine some of the ramifications. Two recent developments have brought it to the fore. First is critical discussion of Karl Barth's appeal to the *tropos hyparxeos* as expressing more adequately what the concept of the person once served to denote.[35] Second (and it is related) is the increasing literature on the concept of the person and the necessity of its redemption, rather than abandonment, if some of the deep problems of both Church and world are to be addressed.

While Barth rejected the concept on the grounds of its irremediable individualism, in recent discussion it has been argued that used *of God* it provides a major weapon against the distortion of *our humanity* in modern anthropology. One of the emphases it enables theology to make is on the ontological compatibility of the one and the many in both instances. In the case of God, it means that to speak of the *koinonia* or communion in which the being of God consists provides a concept of divine oneness in which the individuality of the particular persons is also stressed, because Father, Son, and Spirit in their interrelatedness make God to be the God that he is. This bears not only on our belief in God, but also on the nature of what it is to be a created person, unique and particular yet bound up with the other in patterns of relational being and living.[36]

We can therefore agree with the rejection of the notion of the person as *tropos hyparxeos*. Theologically, it almost certainly fails to avoid at least the suspicion of modalism, even in Barth's most careful formulation. Therefore we must look with especial care at what Torrance makes of Gregory's, and indeed of Calvin's, formulation of the concept. Of Gregory he writes as follows: "the Persons are not just modes of existence but substantial relations subsisting intrinsically in the eternal Being of God . . . . The term "Father". . . is not a name for being (*ousia*) but for *the relation that subsists* between the Father and the Son."[37]And of Calvin's view that persons are subsistences in God's being, Torrance writes that they "are to be understood as more than distinctive relations, for they really subsist."[38]

Really subsist, we may ask, but as what? There are two problems with this development, first whether it is fair to accuse Basil of identifying the persons as modes of being; and second whether "relation" is an adequate way of describing the person. In a passage cited by Torrance, Basil clearly attributes to the Spirit more particularity than that: "the Spirit is living being"(surely better translated "*a* living being") "from which his kinship with God becomes disclosed, while his ineffable mode of existence . . . is preserved."[39] In that passage, the Spirit is neither a mode of existence nor a relation; rather, he is a person existing in a certain relation (*his* mode of being) with the Father. For Basil the persons are not relations; rather, persons are constituted by their relations to one another.

It must therefore be asked whether it is not rather the case that the Cappadocians held not that the *tropoi* were persons, but that they referred to the way in which the persons were distinctly themselves, something in which Torrance himself shows little interest. Without a distinction between persons—as the ones who are each particularly what they are by virtue of their relations (*scheseis*) to one another—and the relations between them, the danger is that their particularity will be lost, as has been the case notoriously in the West with its excessive stress on the principle that the acts of God *ad extra* are undivided. It is significant that one of Torrance's few appeals to Augustine is in support of the notion that persons are relations, and that is surely a Western, not Eastern, way of putting it.[40]

What, then, is the relation between the being and the persons? That is to say, how are being and persons related in the doctrine of the immanent Trinity? Torrance here revises the Cappadocian teaching that *ousia* refers to the being of God in general, hypostasis to the particular persons who constitute God's being, and especially its "recourse to the dangerous analogy of three different people having a common nature."[41] I am sure that he is right about the latter, but let us look carefully at the way he himself states the relation:

> In precise theological usage, *ousia* now refers to "being" not simply as that which is but to what it is in respect of its internal reality, while *hypostasis* refers to "being" not just in its independent subsistence but in its objective otherness. . . . *Hypostasis* denotes being in its "outward reference."[42]

An almost identical point is made in *Trinitarian Perspectives*: "*ousia* denotes being in its internal relations, while *hypostasis* denotes being in its inter-personal objective relations."[43]

I am not sure quite what to make of these formulations. Do they perhaps run the risk of confusing the denotation of a term with its connotation? The obvious meaning of the distinction between the concepts is that which the Cappadocians teach: that *ousia* refers to God's being generally (to God's *oneness*) while *hypostasis* to the particular persons of which that being is constituted, his *threeness*. This is what Torrance in fact elsewhere says: "the three divine Persons in their Communion *are* the Triune Being of God."[44] The two terms are, accordingly, chiefly *denoting* terms, picking out different aspects of the one divine being.

However, when it comes to connotation (to what the terms distinctly mean) should we differentiate between inner and outer in the way that Torrance does? He cannot intend the modalistic teaching that God is outwardly (in the persons) one thing, and inwardly, in his unified being another. But if not, what is the point of the distinction between inner and outer? Do not being and person both refer to God both outwardly (in the economy) and inwardly (in the immanent Trinity)? Surely there is no relational being of God which is not that of the three persons in mutually constitutive perichoresis.

4. *The particular persons and their relations.* Torrance's fairly conventional treatment of the three persons of the Trinity follows the pattern that might be expected in the light of the developments so far. To the Father is attributed, according to the pattern of the creed, the act of creating, and therefore power. But, and here the *homoousion* again makes its presence felt, this is not mere or sheer power, but the power of God made known in what God actually does. "The *homoousion* tells us that the sovereignty of the Father is identical with the sovereignty of the incarnate Son, and the sovereignty of the incarnate Son is identical with the sovereignty of God the Father."[45]

As we have seen, it follows from Athanasius's distinction between the being and will of God that while God is eternally Father, he is not eternally the creator, for creation is, as the first act of his sovereignty, the act of his freedom. The doctrine of God the Son is precisely correlative with this, and marks the place where Torrance's apophatic theology of language comes to clearest expression. The relation between eternal Father and eternal Son, being a spiritual relation, bursts the limits of the analogy which it represents. Patristic appeal to biblical language of light and radiance prevents "any projection into God of the creaturely or corporeal ingredient in the terms 'father,' 'son,' 'offspring'" and yet "also had the effect of making clear that as light is never without its radiance, so the Father is never without his Son or without his Word."[46] The language remains rational and explicatory, but within the strict limits set by the nature of God's spiritual being.

Similarly, in line with what we have already seen, detailed discussion of the person of the Spirit is fairly brief, with Torrance concentrating on his function of ensuring that we conceptualize the truly spiritual nature of God. It is consistent with the drive of Torrance's thought to stress the way in which the being of the persons inheres in the being of the one God:

> [T]he Holy Spirit himself is to be thought of as the ever-living two-way Communion between the Father and the Son in which he is no less fully God than the Father and the Son. Through sharing equally in the one living Being of God, in an essentially *spiritual and onto-relational way*, the Father, Son and the Holy Spirit form and constitute together in their distinctive properties in relation to one another the natural Communion . . . and

indivisible Unity of the Holy Trinity.[47]

Like Augustine, therefore, Torrance conceives the Spirit as the bond of love between the Father and the Son.

What, then, does he make of what has some claim to be the crucial ecumenical crux, at least so far as relations between East and West are concerned? The *Filioque*, as is well known, was the occasion, some would say cause, of the breach between the Orthodox and Roman Churches. It was the occasion because of the West's one-sided political action of adding the offending clause to the creed. Torrance's main contribution, and it is a major one, is to seek to bring together the divided Churches by adopting a position which precedes and so relativizes their differences.[48]

In Athanasius's teaching of the coinherence of the three persons is to be found the proof that the question should not have arisen in the way that it did. What we might call the *homoousial* revelation shows us the coinherence of all three persons in all that happens. It follows that they are also coinherent in being. "Thus for Athanasius the procession of the Spirit from the Father is inextricably bound up with 'the generation of the Son from the Father which exceeds and transcends the thoughts of men.'"[49] In effect Torrance is saying that the solution is to be found in the doctrine that the procession, coming as it does from the being of the Father rather than from his person, involves the whole of the Godhead in such a way that a choice between the two positions should not be required.

Through Western Eyes?

All the questions which should be asked of this consistent, creative, and important doctrine of God center in some way on the relation between the one and the many. As always in these matters, a small emphasis in one area of theology affects all the other dimensions. As we have seen, there are some questions which can be asked about the interpretation of the Fathers, though anyone who ventures to engage with Professor Torrance's formidable learning must proceed with care.

Accordingly, the following items will mainly take the form of a series of questions, and they all center in some way on the query as to whether the immense stress on the *homoousion* does not run the risk of flattening out the particularities, so that divine *being* tends to be stressed at the expense of the divine *persons*. Another way of putting it would be to ask whether the Eastern Fathers have been read rather too much through Western eyes. To be sure, this is to simplify overmuch what are highly complicated issues, as another glance at the historical provenance of this theology will make all too evident.

One of the interesting features of Torrance's work has been his ecumenical work with the Eastern Orthodox. Despite what some may expect, Christians in the Reformed tradition are often able to engage with Orthodox theology in ways not so readily available to the Catholic tradition. The reason is that John Calvin, despite his heavy dependence upon Augustine, was also a careful reader of the Eastern, including the Cappadocian, Fathers, especially in matters Trinitarian. What we find in Torrance is a reopening of a major historical conversation. My query is whether Torrance is still reading our common Fathers rather too much through Augustinian eyes, and I hope that the following questions will serve to clarify what is at stake at this important time in Christian history.

1. One key to Torrance's theology is a vision in some ways more patristic than biblical. Whether that be the case, it is remarkable how little exegesis of Scripture, as distinct from the Fathers, is to be found in the major treatments of Trinitarian themes. It is also the case that (and in this our subject is scarcely different from other theologians) texts appealed to tend to be those supporting the tendency we have already noted, to bring the economic Trinity as close as possible to the immanent. Do the apparently subordinationist texts of 1 Corinthians 15 and some of those in the Fourth Gospel receive the attention they perhaps need if the subordinationist elements of the economic Trinity are to be adequately correlated with the necessarily and rightly egalitarian note in the treatment of the immanent Trinity? They at least appear to be counterevidence to the central thesis, and therefore require careful interrogation.

2. Can we not see in the reading of the Eastern Fathers the dominance of a rather Augustinian eye? We have seen that for Torrance the divine *monarchia* is that of the whole Trinity. The question we must ask of him is whether Athanasius supports his position as clearly as he is claimed to. He is too good a scholar not to cite the crucial evidence, and the following piece is crucial. In it, God is identified by Athanasius as "the all-holy Father of Christ beyond all created being." This is then glossed to mean that:

> When Athanasius applied the term *ousia* to speak of the Being of God the Creator and of God the Father of Christ . . . it is "being" understood in the light of the truth that the Son and the Spirit are each of one and the same being or *homoousios* with God the

Father; or . . . that the fullness of the Father's Being is the Being of the Son and of the Spirit.[50]

Is there a subtle move here from the *homoousion* to something more than that? Does the final move, that "the fullness of the Father's Being *is* the Being of the Son and the Spirit" (my emphasis) follow from what has gone before? May it not at least be asked whether both Athanasius and the Cappadocian Fathers express the particular being of the three persons of the Godhead rather more strongly than that.

3. The strength of the patristic concentration is revealed in the ecumenical importance of the theology. The Fathers are an authority which all branches of the Church have in common, despite the lamentable neglect of them in some places, and here Torrance's achievement is quite remarkable, able as he is to bring together theologians from a wide spectrum of background and confession. The question to be asked concerns his tendency to limit discussion too much to the realms of piety and Churchmanship, the discussion of science excepted. And the point can be sharpened.

The engagement with science, of immense importance as that is, is very much at the level of epistemology and ontology. When we come to more broadly human and social concerns, the trumpet gives a somewhat less certain sound. Do not let me be misunderstood: Torrance has written on ethical and social matters, with authority. But it seems to me that his armory would have been stronger had other themes been treated in his work, and if, for example, there had been rather more engagement with the work of another important ecumenical figure, John Zizioulas, despite (or perhaps because of) their continuing differences over central matters of Trinitarian construction (Zizioulas being more of the school of Basil than of Gregory of Nazianzus).

Torrance shares with Zizioulas the judgement that the Fathers contributed centrally to the development of a new concept of the person.[51] Discussion of this, however, is for the most part rather limited, particularly with respect to what it might mean for human personhood. For it is there that our culture is in desperate need. I need not repeat here the often enough rehearsed contention: that modernity cannot do justice to the being of the human person because it has an impoverished theology.[52] Oscillating between collectivism and individualism (which represent ultimately one and the same failure) it calls desperately for an understanding of the person not as *a relation*, but as one who has his or her being *in relation to* others. This Trinitarian and *ethical* insight flows from a theology of the Trinity in which both the one and the many are given due and equal weight. If Barth is right that all good dogmatics is also ethics, might we not expect this component of theology to be somewhat more strongly represented at this very place?

4. There is another place where discussion of things Trinitarian is broken off where further development might have been of interest, and it is in a cognate realm. The solution of the problem of the *Filioque* is of far more than immanent Churchly or ecumenical concern, and in two areas in particular. The first is the deep-seated weakness of the Western tradition on the doctrine of the Spirit. The reason is Trinitarian. If the Spirit is conceived to proceed from the Son as well as from the Father, he easily comes to be treated as subordinate to the Son, and is therefore effectively reduced to the margins, as functionally appearing to do little more than apply Christ's work in the Church or to the individual believer. It is no accident that, in reaction to this impoverishment, outbreaks of Pentecostal and millenarian enthusiasm, which often overemphasize the Spirit at the expense of the Son, have marked the history of Western Christianity from early times.

Corresponding to this weakness of our tradition, as its *alter ego*, so to speak, is a failure to do justice to the full humanity of the incarnate Son of God. Here, we must be careful to specify what exactly is the point of the question to our author. As always, there are resources in Torrance's work which are waiting to be developed. One of his papers which has long continued to work in my mind is that on "The Mind of Christ in Worship: The Problem of Apollinarianism in the Liturgy."

The thesis of this magisterial paper is that the human Christ has effectively been written out of the liturgy of the Western Church. Here the theme is taken up of the human priesthood of the ascended Christ present in the worship of the Church. "[S]ince he is God become man, who in becoming man was made Priest, it is humanity which is the sphere of his priesthood, and it is the fulfilment of his priestly ministry as man offering himself on our behalf which becomes the focus of our worship of the Father."[53] This is christologically, and therefore Trinitarianly, important, for the neglect of the Holy Spirit and the underplaying of the human life and ministry of Jesus, and especially its continuation in the ascension, are simply two sides of the same coin.

Yet while the humanity of Christ is affirmed and used theologically in Torrance's work, it is surprising how little interest is shown in the *Christusbild*, the detailed Gospel presentations of the life, death, resurrection, and ascension of Jesus. This is particularly marked in treatment of the eternal Sonship of Christ, but is muted even in the discussion of the incarnate Lord. This may, to be sure, be to ask too much, and it might be better to say that here is a question left over for later generations to develop in the light of issues that have recently become prominent.

The second ramification of the *Filioque* requiring consideration is the equally deep-seated failure of the Western tradition to avoid modalism of some kind or other. The problem of modalism in the context of the doctrine of the double procession is the problem of that which ultimately unifies the world and our experience. From the days of the Greeks onwards, the Western mind has sought the basis of experience and reality in the One, whether that One be the God of Israel and Jesus Christ, Heraclitean flux, the Parmenidean or Plotinian One, or the many variations on them which have appeared in philosophy and theology since.

The perennial question, as Coleridge especially among modern thinkers has argued, is whether the unity of things be lodged in some impersonal principle (ultimately some monism or pantheism) or in the personal, Triune God of Scripture. And the perennial temptation of the Western mind has been to seek for the unity of things in some deity or divine principle over and above the Triune revelation. We have seen that Torrance's whole theological calling has been dominated by the establishment of the latter: that the only unity of things is to be found in the almighty Triune creator, thc one made known in his involvement in the created world in his Son and Word.

The problem of the dual procession is the related one of whether it subverts from within this personal and Trinitarian integration of things. Now, I do not wish to adjudicate here on the dispute between, on the one hand, John Zizioulas's view that the only way of maintaining a truly personal basis for reality is by making the Father the source of all things, especially the source or *aitia* of the Triune communion; and, on the other hand, Torrance's view that in some way or other we must understand the Triune communion as a whole to be the metaphysical source of unity.[54] The problem rather is whether the double procession ineluctibly encourages the development of a modalist tendency in theological thought.

The point is this! If the Father is the one from whom the Son is begotten (in the Spirit) and from whom the Spirit proceeds (indeed, through the Son), our enquiries come to an end. There is a final, if mysterious, explanation for the way things are. But suppose that the Spirit does come from the Father *and* the Son. Can we avoid at least toying with the question of the reality which gives the Father and the Son *their* underlying unity?

In other words, a double procession is an invitation to seek a deeper cause than the Trinity, and thus a modalism, even though it may not necessitate it, because while there remain two apparently ultimate principles, however unified in communion, discontented minds will seek that which underlies them. And surely there is a case for saying that some such temptation must explain why it is so difficult for Western minds not to tend to a modalism of some kind.[55]

That is not to suggest that Torrance, any more than Barth, commits the heresy of modalism; it is rather that if its underlying causes are to be removed, more attention perhaps needs to be paid to the concrete ways in which the particular persons of the Trinity present themselves to our experience in the economy of creation and salvation.

Conclusion

In recent years, studies of the Trinity have appeared in ever increasing numbers, in some ways remarkably different from one another, but most of them responding to a real change in theological atmosphere. When I first entered the profession, the dominant names among Torrance's contemporaries and near contemporaries were for the most part critical, if not actively dismissive, of the doctrine of the Trinity. One can recall, for instance, the considerable impact of a paper written by Maurice Wiles in 1957 doubting the biblical basis of the doctrine.[56] And far worse rationalist critiques of the Orthodox tradition were, did we but know it, just over the horizon. To our subject must go much of the credit for refusing to succumb to the loss of confidence in mainstream Christian theology after the last war and for maintaining steadily and faithfully the vision of the classic doctrine of God. The interest in his work shows signs of increasing, and promises that the achievement will be a lasting one.

Notes

1. Karl Rahner, *The Trinity,* trans. Joseph Donceel (London: Burns and Oates, 1970).

2. Now chapter 4 of T. F. Torrance, *Trinitarian Perspectives: Toward Doctrinal Agreement* (Edinburgh: T&T Clark, 1994).

3. Torrance, *Trinitarian Perspectives*, 81.

4. T F.Torrance, "Karl Barth and the Latin Heresy," *Scottish Journal of Theology* 39, no. 3 (1986): 461-82.

5. T. F. Torrance, *The Christian Doctrine of God, One Being Three Persons* (Edinburgh: T&T Clark, 1996), 92.

6. T. F. Torrance, *Space, Time and Incarnation* (London: Oxford University Press, 1969).

7. T. F. Torrance, *Transformation and Convergence within the Frame of Knowledge: Explorations in the Interrelations of Scientific and Theological Enterprise* (Belfast: Christian Journals, 1984), chapter 1.

8. Torrance, *Christian Doctrine*, 84.

9. Torrance, *Christian Doctrine*, 84f., emphasis added.

10. Torrance, *Christian Doctrine*, 85.

11. Torrance, *Christian Doctrine*, 88f.

12. Torrance, *Christian Doctrine*, 91.

13. Torrance, *Christian Doctrine*, 94.

14. Torrance, *Christian Doctrine*, 95.

15. T. F. Torrance, *The Trinitarian Faith: The Evangelical Theology of the Ancient Catholic Church* (Edinburgh: T&T Clark, 1988), 119.

16. Torrance, *Christian Doctrine*, 97.

17. Torrance, *Trinitarian Faith*, 10.

18. See especially Karl Barth, *Church Dogmatics*, trans. and ed. G. W. Bromiley and T. F. Torrance (Edinburgh: T&T Clark, 1957-1975), *Church Dogmatics* 4/1, §59.1.

19. Torrance, *Christian Doctrine*, 42.

20. Torrance, *Christian Doctrine*, 43.

21. Catherine Mowry LaCugna, *God for Us: The Trinity and Christian Life* (New York: HarperCollins, 1991), 223.

22. Barth, *Church Dogmatics*, I/1, §12.2.

23. Torrance, *Christian Doctrine*, 95.

24. Torrance, *Trinitarian Faith*, 89.

25. Torrance, *Trinitarian Perspectives*, 79, citing Rahner, *The Trinity*, 22. The original is in italics.

26. Torrance, *Trinitarian Perspectives*, 80.

27. Torrance, *Trinitarian Perspectives*, 79-80f, citing Rahner, *The Trinity*, 102.

28. E.g., Torrance, *Trinitarian Faith*, 91, 147.

29. Torrance, *Christian Doctrine*, 121.

30. Torrance, *Christian Doctrine*, 124.

31. Torrance, *Christian Doctrine*, 102.

32. Torrance, *Trinitarian Faith*, 90.

33. Torrance, *Trinitarian Faith*, 93.

34. Torrance, *Trinitarian Faith*, 27.

35. See, for example, Alan J. Torrance, *Persons in Communion: Trinitarian Description and Human Participation* (Edinburgh: T&T Clark, 1996).

36. See Christoph Schwoebel and Colin Gunton, eds., *Persons, Divine and Human: King's College Essays in Theological Anthropology* (Edinburgh: T&T Clark, 1992).

37. Torrance, *Trinitarian Perspectives*, 27, emphasis added.

38. Torrance, *Trinitarian Perspectives*, 28; cf. Torrance, *Christian Doctrine*, 127.

39. Torrance, *Trinitarian Faith*, 218.

40. Torrance, *Trinitarian Perspectives*, 29.

41. Torrance, *Christian Doctrine*, 125.

42. Torrance, *Christian Doctrine*, 130. The latter expression is attributed to G. L. Prestige.

43. Torrance, *Trinitarian Perspectives*, 131.

44. Torrance, *Christian Doctrine*, 124.

45. Torrance, *Christian Doctrine*, 205.

46. Torrance, *Trinitarian Faith*, 121.

47. Torrance, *Christian Doctrine*, 126-27.

48. It can, and below will, be argued that underlying the *Filioque* are questions of far more than ecumenical importance alone.

49. Torrance, *Trinitarian Faith*, 235.

50. Torrance, *Christian Doctrine*, 116.

51. John D. Zizioulas, "On Being a Person: Towards an Ontology of Personhood," in Schwoebel and Gunton, *Persons, Divine and Human*, 33-46.

52. Colin E. Gunton, *The One, the Three and the Many: God, Creation and the Culture of Modernity: The 1992 Bampton Lectures* (Cambridge: Cambridge University Press, 1993).

53. T. F. Torrance, "The Mind of Christ in Worship: The Problem of Apollinarianism in the Liturgy," in *Theology in Reconciliation: Essays towards Evangelical and Catholic Unity in East and West* (London: Geoffrey Chapman, 1975), 139-214 (especially 175-76).

54. See the discussion by Alan Torrance, *Persons in Communion*, 283-306.

55. This is not to suggest that the East does not have its own and entirely parallel problems, which also derive from a tendency to platonize the deity. We are very near to the problem, isolated in a celebrated paper by Dorothea Wendebourg, of the way in which the later development of Cappadocian Trinitarianism fell away from its begetters' identification of the being of God with the persons. The problem is that the doctrine of the divine energies interposed in some way between the being and the persons of God, leading to what she has called "The Defeat of Trinitarian Theology." See Torrance, *Trinitarian Faith*, 72, for Torrance's version of this very point, or at least something similar, and his note 70 for references to his earlier treatment of the concept of the energies. Dorothea Wendebourg, "From the Cappadocian Fathers to Gregory Palamas: The Defeat of Trinitarian Theology," *Studia Patristica* 17, no.1 (1982): 194-98.

56. Maurice Wiles, "Some Reflections on the Origins of the Doctrine of the Trinity," *Journal of Theological Studies* n.s., 7 (1957): 92-106. Some of Wiles' points would hold against the particular formulations of Barth, but Torrance's more directly patristic development is less liable to the critique.

Chapter 6

The Dimension of Depth:

Thomas F. Torrance on the Sacraments

by George Hunsinger

Introduction

"All the gifts of God set forth in baptism," wrote John Calvin, "are found in Christ alone" (*Institutes* IV.15.6).[1] The baptismal gifts, for Calvin, were essentially three: forgiveness of sins, dying and rising with Christ, and communion with Christ himself.[2] They were ordered, however, in a particular way. Communion with Christ, Calvin considered, was in effect the one inestimable gift that included within itself the other two benefits of forgiveness and rising with Christ from the dead.[3] Forgiveness and eternal life were thus inseparable from Christ's person and so from *participatio Christi* through our communion with him. Only by participating in Christ through communion could the divine gifts set forth in baptism be truly received. Any severing of these gifts from Christ himself would result only in empty abstractions. No spiritual gift (neither forgiveness nor eternal life nor any other divine benefit) was ever to be found alongside Christ or apart from him. Christ's saving benefits were inherent in his living person. Only in and with his person were they set forth and available to the Church. Communion with Christ was thus bound up with Christ's person in his saving uniqueness. He himself and he alone, for Calvin and for the whole Reformation, was our wisdom, righteousness, sanctification, and redemption (1 Cor. 1:30).[4]

It was only a short step from the centrality of communion with Christ to the idea of one baptism common to Christ and his Church. As the sign and seal of *participatio Christi*, baptism meant that the baptized person was granted a share in Christ's own baptism in the Jordan, which he had undergone for the sake of sinners. A person's baptism here and now partook of Christ and his baptism there and then. Calvin wrote:

> He honored and sanctified baptism in his own body that he might have it in common with us as the most firm bond of union and fellowship that he humbled himself to form with us; and so Paul proves us to be God's children from the fact that we have put on Christ in baptism. (Gal. 3:27)
>
> Thus we see that the completion [*complementum*] of baptism is in Christ, and for this reason we call him the proper object of baptism [*proprium Baptismi obiectum*]. (*Institutes* IV.15.6)
>
> The general reason why Christ received baptism was that he might render full obedience to the Father. And the special reason was that he might consecrate baptism in his own body, that we might have it in common with him.[5]
>
> From baptism our faith receives the sure testimony that we are not only ingrafted into Christ's death and life, but are so united with Christ himself as to partake in all his benefits. (*Institutes* IV.15.6)

In baptism, Calvin believed, we so put on Christ that we enter into inseparable union with him in his dying and rising for our sakes. Our baptism finds its ground and fulfillment not in itself but in him. Baptism testifies that we are so united with Christ that we share in all his blessings. His baptism becomes ours, and ours becomes his, because in his very body he has consecrated baptism for us by making it his own.

Calvin's theology of baptism, obviously very rich, is much richer than can be indicated here. In and with this richness, however, are also certain perplexities and ambiguities. One of these concerns what might be called the complex temporality of salvation. Ever vexing for the Church, this question remains unresolved, right down to the present day. Baldly stated, the question for Calvin is whether he is as consistently Christocentric in his understanding of salvation as his commitments would seem to require.

The basic options come down to two. Either salvation must be spoken of *essentially* in the perfect tense, or else *also* in the present tense *alongside* the perfect tense. (The use of the future tense would coordinate with which option is taken.) If salvation is essentially in the perfect tense, then its present and future tenses must be seen as *modes of receiving and participating in* the one salvation already accomplished in Christ. If, on the other hand, salvation occurs *essentially* also in the present tense alongside the perfect tense, then its present and future tenses must somehow *supplement and complete a process* that Christ initiated in his earthly existence, but did not entirely fulfill.

An image for the first idea would be a circle with its center and periphery, whereas an image for the second would be an ellipse with two foci.[6] The circle would mean that salvation is to be found solely and entirely in Christ the center, whereas the ellipse would mean that Christ at one focal point is the condition for the possibility of a salvation that does not become fully actual until appropriated at the other focal point by the Church.

Either salvation is a perfect actuality in Christ to be received and partaken of for what it is, or else it is an existential possibility that becomes fully actual and complete only upon the Church's reception. In the latter case, the act of reception is constitutive of salvation, in the former, strictly speaking, it is not. In the former case, the act of reception becomes the mode of participation in a salvation complete and perfect in itself.

Calvin's ambiguities at this point, which are often quite subtle, can be no more than suggested. Suffice it to say that his standard remarks about regeneration seem to hover ambiguously around both possibilities, falling now to one side, now to the other, with no real ultimate resolution. Sometimes "regeneration" or "sanctification" seems essentially a matter of *participatio Christi* (option 1), whereas elsewhere it seems more nearly an existential supplement *alongside* justification by the perfect righteousness of Christ (option 2).

For example, the first option would seem to be in view when Calvin writes: "Do you wish, then, to obtain righteousness in Christ (*iustitiam in Christo*)? You must first possess Christ, but you cannot possess (*possidere*) him without becoming a partaker of his sanctification (*sanctificationis eius particeps*), for he cannot be divided" (*Institutes* III.16.1). Here sanctification seems to be essentially a matter of *possidere et participatio Christi*. The accent falls on the totality, indivisibility, and fullness of what is already actual in Christ. The same accent seems evident in the statement with which we began: "All the gifts of God set forth in baptism are found in Christ alone" (*Institutes* IV.15.6).

More in line with the second option, however, would be a statement like this: "We cannot be justified by faith alone, if we do not live in holiness."[7] Here Calvin's wording seems open to the view that living in holiness is a necessary condition for justification, or at least a necessary supplement alongside it, as opposed to its provisional manifestation. Or again: "We obtain regeneration by Christ's death and resurrection *only if* we are sanctified by the Spirit and imbued with a new and spiritual nature" (*Institutes* IV.15.6).[8] Here he would seem close to the idea that being imbued with a new and spiritual nature is the condition for obtaining regeneration, as if regeneration were the uncertain telos instead of the assured basis of whatever takes place *in nobis* through faith.[9]

Whether these latter statements and others like them in Calvin could finally be interpreted as in line with the first option after all, or whether that would even be a good idea, need not be pursued here. What are arguably at least ambiguities in Calvin's discourse, however, became less and less ambiguous as the Reformed tradition went on. Later forms of pietism, Puritanism, and eventually modern liberalism, existentialism, and liberationism undeniably shifted the temporality of salvation away from the first option to the second. The definitive locus of salvation came increasingly to be seen not as what has taken place in Christ, but instead as what takes place in us or among us.

Although the first option had deep roots not only in the New Testament but also in patristic and Reformation theology, its inner logic slipped more or less into obscurity. The idea that the existential moment of salvation could be seen as participating baptismally and Eucharistically in a salvation that it did not constitute but purely received, and whose perfection in Christ remained hidden to faith until the final consummation (cf. Col. 3:3), became at best a distant memory. Emphasis on the objective character of salvation in Christ could be dismissed with ready assent as little more than an obvious absurdity; for example, as a stone thrown down from heaven (Tillich's reproach against Barth). In any case the ellipse with two foci proved inherently unstable over time, tending to resolve itself into another circle with a different center. In modernity (and "postmodernity") humanity and its much vaunted spirituality became the pivotal term, around which all else was thought somehow to revolve.

The immense contribution of Thomas F. Torrance to an understanding of the sacraments in the Reformed tradition can be appreciated in this setting. What Torrance accomplishes is, in effect, to bring Calvin and Barth together into a brilliant new synthesis. Like Calvin (but unlike Barth), Torrance sees baptism and the Lord's Supper as forms of God's Word, establishing and renewing the Church in its union and communion with Christ. Like Calvin, that is, he sees the sacraments as vehicles of testimony that impart the very Christ whom they proclaim (by the gracious operation of the Holy Spirit), as opposed to Barth, who insists on seeing them "ethically" as no more than a grateful human response to a prior divine grace not mediated or set forth by the sacraments themselves. (Indeed, even using the term "sacraments" for baptism and the Lord's Supper is something that Barth notoriously abandons.)

However, like Barth (but unlike Calvin), Torrance has an unambiguous grasp on how salvation must be spoken of essentially in the perfect tense. He thereby uses a consistently Christocentric soteriology to "disambiguate" (to borrow an inelegant term from recent philosophy) Calvin's view of the sacraments. The result is surely the most creative Reformed breakthrough on the sacraments in twentieth-century theology, and arguably the most important Reformed statement since Calvin.

Torrance on the Sacrament of Baptism

Like Barth, Torrance teaches that "the primary *mysterium* or *sacramentum* is Jesus Christ himself."[10] The sacraments of baptism and the Lord's Supper, therefore, point away from themselves to him. The reference to Jesus Christ necessarily brings with it a complex temporality. The risen Jesus Christ is continuously present to the Church, clothed in his Word and his Spirit, as the one who has accomplished the world's salvation in and of himself. What takes place in the present tense (through Word and Spirit) fulfills but does not supplement what has already taken place in the perfect tense (through Christ's Incarnation and perfect obedience). "Baptism sets forth," writes Torrance, "what God has already done in Christ, and through his Spirit continues to do in and to us. . . . Our part is only to receive it, for we cannot add anything to Christ's finished work."[11] Salvation's present tense manifests and fulfills its perfect tense.

Baptism therefore always involves a twofold reference. "Baptism is . . . not a sacrament of what we do but of what God *has done* for us in Jesus Christ, in whom he *has bound* himself to us *and bound* us to himself, before ever we could respond to him" (italics added).[12] That is the first and primary reference. "But it is also the sacrament of what God *now does* in us by his Spirit, *uniting* us with Christ in his faithfulness and obedience to the Father *and making* that the ground of our faith" (italics added).[13] That is the second and dependent reference, internally (not externally) related to the first. The relation of the present to the perfect tense is, we might say, an analytic not a synthetic relation.

The perfect tense of our salvation in Christ becomes what Torrance calls "the dimension of depth" in the sacraments. The perfect tense indicates the "ultimate ground" of the sacraments, that which constitutes "their content, reality and power." The dimension of depth in the sacraments involves not just the perfect tense in general, however, but more specifically "the act of God fulfilled in the humanity of Christ."[14]

It is the reference to Christ's humanity that is crucial. The sacraments can be seen in their depth only when traced back to Christ's humanity in its vicarious significance: "to their ultimate ground in the Incarnation and in the vicarious obedience of Jesus Christ in the human nature which he took from us and sanctified in and through his self-offering to the Father." The efficacy of the sacraments (their content, reality, and power) is ultimately grounded in "the whole historical Jesus from his birth to his resurrection and ascension."[15] Baptism, for example, is focused beyond itself "upon the one saving act of God in Jesus Christ. . . . When the Church baptizes in his name, it is actually Christ himself who is savingly at work, pouring out his Spirit upon us and drawing us into the power of his vicarious life, death and resurrection."[16]

At the heart of the perfect tense for Torrance, and of the sacraments in their dimension of depth, is therefore the idea of Christ's vicarious humanity. This idea involves, as we have seen, the entire history of the Incarnation: "what has been done for us in the birth, life, death and resurrection of Jesus Christ."[17] Vicarious humanity means that everything Christ has done and suffered in his humanity was done and suffered in our place and for our benefit. "Our adoption, sanctification and regeneration have already taken place in Christ, and are fully enclosed in his birth, holy life, death and resurrection undertaken for our sakes."[18]

The perfect tense then determines the present tense. Salvation comes to us "more by way of realization or actualization in us of what has already happened to us in him than as a new effect resulting from [his finished work]."[19] Note that any residual ambiguity in Calvin's soteriology of sanctification has here been dispelled. It is in the vicarious humanity of Christ that the definitive sanctification of our humanity has taken place. In the assumption of our flesh (*assumptio carnis*) to his own person, as lived out in his birth, life, death, and resurrection, our human nature has been judged, purified, and renewed.

Christ's vicarious sanctification of our humanity has, we might say, the status of a "concrete universal": its saving significance resides in its radical particularity. It is unique, all-embracing, and all-sufficient, not just prototypical or provisional. It is a blessing into which we are incorporated, a reality in which we come to participate, not just a model to which we are conformed.[20] Our inclusion in the Church as the body of Christ is based in the perfect tense: "We have been adopted through his incarnational assumption of us into himself, sanctified through the obedient self-offering of Christ in his life and death, and we have been born again in his birth of the Spirit and in his resurrection from the dead."[21]

Vicarious humanity means that when Christ entered into the hopelessness of our plight, he also at the same time took us up into the perfect obedience that he offered to the Father. Having assumed our twisted humanity, he has sanctified and renewed it from within. By virtue of his vicarious obedience (both passively and actively),[22] he himself and he alone is our salvation (its content, reality, and power). "That is why baptism is understood properly only in that dimension of depth reaching back into Jesus Christ himself, for it belongs to the peculiar nature of baptism that in it we partake of a redemption that has already been accomplished for us in Christ."[23]

Seen in this dimension of depth, our baptism involves a twofold movement of simultaneity: from Christ to us and from us to him. As Christ communicates himself to us in baptism, so he also joins us at the same time to himself. Therefore, as we receive him into our hearts, we are also drawn at the same time into living participation in him. Both aspects of this twofold movement find their depth in the perfect tense of his *assumptio carnis*. Having already bound himself to us and us to himself by his Incarnation, he now actualizes and manifests this blessing in a secondary, dependent way.

In baptism, the perfect tense of our salvation in him becomes present to us for what it is (by making us present to itself); its objective reality becomes, as it were, subjectively accessible and actual. On the basis of "his atoning and sanctifying incorporation of himself into our humanity," Christ acts upon us in baptism through his Spirit so that his finished work "takes effect in us as our ingrafting into Christ and as our adoption into the family of the heavenly Father."[24]

Baptism is thus well described, with Irenaeus, as "the sacrament of the incarnational reversal."[25] Just as Adam's disobedience was reversed by Christ's obedience, so also is our lost condition reversed through our participation in Christ's new humanity, first objectively (*extra nos*), then subjectively (*in nobis*). "Hence the reality of our baptism is to be found in the objective reality of what has already been accomplished for us *in Jesus Christ* and is savingly operative in us through union and communion with Christ effected *by the Spirit*" (italics added).[26] Our baptism "is not a separate or a new baptism but a participation in the one all-inclusive baptism common to Christ and his Church, wrought out vicariously in Christ alone but into which he has assimilated the Church through the baptism of the one Spirit, and which applies to each of us through the same Spirit."[27]

In our baptism, then, the risen Christ's saving obedience unto death (perfect tense) and his self-communication (present tense) bring us not only to the point of reception and participation but also into living communion. Again, the perfect tense is the dimension of depth in the present tense; his finished work *pro nobis* the content, reality, power of his self-communication. Christ's self-communication involves at least three things simultaneously: our receiving *of him* into our hearts, our participating *in him* personally, and our communing *with him* eternally.

When we receive the one Jesus Christ by faith, he himself enters our hearts, that he may dwell in us forever, and we in him. Just as there is no present tense without the perfect tense, so also there is no reception without participation, and no participation without communion. Reception and participation take place ultimately for the sake of communion.[28] We might say, very roughly, that reception is oriented to the past, participation to the present, and communion to the future. Reception of Christ means acknowledging who he is and what he has done for our sakes. Participation in Christ means being clothed and renewed by his perfect righteousness.[29] Communion with Christ is eternal life itself. We receive him by grace through faith, partake of him by virtue of his vicarious humanity, and enjoy communion with him in reciprocal love and knowledge.

As the purpose of communion would suggest, the Christocentric reality of our salvation, as manifest in baptism, is also essentially Trinitarian. By virtue of our union with Christ, we are drawn into the eternal communion of the Holy Trinity. The twofold movement from Christ to us and from us to Christ occurs in a specifically trinitarian context. When redescribed from this perspective, it is, as Torrance notes, a movement that comes to us (1) from the Father, through the Son, and in the Holy Spirit while also being, at the same time, a movement bringing us (2) in the Holy Spirit, through the Son, to the Father.

The Incarnation is the vehicle of mediation between heaven and earth, between the Trinity and the community of faith. This mediation moves in two ways at once. It brings God down to us in human flesh in order that, through that same flesh, we might be elevated to communion with God. Through the incarnate Son, who is our

Mediator, the Triune God opens "his inner life and being to communion with us" and "creates genuine reciprocity between us and himself."[30]

> This profound reciprocity in word and act is fulfilled in Christ and in the Spirit: *in Christ*, for it is in hypostatic union that the self-giving of God really breaks through to man, when God becomes himself what man is and assumes man into a binding relation to his own being; and *in the Spirit*, for then the self-giving of God actualizes itself in us as the Holy Spirit creates in us the capacity to receive it and lifts us up to participate in the union and communion of the incarnate Son with the heavenly Father.[31]

By virtue of the humanity of the incarnate Son, God has "opened his divine being for human participation." With the Incarnation our human nature has been assumed once and for all into the mutual relation between the Father and the Son. By our elevation into the eternal life of the Holy Trinity through our union with the incarnate Son, "God interacts with us in such a way as really to give himself to us and make us share in his own inner life and light and love."[32] The "point of contact" between the Trinity and us (as between us and the Trinity) is thus Christ's vicarious humanity, existing as it does in hypostatic union with the eternal Son.

Our union with the person of Christ, which Calvin called an *unio mystica*, presupposes the hypostatic union, but does not reduplicate it.[33] We share in the communion of the Trinity as we are joined to the person of the incarnate Son by virtue of our participation in his vicarious humanity. "Only by way of the Incarnation" are we "given access to, and knowledge of God in his own inner life and being as Father, Son and Holy Spirit."[34] We are thus given a share through the Spirit in the communion of the incarnate Son with the Heavenly Father. That is the deepest reason, theologically, why baptism is administered in the name of the Father and of the Son and of the Holy Spirit.[35]

The vicarious humanity of Christ is the central element in Torrance's understanding of baptism. It is the element that holds together the present tense of salvation with the perfect tense so that the finished work of Christ is properly manifest as the dimension of depth in the sacrament of baptism. At the same time it is also the central element that joins God to us and us to God in a properly Christocentric and Trinitarian way.

As the mediating factor joining Church, Incarnation, and Trinity, it powerfully illuminates the historically vexing *in nobis* aspect of our salvation by clarifying the profound interconnections among reception, participation, and communion. It improves on Calvin by grounding the present tense of sanctification unmistakably in the perfect tense. It improves on Barth by eliminating the false dichotomy that he posits between "witness" and "mediation," as if baptism could be a witness to grace without also being at the same time a means of Christ's self-mediation to us.

Finally, it improves on what Torrance calls "flat" views of the sacramental rite of baptism, as if it were the Church (not Christ himself and Christ alone in and through the Church) which is somehow also the agent and substance of our salvation, or as if salvation were essentially a spiritual process initiated by the sacrament of baptism, rather than Christ's incorporating of us into union and communion with himself in his finished, perfect, and sufficient saving work.[36]

Torrance on the Sacrament of the Lord's Supper

The discussion of the sacraments in Torrance's theology is ecumenical in orientation. We might think of it as attempting to combine "the Protestant principle" with "Catholic substance," though not so much in Tillich's sense as in another sense all his own. The Protestant principle is not diluted to "prophetic protest," nor is Catholic substance reduced to polymorphous "concrete embodiments" of indeterminate spiritual presence. Rather, for Torrance, something more robust and venerable would be meant.

The Protestant (and patristic) principle would mean salvation in and by Christ alone, while Catholic substance would mean baptism and the Lord's Supper as specific sacramental forms of the one saving act of God in Christ and through the Spirit. Again, with the Lord's Supper as also with baptism, salvation's perfect tense is set forth as the dimension of depth informing the present tense, the vicarious humanity of Christ is the element central to them both, and the purpose of reception and participation is eternal life in communion with God.

However, whereas baptism involves our once and for all incorporation into Christ and his community, the Lord's Supper or the Eucharist involves the continual renewal over time of our communion with Christ in the Church. Accordingly, the "dimension of depth" (a term Torrance uses again here) needs to be described in a slightly different way. Although the definitive significance of the perfect tense clearly remains, the accent shifts, when we consider the Eucharist, to Christ's one saving work in its eternal and perpetual validity.

At the same time the inseparability of Christ's person from his work is also accentuated, regardless of whether the focus is on the present or the perfect tense, because there is no person without the work, and no work without the person. The risen Christ lives eternally and perpetually in his one vicarious, perfect, and finished work— even as the work lives also in him. In a way that endures, the work is in his person even as his person is in the work. "What he has done once and for all in history," writes Torrance, "has the power of permanent presence in him. He is present in the unique reality of his incarnate Person, in whom Word and Work and Person are indissolubly one."[37] What he has done in history has validity for both time and eternity.

On the ground of "his one perfect all-sufficient sacrifice," Christ presents us continuously to the Father in a way that calls for "our continuous living communion with him as the Son."[38] His being can never be separated from his action, for in the person of the incarnate Son, "being and act are inseparably one." Therefore, "all that he has done for us in his union with us . . . remains a present hypostatic reality creating and inviting communion with us."[39]

The real presence of Christ in the Eucharist is therefore his presence in the unity of his person and work. His personal presence brings with it the presence of his finished work in all its content, reality, and power. The perfect tense of his work is present, we might say, in and with his person. "It is the whole Jesus Christ whose historical life and passion, far from being past, persist through the triumph of the resurrection over all corruption and decay."[40]

It is thus the whole Jesus Christ who as "continuing living reality" mediates his real presence to us, in the unity of his person and work, "through the Spirit . . . in the eucharistic worship of the Church."[41] In the Eucharist this mediation of the whole Christ takes place by virtue of his real presence to us in his body and blood. "Body and blood," as Torrance keenly perceives, involve a reference to Christ in his priestly significance. "The key to the understanding of the Eucharist is to be sought in the *vicarious humanity of Jesus, the priesthood of the incarnate Son.*"[42] Intercession is the essence of the priestly office.

The intercession of Christ is basically twofold: first, he interceded for us by his sacrificial death in our place and on our behalf; then, upon his resurrection and ascension, he continues to intercede for us by offering himself, and us in union and communion with himself, to the Father. The flesh of the Word made flesh, the body and blood of the incarnate Son, are the perpetual means of our union and communion with Christ, and of his union and communion with us, in the exercise of his priestly role. Through the same body and blood once sacrificed on the cross of Golgotha, he now gives himself to us perpetually in the Eucharist and offers us eternally to the Father.

Torrance writes:

> The union of Jesus Christ with us in body and blood by virtue of which he became our Priest and Mediator before God demands as its complement our union with him in his body and blood, in drawing near to God and offering him our worship with, in and through Christ, while his continuous living presentation of us before the Father on the ground of his one perfect all-sufficient sacrifice calls for our continuous living communion with him as the Son. It is in this union and communion with Christ the incarnate Son who represents God to us and us to God that the real import of the Lord's Supper becomes disclosed, for in eating his body and drinking his blood we are given to participate in his vicarious self-offering to the Father.[43]

> The real presence is the presence of the Savior in his personal being and atoning self-sacrifice, who once and for all gave himself up on the cross for our sakes but who is risen from the dead as the Lamb who has been slain but is alive for ever more, and now appears for us in the presence of the Father as himself prevalent eternally propitiation.[44]

Although Torrance presupposes a real eating and drinking of Christ's body and blood in the Eucharist, he does not, in the essay under discussion, propound a theory of how these might be related to the Eucharistic elements of bread and wine. Similarly, in the baptism essay previously discussed, no theory is set forth for understanding just how the baptismal waters themselves might be related to Christ's cleansing and sanctifying of us by his Spirit, in uniting us with his vicarious humanity.

The general tenor of the essays would seem to suggest, however, that the relations of *signum* and *res* are more nearly instrumental than parallel or symbolic. The elements, in other words, seem to be instruments of Christ through his Spirit, attesting in the sacraments what they mediate, and mediating what they attest. What they attest and mediate in each case, however, is the one whole Jesus Christ in his full depth so that he is acknowledged as perfected in history, present perpetually, and valid eternally in the significance of his vicarious humanity.

Torrance interprets the question of Eucharistic sacrifice along much the same lines as he does real presence. The one priestly sacrifice of Jesus Christ involves a twofold movement in various temporal forms. The twofold sacrificial movement consists of (1) Christ's self-giving to us in the Spirit and (2) his self-offering of us to the Father in such a way that (3) the self-giving and the self-offering are one. Moreover, the one priestly sacrifice of Christ has a definitive and originative form (as signified by the perfect tense) which then serves as the content, reality, and power of all subsequent and derivative forms (as signified by the present tense).

Christ continues to give himself to us today in the Eucharist as the one who has already given himself to us, unsurpassably, in his life, death, and resurrection. The Eucharistic form of his priestly sacrifice participates in the incarnational form, yet without adding to it or supplementing it, as if the incarnational form were not already complete and perfect in itself. The Eucharistic form does not repeat the unrepeatable, but it does attest what it mediates, and mediate what it attests—the one whole Jesus Christ, who in his vicarious humanity, his body and blood, is at once both the Giver and the Gift.

The incarnational form of Christ's one priestly sacrifice is thus perpetually present in and with its Eucharistic form in the Church. Together the two constitute an inseparable unity that nonetheless preserves their necessary distinction—without separation or division, without confusion or change, and with strict precedence accorded to the Incarnation as fulfilled by the Cross. That is, the precedence belongs completely to the incarnational form of Christ's one priestly self-sacrifice. Upon it the Eucharistic form is therefore completely dependent.

With this proviso in place, however, the actual content, reality, and power of the Eucharistic sacrifice is entirely one and the same as that of the Incarnation as fulfilled by the Cross. It is a matter of one reality, one priestly sacrifice of Christ, in two different temporal forms, such that the subsequent form (Eucharistic) participates in, manifests, and attests the originative form (incarnational) that is definitive, finished, and all-sufficient. The Eucharistic sacrifice is not a matter of repetition, but of participation, manifestation, and witness.

"If we are to understand aright what is traditionally spoken of as 'the Eucharistic sacrifice,'" writes Torrance, "it will be important to discern clearly how these two aspects of Christ's one saving work are related to each other, his self-giving to humankind and his self-offering to God." The first aspect involves a movement from God to us. Christ came to participate in the depths of our hopeless plight in order that he might abolish it in himself. By his Incarnation he has bound himself to us while also binding us to himself. Incorporating himself into our humanity, he has given his very self to us, becoming bone of our bone and flesh of our flesh. He has identified with us to the uttermost, "penetrating into the disobedient and corrupt condition of our human being, in order to pour out the love of God upon us, take away our sin and guilt, and endow us with divine holiness."[45] That is his saving work as it moves from heaven to earth. It is the aspect of his self-giving to us.

The second aspect of his saving work is the reverse movement from earth to heaven. It is the aspect of his self-offering to God. The obedience that he offered to God he offered for us vicariously "as our own act towards God." He consecrated himself for us in order that we might be consecrated through him. He offered himself to God, in holy obedience and atoning sacrifice, for our sakes so that "we, through sharing in his self-offering, may offer to God through him a holiness from the side of man answering to his own."[46]

The key to this twofold movement is participation. Aphoristically stated, with the Incarnation, heaven participates in earth that earth might participate in heaven. God participates in human flesh that human flesh might participate in God. Holiness participates in corruption that corruption might be uncorrupted by participating in holiness. Christ binds us to himself in his incarnational self-giving unto death in order that he might bring us into living union and communion with himself in his eternal self-offering to God.

This twofold movement is the dimension of depth in the Eucharist. When we celebrate the Eucharist "in memory of" our Lord, receiving his body and blood with the bread and the cup, "Christ through the Spirit is really present . . . taking up the eucharistic memorial we make of him as the concrete form of his own self-giving and self-offering, assimilating us . . . to himself and lifting us up in the closest union with himself . . . to the presence of the Father." As we celebrate the Lord's Supper in the Church, we "offer Christ eucharistically to the Father through prayers and thanksgiving in his name as our only true worship."[47]

What we do thus stands "in holy analogue and in union with what he has done for us in his self-offering and self-consecration to the Father, for it is done in the same eternal Spirit in whom he fulfilled his atoning sacrifice and now presents himself in our nature before the Father for us."[48] With our Eucharistic sacrifice of praise and thanksgiving, we participate in Christ's own self-offering to the Father. Putting it the other way around, Christ, in his real presence, includes our Eucharistic sacrifice in his and makes it his own. "His self-offering is utterly unique and completely vicarious . . . a self-offering made in our place, in our stead, and on our behalf which we could not make." It was accomplished "once for all and does not need to be repeated." But as such it is "eternally valid" in God, and "eternally prevalent" for us, for the Gift is identical with the Giver, the Giver is identical with the Gift, and the Offering and the Offerer are one.[49]

The Eucharistic sacrifice does not merely correspond to Christ's self-offering; it is a "participation through the Spirit in Christ" in his entire self-giving and self-offering for us.[50] "Thus the Eucharistic sacrifice means that we *through the Spirit* are so intimately united with Christ, by communion with his body and blood, that we participate in his self-consecration and self-offering to the Father and thus appear . . . before the Majesty of God . . . with no other sacrifice than the sacrifice of Jesus Christ our Mediator and High Priest" (italics original).[51] Our sacrifice becomes his, even as his has already become ours, by virtue of his incarnational self-giving and self-offering, in other words, by virtue of his vicarious humanity, first in the perfect and then in the present tense.

Torrance is careful to explain that participation takes place without synergism. "Synergism" does not rule out all modes of cooperation between divine and human willing, but it does rule out all modes in which human willing is thought somehow to effect our salvation, even if in a secondary or subordinate way. Our participation in Christ, and here in particular, our Eucharistic participation in his priestly self-offering to God, occurs strictly in the mystery of the Holy Spirit.

The question is not the fact but the status of human willing and acting before God. As an "act of prayer, thanksgiving and worship," the Eucharist is undoubtedly "the act of the Church." But in the Eucharist as elsewhere, it is the action of the Holy Spirit, not of the Church, that brings us into living union and communion with Christ. The act of Eucharistic worship in the Church must be seen as an act "in which through the Spirit we are given to share in the vicarious life, faith, prayer, worship, thanksgiving and self-offering of Jesus Christ to the Father."[52]

The Eucharist is "not to be regarded as an independent act on our part in response to what God has already done for us in Christ." It is rather an "act toward the Father already fulfilled in the humanity of Christ in our place and on our behalf, to which our acts in his name are assimilated and identified through the Spirit." In the Eucharist we are so intimately united to Christ through the Spirit that in and with our actions "it is Christ the incarnate Son who honors, adores and glorifies the Father."[53] In the Eucharist it is by the Spirit that we truly receive God's self-giving to us in the body and blood of Christ, and so also truly share "in the self-offering of the ascended Son" to the Father, in that same body and blood, as "grounded in his passion and resurrection."[54]

The mystery of Christ's real presence in the Eucharist, like the mystery of our reception of and participation in his body and blood, is a mystery to be adored and glorified, not a mystery to be explained. Torrance writes:

> How he is . . . present is only explicable from the side of God, in terms of his creative activity which by its very nature transcends any kind of explanation we can offer. That is what is meant by saying that he is really present *through the Spirit*, not that he is present only as Spirit, far less as some spiritual reality, but present through the same kind of inexplicable creative activity whereby he was born of the Virgin Mary and rose again from the grave.[55] (italics original)

> In this way [Reformation theology] sought to let the mystery of the real presence of Christ in the objective depth of his divine-human person and the eternal reality of his atoning sacrifice once for all perfected through the offering of his body, continually confront us in the Eucharist, without attempting to explain *how* this actually takes place in terms of causal-spatial connections with which we operate in any natural philosophy, and therefore without having recourse to any other analogy than that which rests upon the hypostatic union of divine and human nature in Jesus Christ himself.[56] (italics original)

The God who created the world out of nothing, who became Incarnate in the Virgin Mary by the Holy Spirit, and who raised our Lord Jesus Christ from the dead is the same God who acts upon us in the Eucharist. By the sheer sovereignty of his grace, this God is free to bring us into freedom, in and through the real presence of Christ. And so in the Eucharist we are brought by a power not our own worthily to receive and partake of Christ's body and blood, which, grounded in his sacrificial death and glorious resurrection, are at once his perpetual self-giving to us as well as his eternal self-offering for us, that we might be brought to eternal life in communion with the Father through the Son and in the Holy Spirit.

The one saving act of God through Christ and in the Spirit assumes, as Torrance understands it, a number of different temporal and substantive forms. One of these is the Eucharist. Everything depends, however, on how the various forms of God's one saving act are ordered in relationship to one another. Like baptism, the Eucharist is no more than a mediating form of the one saving action, and not in any sense its constitutive form. Like the preaching of the Gospel, the Eucharist is always secondary and derivative in relation to the finished work of Christ, the one form of our salvation that is definitive.

No secondary form can do anything more than manifest, attest, mediate, and participate in the one central form, precisely because Christ's finished work of salvation, being once for all, perfect, and all-sufficient, allows for no supplementation, repetition, or increase. In its perfection, however, the finished work of Christ (*opus perfectus*) does allow for secondary forms of self-manifestation, self-attestation, and self-mediation (i.e., Word and Sacrament) which participate in the central form without becoming confused with or changed into it (*operatione perpetuus*).

With this accent on the *opus perfectus*, as focused on Christ's fulfillment of his priestly office, and especially on the vicarious significance of his active and passive human obedience by virtue of his Incarnation, Torrance upholds the Protestant principle that affirms salvation in and by Christ alone. At the same time, with a complementary stress on how the *operatione perpetuus* manifests, attests, mediates, and participates in this one *opus perfectus*, especially as focused here on the body and blood of Christ as the Eucharist's true content, reality, and power, Torrance also upholds Catholic substance. For without violating the Protestant principle, he makes sense of the real presence of Christ's body and blood in and with the bread that we break and the cup that we bless. He also makes sense of the Church's Eucharistic offering of Christ to the Father in a sacrifice of thanks and praise, as an offering that is graciously assimilated by Christ into his own eternal self-offering for our sakes (as grounded in his death and resurrection) to the Father.

The mediating factor that joins the *opus perfectus* of Christ's finished saving work with his ongoing *operatione perpetuus* is again the vicarious humanity of Christ, here particularly its real Eucharistic presence to the Church in the form of his body and blood. Torrance's rich conception of this vicarious humanity amounts to a powerful theological and ecumenical advance in understanding the Eucharist. It improves on Calvin, for example, by accepting while also surpassing his view of the *sursum corda*. For whereas Calvin was correct to stress, in effect, that we are elevated by the Spirit to participate in the incarnate Son's eternal self-offering to the Father, he failed to see clearly at the same time that in and with the bread and the cup Christ is really present to the Church, through the very same Spirit, in the vicarious humanity of his body and blood.[57]

Torrance improves on Barth, furthermore, by again overcoming the unfortunate split Barth posited between the Eucharist as a response to grace and the Eucharist as also an indispensable manifestation, attestation, mediation, and partaking of grace.[58] Finally, he improves on "flat" views of the Eucharist that lose the dimension of depth because they undervalue salvation's perfect tense and blur it indistinguishably into the present tense. They focus improperly on the Eucharistic rite in itself and on the Church's supposedly causal or constitutive action as opposed to the Church's manifestation, attestation, mediation, and participation in the one saving divine action of salvation as historically perfected, perpetually present, and eternally valid by the Father through the Son and in the Spirit.[59]

Notes

1. *Quicquid enim in Baptismo proponitur donorum Dei, in Christo uno reperitur*. Unless otherwise indicated, I am using my own translations, though I tend to follow Allen closely. John Calvin, *Institutes of the Christian Religion*, 2 vols., tr. John Allen (Philadelphia: Presbyterian Board of Education, 1928).

2. Calvin, *Institutes*, IV.15.1, 5, 6.

3. Cf. Wilhelm Niesel, *The Theology of Calvin* (London: Lutterworth Press, 1956), 220.

4. Calvin, *Commmentary on 1 Corinthians 1:30*: "Since there are many who, while they do not wish to withdraw deliberately from God, do however seek something apart from Christ, just as if he alone did not contain all things in himself (*ac si non omnia in se unus contineret*), Paul tells us, in passing, what, and how great, are the treasures with which Christ is provided, and in doing so he seeks to describe at the same time our mode of existence (*modus subsistendi*) in Christ . . . . Finally, let us not seek the half, or some part (*non dimidium aut partem aliquam*), but the totality of the benefits in Christ (*bonorum omnium*) which are listed here. For Paul does not say that he has been given to us as something to add on to, or to be a buttress (*in supplementum vel adminiculum*) to righteousness, holiness, wisdom and redemption, but he ascribes to Christ alone the complete fulfillment of them all (*sed solidum omnium effectum ei soli assignat*)." John Calvin, *The First Epistle of Paul to the Corinthians* (Grand Rapids, Mich.: Eerdmans, 1960), 45-47. Significantly, a survey of the standard Scripture index to Calvin's *Institutes* indicates that in that work no New

Testament passage is cited more frequently than 1 Cor. 1:30 (though it is twice matched by John 20:23 and Matt. 16:19). The frequency is twelve citations.

5. *Commentary on Matthew 3:13.*

6. These images, of course, have been famously proposed by Karl Barth, who saw what was at stake, and who powerfully urged the first option. For a discussion unsurpassed in its incisiveness, whether in Barth's own corpus or elsewhere, see his *Church Dogmatics*, vol. 1, part 2 (Edinburgh: T& T Clark, 1956), 250-57.

7. *Non posse nos gratis iustificare sola fide, quin simul sancte vivamus. Commentary on 1 Corinthians 1:30.*

8. *Regenerationem vero ita demum ab euis morte et resurrectione consequimur, si per Spritum sanctificati imbuamur nova et spirituali natura.* Here I have cited from the Battles translation: Calvin, *Institutes of the Christian Religion* (Philadelphia: Westminster, 1960), 1308 (my italics). My point is not that this translation is necessarily the best rendering of the Latin, only that Calvin's wording is ambiguous enough that it can be pressed in this direction. Allen and Beveridge, in their different translations, both soften the *si* to "when."

9. In context, in these passages as elsewhere, Calvin is clearly concerned to counter Catholic criticisms that justification, as taught by the Reformation, abolishes sanctification. Too often, however, in countering this allegation, Calvin resorts to formulations that leave him open to misunderstanding on another flank. What he seems to mean is that justification, properly understood, is not only compatible with sanctification, but also includes it. But the perfect tense of sanctification in Christ seems threatened (or at least rendered ambiguous) in various ways, for example, by his use of conditional clauses beginning with the word "if" (or its equivalent).

10. Thomas F. Torrance, "The One Baptism Common to Christ and His Church," in *Theology in Reconciliation: Essays towards Evangelical and Catholic Unity in East and West* (Grand Rapids, Mich.: Eerdmans, 1975), 82.

11. Torrance, *Reconciliation*, 87-88.

12. Torrance, *Reconciliation*, 103.

13. Torrance, *Reconciliation*, 103.

14. Torrance, *Reconciliation*, 82-83.

15. Torrance, *Reconciliation*, 82.

16. Torrance, *Reconciliation*, 83.

17. Torrance, *Reconciliation*, 88.

18. Torrance, *Reconciliation*, 89.

19. Torrance, *Reconciliation*, 89.

20. Cf. the phrase drawn from Cranmer's great Eucharistic Prayer of Thanksgiving: "that we are members incorporate in the mystical body of thy Son, the blessed company of all faithful people." *The Book of Common Prayer* (New York: Oxford University Press, 1979), 339 (Rite 1). For U.S.

Presbyterians, a similar phrase could still be found in *The Book of Common Worship* (Philadelphia: The Board of Christian Education of the Presbyterian Church in the U.S.A., 1946, 1960), 164. In the newer Presbyterian *Book of Common Worship* (Louisville, Ky.: Westminster/John Knox Press, 1993), the phrase completely disappears.

21. Torrance, *Reconciliation*, 89.

22. Torrance, *Reconciliation*, 94. "The implication of this for an understanding of the saving life and activity of Jesus is immense. It laid the emphasis not only on what was called Jesus' 'passive obedience,' in which he submitted to the divine judgment upon us, but also upon his 'active obedience,' in which he took our place in all our human activity before God the Father, such as our acts of faith, obedience, prayer, and worship. To be united with Christ is to be joined to him in his life of faith, obedience, prayer, and worship, so that we must look away from our faith, obedience, prayer, and worship to what Christ is and does for us in our place and on our behalf." Thomas F. Torrance, "The Distinctive Character of the Reformed Tradition," The Donnell Lecture delivered at the University of Dubuque Theological Seminary, 1988, published in Christian D. Kettler and Todd H. Speidell, ed., *Incarnational Ministry: The Presence of Christ in Church, Society, and Family* (Colorado Springs, Colo.: Helmers & Howard, 1990), 6-7. Although they share the same basic Christocentric emphasis on salvation's perfect tense, Torrance characteristically places much more weight than Barth on the priestly, vicarious, and mediating nature of Christ's active obedience.

23. Torrance, *Reconciliation*, 89.

24. Torrance, *Reconciliation*, 88.

25. "For Irenaeus Baptism is certainly the sacrament of the whole incarnational reversal of our lost and disobedient estate in Adam which was carried through in the penetration of the Son of God into our alienation in the birth of Jesus, in the whole course of his obedient and saving humanity from infancy to maturity, in his death and resurrection and ascent to the right hand of the Father. As such the reality of our baptism is to be found in the objective reality of what has already been accomplished for us in Christ alone." Thomas F. Torrance, "Baptism in the Early Church," *1956 Interim Report of the Special Commision on Baptism* (The General Assembly of the Church of Scotland), 13-14.

26. Torrance, *Reconciliation*, 94.

27. Torrance, *Reconciliation*, 88.

28. By distinguishing "participation" from "communion" (words which can overlap in meaning), I am using the former in the ontic sense of "real union" and the latter in the more noetic sense involving cognition and volition.

29. Torrance does not reject the Reformation idea of "imputation," but following Luther, Calvin, and Barth, he places it in the context of participation. Justification has to be understood, he writes, "not just in terms of imputed righteousness but in terms of a participation in the

righteousness of Christ which is transferred to us through union with him." Torrance, "Reformed Tradition," 7. The forensic imagery of imputation, as Torrance is keenly aware, although helpful, is not sufficient. Its great value lies in clarifying that Christ's righteousness is not bestowed upon us piecemeal but as an indivisible whole. Its insufficiency, on the other hand, lies in the misleading implication, seized upon by opponents of the Reformation, that our righteousness in Christ is no more than a "legal fiction." The context of union and communion with Christ helps overcome this misunderstanding—as also does the free, gracious, and miraculous nature of the transaction that Luther and Calvin in particular grasped especially from their reading of Romans 4, in which the justification of the godless, through their being clothed in the righteousness of Christ, is perceived as being just as much a free miracle of grace as the creation of the world *ex nihilo* and the resurrection of Christ from the dead. See Thomas F. Torrance, "Justification: Its Radical Nature and Place in Reformed Doctrine and Life," in *Theology in Reconstruction* (Grand Rapids, Mich.: Eerdmans, 1965), 150-68, esp. 153, 155.

30. Torrance, *Reconciliation*, 100.

31. Torrance, *Reconciliation*, 100.

32. Torrance, *Reconciliation*, 101.

33. Two possible mistakes need to be avoided here. One is to reduce the *unio hypostatica* downwards to the *unio mystica*. This is the typical mistake of modern liberal theology. The other moves in the opposite direction by dissolving the *unio mystica* upwards into the *unio hypostatica*. This is the typical mistake of various high sacramental ecclesiologies. By seeing the *unio hypostatica* as absolutely *sui generis* and the *unio mystica* as pertaining to our union with the person of the incarnate Son by virtue of our participation in his vicarious humanity, Torrance preserves their proper distinction, and so the proper unity-in-distinction (and distinction-in-unity) between Christ and his Church.

34. Torrance, *Reconciliation*, 100.

35. Torrance, *Reconciliation*, 102.

36. Torrance, *Reconciliation*, 83, 98-99.

37. Torrance, "The Pascal Mystery of Christ and the Eucharist," in *Reconciliation*, 106-38; on 120.

38. Torrance, *Reconciliation*, 111.

39. Torrance, *Reconciliation*, 135.

40. Torrance, *Reconciliation*, 135.

41. Torrance, *Reconciliation*, 135.

42. Torrance, *Reconciliation*, 110.

43. Torrance, *Reconciliation*, 111.

44. Torrance, *Reconciliation*, 120.

45. Torrance, *Reconciliation*, 117.

46. Torrance, *Reconciliation*, 117.

47. Torrance, *Reconciliation*, 118.

48. Torrance, *Reconciliation*, 118.

49. Torrance, *Reconciliation*, 133.
50. Torrance, *Reconciliation*, 136.
51. Torrance, *Reconciliation*, 134.
52. Torrance, *Reconciliation*, 109.
53. Torrance, *Reconciliation*, 109.
54. Torrance, *Reconciliation*, 118. The focus on Christ's blood, though often repugnant to modern and Gentile sensibilities, is profoundly Hebraic in its priestly significance. See "Meditation on the Blood of Christ," in George Hunsinger, *Disruptive Grace* (Grand Rapids, Mich.: Eerdmans, 2000), 361-63.
55. Torrance, *Reconciliation*, 120.
56. Torrance, *Reconciliation*, 126-27.
57. Torrance, *Reconciliation*, 118, 128.
58. Torrance, *Reconciliation*, 109, 129.
59. Torrance, *Reconciliation*, 120, 122-25, 131.

Chapter 7

Reading T. F. Torrance as a Practical Theologian

by Ray S. Anderson

Introduction

As a former student of Thomas Torrance, I was as much impressed with his commitment to the Church and its ministry as by his scholarly acumen and theological brilliance. At the time, while I appreciated both dimensions to his life and teaching, I did not comprehend the inner logic which bound them together. For one thing, the discipline of practical theology had not yet emerged from the unfortunate dichotomy between the so-called pure theology as an academic discipline and applied theology as a set of skills and practices. Torrance's lectures and writing were not texts which one might read as prima facie principles for the effective practice of ministry. Reading Torrance with a conventional dualism between theology and ministry (as theory is related to practice), one could easily place him on the purely theoretical side of the theological enterprise.

Now, some twenty-five years later, I have come to see that it was this very dualism which Torrance sought to overcome through his rigorous insistence upon the correlation between revelation and reconciliation. Following Karl Barth's christological epistemology, Torrance grounded the revealed knowledge of God in the personal ministry of Christ as the one who discloses to us the innermost being of God in the same act of reconciling estranged and sinful humanity to God. This is the inner logic at the heart of the atonement which binds humanity to God in a saving way and God to humanity in a knowing way. Torrance puts it this way:

> Knowledge of God takes place not only within the rational structures, but also within the personal and social structures of human life, where the Spirit is at work as *personalising Spirit*. As the living presence of God who confronts us with His personal Being, addresses us in His Word, opens us out toward Himself, and calls forth from us the response of faith and love, He rehabilitates the *human subject*, sustaining him in his personal relations with God and with his fellow creatures.[1]

Citing John Duns Scotus, Torrance made a distinction between *theologia in se* and *theologia nostra*. As important as it is for theology to be grounded in God's own being (*theologia in se*), it is equally necessary that theology be mediated through the bounds and conditions of our life (*theologia nostra*).[2] While Torrance does not here speak of practical theology as a theological discipline, he insists that theology cannot properly be a science without being grounded in God's actual interactions with the world and with humans as recipients and interpreters of divine self-revelation.

The emergence of practical theology as a theological discipline and not merely the application of practice to theory, makes it possible to read Torrance not only as a dogmatic theologian, but as a practical theologian par excellence. Practical theology demands a very specific understanding of the nature of theology. Theology is not simply something to be known; theology is something which is lived and experienced by a particular community.

Thus, in contrast to models of theology which focus on the cognitive and rational aspects of theological knowledge alone, the discipline of practical theology focuses on *whole person knowledge*. Human beings are lovers and worshippers as well as thinkers, and all of these aspects are potential sources of theological knowledge.

Torrance places himself firmly in the arena of practical theology when he says:

> As the incarnate presence of the living God in space and time, he presents himself to our faith as its living dynamic Object. This has the effect of calling for a living theology, a way of thinking which is at the same time a way of living, that cannot be abstracted from the life-giving acts of Christ in the depths of human being and must therefore affect man radically in his daily life and activity.[3]

At its simplest, practical theology is critical reflection on the actions of the Church in the light of the Gospel and Christian tradition. Don Browning defines it as "the reflective process which the church pursues in its efforts to articulate the theological grounds of practical living in a variety of areas such as work, sexuality, marriage, youth, aging and death."[4] James Fowler adopts a similar understanding of the nature of practical theology, but adds an important dimension. "Practical theology is theological reflection and construction arising out of and giving guidance to a community of faith in the praxis of its mission."[5] Stephen Pattison astutely observes, "Only in action can the meaning of love and compassion be revealed."[6] Critical, analytical thinking is important, but it is not omniscient. Practical theology, as Ballard and Pritchard say,

> must take on the characteristics of theology as such. It too is a descriptive, normative, critical and apologetical activity. It is the means whereby the day-to-day life of the Church, in all its dimensions, is scrutinized in the light of the gospel and related to the demands and challenges of the present day, in a dialogue that both shapes Christian practice and influences the world, however minimally.[7]

In summary we can say that practical theology is a dynamic process of reflective, critical inquiry into the praxis of the Church in the world and God's purposes for humanity, carried out in the light of Christian Scripture and tradition and in critical dialogue with other sources of knowledge. As a theological discipline, its primary purpose is to ensure that the Church's public proclamations and praxis-in-the-world faithfully reflect the nature and purpose of God's continuing mission to the world, and in so doing authentically addresses the contemporary context into which the Church seeks to minister.[8]

Reading Thomas Torrance as a Practical Theologian

Understanding the discipline of practical theology as defined above, we can now read Torrance in a nondualistic way with regard to the relation of theology and ministry (or theory and practice).

> The spiritual reality to which we belong has a range of content which we cannot infer from what we already know, but which we may get to know more fully only through heuristic acts of exploring entirely new ground and grappling with novel connections and ideas. . . . Hence intensely personal acts of relation, discernment and judgment belong to the epistemic act in every

field of rational knowledge and fundamental science.[9]

This kind of heuristic thinking is what Torrance has called a "backwards kind of thinking." There is a "backward correlation" from the new to the old (cf. Matthew 13:51).[10] This is also similar to what Torrance calls axiomatic inquiry. Axioms are formulated out of experience and used to penetrate deeper into the inner logic of that which is to be known. While axioms are unprovable, they serve as keys to penetrate into the inner structure of reality in order to cause this inner reality to reveal itself to us.

The hermeneutical criterion for this reading of Torrance is the concept of *praxis* as opposed to practice. Praxis is quite different from the mere application of truth or theory. The word "practice" ordinarily refers to the methods and means by which we apply a skill or theory. This tends to separate truth from method or action so that one assumes that what is true can be deduced or discovered apart from the action or activity which applies it in practice. In this way of thinking, truth is viewed as existing apart from its manifestation in an event or an act. Practical theology seeks to overcome this dichotomy through the concept of praxis.

Aristotle defined praxis when he distinguished between *poiesis* as an act of making something where the *telos* lay outside of the act of making, and *praxis* as an act which includes the *telos* within the action itself. The *telos* of something is its final purpose, meaning, or character.[11] In praxis, God's truth is revealed through the structures of reality by which God's actions and presence are disclosed to us through our perception of God's actions as part of our experience. It is not our human actions that constitute the praxis of God. Rather, God acts through our human actions to reveal the truth.[12]

Praxis reveals theology in a very tangible form. In this sense *actions are themselves theological* and, as such, are open to theological reflection and critique. Thus the praxis of the Church is in fact the embodiment of its theology. Elaine Graham elaborates on practical theology as praxis when she says:

> Christian praxis is understood as the medium through which the Christian community embodies and enacts its fundamental vision of the gospel. Theology is properly conceived as a performative discipline, in which the criterion of authenticity is deemed to be orthopraxis, or authentic transformatory action, rather than orthodoxy (right belief).[13]

The truth of God's Word, for example, is not something which can be extracted from the Bible by the human mind so that one can possess this truth as a formula or doctrine without regard to its purpose of bringing us "into the truth." There is also true doctrine as opposed to false doctrine. But God's truth does not end with our concept of truth, nor is the human mind the absolute criterion for God's truth. God is the authority for what is true of God. How could it be otherwise? "Let God be proved true," wrote Paul, "although every one is a liar" (Rom. 3:4).

Reading Torrance as a practical theologian with the concept of praxis as a hermeneutical criterion, we can discern several contours of practical theology; practical theology as Christopraxis; as Ecclesial Praxis; as Missiological Praxis, and as Pastoral Praxis.

Practical Theology as Christopraxis

As with Karl Barth, under whom he studied, Torrance held that the act of God is the hermeneutical criterion for the being of God. This becomes a christological statement when Christ is viewed as the definitive act of the self-revealing God binding the historical people of God through Israel to the incarnation of God in the historical person of Jesus Christ for the sake of and on behalf of all humankind. In a masterful summary statement Torrance writes:

> And at last in the fullness of time the Word of God became man in Jesus, born of the Virgin Mary, within the embrace of Israel's faith and worship and expectation, himself God and man, in whom the covenanted relationship between God and Israel and through Israel with all humanity was gathered up, transformed and fulfilled once for all. In Him the revealing of God and the understanding of man fully coincided, the whole Word of God and the perfect response of man were indivisibly united in one person, the Mediator, who was received, believed and worshipped together with God the Father and the Holy Spirit by the apostolic community which he creatively called forth and assimilated to his own mission from the Father. Thus as both the incarnate revelation of God and the embodied knowledge of God, Jesus Christ constitutes in himself the Way, the Truth and the Life through whom alone access to God the Father is freely open for all the peoples of mankind.[14]

The knowledge of God which results from the historical act of God's self-revelation in Christ is not only *revealed knowledge* of God's inner being as grounded in the eternal relations of Father, Son, and Holy Spirit (*theologia in se*), but is also a *vicarious participation* of humanity in that intradivine relation as the basis for a *saving knowledge* of God (*theologia nostra*).[15]

> Our knowledge of the Father and the Son, of the Father in the Son and of the Son in the Father, is mediated to us in and through Jesus Christ in such a way that in a profound sense we are given to share in the knowledge which God has of himself within himself as Father and Son or Son and Father, which is part of what is meant by our knowing God through the Spirit of God who is in him and whom he sends to us through the Son. Now it is because we do not know the Father or the Son except through the revealing and reconciling work of Jesus Christ, that our knowledge of the Father and of the Son and of the Holy Spirit is, as it were, a function of our knowledge of Jesus Christ.[16]

As Torrance indicates in the following quotation, through the incarnation, the divine Son assumed the humanity common to all descendents of Adam and Eve through the humanity of Jesus of Nazareth. In his life, death, and resurrection, Jesus thus served as a vicarious representative of all humanity in his priestly ministry of bearing the consequence of sin in his death and delivering humanity from the power of sin through his resurrection.

> [T]he key to the understanding of the Eucharist is to be sought in the *vicarious humanity of Jesus, the priesthood of the incarnate Son*. Eternal God though he was, he condescended to be our brother, and since we are children sharing in flesh and blood, he partook of the same, made like unto his brothers in every respect, so that he might be a merciful and faithful High Priest in the affairs *towards* God to make expiation for the sins of the people.[17]

The substitutionary atonement is thus grounded in the substitution of the humanity of Jesus for our humanity, not only on the cross, but through his entire life of prayer, worship, and obedience unto death. For Torrance, revelation is always knowledge of the self-revealing God mediated to us through Jesus Christ. Simultaneous with that act of self-revelation, not sequential to it, a corresponding movement from below to above constitutes an act of reconciliation by which humanity is vicariously represented in the personal life, death, and resurrection of Jesus Christ. The twofold significance of the vicarious humanity of Christ means that through the person of Christ all that belongs to the innermost being of God is revealed to us through Christ and all that is demanded of God from humanity is fulfilled through Christ.

This can be expressed more clearly in the following diagram:

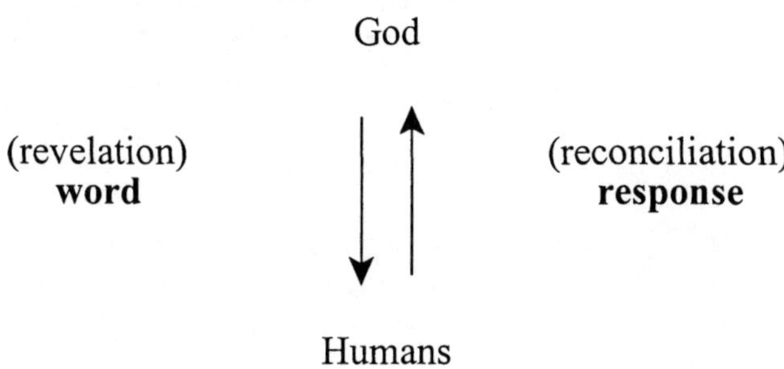

This movement provides the ontological and objective basis for the life and ministry of the Church in its continuing praxis of Christ's revelation and reconciliation. The Holy Spirit mediates the very Person of Christ to us, not merely the benefits of Christ's death. The whole of Christ's life of obedience, prayer, and worship thus becomes the objective and ontological basis for the Christian's life of faith. The Church, as the body of Christ, participates in Christ's ongoing ministry of revelation and reconciliation. Through the incarnation the Son of God penetrated into the ontological structures of fallen humanity in order to restore humanity to its proper and divinely purposed existence through the reconciling ministry of Christ which continues as the ministry of the Church. This is the incarnational basis for a practical theology of the Church's life and existence.

> What is supremely needed, therefore, in all the churches today, is a far profounder understanding of the Incarnation, the coming of God himself into the structures of creaturely and human being, in order to restore the creation to its unity and harmony in himself—that is, a Christology with genuine *substance* in it once more, the theology of the incarnate Son of God, the one Lord Jesus Christ, "*being of one substance with the Father, by whom all things were made*." And then in intimate correlation with such a Christology, what is supremely needed also is a far profounder understanding of the Church as divine creation within the ontological structures of the universe, entrusted with the mission of healing and reconciliation in the depth of being.[18]

This continuing ministry, or praxis of Christ through the power of the Holy Spirit, takes place in and through the life of the Church without making the ministry of Christ subject to human manipulation and control. "That is the living God who still acts here and now through Jesus Christ in the Spirit, but *in the Spirit* means in God's own distinctive way and with God's own distinctive kind of power, and therefore beyond any realm of human control and manipulation."[19]

Practical Theology as Ecclesial Praxis

The Word of the Gospel (*kerygma*) which the Church proclaims, says Torrance, "is in the fullest sense the sacramental action of the Church through which the mystery of the Kingdom concerning Christ and His Church, hid from the foundation of the world, is now being revealed in history . . . in *kerygma* the same word continues to be 'made flesh' in the life of the Church."[20]

Correspondingly, says Torrance, "the church constitutes the social coefficient of our knowledge of God, for in the nature of the case we are unable to know God in any onto-relational way without knowing him in the togetherness of our personal relations with one another."[21]

> Thus if the Word of God is to enter the forum as speech to man through the medium of human words it must be directed to man in community, and if that Word creates reciprocity between God and man it must create a community of such reciprocity within human society as the appropriate medium of its continuing communication to man.[22]

It is for this reason that Torrance places such importance upon the empirical content of knowledge of God revealed through the Church's praxis of life in the Spirit as the basis for our cognitive and theoretical theological formulations.

> It is, I believe, still within the matrix of Eucharistic worship and meditation upon the Holy Scriptures, and evangelical experience in the fellowship and mission of the church, that the empirical and theoretical components in our knowledge of God are found fused together, in a kind of stereoscopic coordination of perceptual and auditive images, and thus provide us with the cognitive instruments we need for explicit theological understanding of God's interaction with us.[23]

Practical theology, as critical and constructive reflection on ecclesial praxis is the process of ongoing critical reflection on the acts of the Church in the light of the Gospel and in critical dialogue with secular sources of knowledge with a view to the faithful transformation of the praxis of the Church-in-the-world. Secular sources are drawn upon not only to improve technique, but also to clarify the nature of the ecclesial praxis, to uncover the meanings which lie behind and are present within the praxis of the Church, and even to challenge and clarify particular understandings of theological concepts.[24] Contrary to models of theology which suggest that theology is done primarily within the academy, a model of practical theology which focuses on ecclesial praxis points towards the fact that *ecclesial praxis is the place where theology is done.*

> The implication of this is that we may know God and interpret his self-revelation only in the attitude and context of worship and within the fellowship of the church, where to the godly reason God is more to be adored than expressed. It is only as we allow ourselves, within the fellowship of faith and through constant meditation on the Holy Scriptures, to come under the creative impact of God's self-revelation that we may acquire the disciplined spiritual perception or insight which enables us to discriminate between our conceptions of the Truth and the Truth itself.[25]

By focusing critical reflection on ecclesial praxis, the practical theologian seeks to examine the meaningful acts of the Church and to critically assess, challenge, and seek the transformation of particular forms of praxis in the light of the mission of God and in critical dialogue with the Christian tradition and the world. The practical theologian seeks to interpret Scripture, tradition, and praxis in order that the contemporary praxis of both Church and world can be transformed. Torrance says:

> In order to think out the relation of the Church in history to Christ we must put both these together—*mediate horizontal relation* through history to the historical Jesus Christ, and *immediate vertical relation* through the Spirit to the risen and ascended Jesus Christ. It is the former that supplies the material content, while it is the latter that supplies the immediacy of actual encounter.[26]

An adequate understanding of the theological validity of Christian praxis as a form of practical knowledge allows practical theology to hold together in constructive tension theory and practice, Church and world, normativity and transformation, and enables a constructive and mutual dialogue to take place between all of these elements and other sources of knowledge.

The interaction between the mediate horizontal dimension and the immediate vertical dimension of divine revelation is similar to what James Fowler says about the twofold axis of practical theology, which

> is critical and constructive reflection on the praxis of the Christian community's life and work in its various dimensions. As such practical theology is not self-sufficient as a discipline. Though it has and must exercise direct access to the sources of faith and theology in Scripture and tradition, it does not do so in isolation. Practical theology is part of a larger, theological enterprise that includes the specialties of exegetical, historical, systematic, and fundamental theological inquiry and construction.[27]

Practical theology, for Fowler, revolves around his concept of *ecclesial praxis* which he describes as the specific way in which the Church attempts to work in partnership with God and to remain faithful to Him and His mission. Fowler sees practical theology as existing at the critical interface between the Church and the world.[28] In Fowler's model, theory and practice are drawn together in his understanding of practical theology as a type of *practical wisdom;* a kind of knowing that guides being and doing.[29] This is a knowing "in which skill and understanding cooperate; a knowing in which experience and critical reflection work in concert, a knowing in which the disciplined improvisation, against a backdrop of reflective wisdom, marks the virtuosity of the competent practitioners."[30]

Thus theory and practice are united within this form of practical knowledge which works itself out within the praxis of the Church. This model of practical theology with its emphasis on ecclesial praxis and the attainment of practical knowledge goes a long way towards healing the rift between theory and practice. Torrance's insistence on the ecclesial context, where prayer, worship, and obedient response to the Word of God take place fits well within the scope of practical theology as we now understand it.

Practical Theology as Missiological Praxis

The outpouring of the Spirit at Pentecost, argues Torrance, not only constituted the "re-birth" of the Church as the people of God, it called forth and empowered the Church to be the missionary people of God.

> Not only did he pour out his Spirit upon the Apostles inspiring them for their special task, and not only did he pour out his Spirit in a decisive and once for all way, at Pentecost, constituting the people of God into the New Testament Church which is the Body of Christ, but within that Church and its Communion of the Spirit he continues to pour out special gifts for ministry, with the promise that as the Gospel is proclaimed in his Name he will work with the Church confirming their ministry of Christ to others as his own and making it the ministry of himself to mankind.[31]

Between the word of the Kingdom and its power of healing there is what Torrance once called an "eschatological reserve" in which the Word is borne in hope and faith.[32] The incarnational community lives and functions between these two moments, between the cross and the *parousia,* between the evangelical word of forgiveness and the final act of restoration and reconciliation.

The Christ proclaimed in the Gospel through the Church has a counterpart in the Christ clothed with the needs of the world. In one of his most eloquent missiological utterances, Torrance says:

> The Church cannot be in Christ without being in Him as He has proclaimed to men in their need and without being in Him as He encounters us in and behind the existence of every man in his need. Nor can the Church be recognized as His except in that meeting of Christ with Himself in the depth of human misery, where Christ clothed with His gospel meets Christ clothed with the desperate need and plight of men.[33]

The theme of the vicarious humanity of Christ reappears in Torrance's discussion of the role of Christ in the mission of the Church to the world. "We are to think of the whole life and activity of Jesus from the cradle to the grave," says Torrance, "as constituting the vicarious human response to himself which God has freely and unconditionally provided for us."[34] Any presentation of the Gospel which strips Christ of the saving significance of his humanity is "unevangelical," argues Torrance. "How, then, is the Gospel to be preached in a genuinely evangelical way? Surely in such a way that full and central place is given to the *vicarious humanity of Jesus* as the all-sufficient human response to the saving love of God which he has freely and unconditionally provided for us."[35]

The Church's mission of evangelism must not strip the Gospel of the humanity of Christ as the objective basis for saving faith. Rather, the unconditional grace of God not only makes an unconditional demand upon humans to acknowledge their desperate need of God's saving grace, but provides in Christ's own human response the actuality and possibility of every person's response of faith.

> To preach the Gospel of the unconditional grace of God in that unconditional way is to set before people the astonishingly good news of what God has freely provided for us in the vicarious humanity of Jesus. To repent and believe in Jesus Christ and commit myself to him on that basis means that I do not need to look over my shoulder all the time to see whether I have really given myself personally to him, whether I really believe and trust him, whether my faith is at all adequate, for in faith it is not upon my faith, my believing or my personal commitment that I rely, but solely upon what Jesus Christ had done for me, in my place and on my behalf, and what he is and always will be as he stands in for me before the face of my Father.[36]

Practical theology, as envisioned by Torrance, therefore calls theology and the Church back to its roots as a fundamentally missionary church with a particular vision and a specific task to perform in the world. As a missionary church it is crucial that it remains faithful to its missiological task and vision. One of the primary tasks of the practical theologian is to ensure that the Church is challenged and enabled to achieve this task faithfully.

Practical Theology as Pastoral Praxis

Woven through the tightly knit fabric of Torrance's erudite and sometimes obscure theological essays, one finds the refreshing spring of a personal experience of Jesus Christ flooding its banks, revealing a passionate and compassionate pastoral heart. Only rarely does he speak of his own relation with God, and when he does it is a voice of serenity and sanity as of a soul in the grip of grace.

> If I may be allowed to speak personally for a moment, I find the presence and being of God bearing upon my experience and thought so powerfully that I cannot but be convinced of His overwhelming reality and rationality. To doubt the existence of God would be an act of sheer irrationality, for it would mean that my reason had become unhinged from its bond with real being.

> Yet in knowing God I am deeply aware that my relation to Him has been damaged, that disorder has resulted in my mind, and that it is I who obstruct knowledge of God by getting in between Him and myself . . . . But I am also aware that His presence presses unrelentingly upon me through the disorder of my mind, for He will not Himself be thwarted by it, challenging and repairing it, and requiring of me on my part to yield my thoughts to His healing and controlling revelation.[37]

Pastoral praxis is the continuing diaconal ministry of Christ grounded in the heart of divine compassion and poured out lavishly and freely upon bruised and burdened human lives.

> Christ was Himself the *diakonos par excellence* whose office it was not only to prompt the people of God in their response to the divine mercy and to be merciful themselves, not only to stand out as the perfect model or example of compassionate service to the needy and distressed, but to provide in Himself and in His own deeds of mercy the creative ground and source of all such *diakonia*. He was able to do that because in Him God Himself condescended to share with men their misery and distress, absorbed the sharpness of their hurt and suffering into Himself, and poured Himself out in infinite love to relieve their need, and He remains able to do that because He is Himself the outgoing of the innermost Being of God toward men in active sympathy and compassion, the boundless mercy of God at work in human existence, unlimited in His capacity to deliver them out of all their troubles.[38]

Fully aware of the contradiction between God's creative moral goodness and the human experience of gratuitous evil, Torrance undergirds pastoral concern with solid practical theology. One of the greatest challenges to a pastoral theology is the problem of evil. When tragedy in the form of catastrophic illness and violent death, birth defects, child abuse, genocide and mass murder strikes, ordinary means of pastoral care built upon psychological strategies and techniques fail. Presenting the arguments of traditional theodicy (defense of God in the face of evil) to those who grieve or to the victims of violence often adds insult to injury.

The questions easily become accusations. "If you are an all powerful God, why do you not intervene when evil threatens to strike down the innocent?" "If nothing happens except that God knows in advance and determines all things, how can we love and trust a God who causes such evil?" "What good purpose could God possibly have that would justify him allowing children to suffer violence?"

The challenge to a practical theologian in the face of such agonizing questions is to expand the reality of God's love and the reality of human suffering without breaking the two apart.

Torrance does not fail us. He reminds us that God does not attack evil with the kind of power which would destroy it, but through the power of suffering love attacks it from within and from below:

> This movement of God's holy love into the heart of the world's evil and agony is not to be understood as a direct act of sheer almighty power, for it is not God's purpose to shatter and annihilate the agents and embodiments of evil in the world, but rather to pierce into the innermost centre of evil power where it is entrenched in the piled-up and self-compounding guilt of humanity in order to vanquish it from within and below, by depriving it of the lying structures of half-truth on which it thrives and of the twisted forms of legality behind which it embattles itself and from which it fraudulently gains its power. Here we have an entirely different kind of and quality of power, for which we have no analogies in our experience to help us understand it, since it transcends every kind of moral and material power we know.[39]

Torrance goes on to suggest that only through the cross of Jesus Christ can we see and understand how God deals with evil in this world. The reality of God's love as enfleshed in the humanity of Jesus is the hermeneutic of God's power. All questioning from the side of human pain is now "Questioning in Jesus Christ," the title of a chapter in one of Torrance's early books.[40]

> Yet this is only at the cost of an act, utterly incomprehensible to us, whereby God has taken the sorrow, pain, and agony of the universe into himself in order to resolve it all through his own eternal righteousness, tranquillity, and peace. The centre and heart of that incredible movement of God's love is located in the Cross of Christ, for there we learn that God has refused to hold himself aloof from the violence and suffering of his creatures, but has absorbed and vanquished them in himself, while the resurrection tells us that the outcome of that is so completely successful in victory over decay, decomposition, and death, that all creation with which God allied himself so inextricably in the incarnation has been set on the entirely new basis of his saving grace. . . . The Cross of Christ tells us unmistakably that all physical evil, not only pain, suffering, disease, corruption, death, and of course cruelty and venom in animal as well as human behavior, but also

'natural' calamities, devastations, and monstrosities, are an outrage against the love of God and a contradiction of good order in his creation.[41]

In stressing that the atonement is grounded in the incarnation of God and not merely in his death on the cross, Torrance has often cited the statement of the Cappadocian father, Gregory of Nanziansus, that "what Christ has not assumed is not healed; but that which is united with his Godhead is also saved."[42] In becoming human flesh, the divine Logos assumed not only the form of humanity but humanity under the burden of physical, mental, emotional, and spiritual pain and suffering. It is in the very person of Christ, Torrance argues, that God takes upon himself the consequence of the fall and the resulting distress which humans experience as subject to natural catastrophes, moral evil, and demonic oppression. The cross became the focal point for violence against humanity in the person of Christ as the powerless Word, but also the decisive point for the power of God, grounded in love, to overcome the power of evil through resurrection from the dead.

As Torrance states, the cross of Christ makes clear the fact that evil is not only a violation of humanity, but it is also a contradiction to God's moral order. The incarnation places God's sovereignty and moral order on the side of humanity in opposition to evil. No longer is there a basis for interpreting the tragic events which threaten human good as somehow linked directly or indirectly to God's providence as though evil contributes eventually to some divinely ordained good.

The implications for pastoral theology are significant. Instead of relying upon psychological strategies alone to assist persons in dealing with their anger and pain, the pastoral caregiver can bring God to the side of the person who is suffering as one who becomes an advocate (paraclete). God's anger and outrage at evil can be expressed as more than divine affect; through Christ God has entered into the "godforsaken" place (Matthew 27:46) where the absence of God's supernatural power is countered by the presence of God's suffering love.

The christological foundations for Torrance's theology are as significant for the practical theologian as for the dogmatician. Dogmatic theology, as Torrance learned from his mentor Karl Barth, has no other basis than the incarnate Word of God which penetrates through the Kantian barrier between the noumenal and the phenomenal so as to create a real, not mythical, epistemological basis for our knowledge of God. In the same way, Torrance has gone beyond Barth in demonstrating how the self-revealing Word of God through Christ (dogma) also becomes the basis for the ongoing priestly ministry of Christ (praxis). As Torrance likes to put it, God "rehabilitates the human subject, sustaining him in his personal relations with God and with his fellow creatures."[43] This is the christological basis for an authentic practical theology.

Comments and Critique

In this chapter I have presented a case for reading Thomas Torrance as a practical theologian. This is intended to be taken both ways. As a practical theologian, I now read Torrance as one who contributes to the discipline of practical theology through a theology which continues to interpret divine revelation through the praxis of Christ's ministry of reconciliation from below. But I also now read Torrance as himself being a practical theologian due to what he called a "living theology" as opposed to a static and sterile dogmatic theology.[44] Torrance's contribution to the discipline of theology proper, especially his extensive work in the area of theology and science, has become well known and subject to a great deal of critical debate as well as acclaim. At the same time, his contribution to the newly emerging discipline of practical theology has gone largely unnoticed.

There are at least two reasons for this. First, as I indicated at the outset of this discussion, Torrance's literary style and scholarly erudition tend to baffle if not discourage all but the most tenacious reader, willing to read and reread, ponder and reflect. Second, even by my attempt at reading Torrance as a practical theologian, it must be admitted that he seldom ventures onto the turf where practical theologians ply their trade.

The two questions put forth by Don Browning, for example, in his seminal work on practical theology are not explicitly raised by Torrance: "What should we do? And how should we live?"[45] These "inner core" questions, argues Browning, provide the critical starting point to which all theological reflection must return if it is to contribute toward a knowledge of God which guides human life as well as thought. When these questions are forced upon one by the circumstances of life, Torrance can be read with profit provided that the connection between his christological praxis and the praxis of the Holy Spirit is supplied by the reader. Knowing Torrance's deep commitment to the life and ministry of the Church, one hesitates to suggest that he, nonetheless, wrote more for the student of dogmatic theology than for the practical theologian. Would Torrance himself agree with my assessment? Would he be comfortable with my reading of him as a practical theologian? I would be interested in what he has to say at this point.

This leads me to a more serious problem that I find with Torrance, despite my bias toward reading him as a practical theologian. The Trinitarian matrix of Torrance's theology is deeply imprinted upon every chapter, if not on every page of his work. This leads to a creative and constructive epistemology—knowledge of God is simultaneously knowledge of God as Father, Son, and Holy Spirit. The soteriological implications are traced out by Torrance extensively.[46]

What I find lacking, however, is the hermeneutical coordinates in this matrix. Torrance's firm grounding in the reformed theology tradition tends toward an epistemology of the Holy Spirit rather than a praxis of the Holy Spirit. This is reflected in his otherwise perceptive and helpful essay "The Epistemological Relevance of the Holy Spirit."[47] The contemporary presence and work of the Holy Spirit constitutes the praxis of Christ himself, as Torrance has suggested. Then should we not be able to say that the work of Christ in the present activity of the Holy Spirit constitutes a hermeneutical criterion for reading and interpreting the Word of Christ (Scripture)? Rather than restricting the Holy Spirit to illuminating the text of Scripture, as Reformed theology tends to do, should we not be willing to give hermeneutical weight to the actual work of the Holy Spirit in the context of the Church's life and ministry in the world? That is, the question is not only "What should we do?" but "What is the Spirit of Christ doing?"[48]

I read Torrance as tending more toward following Barth's concern for a Trinitarian exposition of dogma than following Bonhoeffer's concern for a practical application of theological ethics. While Bonhoeffer assumed Barth's theology of Christ as the very revelation of God, he pressed for a more contemporary answer to the question "Where is Christ in the world today and what am I to do as an obedient disciple?" The ethical question is there in Torrance's theology of the vicarious humanity of Christ, but it lies undiscovered and unappreciated in his major writings. The relation of Christ to God, and of God to humanity, is brilliantly displayed in Torrance's theology. The relation of Christ to culture lies hidden in the shadows, waiting to be brought forth into the light. I wonder if Torrance would not agree with me that the vicarious humanity of Christ has as much to do with contemporary ethical issues as it does with the more classical issues of epistemology and soteriology. Torrance has recently affirmed the practice of ordaining women for pastoral ministry in the Church based on the "new humanity" of Christ.[49] Would he be equally affirming of the inclusion of gay Christians in the Church, if not also for ordination? And if not, why not?

The questions which I raise concerning Torrance's theology from the perspective of practical theology are basically methodological. I have argued that Torrance's theological matrix itself contains an inner logic that overcomes the older dualism between theory and practice. His christological and incarnational theology binds revelation as true knowledge of God to reconciliation as the saving praxis of God. Without the saving praxis of Christ's ministry of reconciliation, knowledge of God becomes partial and abstract, leading only to theory without practice and, in fact, no longer truth. Without the divine self-revelation of God entering into our time and space continuum demanding conformity of mind as well as will, ministry in the name of God quickly dissolves into the pragmatism of practice without theory. It is to the credit of Thomas Torrance that he recognized the fatal flaw in this dualism and gave us a theology which not only has diagnostic value in exposing the dualism, but also has creative and constructive value in pointing the way toward an authentic praxis of practical theology. We would do well to read Thomas Torrance again as a practical theologian!

Notes

1. Thomas F. Torrance, *God and Rationality* (London: Oxford University Press, 1971), 188 (emphasis added). "He is in Himself not only God objectifying Himself for man but man adapted and conformed to that objectification, not only the complete revelation of God to man but the appropriate correspondence on the part of man to that revelation, not only the Word of God to man but man obediently hearing and answering that Word. In short, Jesus Christ is Himself both the Word of God as spoken by God to man and that same Word as heard and received by man, Himself both the Truth of God given to man and that very Truth understood and actualized in man." Thomas F. Torrance, *Space, Time, and Resurrection* (Grand Rapids, Mich.: Eerdmans, 1976), 63-64.

2. Thomas F. Torrance, *Reality and Evangelical Theology* (1982; reprint, Grand Rapids, Mich.: Eerdmans, 1999), 21ff.

3. *Evangelical Theology*, 138. Christoph Schwöble has spoken insightfully to this situation and his comments are worth quoting in full: "This essential interconnection between the practical questions of the life of the Church and the theoretical problems of the theological understanding of the Church, and their relation to the focal point of the nature of Christian faith and its constitution, is so important because we are today painfully aware of the gap between the factual existence of the Church in society and the theological fomulae in which its nature is expressed. This leads to a situation in which the practical questions of day-to-day living in the Church are often decided on the basis of pragmatic and wholly untheological considerations, while the ecclesiology of academic theology, operating, as it seems, at one remove from the social reality of the Church, seems often unable to relate to the practical questions which face the Church in its struggle for survival in a society more and more shaped by a plurality of religious and quasi-religious world views. The challenge of the ecclesiology of the Reformers is the challenge of a theological reflection on the Church which is closely related to the practical problems of Christian life in the Church, and which is at the same time theoretically rigorous." Christoph Schwöble, "The Creature of the Word: Recovering the Ecclesiology of the Reformers," in *On Being the Church: Essays on the Christian Community*, ed. Colin E. Gunton and Daniel W. Hardy (Edinburgh: T&T Clark, 1989), 117.

4. Don S. Browning, *The Moral Context of Pastoral Care* (Philadelphia: Westminster, 1976), 14.

5. James Fowler, "Practical Theology and the Shaping of Christian Lives," in Don S. Browning, ed., *Practical Theology* (San Francisco: Harper & Row, 1983), 49.

6. Stephen Pattison, *Pastoral Care and Liberation Theology* (London: Cambridge University Press, 1994), 32.

7. Paul Ballard and John Pritchard, *Practical Theology in Action: Christian Thinking in the Service of Church and Society* (London: SPCK, 1996), 12.

8. I have discussed the nature of practical theology as a discipline in my book, Ray S. Anderson, *The Shape of Practical Theology: Empowering Ministry with Theological Praxis* (Downers Grove, Ill.: InterVarsity Press, 2001).

9. Thomas F. Torrance, *Reality and Scientific Theology*, vol. 1, *Theology and Science at the Frontiers of Knowledge* (Princeton, N.J.: Scottish Academy Press, for Center of Theological Inquiry, 1985 [Lectures 1970]), 111.

10. Torrance, *Rationality*, 15ff.

11. See Aristotle "The Nichomachean Ethics," in *The Works of Aristotle,* trans. W. D. Ross (London: Oxford University Press, 1915), IX, vi. 5. The use of the term 'praxis' in contemporary theology has been greatly influenced by the quasi-Marxist connotation given to it by some Latin American Liberation theologians. My own attempt in using the word

is to recover the authentically biblical connotation of God's actions which reveal his purpose and truth. I appreciate the concept of praxis as used by Orlando Costas' *The Church and Its Mission: A Shattering Critique from the Third World* (Wheaton, Ill.: Tyndale House, 1974). I have discussed this further in my essay, Ray S. Anderson, "Christopraxis: Competence as a Criterion for Theological Education," in *Theological Students Fellowship (TSF) Bulletin,* (January-February 1984); see also Ray S. Anderson, *Ministry on the Fireline—A Practical Theology for an Empowered Church* (Downers Grove, Ill.: InterVarsity Press, 1993), 27ff; Ray S. Anderson, "Christopraxis: The Ministry and the Humanity of Christ for the World," in *Christ in Our Place—Essays in Honor of James B. Torrance*, ed. Trevor Hart and Daniel Thimell (London: Pasternoster Press, 1989), 11-31.

12. James Will points to the necessity of a praxis theology when he says, "If incomplete and ideologically distorted persons nevertheless have the dignity of participation with their Creator in the preservation and completion of the creation, then praxis is a necessary dimension of theology. But praxis must not be misunderstood as practice. Practice has come to mean the use of external means to attain a theoretically defined end. It suggests that finite and sinful persons may so understand the meaning of God's peace as to be able to devise economic, political, diplomatic, and even military means to attain it. The end of peace is thought to be a transcendent value that appropriate external means may effect. Praxis, on the other hand, is a dialectical process of internally related events from which a result dynamically emerges. Given the finite and ideological character of our preconceptions of peace, they cannot be treated as sufficient definitions of an eternal value to guide our practice. Rather, we need a praxis; that is, peace must be allowed to emerge from a dialogical and dialectical process that may continuously correct our ideological tendencies. Praxis is thus a process of struggle, negotiation, and dialogue toward a genuinely voluntary consensus." James Will, *A Christology of Peace* (Louisville, Ky.: Westminster/John Knox Press, 1989), 24-25.

13. Elaine L. Graham, *Transforming Practice: Pastoral Theology in an Age of Uncertainty* (London: Mowbray, 1996), 7.

14. Thomas F. Torrance, *The Mediation of Christ* (Colorado Springs, Colo.: Helmers and Howard, 1992), 9.

15. "He is in Himself not only God objectifying Himself for man but man adapted and conformed to that objectification, not only the complete revelation of God to man but the appropriate correspondence on the part of man to that revelation, not only the Word of God to man but man obediently hearing and answering that Word. In short, Jesus Christ is Himself both the Word of God as spoken by God to man and that same Word as heard and received by man, Himself both the Truth of God given to man and that very Truth understood and actualized in man." Thomas F. Torrance, *Theological Science* (London: Oxford University Press, 1969), 50.

16. Torrance, *Mediation*, 55.

17. Thomas F. Torrance, *Theology in Reconciliation: Essays towards Evangelical and Catholic Unity in East and West* (Grand Rapids, Mich.: Eerdmans, 1975), 111 (emphasis in the original).

18. Torrance, *Reconciliation*, 283. "This in turn transforms the whole conception of the analogical relation in the sacramental participation. Not only is it one which has Christological content, but it is an *active analogy*, the kind by which we are conducted upward to spiritual things, and are more and more raised up to share in the life of God. This is an elevation or exaltation into fellowship with the divine life through the amazing condescension of the Son who has been pleased to unite Himself with us in our poverty and unrighteousness, that through redemption, justification, sanctification, eternal life, and all the other benefits that reside in Christ we may be endowed with divine riches, even with the life and love that overflow in Christ from God Himself." Thomas F. Torrance, *Conflict and Agreement in the Church*, vol. 2 (London: Lutterworth Press, 1960), 145.

19. Torrance, *Reconciliation*, 291. "That is the epistemological relevance of the doctrine of the Spirit. Certainly the history of Christian doctrine makes it clear that wherever the Church has allowed the reality of the historical Jesus Christ to be depreciated there it has also lost a doctrine of the Holy Spirit, through the dissolving of the Spirit into the immanent reason or into man's own attempts at understanding. The doctrine of the Spirit, i.e. of the objective reality and personal Being of the Spirit, stands or falls with the acknowledgment of the active coming and activity of the Being of God himself within our space and time in Jesus Christ." Thomas F. Torrance, *Theology in Reconstruction* (London: SCM; Grand Rapids, Mich.: Eerdmans, 1965), 235.

20. Torrance, *Conflict and Agreement,* vol. 2, 158-59.

21. Torrance, *Evangelical Theology*, 46.

22. Torrance, *Rationality*, 146-47.

23. Torrance, *Evangelical Theology*, 49. "In so far as worship and prayer are through, with and in Christ, they are not primarily forms of man's self-expression or self-fulfilment or self-transcendence in this or that human situation or cultural context, but primarily forms of Christ's vicarious worship and prayer offered on behalf of all mankind in all ages. . . . Hence when worship and prayer are objectively grounded in Christ in this way, we are free to use and adapt transient forms of language and culture in our worship of God, without being imprisoned in time-conditioned patterns, or swept along by constantly changing fashions, and without letting worship and prayer dissolve away into merely cultural and secular forms of man's self-expression and self-fulfilment." Torrance, *Reconciliation*, 213.

24. Fowler suggests that, in fact, this kind of critical reflective activity may even be a source of revelation in and of itself, in a way that is both dialectical and emergent. Fowler argues that while it does not "go so far, as yet, as to suggest that the moments of emergent truth generated in the

dialectic of interpretation between theory and praxis have the status of revelation, this kind of claim seems to me to be a logical extension [of this position]." Fowler, "Practical Theology," 55.

25. Torrance, *Evangelical Theology*, 120.

26. Torrance, *Resurrection*, 147 (emphasis in the original).

27. Fowler, *Theological Education*, 149. "Ecclesial praxis is located between the normativity of the Christian story and vision (Scripture and tradition) and the present historical contexts of mission and praxis (present experiences and situations). Practical theology, as critical and constructive reflection on and guidance for the praxis of the community, draws on the tradition and Scriptures with the hermeneutical aid of the various specialized theological disciplines (exegetical, historical systematic-ethical, and fundamental theology). In its efforts to interpret and respond to present contexts and issues of praxis, it draws on the hermeneutical aids of a variety of humanities and social scientific disciplines. In its own sub-disciplinary foci, practical theology attends to various particular dimensions of ecclesial praxis as models of action in and interaction with persons and contexts of personal and social formation and transformation." Fowler, *Theological Education*, 50.

28. Fowler's concept of ecclesial praxis is not dissimilar to Farley's suggestion of ecclesial presence as being the place where the fragmented aspects of faculty theology can find their unification. "The unifying region of theological studies is ecclesial presence. To grasp ecclesial presence is to engage in a complex, historical undertaking since ecclesial presence is a certain corporate historical way in which faith occurs in the world. At the same time it is also to grasp the normative claims set by that presence, to struggle, in other words, with reality and truth." Fowler, "Practical Theology," 38-39.

29. James W. Fowler, *Faith Development and Pastoral Care* (Philadelphia: Fortress Press, 1987), 17.

30. See John Wesson, "How Cinderella Must Get to the Ball: Pastoral Studies and Its Relation to Theology," in *The Foundations of Pastoral Studies and Practical Theology*, Paul Ballard, ed. (Cardiff, Wales: Board of Studies for Pastoral Theology, The Faculty of Theology, University College, Cardiff, 1986), 60.

31. Torrance, *Resurrection*, 121.

32. Torrance, "The Ministry and the Sacraments of the Gospel," in Thomas F. Torrance, *Conflict and Agreement in the Church*, vol. 1, *Order and Disorder* (London: Lutterworth Press, 1959), 159. See also Thomas F. Torrance, *Royal Priesthood—A Theology of Ordained Ministry*, 2d ed. (Edinburgh: T&T Clark, 1993), 45-47.

33. Thomas F. Torrance, "Service in Jesus Christ," in *Theological Foundations for Ministry*, Ray S. Anderson, ed., (Grand Rapids, Mich.: Eerdmans, 1979), 724.

34. Torrance, *Mediation,* 80.

35. Torrance, *Mediation*, 94 (emphasis in the original).

36. Torrance, *Mediation*, 94-95.
37. Torrance, *Theological Science*, v.
38. Torrance, "Service in Jesus," 718.
39. Thomas F. Torrance, *Divine and Contingent Order* (Oxford: Oxford University Press, 1981), 136.
40. Torrance, *Reconstruction*.
41. Torrance, *Contingent Order*, 138-39.
42. Torrance, *Reconciliation*, 154.
43. Torrance, *Rationality*, 188.
44. "As the incarnate presence of the living God in space and time, he presents himself to our faith as its living dynamic Object. This has the effect of calling for a living theology, a way of thinking which is at the same time a way of living, that cannot be abstracted from the life-giving acts of Christ in the depths of human being and must therefore affect man radically in his daily life and activity." Torrance, *Evangelical Theology*, 138.
45. Don S. Browning, *A Fundamental Practical Theology*, (Minneapolis: Fortress Press, 1991), 10-11.
46. See his essay on "The Atonement and the Holy Trinity," in Torrance, *Mediation*, 99-126.
47. Torrance, *Rationality*, 165ff.
48. I have written further on this in Ray S. Anderson, "The Resurrection of Jesus as Hermeneutical Criterion—A Case for Sexual Parity in Pastoral Ministry," *TSF Bulletin* (March-April 1986); see also Ray S. Anderson, *The Soul of Ministry: Forming Leaders for God's People* (Louisville, Ky.: Westminster/John Knox Press, 1997), 25-32, 164-65.
49. See the preface to the new edition of Torrance, *Royal Priesthood*, xi-xiv; also Thomas F. Torrance, *The Ministry of Women* (Edinburgh: Handsel Press, 1992).

Chapter 8

Revelation, Scripture, and Mystical Apprehension of Divine Knowledge

by Kurt Anders Richardson

Revelation in Torrance's works is divine self-disclosure: God communicates himself in an act of revelation and attendantly creates knowledge of himself in the human knower. For Torrance, Scripture presents us with positive knowledge of God used to implant knowledge of himself within us as readers. This knowledge of God results from a creative act by God. God is knowable because creation derives its being from God's will to be Creator and because it continuously participates in the life of God.

True to classic Christian themes, the Creator communicates himself to the creation, needy of redemption, through the chief act of redemption, the revelation of himself in the man, Jesus Christ. The Person and Work of Christ, so fully a Trinitarian work, includes the Holy Spirit who has generated not only the creation of life itself, but inspired the great prophets and apostles with the living Word embodied in Scripture.

The great correspondence created in the inspired Scriptures between the dynamic revelation of God and the text is the *depositum fide*, the deposit of faith, which reaches its fulfilment in the *kerygma* concerning Christ. In Torrance's theology, revelation determines both Scripture and the *depositum fide* that is the gracious and therefore relational knowledge of God on the part of the human creature. This deposit makes future understanding possible in an authoritative and yet more than authoritative way, for the deposit of faith generates a mystical or participatory knowledge of God in the human knower. In this essay, I try to lay out the essentials of Torrance's understanding of revelation and Scripture and to point out the mystical dimension of his scientific theological method.

In Barthian fashion, Torrance emphasizes the exclusivity of the revelation of Jesus Christ. Scripture is inspired,[1] but the knowledge of God cannot be coterminus with a knowledge of Scripture. While the words of Scripture are truly revelatory, they achieve their goal as knowledge of God through the hermeneutical guidance of the Holy Spirit in the life of the Church and in the believer. What God reveals by inspired Scripture is truly his Word, but the Scripture leads the hearer/reader beyond itself to the God who communicates himself through Scripture by that same Spirit.

Granted, Scripture contains many texts that are not christological, though they can bear a christological interpretation, but that does not mean that they attain what the New Testament fully means by *apokalypsis*.[2] Revelation is a fulfillment. Revelation is fulfilled when a knowledge relation is attained between the Creator and the human creature, and on this basis among other creatures, especially in the Church.

Torrance, throughout his oeuvre, places great emphasis upon a reconciliation of the objective/realist and subjective/idealist forms of knowledge in science through scientific intuitionism.[3] The objective knowing of facts is always interpreted subjectively according to the relations to facts in other disciplines and realms of knowing, finally building into anthropological, cosmological, and ultimately theological modes of reasoning. Yet divine self-knowledge can never be confused with creaturely knowing of the divine. A dualism between the objective and subjective is also intolerable since it misses something fundamental about reality, that the Creator has formed the world not only to be but also to be known.

The contingent and therefore ordered cosmos is intelligible to human beings created in God's image because in a fundamental way human cognition has been created to correspond to the *arche* of divine intelligence. Although contingent itself, the capacities of human rationality in the face of the intelligibility of the universe preclude dualism in every form. The relationality of divine and the human intelligence is not one where both share a single mind, but one where the rational features of the created relation between the two are made naturally to cohere.

While this is an objective knowing by subjects, both divine and human, its overall condition is a mystical and participatory one, where the features of knowing cognition are satisfied without a constructivist move to the mythic. By mystical interpretation then

Torrance means a kind of intuition that is occasioned by the unique relational knowing of God by the creature.[4]

One way that mystical reading entered into early Reformation theology was the full explication of various renderings of *ordo salutis*. Barth recovers the *ordo* this way: illumination, justification, new obedience, mystical union—the mystical (not an actual mystic*ism*) being not salvific but experiential in Christ. Through mystical union with Christ nurtured by the Holy Spirit there results an illumination, an understanding of the Gospel on God's terms where revelation begins to achieve its fulfillment, an understanding that arises from participation in the gracious life of God.

Torrance grew into his own view of the mystical apprehension of divine knowledge through the Fathers and the balance of the *apophatic* and *kataphatic* traditions. Rather than drawing upon the Dionysian or Eckhartian traditions, Torrance looks to Athanasius and the Cappadocian Fathers for his orientation toward the mystical.

Works such as St. Basil the Great's *Epistle 234* offers us a fine example of the apophatic, mystical theology in the Orthodox tradition. In contemplating the being of God, Basil argues that what the theologian knows is not the essence of God but only his works and his attributes through a revelation which itself can never be ultimate:

> [God's] operations are various,
> And [his] essence simple,
> But we say that we know our God from his operations,
> But do not undertake to approach near to his essence.
> His operations come down to us,
> But his essence remains beyond our reach.

Basil's distinction between the operations and essence becomes fundamental for a proper reception of divine knowledge.

Although revelation comes by divine initiative in self-disclosure, it is never more than the words or actions chosen by God to accomplish this self-disclosure within the created realm. Created signs are for creatures. Neither God's essence/being nor the fullness of his works/operation can be contained in these signs, but only referred to by them. This is the apophatic nature of the gracious signs of revelation which come to us primarily in Scripture, for all find their focus and fulfillment in Jesus Christ. The function of the scriptural signs must be grasped first by understanding what they are not in order to move on to a comprehension of what they are positively or in a kataphatic way.

The apophatic is not to be separated from the kataphatic of course, as the quote above from Basil shows. The operations of God have reached humanity in the Son's becoming human, in self-giving atonement, and in victorious resurrection. Indeed, according to Torrance, there is a profound relation between God's self-giving in the reconciling work of atonement and his self-giving in revelation embodied in Scripture. Here the unity of reconciliation and revelation can be perceived. Revelation in terms of Scripture's concrete and particular forms presupposes reconciliation, and reconciliation presupposes the self-revealing God who does so entirely according to his gracious purpose. There is no revelation without reconciliation.

Furthermore, in Scripture the operations of God are no more immediately accessible than the being of God and yet, since the truth of both are conveyed, positive knowledge, created by the Spirit within the knower, can be attained. Torrance's now famous notion of the simultaneous knowing of God's being in his action, while knowing his action in his being, sums up this relation with great precision.

More comprehensive even than the unity of reconciliation and revelation is the Christology of revelation flowing from the unique time of Christ's appearing and its extension, by the Holy Spirit, through the kerygma of the New Testament Gospels. It is in this sense that Torrance accounts for Scripture as the unique medium of divine knowledge. The deposit of faith embodied in Scripture communicates God's self-revelation in Jesus Christ through the illumination of the Holy Spirit. For our purposes here, the collection of essays *Divine Meaning: Studies in Patristic Hermeneutics*[5] will be our primary resource. In these studies, Torrance gives one of his fullest accounts of the doctrine of Scripture as the vehicle of revelation in relation to the Church's divine knowledge and understanding.

Divine Self-Revelation and Scripture in Torrance

Torrance begins with this statement: "The Source of all our knowledge of God is his active revelation of himself. Although the context of this knowledge is God's creation and presence to his people, the church of old and new covenants, this context surrounds the production of the Scriptures."[6] The Scripture is not "active revelation" apart from the presence of the Holy Spirit working everywhere and at all times with its readers in the Church.

The Spirit's constant action upon the text within the ecclesial context makes for the transcendent knowledge of himself as the Scripture points beyond itself to the God who would communicate with humanity through its statements and signs. What Torrance sets up is a distinction between the Word of God, that is God's self-communication to humanity ultimately as the Person of Christ, and Scripture as the product of the Spirit's inspiration of prophets and apostles among the people of God, yet the Word of God that is Scripture.

In rather traditional fashion, the inspiration of the Scripture by the Holy Spirit and the providential preservation and dissemination of that Scripture are stated plainly by Torrance. Scripture is "the written form of the Word of God." Revelation through Israel was "translated appropriately" into human speech so that in this covenantal community the Word of God might be "assimilated and understood," ultimately including all humanity.[7] This prophetic word reaches its fulfilment in Jesus, the incarnation of the divine Word in Person. And again, through the apostolic witness and tradition, i.e., *kerygma* and *didache*, Jesus Christ the risen Lord communicates himself as the one and only Mediator to the Father and Savior of all through the great deposit of faith that is the apostolic testimony together with the prophet of the Old Testament.

As such, the Scriptures are only and always the "source and norm of all revealed knowledge of God and his saving purpose in Jcsus Christ."[8] All Christian doctrine emanates from the scriptural sources, and therefore close readings and constant reexamination of the texts are necessary for determining the function and essence of this source and norm. The Church's kerygma and didache must come under continual review; because of their very fallible nature, they have always only approximated the revealed truth. Because the Scriptures alone are divinely inspired, they alone mediate the divine ground upon which all other human statements can be judged.

Torrance emphasizes that it is by the Scriptures that "the truth as it is in Jesus" (Eph. 4:21) is acquired and the *hupachoe pisteos*—"the obedience of faith" (Rom. 1:5; 16:26) verifies that the Word of God has been truly heard.[9] Action that is not the result of the free response to this Word is not actually the obedience of faith but the product of the Church's religious imagination. Drawing upon the hermeneutics of *Theological Science*, Torrance refers to the genuine *audits* that result from hearing the Word of God through Scripture, a Word one can hear no place else.[10] "Genuine audits" are those faithful notions that correspond to Scripture and can only arise from it. Doctrinal norms (faithful notions that derive consensually from Scripture) formulated in the Church's confessions then require constant testing of their conformity to Scripture which alone mediates divine revelation.

What is vital here is Torrance's claim that this doctrine of Scripture (faithful to Scripture and tradition) is necessary to the proper "understanding and interpretation of the witness and testimony of the Holy Scriptures."[11] Acknowledging this view of Scripture will in turn aid in avoiding bifurcations between form (human words) and content (divine self-comunication) in receiving and understanding revelation.

Torrance offers four theses as essential to the doctrine of Scripture.

1. The Scriptures are the written form of the Word of God, so that the Word of God is heard through them. Such a claim cannot be substantiated by evidence other than what God offers on its behalf. God is not, after all, at our disposal, probative or otherwise. Only self-critical humility, yieldedness and receptiveness on the part of the faithful hearer can begin to adequately engage with this form of divine revelation.

2. The Bible is the vehicle of the voice of God which speaks through the words of prophetic and apostolic men and ultimately the man Jesus. The Bible is not sacramental, it is more; it is the human verbal instrument that has been appropriated by God and is analogous to the unity of the divine and human in the one and the same Jesus, Son of God. But there is no hypostatic union between the voice of God and the voice of humanity in Scripture—there is only one incarnation, the God/man, Jesus Christ.

Thus it is by participation in the divine reality of revelation that the form of Scripture achieves its status as Word of God. The inspired Scriptures and the Word of God do not undergo a *communicatio idiomatum*; the human word is always dependent upon the divine, always remains a fully human word and must never be confused with the divine Word. Indeed, there is a "real text" that we are after and that is the "*humanity* of Jesus Christ,"[12] since we only hear the Word of God when we hear him in the words of inspired Scripture.

3. The Scriptures, for all their greatness, do not display the divine glory, but are a dim mirror and a partial testimony to it (1 Cor. 13:12). Indeed, just as the flesh of Christ itself originated from our fallen humanity and bore all the marks of its fallenness and corruption, so the Scripture reflects our corruption as well. Torrance expounds upon this:

> The written form which the Word of God has taken in the Bible is in accord with the actual way taken by the Word of God when

> he became incarnate in Jesus Christ in the likeness of our flesh of sin but in such a way as to condemn sin in the flesh. . . . so we must think of the Word of God in the Scriptures not only as accommodating himself to us in our weakness and littleness but as condescending to enter into our alienated and contradictory ways of thought and speech in order to reach us with his message and to restore us to converse with God in truth. Thus the Word of God comes to us in the Bible not nakedly and directly with clear compelling self-demonstration of the kind that we can read it off easily without pain and struggle of self-renunciation and decision, but it comes to us in the limitation and imperfection, the ambiguities and contradictions of our fallen ways of thought and speech, seeking us in the questionable forms of our humanity where we have to let ourselves be questioned down to the roots of our being in order to hear it as God's Word. . . . It is because the Word of God comes to us in this way that either we are offended at it and reject it in order to cling to ourselves, or we believe in it through a decision against ourselves and so hear it by committing ourselves to its action upon us.[13]

Torrance is indicating that Scripture is to the Word of God what the flesh of Christ is to the flesh of all humanity, something on the order of the second *homoousion* of the Chalcedonian formula. Borrowing an analogy from Luther, the Word of God of the Bible is heard only through a kind of redemptive reading that corresponds to a *theologia crucis* over against a *theologia gloria*. With the former there is an acknowledgment of human corruption and an embracing of this offense, rather than the latter and its controlling presupposition of immediate perfection and a self-demonstration of transcendent deity.

4. Indeed carrying the paradigm of *theologia crucis* still further, for the Bible to be heard for what it is, the Word of God, it must be heard within the experience of God's saving action in Christ. Scripture is part of the unity of divine action in revelation and reconciliation, in "self-impartation" and "atoning propitiation" (cf. Eph. 2:12-22). The appropriation of the "wayward and recalcitrant" human word by the Divine Word to bring that human word into conformity and obedience to the divine purpose is analogous to the seizing by Christ of our fallen humanity in the incarnation and bringing it under the judgment of God in order to redeem it.

The Bible speaks to corrupted creation because it is the instrument selected out of that same creation to bear the redemptive Word itself, an instrument requiring "the cleansing and atoning activity of the cross." Strikingly, Torrance cites Hebrews 9:19 where the atoning act of sacrifice cleanses the text of Scripture as well as the people who hear its word of reconciliation. Taken as a mere literary phenomenon, the Bible is an imperfect and inadequate text. Yet this is not what it actually is, as the Scriptures, when appropriated by "God's inerrant Holy Word," are made to "serve his reconciling revelation and the inerrant communication of his Truth."[14]

Just as there is to be no christological "confusion of attributes," there is also no "communication of attributes" until the corrupt form of the dying humanity of Christ (the "likeness of sinful flesh," see Rom. 8:3; Phil. 2:7) is exchanged for glorified humanity in resurrection. Scripture participates in the present, yet to be redeemed, nature of creation and will itself pass away with the present form of this world, but "the Word of God which it has been inspired to convey to us does not pass away but endures for ever."[15]

The Scriptures, in all they communicate and in every part, cannot but be the vehicle of the Word of God himself. Yet at the same time, the Word of God cannot be confused with what the Scriptures are, the inspired word of humanity, participating in the sanctity of the Word but not yet the glory of the same. Scripture too, as it were, awaits the consummation.

Torrance moves on to the hermeneutical essentials connected with reading the Scripture in order that the divine/human unity that it is can be properly attended to. The rules of reading Scripture[16] go beyond a mere attentiveness to the text, and must become a form of "scientific hermeneutics." While universal rules of understanding apply, they reflect only a way of working with the basic meaningfulness of linguistic communication. But as Scripture directs its readers' attention to God, biblical hermeneutics creates itself because of the compelling content of the communication. And since the Bible so often is involved as the text of inquiry in hermeneutics in general, the two are virtually inseparable.

Thus in the call to hear the Word of God from the Bible, one learns about "hearing" from texts, i.e., the openness that is a listening without the imposition of our own communication and thereby a violation of Scripture's communication. It is upon the truth that God communicates with humanity in personal terms that we understand what interpersonal communication is truly about and fashion our hermeneutical rules accordingly.

Far from being a postmodern hermeneutic of indeterminate meaning from disparate localities, Torrance asserts (reflecting Barth's denial of a "special hermeneutics" for theology[17]) that a universally valid hermeneutics is always in view. Torrance agrees with Barth's caution that biblical hermeneutics does not present "a mysterious thing . . . which applies only to the Bible."[18]

In the Bible then, human language has been, in Torrance's words, "assimilated to the communication of God's Word" so that it has as human speech "healing and redemptive significance."[19] And because the biblical text draws human beings into relation with God as a text, it shapes other forms of general knowing through texts as well.[20] Citing Schleiermacher's axiom that Christianity exerts a "language moulding"[21] influence over every other use of language gets at what Barth and Torrance are after here. This is the result of the Bible's unique "*idiomata*" that require special study and reflection. In this way of reading Scripture, its truly theological sense[22] comes through, and it is apprehended through a kind of mystical and participatory process of knowing.

Mystical Apprehension of Revelation in Torrance

If we are to consider what Torrance means by the mystical moment in the apprehension of the knowledge of God in revelation through Scripture, we must first of all be clear about what he does not mean. First and foremost, it means that there is no mystical knowing of God apart from or beyond Christ. In every aspect of God's revelation beginning with the prophets and continuing through the apostles there is no vehicle independent of Christ for the knowledge of God, as God is known only through him.

The native spiritual resources of the human are damaged and misdirected in such as way that the mystical path cannot achieve what God has offered to humanity in the incarnation of the Son. Second, the gnostic path of mystic speculation is also closed in that its metaphysical pattern simply does not correspond to whom God truly is as known in Jesus Christ. Finally, the classic philosophical path that is determined to place the impersonal cosmos and its ultimate forces and truths ahead of the personal and living God as revealed in Scripture is also a mystical path bypassed by Torrance, for it wrests those Scriptures from their intentional bases to supply them with unintended meaning through allegorical interpretation.[23]

Where Torrance discerns the mystical is in the communion of the redeemed with the Redeemer and therefore in participation with God in God's own Triune life. In this communion, the human knower is raised up through the statements of Scripture to a knowledge of God that grasps the Trinitarian whole (Father, Son, and Holy Spirit) of that which has been revealed by Christ, elicits a personal knowing that is interpersonal and inclusive of the creature, and results in true *theologia*, real knowledge of God in God's own Trinitarian reality. This is nothing less than the gracious participation of redeemed existence proleptically enjoyed by faith, and mediated under the aid and guidance of Scripture.

Torrance derives this mystical apprehension (the true *theologia* of Christian knowledge) from the Greek Father's methodology, especially Athanasius (ultimately Origen). Torrance develops this methodology further through his appropriation of Polanyi's "tacit knowing" and more importantly the concept of "indwelling."[24] The following extended quote lays out Torrance's perspective quite well:

> it presupposes the all-important level of intuitive intellective contact with divine reality which is the creative source of our basic convictions and primary concepts and relations. It is through religious experience, in the context of tradition in the continuity of the life of the Church where learning through others, meditation upon the message of the Holy Scriptures, prayer and worship regularly take place, that these basic convictions and primary concepts take their rise. As in every other area of human knowledge this is the level on which we participate in the natural organisation created in the empirical field under the compelling structure of objective reality, and thereby gain our initial insight into the fundamental pattern of things and acquire the first significant clues which prompt and direct further inquiry at a deeper level. It is then at this level (which of course we never leave behind) that we engage in what Polanyi calls *tacit knowing*, in which we come to know more than we can actually tell at the time, but in which we may begin to pass from implicit to explicit awareness through the process which he describes as *indwelling*. This is the activity in which we let our minds dwell within some context of experience, using the framework which it supplies to help us gain access to deeper and fuller meaning. It is significant that Polanyi should use here the language found in the Fourth Gospel, where Jesus speaks of the mutual indwelling between himself and his disciples, their dwelling in his Word and his dwelling in them through the Spirit, enabling them to enter into more intimate knowledge of his mind as the revelation of the Father, and so be led forward into the truth. It is in this way that there take shape in our minds the primary concepts which are directly and intuitively connected with the basic complex of Christian experience, and which we need for scientific theological activity.[25]

All of the background elements of the mystical dimension of

theological knowing are here: the doxological, the suprarational, the transcendent, the experiential, the surplus of knowing, mutual indwelling, and divine participation, all in the encounter with the Scripture.

An added dimension comes through a little later in the essay where Torrance describes humanity as contingently constituting "the boundary conditions" between heaven and earth, the transcendent and the immanent. Humanity is the place where "the universe is kept open to its transcendent ground which is the source of its meaning."[26] Torrance continues:

> Looked at in this way, it may well be said that religious experience and theological understanding can and should play a fundamental role in the development of science in helping it both to overcome the materialist obsession with perceptible, tangible magnitudes and to break free from the paradigmatic preoccupation of western culture with observational images, but also more positively in cultivating in human society the ability to apprehend imperceptible, intangible magnitudes, upon which science more and more relies as it penetrates more and more deeply into the non-observable structures regulating the universe and our understanding of it. Only as man's mind is constantly lifted up in wonder and worship toward God the Creator of the space-time universe so that his thought is ultimately anchored in factors that transcend the universe altogether, will he be able to think in detachment from the refractory effects of split space and time and the reductionist observationalism and materialism that seem regularly to result from the old homogeneous geometrical structures of space independent of time.[27]

In light of this last quotation, precisely what Torrance means by mystical appropriation of the truth of Scripture comes into view.

In Torrance's theology, mystical appropriation in the knowing of God through the Scripture must not be confused with mystical exegesis, allegorical exegesis, or spiritual/speculative exegesis—or a kind of eisegesis actually. The most Torrance wants is a Justinian typological reading with the understanding that Scripture needs to be translated into participatory understanding and worship.

What Torrance finally seems to be after is a *mystical realism* of reading Scripture in communion with God by the Spirit who inspired the Scripture. It is not allegorical or "eisegetical" interpretation that comes into view, but an interpretation that "must seek to lay bare the *internal hermeneutic* already embedded within the Scriptures."[28] Torrance speaks commonly here of a mystical apprehension that strips itself of all preconceptions and yields the mind wholly to the impressions that the text will make upon it.

In this way the "internal hermeneutic" mediated by the presence of the Holy Spirit will produce the fruit of the knowledge of God's reality. This apprehension must move on to appropriate doctrinal formulation that does not go beyond the text (nor need it to), since interpreting Scripture should function to advance the communion between God and rational creatures.

Yet even theological/doctrinal statements, once they have been grounded in the interpersonal knowledge elicited by Scripture and the Spirit, must not be formulated in such a way that they become closed systems of reference. Technical and dogmatic statements in Christian knowledge and worship also must always "point away from themselves" so that they too serve the communion of the Church with her Lord and thereby more fully correspond to the realities of the reconciled relationship with God.

The Convergence of Dogmatic and Mystical Theology

Torrance develops the epistemology legacy of Einstein and agrees with Polanyi's statement that the "Einsteinian process of thought" is "a new epistemological method of speculative discovery."[29] This kind of "creative scientific discovery . . . is unformalisable."[30] This further comports, according to Torrance, with James Clerk Maxwell's "new mathesis" that typifies modern science. Basically, Maxwell means a kind of disciplined use of scientific axioms that are revisable as new discoveries are made,[31] much like the Popperian paradigm for theorectical progress.

This kind of rigorous theoretical openness will form the basis for what Torrance wants in theological science, an "axiomatic dogmatics." In such a theological orientation, dogmatics in theology is not only "grounded in and informed by divine revelation, but a dogmatics operating with fluid axioms in the modern style." This kind of theology, while remaining singularly devoted to the "material or doctrinal content of Christian knowledge of God," will avoid the sterility of "axiomatisation in the old sense leading to closed logico-deductive systems."[32]

Taking a cue here also from Kurt Gödel's theorem of the impossibility of any system containing a principle of complete self-explanation, Torrance advocates an orientation in theology whereby "dogmatic structures . . . cannot be complete in themselves if they are to be meaningful and consistent. They must have constituent elements or basic concepts that are not decidable or provable within the systematic organisation of the general body of our theological concepts."[33]

In this way the ongoing task of theology becomes the progressive clarification of understanding, the uncovering of heretofore unrecognized relations between the knowledge of God and of created reality, and most importantly, transcendent knowledge in relation to the living, personal God himself. This, finally, affords Torrance the occasion to introduce the full extent of his thinking about theological knowledge as it is apprehended at its uppermost levels in human experience:

> That is to say, dogmatic theology may be axiomatised in a consistent and meaningful way only if at decisive points it is correlated with *mystical theology*, for it is in mystical theology that the boundary conditions of our dogmatic formalisations are kept open toward the transcendent and unlimited Rationality and Freedom of the living God. Dogmatic theology of this kind is informed by concepts that are both worthy of the nature of God and empirically relevant in the world he has made.[34]

One of the "decisive points" is the reading of Scripture, which for Torrance is ever present in every account of what he means by the reality and reception of the knowledge of God.

Torrance's introduction of this relationship of mystical theology to dogmatic theology is only surprising when we either do not see its relationship to everything else he has proposed or if we neglect to see how so much of what he had been claiming about the human knowledge of the divine through Jesus Christ and the Scriptures already manifested this dimension. One can hardly miss the frequent references to the epistemological portrayals of Polanyi's "tacit dimension" and what Torrance regards as "the inarticulate grasp of reality . . . upon which all rational knowledge and all scientific inquiry rely."[35]

In a fascinating way, Torrance unfolds his convictions about an immediate apprehension of all the objects of knowing in this way as an essential aspect of all knowing. "In itself it is a non-formal apprehension of reality, but it constitutes the necessary ground or condition for all explicit knowledge such as we develop in the various sciences" (obviously and especially theological science).[36] Only this understanding of our intelligent relation to the intelligibility of the universe and of God can maintain our ever knowing and coming to know more of the "finite but unbounded universe which he has created."[37] Mystical theology characterizes a dimension of depth in the task and joy of knowing God and can best be understood in terms of the tacit dimension of all human knowing.

It is in a discussion of the "social coefficient of knowledge" that Torrance elaborates upon what he means by the inclusion of the mystical dimension in theology. He writes of four emphases inherent in the social coefficient of the knowledge of God: the first being the hearing and obeying of God's Word in the life of the Church; the second, within the wider world of knowers, scientific and otherwise. The third emphasis requires that the "theologian must find a place in his inquiry into the knowledge of God for *mystical theology*."[38] Fourth, here the "extra-logical relation to God" can flourish since there is no way to formalize this relation anyway. In this way "dogmatic theology cannot afford to neglect the function of mystical theology in sustaining the bearing of his mind ontologically upon God himself, if it is to assume the epistemological unity of form and being both in what he knows and in his knowing of it."[39]

Indeed, like all rational concepts, there must be in theology an indeterminacy at some point in all doctrines because they refer to realities beyond the concepts, and therefore beyond a single level of epistemological reference. They require a "meta-theological reference to a higher level in order to be ontologically significant as well as theoretically consistent." Access to this higher level comes through "an informal, intuitive apprehension of God who is infinitely greater than we can comprehend within the bounds of our conceptual patterns and dogmas."[40] Thus we arrive at the level of mystical theology.

Mystical theology, as a dimension of theological science, is the intuitive counterpart to the Church's worship and meditation and is also a corrective, "restraining the systematic impulse of dogmatic theology."[41] The fullness of theology does give expression to the full range of what humans may know and experience in relation to God, which at certain points must be understood in mystical terms. Systematics is not at all eliminated, but restrained, so that it does not overstep its own limitations thereby attempting to cancel out the intuitive, the participatory, the mystical metatheological dimension of dogmatic theology.

Torrance finds this restraining function in John of Damascus's masterful account of the apophatic in theology.[42] Revelation comes to humanity through specially created coordinates within created reality (in this case, the Scriptures). When appropriated through the mystical dimension, revelation then leads the knower "to the ineffable Being and spiritual Reality of God, in such a way that it not only reminds us of their finite limitations but keeps them ever open toward the inexhaustible Mystery of God's Love."[43]

By this means the individual and the community of faith have a way to express their participatory knowledge of God who transcends the particular, historical, and finite of all those vehicles of knowledge and experience by which God has chosen to reveal himself. But in the case of the mystical dimension there is an elevation of knowledge beyond the contextual to a relational knowing of God which is "to be transported in wonder, and in wonder to think ahead of concept and word, and reach an apprehension of God that outstrips what can be formalised."[44]

This is not, however, the reintroduction of a *theologia gloria* which the Reformation, especially in Luther, so roundly condemned in favor of the biblical *theologia crucis.* Torrance does not imply that there is a kind of "heavenly context" into which one ascends to acquire a mystical *visio dei* thereby rendering the biblical text inferior in respect to what is already available to the mystical adept. Instead, along Trinitarian lines, the mystical dimension of God's active interpersonal communication with us leads us to express, however informally, the reality of this divine/human communion.[45] It is a part of theological knowledge that must not be relegated to a separate sphere of piety or devotion.

The mystical dimension in theology must find expression because theology itself presents us with a stratified account of truth.[46] Dogmatic theology must demonstrate its "correlation with divine revelation which it needs if it is to fulfill its task in a godly way worthy of the Being and Nature of God."[47] When theology stops short in historical-critical exegesis, systematic formulation or even natural theology of its fullest mystical and participatory expression, it fails to offer its unique contribution to other fields of human knowing in the sciences. Beyond offering a certain *mythos* to the sphere of religious systems in the world, the mystical dimension in theology gives expression to the reality of humanity's essential relatedness to God. This is something only theology is called upon to do and it is a tragic failure if it does not find appropriate modes of expression and voice to do so.

Critical and Postcritical Movement

I offer here a few short reflections upon Torrance's approach to Scripture.

1. There is no doubt that Torrance's theology of revelation and mystical appropriation are profound contributions, but here one must

consider whether he has not hindered understanding as well as aided it. There are a couple of reasons for this, not least of which is the nature of mystical experience, something not everyone enjoys. There are surely many believing exegetes for whom the very idea of mystical apprehension of divine knowledge sounds strange at best and anti-thetical to proper exegesis at worst. Also, there are numerous mystical schools and methods of mystical reflection. Torrance takes pains to show that the Western traditions tend to be dualistic while the Easterners appear to him to have a much better grasp of "unitive" thinking. Granted, the mystical reading has for its advantage the promise of a kind of knowing that participates in the being and acting of what is known. The problem is the lack of a universally accessible experience of this type of knowing and also a multitude of proposed ways by which one can get there.

2. Scripture's inspiration, it seems, could bear a more exalted role in Torrance's account. While theologians should not attribute perfection to the text of Scripture at any time in its history, Torrance could acknowledge more how the sacredness and authority of the text is always evident to the ecclesial reader(s) and that this is the basis for the confidence in the Scriptures that inspires mystical readings. Rather conspicuously, Torrance uses quite a bit of Western critical thinking about the text of Scripture, but does not employ much of the Western mystical tradition—rightly so, I would add. But it is curious that he can at crucial points leave out the Eastern esteem for the sacredness of the text which goes hand in hand with the Eastern approaches to mystical reading.

3. The inspired Scripture and its disciplined exegesis must be allowed to critique or at least reinforce theology more than it does in Torrance's perspective. Torrance has not yet shown us how this might be done—this is a bit ironic since many of the Fathers and, of course, Calvin himself were simultaneously great theologians and exegetes of Scripture. No doubt Torrance is profoundly aware of recent trends toward a confluence of theological and exegetical reflection and in many ways he actually has helped pave the way for a new openness in this regard.

4. I want to press for a bit more caution on the use of mystical theology since in some ways Torrance seems to be too uncritical of the tradition. There is no doubt that Orthodox theology governs the tradition, but there are significant speculative and ontological issues that occasionally arise. Few Western theologians have been willing to adopt mystical modes of reflection. There is of course a great deal of new scholarship on the mystical tradition, particularly the apophatic type, but it has yet to make a convincing case to a great

many theologians for a modification of their theological practice.

5. None of the above presents fundamental or insuperable problems—there is too much right with Torrance. Torrance's intent is to follow the Scripture to its appointed end: participation in the divine knowledge of the divine and the human. This kind of participatory knowledge of God is wonderfully advanced through his work. His vast contribution then lays the ground work he has so carefully developed for much advancement in theological reflection in the next generation.

Notes

1. Torrance very much reflects Karl Barth on the matter of inspired Scripture and its reality as the sole concretion of the Word of God to humanity. Quoting Barth approvingly: "If God speaks to man, he really speaks the language of this concrete human word of man. That is the right and necessary truth in the concept of verbal inspiration. If the word is not to be separate from the matter, if there is no such thing as verbal inspiredness, nevertheless the matter is not to be separated from the Word, and there is real inspiration: hearing the Word of God, only in the form of verbal inspiration, hearing the Word of God only in the concrete form of the biblical word." Karl Barth, *Church Dogmatics*, I.2, ed. G.W. Bromiley and T. F. Torrance (Edinburgh: T&T Clark, 1956), 532-33, cited in Thomas F. Torrance, *Karl Barth, Biblical and Evangelical Theologian* (Edinburgh: T&T Clark, 1990), 88-89.

2. Cf. Rom. 16:25; 1 Cor. 14:26; Eph. 1:17.

3. Cf. Gabriel Fackre's recent work on revelation and his indebtedness to Torrance in Gabriel Fackre, *The Doctrine of Revelation: A Narrative Interpretation* (Grand Rapids, Mich.: Eerdmans, 1997), 28-30.

4. Cf. Jürgen Moltmann, "Theology of Mystical Experience," *Scottish Journal of Theology* 32 (1979): 501-20; Steven T. Katz, "Language, Epistemology, and Mysticism," in *Mysticism and Philosophical Analysis,* ed. Steven T. Katz (London: Oxford University Press, 1978), 22-74; Anthony N. Perovich, "Mysticism and the Philosophy of Science," *Journal of Religion* 65 (1985): 63-82; Norman Melchert, "Mystical Experience and Ontological Claims," *Philosophy and Phenomenological Research* 37 (1977): 445-63.

5. Thomas F. Torrance, *Divine Meaning: Studies in Patristic Hermeneutics* (Edinburgh: T&T Clark, 1995).

6. Torrance, *Divine Meaning,* 5.
7. Torrance, *Divine Meaning,* 5.
8. Torrance, *Divine Meaning,* 5.
9. Torrance, *Divine Meaning,* 6.
10. Torrance, *Divine Meaning*, 6.
11. Torrance, *Divine Meaning*,6. The obvious circularity of this formulation is quite consistent with Torrance's view of theological science, since its whole pattern of knowing, like any other field, is grounded and shaped by the object to be known, rather than a priori notions or constructs foreign to the object.
12. Torrance, *Divine Meaning*, 7.
13. Torrance, *Divine Meaning*, 9.
14. Torrance, *Divine Meaning*, 10.
15. Torrance, *Divine Meaning*, 10.
16. Not unlike what Peter Ochs introduces in his "The Rules of Scriptural Reasoning," Web-published essay with responses, from the *Society for Scriptural Reasoning* (SSR), <http://www.depts.drew.edu/ssr/nationalssr/NSSR1999rulesSR.html> (1999). These rules reflect his significant reflection upon the work of Charles Peirce from the former's perspective as a Jewish theologian.
17. Citing Barth, *Church Dogmatics,* I.2, 466, Torrance quotes Barth, "It is not at all that the word of man in the Bible has an abnormal significance and function. We see from the Bible what its normal significance and function is. It is from the word of man in the Bible that we must learn what has to be learned concerning the word of man in general." Torrance, *Divine Meaning,* 12.
18. Barth, *Church Dogmatics,* I.2, 472.
19. Torrance, *Divine Meaning*, 12.
20. A point central to Kevin J. Vanhoozer's arguments in *Is There a Meaning in This Text?* (Grand Rapids, Mich.: Zondervan, 1998).
21. Torrance cites Friedrich Schleiermacher, "Die sprachbildende Kraft [*sic*] des Christentums," in *Hermeneutik und Kritik mit besonderer Beziehung auf das Neue Testaments*, *Sämtliche Werke*, I.7 (Berlin: Walter de Gruyter and Co., 1938), 68.
22. Torrance cites Athenagoras in this connection and his *phusikos kai theologikos logos* from his *An intercession on behalf of Christians,* 13.1. There is a further import to this citation for understanding Torrance himself as a theologian who takes the knowledge of God in Scripture and in the Church in such a realistic way that those searching for or merely resting in the apologetical tradition of theology will be sorely disappointed. Instead, with Torrance we have a confidence in the presence and knowledge of God that one must become accustomed to such weighty theological reflection.
23. Torrance, *Divine Meaning*, 15-34.
24. Cf. Thomas F. Torrance, "The Integration of Form in Natural and Theological Science," in *Transformation and Convergence in the Frame of Knowledge: Explorations in the Interrelations of Scientific and*

Theological Enterprise (Grand Rapids, Mich.: Eerdmans, 1984).

25. Torrance, *Transformation*, 93.

26. Torrance, *Transformation*, 98.

27. Torrance, *Transformation*, 99.

28. Torrance, *Divine Meaning*, 419.

29. Cf. Michael Polanyi, *Science, Faith, and Society* (Chicago: University of Chicago Press, 1964), 87.

30. Cf. Michael Polanyi, "The Unaccountable Element in Science," *Transactions in the Bose Research Institute* 24, no. 4 (1961): 175-84.

31. Cf. James Clerk Maxwell, *Scientific Papers*, ed. W. D. Niven, vol. 2 (Cambridge: 1980), 235, cited in Thomas F. Torrance, *Reality and Scientific Theology* (Edinburgh: Scottish Academic Press, 1985), 79.

32. Torrance, *Scientific Theology*, 93.

33. Torrance, *Scientific Theology,* 93.

34. Torrance, *Scientific Theology,* 93 (Torrance's italics).

35. Torrance, *Scientific Theology*, 112.

36. Torrance, *Scientific Theology,* 112.

37. Torrance, *Scientific Theology,* 118.

38. Torrance, *Scientific Theology,* 123.

39. Torrance, *Scientific Theology,* 123.

40. Torrance, *Scientific Theology,* 124.

41. Torrance, *Scientific Theology,* 124.

42. Torrance, *Scientific Theology,* 124. cf. *De Fide Orthodoxa* I.2; 4.

43. Torrance, *Scientific Theology,* 125.

44. Torrance, *Scientific Theology,* 125.

45. Torrance, *Scientific Theology,* 179-200.

46. Torrance, *Scientific Theology,* 144-46.

47. Torrance, *Scientific Theology,* 126.

Chapter 9

A Scientific Theological Method

by Elmer M. Colyer

Theology is the unique science devoted to knowledge of God, differing from other sciences by the uniqueness of its object which can be apprehended only on its own terms and from within the actual situation it has created in our existence in making itself known.[1]

Thomas F. Torrance

Introduction

My encounter with Tom Torrance's theology on the topic of theological method now spans two decades. It is the subject that first generated my interest in his work during my years in seminary when I first read Torrance's highly methodological little book, *Reality and Evangelical Theology*,[2] for a course in pastoral care. My first reading of Torrance was frustrating due to the difficulty of his writing style and his theological perspective which seemed unusual to me. But what I found captivating and valuable was that Torrance had clearly read modern natural science, critical philosophy, and historical/critical biblical studies, and faced the challenges they posed for evangelical and Trinitarian theology head on. Moreover, Torrance had an uncanny ability to expose the assumptions behind these streams of thought and point out their inadequacies with an unparalleled depth and breadth of insight.

As I read Torrance over the years, my admiration for his theology grew as I began to more fully understand what he was trying to accomplish. This is especially true of his integration of rigorous theological method with the evangelical, doxological, Christocentric, and Trinitarian content of Christian faith and theology. Here I find his work to be without peer within evangelical theology.

So I am unashamed of my appreciation of Torrance's work, not the least in the area of theological method. Throughout the body of this chapter, I discuss the contours of his theological method with which I am in essential agreement. The final section will pose a series of questions concerning Torrance's approach to theological method.

A Scientific Theology?

Though it might not be evident from examining a bibliography of Torrance's early publications, the dialogue between theology and natural science and its bearing on theological method have been crucial for Torrance since his undergraduate studies. His interest in this area predates his first encounter with Karl Barth in the mid-1930s. The subject of a *scientific* theological method remains at the center of Torrance's work throughout the rest of his career, even if it only becomes conspicuous in his writings after his groundbreaking book, *Theological Science* (1969), which won the first Collins Award.

The linking of the two terms, scientific and theological, has created significant misunderstanding (and misgiving) about Torrance's theological and methodological vision for many. What exactly does Torrance mean by theological science? Interpreters who employ a preconceived idea of *science* as a *universally applicable method* (*scientia universalis*) will completely miss what Torrance has in mind.

For Torrance, there is no *scientia universalis* with presuppositions and/or procedures to which all special sciences (*scientiae speciales*), including theology, must conform if they are to be *scientific*. In fact, in Torrance's perspective, theology must *not* conform to the presuppositions/procedures of other sciences. For Torrance, theological science, like every special science, *has its own particular scientific requirements and material procedures determined by the unique nature of its object or subject matter.*[3]

There are only various special sciences, according to Torrance, which manifest particular similarities as human forms of inquiry within the same space-time universe. These formal similarities together constitute *scientia generalis* (general science) which has no life or reality apart from the existence of the various special sciences.

Special sciences can and do learn from one another, as Torrance has demonstrated in his dialogue with natural science. Yet each science has to be developed *kata physin*, in strict conformity to the nature of the object it investigates in every aspect of its inquiry (an example of a formal similarity), and when it does so, it is *scientific*. Knowing *how* we know is only one domain of knowledge and cannot be separated from *what* we know.

Thus from Torrance's perspective, theology can be scientific *if* there is a knowable God and *when* theology proceeds in strict accordance with the nature of that knowable God—when it allows actual knowledge of God to determine the appropriate mode of knowing, to disclose the inherent relations in that knowledge, and to generate the conceptual structures and their interrelations appropriate to that knowledge. A scientific theological method is one in which every aspect of method is determined (*kata physin*) by the nature of its "object" or subject matter.

The Basic Principle of Torrance's Scientific Theology

This is the basic principle that runs throughout Torrance's publication on theological method: "It is always the nature of things that must prescribe for us the specific mode of rationality that we must adopt toward them, and prescribe also the form of verification apposite to them, and therefore it is a major part of all scientific activity to reach clear convictions as to the distinctive nature of what we are seeking to know in order that we may develop and operate with the distinctive categories demanded of us."[4] Thus, Torrance defines theology, as we saw at the beginning of this chapter, as "a dogmatic, or positive and independent, science operating on its own ground and in accordance with the inner law of its own being, developing distinctive modes of inquiry and its essential forms of thought under the determination of its given subject-matter."[5] This means that, for Torrance, while we may distinguish between method and content, we must develop method in rigorous correlation with theological content.

Interpreters repeatedly misunderstand Torrance's theological method because they fail to clarify this basic point and read Torrance in light of it.[6] What Torrance really has in mind regarding theological method only comes fully into focus when one is clear about his theological vision regarding the "distinctive nature" of God. So what is "the distinctive nature" of God which must condition every aspect of theological method? Torrance discloses something of his theological vision in several important autobiographical essays where he recounts his early encounters with Schleiermacher and Barth.[7]

Torrance's Theological Vision

During his undergraduate studies at New College in Edinburgh, Torrance read Schleiermacher's *The Christian Faith* and found himself "captivated by the architectonic form and beauty of Schleiermacher's method and his arrangement of dogmatics into a scientific system of Christian doctrine."[8] But Torrance was significantly disturbed because the "fundamental presuppositions of Schleiermacher's approach did not match up to the nature or content of the Christian gospel" (the distinctive nature of theology's subject matter!), and concluded that Schleiermacher's "whole concept was wrong."[9]

Torrance decided that there had to be a more adequate way to develop a "scientific" theology and recounts that "I was determined from then on to make it one of my primary objectives."[10] At this early stage in his career, Torrance was absolutely clear "that any rigorous scientific approach to Christian theology must allow actual knowledge of God, reached through his self-revelation to us in Christ and in his Spirit, to call into question all alien presuppositions and antecedently reached conceptual frameworks, for form and subject-matter, structure and material content, must not be separated from each other."[11]

It was when Torrance turned to Karl Barth's theology (the chapter on the revelation of the Triune God in the *Church Dogmatics* I.1.2), that he began to find what he was searching for "in the doctrines of the *hypostatic union* between the divine and human natures in Christ, and the *consubstantial communion* between the Persons of the Holy Trinity."[12] Here Torrance sensed that he was "probing into the essential connections embodied in the material content of our knowledge of God and his relation to us in creation and redemption and that it might be possible to develop a coherent and consistent account of Christian theology as an organic whole in a rigorously scientific way in terms of its objective truth and inner logic, that is to say, as a dogmatic science pursued on its own ground and in its own right."[13]

Torrance believed that he had discovered the basis for a scientific account of theology "from its Christological and soteriological centre and in light of its constitutive trinitarian structure,"[14] a theology "deeply Nicene and doxological (theology and worship going inextricably together), with its immediate focus on Jesus Christ as

Mediator, and its ultimate focus on the Holy Trinity."[15] A rigorous scientific methodology, Torrance believed, could "isolate the core of basic and central theological concepts and relations, as few in number as possible . . . in order to grasp something of its [theology's] inner coherence and unity, and then use it as an instrument with which to comb through the whole corpus of accumulated beliefs and doctrines in the service of clarification and simplification."[16]

Whenever one reads Torrance's methodological works, one must keep the soteriological/christological center and the overall Trinitarian structure of his theology in mind, and also the goal of a core of basic concepts and relations that will enable theology to grasp the essential organic structure of our actual knowledge of God through Jesus Christ and in the Holy Spirit. When you think of Torrance's theological method, you have to think of how it is that we come to apprehend God through Jesus Christ and the Gospel in the Holy Spirit, how we understand and articulate the basic relations which define these central realities of the Christian faith, and how the doctrines of the *homoousion*, the *hypostatic union*, and the Trinity arise out of our evangelical and doxological knowledge of God.

For Torrance, scientific theology and a scientific theological method can never be more than a clarification and extension of our evangelical and doxological knowledge of God through Jesus Christ in the Holy Spirit mediated through the Old and New Testament of the Bible.[17] It is this theological vision of a *Living* God who *interacts* with us through Jesus Christ and in the Holy Spirit within this universe of space/time, in such a way that we can really know God, that leads to Torrance's incessant conflict with ancient and modern forms of dualism and to his holistic, integrative, and realist theological alternative.

Rejection of Dualism/Affirmation of Realism and Holism

Torrance's rejection of dualism clarifies several crucial aspects of his theology in relation to theological method: his conception of the God-world relation, his understanding of the dynamic interrelationality of reality (ontology—form inherent in being), and his critical realist epistemology (the kind of integration of form in knowing required in order to grasp the form inherent in being). Torrance sees dualism as a perennial temptation for the Church and Christian theology, especially in the patristic and modern periods.[18]

Dualism signifies the separation of reality into two isolated or incompatible domains.[19] In cosmological dualism there is a chasm or gap between God and the world. The Early Church had to cope with Greco-Roman forms of this dualism, whereas in the modern period, Newtonian, deistic, and other forms have been the problem. Yet whether ancient or modern, these cosmological dualisms open up a deep gulf between God and the world which makes any direct involvement of God in the universe of space/time problematic (God's activity becomes a violation of "natural law") or simply impossible.

Those who embrace a dualist cosmological perspective have difficulty accepting at face value what the Bible has to say about God's activity in the world and history. They often view the scriptural witness to God's Agency in the world as premodern mythology or a nonliteral symbolism subject to allegorical or demythological methods of interpretation which allow readers to extract or comprehend the meaning that lies embedded in the mythical or symbolic account.

In epistemological dualism the chasm or disjunction is between the human knower and the object or reality the human subject attempts to know. This kind of dualism asserts that we cannot actually know reality in itself (the *Ding an sich* of Kant's philosophy), because human knowing is always conditioned by the culture, language, and structures/activities of the human mind operative in the process of knowing. What we really know is how the reality appears to us colored by the configurative synthesis of these various elements that are part of human cognitive activity.[20]

In contrast to cosmological dualism and its separation between God and the world (or a panentheist inner identity between God and the world), Torrance characterizes the biblical perspective as "realist" or "interactionist." God closely interacts in a personal way with nature and history, though remains distinct from nature and history.

This interactionist God-world relation enables Torrance to develop a "realist" interpretation of God's dealings with the nation of Israel (reflected in the Old Testament) and of God's self-revelation in the incarnation in Jesus Christ and the outpouring of the Holy Spirit at Pentecost. Torrance conceives of revelation as a real and redemptive *self*-communication by a living God who is free to enter the world of space/time and act within the universe God has created. Torrance rejects a view of revelation as symbols or myths constructed by the human imagination out of heightened religious experience.

Torrance also argues for a critical "realist" epistemology where reality (created or Divine) discloses itself in a manner in which the human knower is able to achieve real understanding. There is a *possible* isomorphism, a *potential* correlation, between the human subject and object that is *presupposed* (an *ultimate belief*) by human beings everywhere in day-to-day life in the world and also *confirmed* by the success of scientific endeavor. Thus Torrance sees *not* a radical disjunction between subject and object that makes knowledge impossible, but an astonishing *continuity* which invites our trust even while it eludes our complete explanation.[21]

Yet, for Torrance, human knowledge is not automatic. There is no *necessary* or *inherent* isomorphism between human subject/mind/thought and reality (there are no final categories in the Kantian sense, no analogy of being in knowledge of God).[22] There can be an actual correlation *if* the human subject actively responds to the self-disclosure of reality in the *appropriate* way.[23] When this takes place there is real knowledge or a transparence between reality and human thought/language.[24] Genuine knowledge (of the created order or God) is possible but not inevitable.

This means that Torrance's realism is *critical*. The human subject does play an active role in all knowledge which always requires the *generation* (discovery and creation) of the appropriate forms of thought and speech (and even life) in order to grasp and understand reality in its intrinsic interrelations and intelligibility (form inherent in being).[25] We will return to a precise discussion of Torrance's understanding of the integration of form in human knowing in a moment.

This brings us to Torrance's holism, a third crucial theme in his rejection of dualism. Torrance's holism is grounded in his ultimate belief about the dynamic interrelationality of reality (ontology—form intrinsic in being) and the kind of inquiry demanded if we are going to apprehend and articulate this interrelatedness (integration of form in knowing).

Torrance calls these interrelations *onto-relations*, relations so fundamental that they are characteristic of, and inseparable from, what realities *are*. The only way to really understand realities is to examine them, not in isolation, but within the web of their interconnections, for realities are what they are by virtue of their interrelations.[26]

The goal of a scientific theology, in Torrance's perspective, is to investigate and bring to articulation (integration of form in knowing) the essential interrelations or intrinsic structure (form inherent in being) embodied in our actual knowledge of God through Jesus Christ and in the Holy Spirit. The goal of scientific theological *method* (Torrance prefers *philosophy of theological science*) "is to clarify the process of scientific activity in theology, to throw human thinking of God back upon Him as its direct and proper Object, and thus to serve the self-scrutiny of theology as a pure science."[27]

Philosophy of theological science helps theology proceed in strict accordance (*kata physin*) with the essential interrelations or intrinsic structure of God's self-revelation (the interactionist God-world relation) and seeks to insure that the conceptual patterns (doctrines) which arise out of critical holistic realist epistemology (integration of form in knowing) express these essential interrelations (form inherent in being).

How does one enter cognitively the dynamic interrelationality of reality in which form and being are inseparable and complex, and have to be grasped and articulated together, simultaneously, as a differentiated whole? Torrance thinks that we cannot proceed by analyzing and isolating discrete particulars or facts and then deducing or abstracting the theoretical element from them. It requires an integrative epistemology.

Epistemology: The Integration of Form[28]

The Integration of Form from Hume through Kant

Torrance accepts the insight crucial to historical consciousness that we are "inevitably and inseparably inside the knowledge relation, from the start to the end, and so cannot step outside of ourselves to an indifferent standpoint from which to view and adjust the relations of thought and being."[29] It was the infamous David Hume who was among the first to call attention to the fact that the act of knowing, even in modern natural science, conditions our knowledge of the real.

Hume raised serious questions concerning Isaac Newton's account of the discovery of scientific concepts. Newton viewed modern natural science as an inquiry into the interconnections between material realities understood in terms of what he called "manifest principles" and their articulation in scientific concepts. These manifest principles and their related concepts, Newton claimed, are *derived by way of abstraction* from observation or *deduced* from phenomena (Newton's conception of the integration of form).[30] Natural science yields *indubitable truth* about nature stated as natural laws (directly abstracted or deduced from observation or phenomena) which express the mathematical characteristics of the natural world (for example, gravity and motion).[31]

The problem in Newton's account of the integration of form (the generation of concepts) which Hume exposed is that important theoretical or conceptual elements like time, space, and causality are not "given" in sense perception and are not directly deduced from observation.[32] Hume's astute and clever analysis demonstrated that no real relation is *observed* between one immediately perceived fact and another in an account of the generation of concepts based *solely* on sense perception.[33] As Hume stated it, "Objects have no discoverable connexion together; nor is it from any other principle but custom operating upon imagination, that we can draw inference from the appearance of one to the existence of another."[34]

When a stone shatters a window, for instance, what we see is a series of sense perceptions. We maintain that the stone "causes" the shattering of the window. Yet the senses only provide a sequence of impressions of the stone and the window. No cause is perceived in light of a strict analysis of sensory perception.[35] So Hume defines cause as "an object followed by another, and whose appearance always conveys the thought to that other."[36]

While this seems contrary to ordinary human experience, Hume's critique created a major impasse for Newton's conception of the integration of form, and therefore for Newtonian natural science, for many crucial scientific concepts, like causality, relation, and substance, are not deduced or abstracted directly from observation.[37] It was Hume's critique that awakened Immanuel Kant from what Kant called his "dogmatic slumber," for it demonstrated the inadequacy of an exclusively empirical approach to knowledge.

Kant developed an alternative account of the integration of form in which a theoretical or conceptual component (not derived by observation) operates together with empirical elements in all human knowledge from ordinary experience to scientific endeavor. The theoretical ingredient, however, is thus transferred to the human pole of the knowing relation. These categories and structures of the mind are a priori and organize the a posteriori empirical component (the data provided by the senses), rendering it intelligible.[38]

This synthetic epistemological perspective which combines the a priori categorical structures of the mind (which are the necessary condition for intelligible experience) with an a posteriori element is Kant's clever contribution to the evolution of epistemology in Western thought, for it develops the fact that the act of knowing conditions all of our cognitive intercourse with the world around us. The problem, however, is that since the categorical structures of the mind are unchanging, Kant was forced to concede that the *human mind is the origin of the uniformity and laws of nature*.[39]

Torrance notes that there is "a profound element of truth here" for "in all our knowing there is a real interplay between what we know and our knowing of it," and "we do not apprehend things apart from a theoretic structure."[40] Yet, Torrance argues that if the categorical structures of the mind determine our apprehension of reality, then objective reality and its intrinsic interrelations play no substantive role in human knowledge which becomes primarily *constructive* and *subjective*.

There is, Torrance grants, a constant coordination of theoretical and empirical ingredients in cognitive activity in which the theoretical component is not directly deduced from phenomena. Yet he asserts that the way beyond Kant "requires a theoretic structure which, while affecting our knowledge, is derived from the intrinsic intelligibility of what we seek to know, and is open to constant revision through reference to the inner determinations of things as they come to view in the process of inquiry."[41]

Torrance thinks that this kind of integration of form is not only possible, but actually takes place both in ordinary human knowing and in successful scientific endeavor (natural and theological).[42] The integration of form occurs through a process of *indwelling* and the *tacit dimension* it involves.

Indwelling

The kind of constant coordination between theoretical and empirical ingredients in human knowing which Torrance envisions is one in which the theoretical affects our knowing, but is open to constant revision in light of the interrelations of things as they come into view in the process of inquiry. This coordination takes place through *indwelling* the inherent interrelations of a particular field of investigation.[43] Indwelling is a holistic, integrative, heuristic, and highly informal process of investigation.

This practice of indwelling leads to an anticipatory insight, an intuitive foreknowledge, what Torrance also calls a *prolepsis* which "takes shape in our understanding under the imprint of the internal structure of that into which we inquire, and develops within the structural kinship that arises between our knowing and what we know as we make ourselves dwell in it and gain access to its meaning."[44] The structural kinship (integration of form) that arises is neither inherent in the human mind, nor deduced from observation, but is nevertheless *real*.[45]

How do we begin in any new arena of inquiry? How do we develop an integrated understanding of Torrance's complex and interconnected theology from his diverse publications? In Torrance's perspective, we *indwell* his work. We research, read, compare, etc., his writings until we assimilate it and arrive at an insight, a clue into the internal relations of his thought which we test and refine through continued heuristic and integrative inquiry so that a structural kinship develops in our knowledge and we find the appropriate concepts with which to understand and articulate his theology. This includes an undeniable ingredient of creative imagination, but an imagination shaped from beyond the human mind by the intrinsic interrelations of field of inquiry.

The Tacit Dimension

This kind of informal, holistic, integrative, and heuristic process of indwelling entails a *tacit dimension*. Crucial to Torrance's epistemology and theological method is his contention that *we know more than we can tell*, for "in addition to our 'focal awareness' and the explicit knowledge to which it gives rise, we always operate with a 'subsidiary awareness' and an implicit knowledge on which we rely in all our explicit operations."[46]

This implicit knowledge develops over a lifetime. Torrance notes that "much of our basic knowledge on which we rely throughout life is gained in our earliest years, as we learn to speak and adapt ourselves to the physical and social world around us."[47] In fact, a child learns more physics by the age of five than she will be able to understand even if she becomes a great scientist.[48] Within scientific endeavor, an implicit knowledge arises in the process of investigation as we indwell the particular field of inquiry. Torrance argues that this implicit informal knowing plays a significant role in all explicit understanding and scientific inquiry.

If, in fact, theories and concepts are coordinated with reality through the tacit coefficient or dimension out of which they arose, Torrance maintains that this requires "a significant modification in what we understand by knowledge, for knowledge cannot then be defined merely in terms of what is explicit, and also in what we understand by reality, for correspondingly, reality cannot be defined in terms of what is only correlated with explicit concepts and statements."[49]

An example of the tacit dimension and place of a subsidiary element in focal awareness which is at the heart of tacit inference is the popular *Magic Eye* pictures. The *Magic Eye* at first appears to be a collage of tiny unrelated figures. However, if one holds the *Magic Eye* near to one's face and slowly moves it away from one's eyes without focusing on the details, one will (may) suddenly "see" an astonishing three-dimensional image. *Magic Eye* pictures "work" because the human mind is able to integrate subsidiary clues to a matrix of intrinsic *interrelations* between the tiny figures which compose the three-dimensional whole (clues that are in one sense hidden amidst the tiny figures). As the mind integrates these subsidiary clues, the 3-D image of the *Magic Eye* comes into focal awareness.[50]

The 3-D image (form) is *intrinsic* to the *interrelations* of the detail of the *Magic Eye* (form inheres in being). The human mind must assimilate and integrate the details *in their intrinsic interrelations* for the 3-D image to come into view (integration of form in knowing).

Another example of the integration that visual perception entails (including the tacit dimension, the process of indwelling, and the informal learning it involves) is the experiments utilizing inverting spectacles.[51] With inverting spectacles, one sees things upside-down or reversed from right to left, and one enters a state of significant disorientation that makes even the most simple everyday tasks extremely difficult. It takes a long time (about eight days) before one can "properly" perceive the world again. Throughout the eight-day period, one passes through a process of tacit learning, as well as active experimentation, not unlike what happens to a child as he first coordinates his vision with his environment.

What is interesting in this experiment where the inverting spectacles alter the *visual* image is that it is the *mental* image (integration of form) that changes by the end of eight painful days of "indwelling" the altered environment.[52] The fact that this change occurs, reveals, Torrance maintains, "how the visual and the conceptual images operate inseparably together in our orientation to the objective structure of the world around us,"[53] and does so through tacit learning. The conceptual ingredient is neither imposed upon, nor deduced from, the visual element, but is *integrated* with it in a way that is holistic, complex, and defies expression in entirely explicit terms. Yet, while to a large degree *tacit*, the integration that occurs is *real*: the theoretical and empirical (the mental image and the perceptual image) are realigned in our apprehension (integration of form in knowing) and again reflect the configuration of form and being in the world around us (form inherent in being).[54]

The Integration of Form in Science

The integration of form in scientific inquiry embodies a similar pattern in which we *indwell* the field we are investigating (sort of like the informal tacit learning and active experimentation that takes place in the eight-day process of reorientation that occurs in the inverting spectacle experiment) until a structural isomorphism arises between what we seek to know and our knowing of it (kind of like the 3-D image we come to perceive in the *Magic Eye* picture). This structural kinship is neither inherent in the mind nor deduced from observation, but is contingent upon the dynamic, interactive, and integrative process of *indwelling* (that entails a tacit dimension) and leads to a *prolepsis* or insight which we develop, refine, and test until we are sure that it is an accurate theory or concept disclosive of the intrinsic interrelations of the reality we are investigating.

It is the fusion of form in being (the interrelationality of reality), Torrance contends, that demands this kind of holistic, integrative, informal, and heuristic epistemology beyond analyzing and isolating particulars or data and then deducing knowledge from them or abstracting knowledge from observation (just as we cannot perceive the *Magic Eye* picture by analyzing and isolating the tiny figures and deducing or abstracting the 3-D image from it).[55] This is in no way to depreciate the significance of analytic and deductive activities which can be of immense help in testing the coherence of the theory and developing its implications.

However, it does mean that Torrance is skeptical concerning the possibility of rendering the integration of form in terms of entirely explicit operations or any kind of a logical bridge between the human mind/concepts/theories and the objective, intrinsic interrelations constitutive of reality. As Daniel Hardy points out, Torrance's understanding of the integration of form and the conceptual frameworks that arise out of it are not like Kant's unalterable categories or Bernard Lonergan's structures of consciousness. Torrance's account of the mind's integrative abilities is "far less consciousness-centered, and far less bound by the limits of rational accounts of the conscious mind."[56]

If there is an ineradicable extralogical relation, an informal tacit dimension, in the integration of form in scientific discovery, Torrance agrees with Polanyi that "any critical verification of a scientific statement requires the same powers for recognizing rationality in nature as does the process of scientific discovery."[57] In the end, the "meaning, the success and the validity of a scientific theory depend," Torrance asserts, "on its *ontological import*, i.e. its *power of objective reference* to point to and reveal the hidden structure in the world to which it is correlated, and which determines its cognitive and heuristic values."[58]

The kind of integration of form Torrance advocates involves

personal agency, but not necessarily *subjective* personal agency, for personal knowledge and personal judgment can be grounded in, and arise out of, the *participatory* process of indwelling the field of inquiry. It is personal knowledge and judgment *in light of* the intrinsic interrelations which come into focus in the course of investigation and provide an objective element for personal knowledge and judgment.[59]

In fact, Torrance argues that "only persons are capable of distinguishing what they know from their knowing of it, and of engaging in sustained self-critical operations in the interest of objectivity and consistency."[60] Thus for Torrance, genuine objectivity and personal agency do not have to be pitted against one another, for personal being is, in fact, the *bearer of objectivity*.[61]

In the end, it is personal participation through the process of indwelling that prevents personal knowledge and personal judgment for being merely subjective, for the structural kinship (integration of form) only arises out of actually engaging the field of inquiry in active experimentation and informal tacit knowing.[62] This element of personal participation is also the reason why, in Torrance's perspective, theology can never be built upon natural science (or vice versa), for theology and natural science involve *dramatically different kinds of personal participation*, so that each must develop its *own distinctive conceptualities and methodologies* in light of the *nature* of the realities each science investigates and indwells, the Living Triune God or the space-time universe.

The Integration of Form in Theology

The Problem of Dualism

However, what Torrance did discover in his encounter with natural science is that natural science and theology have struggled with similar difficulties in the modern period because of the cosmological and epistemological dualisms in the received framework of thought.[63] In fact, Torrance finds that modern theology and critical biblical studies often generated parallel accounts of how form is integrated characterized by analytic, abstract, deductive, and mechanistic procedures similar to those in the history of modern philosophy and natural science from Newton to Kant.[64]

Newton said that he proceeded by observing phenomena and/or isolating data, and on the basis of this "empirical data" he deduced or abstracted his concepts or natural laws.[65] The real problem with this approach is much deeper than Hume's critique revealed and only came into focus after Einstein's work on relativity: the analytic isolation of "empirical data" tends to fragment the *interrelational* character reality (form intrinsic in being), like the electromagnetic field for example (or the space-time continuum), into discrete particles (externally related to one another). This effaces the actual intrinsic relations which are characteristic and constitutive of what realities are (the relations between particles in the electromagnetic field, for example).[66]

Torrance finds parallel problems in modern critical biblical studies and theology which employ modes of inquiry designed to move back through the biblical witness and isolate various textual and pretextual materials in order to arrive at authentic (probable) historical sources (data) out of which to deduce or construct an accurate historical and/or theological portrayal of Jesus, for example. This is necessary, according to modern constructivist epistemology, because the human mind *imposes* its categories (in Kant, a priori, though today more often *cultural-linguistic* or culturally-acquired categories) upon everything it attempts to apprehend. Streams of critical biblical studies and modern theology, Torrance argues, explain the theological cohesion of the Gospels, of the whole New Testament, and of the Old and New Testaments in terms of the Church *imposing* its theological perspective on the earlier sources.[67] Needless to say, the "real" historical Jesus constructed from the "empirical data" isolated by critical historiography bears little similarity to the Jesus Christ of classical ecumenical Christian faith which comes to expression in the Nicene Creed.

The problem with the various versions of this basic modern critical approach, according to Torrance, is that it fragments the intrinsic interrelations of Scripture and of the realities to which Scripture bears witness (form inherent in being) by separating the various books of the New Testament from one another, breaking up the natural cohesion of the Gospels into various fragmentary sources, and even severing the Old and New Testaments. This kind of analytic isolation of data effaces the very intrinsic interrelations characteristic and defining of Jesus Christ and the Gospel, for Torrance argues that the Old Testament constitutes the very matrix of relations between God and humanity, the suitable forms of thought, speech, and life in Israel (adapted by God over the centuries of God's interaction with the Jewish people), within which alone Jesus Christ could be recognized as the Son of God, the Savior of the world, and his death on the cross interpreted as an atoning sacrifice for human sin.[68]

Think of the Bible as somewhat like a giant literary *Magic Eye* which bears the imprint (form intrinsic in being) of God's *oikonomia* (the divine *Realities* and saving events of God's self-revelation) amidst clues imbedded in the Bible's massive detail. In Torrance's perspective, breaking up the Bible by isolating the sources makes it impossible to grasp God's *oikonomia*, somewhat like breaking up the *Magic Eye* and merely analyzing its detail hampers one's capacity to *integrate* the clues to the distinctive intrinsic interrelations of the detail and apprehend the 3-D image embedded in the picture. Torrance argues that God's *oikonomia* only comes into view as we indwell the conjoint witness of Scripture (OT and NT, all of the Gospels and Epistles) until we assimilate it (and it assimilates us) in an *integrative* perception of its witness to God's self-revelation and self-communication, somewhat analogous to the way our subsidiary awareness of marginal clues leads to an integration and focal awareness of the 3-D image of the *Magic Eye*.

Any perspective or method (like those of modern critical biblical studies and theology mentioned above) that prohibits an integrative, holistic, and theological approach to the interpretation of the Bible is suspect on several levels from Torrance's theological and methodological orientation. These kinds of methods seldom lead to robust Trinitarian theology (the distinctive *Christian* doctrine of God) of classical ecumenical Christian consensus. In addition, similar perspectives and methods have been radically questioned and set aside in natural science due to the scientific advance that has taken place in Maxwell, Einstein, Polanyi, and others. If similar perspectives and methods are inadequate in those fields, Torrance thinks we should be suspicious of parallel approaches in theology.[69]

Torrance's Integrative, Holistic, and Theological Approach

The first step to be taken in the approach Torrance advocates is that we *indwell* biblical witness until a structural kinship develops between the human mind and the intrinsic pattern of God's *oikonomia* (the distinctive Trinitarian pattern of God's revealing and saving activity in Jesus Christ and the Holy Spirit within Israel) out of which Scripture arose and to Scripture bears witness.[70] Since this order is complex and interrelated and must be grasped holistically (we have to understand Jesus Christ and the Gospel within the matrix of Israel, for example), the method employed must be comprehensive and integrative. Indwelling is the informal integrative process that enables our minds to expand, attend to all that the biblical witness entails, and assimilate it holistically until we attain the clues or insights which allow us to begin to apprehend and articulate the complex order and intrinsic interrelations with which theology is concerned.[71]

Of course, it is this complex fusion of form (the intrinsic interrelations) in God's *oikonomia* that requires an integrative and holistic kind of knowing far beyond merely analyzing sources, isolating this historical data, and then deducing theoretical elements from what is left (which is an inadequate approach to the complexity of electromagnetic fields, the space-time continuum, or God's *oikonomia*). What is radically different in theological inquiry, compared to natural science, at this point, is that theology is concerned with a scriptural witness to a Living God who has come to us in *redemptive* self-communication. This calls for a level of participation beyond what we find in natural science. The clues or insights important to theology only develop out of a personal, intimate, ongoing, and participatory contact with, and indwelling of, the Living Reality of God's *oikonomia* through the conjoint witness of the Bible.

The Role of the Church and Tradition in Theology

For Torrance, the place where we indwell the Scriptures and the kind of order theology investigates, and gain the insights or anticipatory conceptions theology develops into doctrinal formulations, is within the Church, the people of God in worship, fellowship, and service of Jesus Christ: "It is through religious experience, in the context of tradition in the continuity of the life of the Church where learning through others, meditation upon the message of Holy Scripture, prayer and worship regularly take place, that these basic convictions and primary concepts take their rise."[72]

The reason for this is that the Bible is more than simply a collection of historical documents with complicated textual and pretextual histories; it is the divinely inspired medium through which God continues to speak and draw people into participation in the *Realities* to which it bears witness. Torrance maintains that in a similar way that a child learns more about physics in her first five years than she will be able to fully understand if she becomes a brilliant physicist, so we come to know more about God within the Church that participates in the Gospel than we will ever be able to comprehend and articulate.[73]

All scientific pursuits are related to communities and their perspectives and paradigms within which we live and think. Torrance thinks that all knowledge includes a personal and social coefficient, including the knowledge of God that theology develops.[74] This is merely an implication of the fact that we are always already within the knowing relation and that we do not apprehend anything without a conceptual framework that is learned rather than innate.

In Torrance's theology, God's relation to humanity is not merely an event, for God's self-revelation calls into existence a *community of reciprocity* in active relation to God, progressively molded by God through space-time, first in the nation of Israel, then in the Apostolic community Jesus Christ drew to himself (within Israel), and now in the Church as the Body of Christ.[75] The Church provides what Torrance calls "the semantic focus" within which people's apprehension of and relation to God is established and nurtured.[76] Theology is always faith seeking understanding in an attitude of prayer and thanksgiving within the evangelical and doxological life of the Church.[77]

Torrance finds this is the kind of theological inquiry taking place throughout the history of the Church and particularly in certain crucial periods. Though not uncritical of tradition, Torrance maintains that real apprehension and articulation of the intrinsic interrelations constitutive of the *Realities* with which theology is concerned is not only possible, but has in fact taken place, for example, in the classical conciliar theology that came to expression in the Niceno-Constantinopolitan Creed and in the Reformation.

For this reason, Torrance's theological method includes substantive dialogue with the history of theology in light of which he develops his own theological position. Daniel Hardy has correctly identified the way Torrance utilizes what he learns from his historical work to discriminate genuine advance from various distorted developments in this history.[78] This is not a naive circularity, but rather a critical yet sympathetic correlation between truth apprehended in the past and truth appropriated ever anew in the present. The success of this correlation reinforces Torrance's critical realist methodology and, in Hardy's words, "provides a powerful argument for the normalcy—as against alternatives—of both the content and the method which he [Torrance] advocates."[79] Of course, Torrance's use of tradition is always in service of his scientific intent: to allow the nature of the reality which theology investigates, God in God's self-revelation, to be the determining factor of every aspect of theological inquiry.

Scientific Theology

The fundamental insights and clues into the intrinsic interrelations in God's redemptive self-revelation which scientific theology refines and develops arise within the Church where we encounter Jesus Christ and the Gospel (and respond in faith, worship, and obedience) as the Christian community indwells the biblical witness.[80] Theology is always a refinement and amplification, Torrance argues, of *this* knowledge of God through Jesus Christ and in the Holy Spirit at the evangelical and doxological level where we are spiritually, personally, and intellectually implicated in the patterned activity of God beyond our ability to fully comprehend and articulate.[81] Torrance is adamant that "this ground level of evangelical experience and apprehension remains the necessary basis, the *sine qua non*, of the other levels of doctrinal formulation developed from it."[82]

The goal of scientific theological activity is to refine, unify, and extend this knowledge of God, and test the proclamation and life of the Church in light of it. The theologian returns to the biblical witness with those basic insights and clues which arise within the life and tradition of the Church and "indwells" the conjoint focus of the Old and New Testament in their witness to God's self-revelation so that the theologian's mind "becomes assimilated to the *integration* of the different strata [of the biblical texts] in their bearing upon the objective events and realities they intend."[83]

Torrance never defines all that "indwelling" entails, since by its very character it is an *integrative* and *holistic* activity that involves the *informal* tacit dimension and *personal* participation which cannot be rendered fully explicit. But the process of indwelling includes all the normal hermeneutical tools, including the historical-critical method which Torrance says is "scientifically obligatory," even if it is helpful only up to a point.[84] Torrance occasionally provides "general guidelines" for the actual task of theological interpretation of the Bible, though we cannot discuss them here.[85]

This kind of interpretation of Scripture in its witness to the *Realities* of God's redemptive self-revelation demands, Torrance contends, a *theological* exegesis in order to apprehend and articulate God's *oikonomia* out of which the Bible arose. It involves a proper circularity in which the interpretation of the Bible is guided by a theological understanding of the divine *Realities* and truths it mediates, while at the same time that theological understanding is itself regulated by the exegesis and interpretation of the Scripture witness.[86]

This has the effect, Torrance grants, of "allotting to the Scriptures a subsidiary status" to the *Realities* they intend.[87] But this does not undercut the significance of the Bible in Torrance's theological method, for "without all that the Scriptures in the saving purpose of

God have come to embody, we would not be able to know God or to have intelligible communion with him within our continuing human and historical existence."[88] It does, however, demand a thorough rethinking of the doctrine of Scripture in relation to God's self-revelation.[89]

Examples of Effective Integration of Form in Theology

Time and again in the history of the Church, Torrance discerns an example of the kind of integration of form he intends as "something like the doctrine of the hypostatic union . . . keeps on forcing itself upon our minds and we are convinced that here we have penetrated deeply into the inner logic of the evangelical material."[90]

A further illustration of an effective integration of form is the *homoousion*, that Jesus Christ is one being with God the Father. The *homoousion* is a faithful exegetical and theological concept that is neither deduced from the biblical text, nor imposed on it. Nor is it even the conclusion of an inductive examination of all the scriptural texts which speak Jesus Christ's relationship to God. It is a faithful distillation not simply of the fundamental sense of the New Testament, but an articulation of the basic constitutive relations in the revealing and redemptive activity of God in Jesus Christ.[91]

The *homoousion* crystallizes the evangelical conviction that Jesus Christ is not a created intermediary between God and humanity, nor a paradigmatic instance of a panentheist God-world relation, but rather the very eternal Word and Son of *God* who is made flesh for us and our salvation in Jesus Christ. The *homoousion* gives careful and cogent expression to the interrelations implicit in God's *oikonomia*, and informally apprehended at the evangelical and doxological level that in Jesus Christ and the Holy Spirit we are directly in touch with the ultimate Reality and Presence of God: "*what Jesus Christ does for us and to us, and what the Holy Spirit does in us, is what God himself does for us, to us, and in us.*"[92]

Thus Torrance argues that *homoousion* give "compressed expression in exact and equivalent language, not so much to the biblical terms themselves but to the objective meaning or reality they were designed to point out and convey."[93] The theological activity (integration of form) involved in the development of the *homoousion* is not a speculative movement of thought that leaves the evangelical and doxological life of the Church behind, for it gives careful articulation to the core of the Gospel in which the faithful know that it is *God* who loves them to the uttermost in Jesus Christ, and in the fellowship of the Holy Spirit it is *God* who opens their lives to the Gospel and lifts them up in faith and hope to share in the love that God is as Father, Son, and Holy Spirit.[94] The *homoousion* discloses and articulates the profound depth of Truth in the mystery of the simple Gospel.[95] It expresses that what God is and has done for us in the Gospel is ultimately grounded in who God is and always will be in God's own eternal being, nature, and life.

When this kind of theological activity is carried a stage further, Torrance thinks that "we penetrate into a higher level of unity and simplicity [the Trinity] which gives coherent order to the whole stratified structure of our theological concepts."[96] Though the doctrine of the Trinity is a human apprehension and articulation of God that falls short of the *Reality* of the Triune God, Torrance argues that it constitutes what we must say and think about God if we are to be faithful to God's self-revelation and self-communication as Father, Son, and Holy Spirit in the Gospel itself. As such, the doctrine of the Trinity is a par excellence example of the kind of scientific theological activity Torrance has in mind.

Torrance believes that the *hypostatic union*, the *homoousion*, the doctrine of the Trinity, along with several other key theological concepts, enable us to enter the inner matrix of relations and apprehend and articulate the intelligible pattern intrinsic in God's *oikonomia* to which the Old Testament and New Testament Scriptures bear witness.[97] Together they provide a *disclosure model* which clarifies and simplifies the whole structure of our knowledge of God, though in a way that is always revisable in light of the *Realities* they intend.[98] This kind of doctrinal disclosure model brings theological order to our day-to-day experience of, and faith in, God and enables us to integrate the enormous complexity of the Bible in a way that illuminates the *Realities* and events of God's *oikonomia* and thereby also deepens our faith and experience.[99]

This, of course, means that doctrines are not simply propositions (deduced from Scripture) that correspond to objective *Realities*, since this is a misinterpretation of the relation between the human mind/concepts and reality. Neither are doctrines nondiscursive symbols constructed out of preconceptual religious experience as in the experiential-expressivism characteristic of much of modern theology. Nor are doctrines second-order rules dictating the dynamics of first-order Christian discourse (George Lindbeck's cultural-linguistic paradigm). In Torrance's theology doctrines are effective integrations of form, or *disclosure models*, arising out of the complex theological activity described above, and which are progressively disclosive of the *Realities* they signify.

Authority in Theology

Torrance is adamant that there "is not and cannot be any logical bridge between concepts and experience."[100] There is no logical bridge between doctrines and the *Realities* they are designed to disclose, for doctrines are correlated with God's *oikonomia* through indwelling, participatory knowing, and the informal tacit dimension at the evangelical and doxological level out of which arose the clues or insights that are developed into doctrines.[101] Since doctrines do not evolve out of a formal process that can be rendered entirely explicit (deduction, abstraction, or induction), the application of doctrines to the divine *Realities* and saving events (which doctrines express) entails unformalizable and integrative discernment and recognition not dissimilar from those out of which the doctrines arose in the first place, for the *relation* between our concepts and reality cannot be reduced to the relations that exist between ideas.

At several points above we noted that, for Torrance, Jesus Christ is a *self*-revelation of God. This means that in Christ, God communicates not simply truths about himself, but the *Supreme Truth* of God's very *self*. In light of this, Torrance thinks that all theological understanding and doctrinal formulation is relativized by this Truth, and doctrinal formulations are true in so far as they are truly related to the Truth through the integrative and participatory matrix out of which theological understanding and doctrinal formulations arise.

In other words, Torrance argues that "theological concepts and statements have their justification through the Grace of God alone."[102] Doctrinal formulations have their truth not through a process of verification which we control, for we cannot force God to be the content of our thought or our doctrinal affirmations.[103]

The Church is called by God to think and speak truthfully and correctly about God in its doctrine which is what "orthodoxy" means, Torrance contends. But the verification of doctrinal formulations requires the same kind of integrative and participatory relation to the divine *Realities* and saving events that is the source of the theological concepts at the evangelical and doxological level in their genesis.[104]

Yet God's self-revelation and self-communication has created a profound reciprocity and corporate medium of relations and structures in space-time in the thought, speech, and life of Israel and of the apostolic nucleus and New Testament community embodied in the Old and New Testaments as the inspired creaturely instrumentality through which that self-revelation and self-communication continue to meet us. God honors this creaturely instrumentality which God called into contrapuntal relation with this *self*-revelation. Therefore Torrance argues for "secondary authorities or delegated authorities whose function it is to serve his [God's] supreme Authority . . . in such a way as not to obscure it but let it appear in all God's Prerogative and Majesty."[105] Holy Scripture is authoritative for theological understanding and doctrinal formulation, though what is crucial for Torrance is God's self-revelation that resounds through the Bible.[106]

While the ultimate authority for faith and doctrine is the self-revelation of God through Scripture, when this authority is acknowledged and given primacy, Torrance thinks that the Church and tradition are also authoritative and ought to be respected and revered, so long as the Church's tradition, faith, and life stay open to the objective Source of Truth and Authority, Jesus Christ himself.

In Jesus Christ, Torrance contends, we meet the ultimate *Truth* of God face to face. All of the levels of truth and authority are united indivisibly in Christ's divine-human Person.[107] As such, Jesus Christ is the Truth of God to humanity and the true human response to God, the *self*-revelation of God and the perfect human correlate of that revelation in thought, word, and deed, and therefore the ultimate norm for all Christian doctrinal formulation with reference to God, God's relation to the world, and all of Christian faith, life, and mission in the world. As *the Truth*, Jesus Christ himself is both the decisive embodiment of God's Truth and final *authoritative Judge* of theological understanding and doctrinal formulation.[108]

Dialogue with Torrance

I indicated my sympathy with Torrance's overall theological vision and his theological method in the introduction. I find the rigor, depth, and breadth of Torrance's reflection on scientific theological method unsurpassed within evangelical theology (and with few equals in the wider theological community). This is especially the case with his integration of method and content, the clarity of intent and development of the thesis that method has to be forged in light of the nature of theology's "object," God in God's self-revelation which, thus, makes scientific theological method radically biblical, evangelical (soteriological and participatory), Christocentric, and Trinitarian.

In addition, Torrance's level of engaging the history of epistemology/method in modern science, philosophy, theology, and critical biblical studies (and especially their interrelations) is virtually unique. This enables Torrance to restate the critical realist epistemology demanded by biblical and Trinitarian Christian faith in a sophisticated and compelling manner after the collapse of the modern foundationalist paradigm. Torrance's position is a viable alternative to the kind of radical postmodern perspectivalism and, at times, cognitive relativism which I believe is a danger to Christian faith, as well as to Western culture, and which represents an unnecessary overreaction against the pretentious modern quest (with its often imperialist consequences) to render the conditions for indubitable knowledge entirely explicit.

For the rest of this chapter, I want to engage Professor Torrance in critical dialogue about several points in his account of theological method.

1. The first of these is his notion of a *scientific* theological method. Torrance has been repeatedly criticized for building his theology on natural science or philosophy of science. Some contend that too much of the physics lab finds its way into Torrance's account. Others argue that his work is severely rationalistic.

These criticisms, I believe, miss the mark for two reasons and I want to know if Professor Torrance agrees with my analysis. First, this kind of criticism fails to take into account Torrance's rejection of any *scientia universalis* to which theology must conform, and also his affirmation that a scientific theology has to be determined by the unique nature of its "Object." Once these points are in place, it becomes clear that the only *scientific* approach to theology, in Torrance's perspective, is one that is evangelical and doxological within a *participatory* relation of God through Christ in the Holy Spirit in the matrix of the Church (*theologia=eusebia*, as Athanasius stated it).

Second, I think what confuses Torrance's readers is that his publications tend to focus on either method or on positive theological content, and so unless his interpreters figure out the interconnection, they read his account of method in light of their preconceptions of what is scientific, rather than in light of Torrance's understanding of the nature of theology's object, God in God's self-revelation and evangelical and doxological approach this demands. I invite Torrance to confirm whether I have appropriately interpreted his theology on this point.

2. Is Torrance a *foundationalist*? Few epistemological positions have more negative connotations in theology and philosophy today than foundationalism. Ronald Thiemann was one of the first to lodge this criticism against Torrance, arguing that Torrance is a foundationalist because he "uses the term *intuition* to signify the indubitability and incorrigibility of this *causally imposed knowledge*."[109] Yet, Torrance repeatedly asserts that "no rational

knowledge is merely *per modum causalitatis* . . . [for] even though I think rationally as I am compelled to think . . . I am free and not a puppet."[110] Torrance rejects the kind of "mechanization of knowledge" found in many forms of foundationalism and argues that human knowing and reality are "found to be much too subtle and flexible . . . to be open to explanation or understanding within the old framework of 'necessity and chance.'"[111]

In place of *this* kind of foundationalism, Torrance advocates *personal* participatory knowledge rooted in indwelling and the tacit dimension. My question for Torrance is that while the tacit dimension is affected by one's cultural-linguistic framework (and therefore all of the issues of sociology of knowledge) and is open to critical modification as inquiry proceeds, does it not still provide some kind of foundation in his epistemology?[112] I suspect that Torrance's answer to this lies in his account of ultimate beliefs and fiduciary frameworks. In the end, even after adding elements of communal consensus and indirect testing via the long-term fruitfulness of theories, it is endemic to the human condition that we must all say, "I believe it is so," though for Torrance proper belief is itself always objectively oriented toward reality through participation in the tacit dimension.

3. Daniel Hardy raises the most serious critique of Torrance's theological method to date. Overall Hardy is appreciative of Torrance's contributions. Yet Hardy also argues that the obscurity of Torrance's position is due not simply to the difficulty of the subject matter or Torrance's complex writing style. It is ultimately because the nature of the position Torrance adopts, Hardy contends, "which verges on the private and publicly inexpressible."[113] For Torrance, the verification of the knowing relation requires the same participatory relation that generated the knowledge in the first place. Those already in the knowing relation can only speak or write in such a way, Hardy argues, "that their words and ideas are transparencies through which others may see[114] (somewhat like trying to help another person see the 3-D image in the *Magic Eye*). When it is all said and done, either you see it or you do not, though it is possible to convince some people that the 3-D image is there, even when they do not see it!

While Hardy praises Torrance for his careful documentation that real knowledge "occurs" in the history of theology and the natural sciences, Hardy faults Torrance for remaining at the level of the "fact" that the knowing relation "occurs." This criticism has to be qualified at several points to make it fair to Torrance's position, rather than Hardy's caricature of it. First, for Torrance, the knowing relation does not just occur, it arises out of the detailed, intimate, and rigorous process of indwelling and yields cognitive structures (doctrines in theology) disclosive of the reality one indwells.

Second, Torrance argues at length that the process of indwelling is *by its very character* not fully formalizable. This appears to be the real thrust of Hardy's criticism, and if so, it means that Hardy seems to be calling for a return to a form of foundationalism where the conditions for knowledge are made completely explicit.

Hardy points to two additional difficulties in the position Torrance advocates: (1) the privileged position of those who are in the knowing relation; and (2) the "exclusivist" claims for the knowledge thus attained.[115] These criticisms are germane to all participatory epistemologies, for each promises *real* knowledge for *those* who participate in the occurrence of the knowing relation, not unlike those who "see" the *Magic Eye* and tell others that they too will see the 3-D image *if* they hold the picture close to their faces and slowly move it away without focusing on the detail. The difference in Torrance's position is his emphasis on the living Reality and Agency of the Triune God which is at the center of his theology and epistemology. This both complicates Torrance's approach (even though we engage in rigorous theological activity, we are ever dependent upon God's activity in our knowledge of God), but also provides resources for engaging Hardy's criticism not available to other participatory approaches which discount the reality of this kind of God. I am particularly interested in Torrance's response to these criticisms.

4. Finally, other perspectives which appeal to a participatory epistemology could (and do) also claim to be rooted in the tacit dimension (certain feminist epistemologies, for example). Yet they end up in very different positions than Torrance does. This fact tends to reinforce historical consciousness and indicate that the tacit dimension reflects the limitations of the person, the person's experience and social location, and then a radical perspectivalism and relativism is not far away. How does Torrance avoid this kind of account of the tacit dimension (or Hardy's charge of special "privilege") without embracing a form of foundationalism?

Torrance needs to engage these kinds of criticisms so that his scientific theological method can stand out as *the* most viable alternative to the various postmodern approaches clamoring for attention after the collapse of foundationalism at the dawn of the new millennium.

Notes

1. See Thomas F. Torrance, *Theological Science* (London: Oxford University Press, 1969), 281.

2. Thomas F. Torrance, *Reality and Evangelical Theology* (Philadelphia: Westminster Press, 1982.).

3. Torrance, *Theological Science*, 106-40. See the introduction in Elmer M. Colyer, *How to Read T. F. Torrance: Understanding His Trinitarian and Scientific Theology* (Downers Grove, Ill.: InterVarsity Press, 2001). See chapter 9 of this book for a more developed account of Torrance's theological method. There are significant parallels between that chapter and this chapter since they are on the same subject and I wrote them within a few weeks of one another.

4. Torrance, *Theological Science*, xii.

5. Torrance, *Theological Science*, 281.

6. Interpreters must read Torrance's methodological publications and his constructive theological work together.

7. See especially Torrance's essay, "My Interaction with Karl Barth" in *How Karl Barth Changed My Mind*, ed. Donald K. McKim (Grand Rapids, Mich.: Eerdmans, 1986), 52-64.

8. McKim, *How Karl Barth*, 52.

9. McKim, *How Karl Barth*, 52.

10. McKim, *How Karl Barth*, 52.

11. McKim, *How Karl Barth*, 52.

12. McKim, *How Karl Barth*, 54.

13. McKim, *How Karl Barth*, 54.

14. McKim, *How Karl Barth*, 54. Also see I. John Hesselink, "A Pilgrimage in the School of Christ—An Interview with T. F. Torrance," *Reformed Review* 38, no.1 (autumn 1984): 53.

15. R. D. Kernohan, "Tom Torrance: The Man and Reputation," *Life and Work* 32, no. 5 (May 1976): 14. Also see Thomas F. Torrance, *The Christian Doctrine of God: One Being Three Persons* (Edinburgh: T&T Clark, 1998), 146.

16. Thomas F. Torrance, *Reality and Scientific Theology* (Edinburgh: Scottish Academic Press, 1985), 156.

17. Thomas F. Torrance, *God and Rationality* (New York: Oxford University Press, 1971), 9-10, 91.

18. See Thomas F. Torrance, *The Mediation of Christ*, 2d ed. (Colorado Springs, Colo.: Helmers & Howard, 1992), 1-3, 47-50, and Thomas F. Torrance, *The Trinitarian Faith* (Edinburgh: T & T Clark, 1988), 35-43, 47-54, 102-4, 106-9, 111-15, 136-39, 149-54, 273-78.

19. For further discussion see Colyer, *How to Read*, chapter 2.

20.Torrance argues that dualist ways of thinking have damaged our knowledge of God, for their effect has been "to detach Jesus Christ from God, to detach Jesus Christ from Israel, and to detach Christianity from Christ himself." Torrance, *Mediation*, 1. Epistemological dualism makes it difficult if not impossible to know all that much about Jesus himself, since the New Testament is a collection of accounts about Jesus by various authors/communities who inevitably construed Jesus in light of their agendas and contexts.

This creates a double problem for modern interpreters, for the New Testament Jesus is not necessarily the real historical Jesus and modern readers are historically and culturally distant from the first/second-century Christianity reflected in the New Testament. It is not uncommon for modern cosmological and epistemological dualisms to coalesce and operate together at this point. Cosmological dualism interprets what the Bible says about God's activity in the world in Jesus Christ (the resurrection, for instance) in terms of the mythopoetic or apocalyptic imagery of early Christian faith historically distant from modern/postmodern readers/communities.

A classic modern example of what Torrance has in mind here is David Strauss and his controversial work, *The Life of Jesus Critically Examined*, ed. and trans. Marian Evans (London: SCM Press, 1973), originally published in 1835. Strauss viewed the miraculous events in the Gospels as myth, "the representation of an event or of an idea in a form which is historical, but, at the same time characterized by the rich pictoral and imaginative mode of thought and expression of the primitive ages." Strauss contended that "the sages of antiquity . . . deficient themselves in clear abstract ideas, and in ability to give expression to their dim conceptions . . . sought to illumine what was obscure in their representations by means of sensible imagery." Strauss, *Life of Jesus*, 53-54. He further maintains that the biblical writers had "a ready disposition to derive all things . . . as soon as they appear particularly important, immediately from God. He . . . gives the rain and the sunshine . . . he hardens hearts and softens them. . . . Our modern world, on the contrary, after centuries of tedious search, has attained a conviction that all things are linked together by a chain of causes and effects, which suffers no interruption." Strauss, *Life of Jesus*, 78. Also see Colin Gunton, *Enlightenment and Alienation* (Grand Rapids, Mich.: Eerdmans, 1985), 116-17.

Thus in Strauss we find the cosmological dualism of a cause and effect universe that "suffers no interruption" from a God outside of it. But we also see epistemological dualism, at least for primitive peoples, "deficient in abstract ideas," whose "mythological" modes of apprehension, thought, and expression are incapable of generating enlightened knowledge of reality, though Strauss seems to think that the modern Western science/scholarship is much more epistemologically adept.

21. Torrance, *Theological Science*, x-xi.

22. Torrance rejects traditional natural theology. See Colyer, *How to Read*, chapters 4 and 5.

23. Daniel Hardy is one of the few interpreters who correctly understands Torrance on this point. See Daniel Hardy, "Thomas F. Torrance," in *The Modern Theologians: An Introduction to Christian Theology in the Twentieth Century*, ed. David Ford (Oxford: Basil Blackwell, 1989), 1:77.

24. Hardy, "Torrance," 77.

25. Torrance, *Mediation*, 7.

26. Torrance, *Mediation*, 3-4. An example of holism in physics is the development of field theory. Torrance, *Mediation*, 47-49. Torrance rejects any kind of dualism between form and being.

27. Torrance, *Theological Science,* xvii. Also see Torrance, *Scientific Theology*, xi-xiii.

28. See Colyer, *How to Read*, chapter 9, and Elmer M. Colyer, *The Nature of Doctrine in T. F. Torrance's Theology* (Eugene, Oreg.: Wipf & Stock, 2001), chapters 1 and 2.

29. James Brown, *Subject and Object in Modern Theology* (New York: Macmillian, 1955), 170. See Torrance, *Theological Science*, 1.

30. Thomas F. Torrance, *Transformation and Convergence in the Frame of Knowledge* (Grand Rapids, Mich.: Eerdmans, 1984), 14. Thus, Newton asserts, "I frame no hypotheses," for "whatever is not deduced from phenomena, is to be called an hypothesis; and hypotheses, whether metaphysical or physical, whether occult qualities or mechanical, have no place in experimental philosophy. In this philosophy particular propositions are inferred from the phenomena, and afterward rendered general by induction." Isaac Newton, *Philosophiae Naturalis Principia Mathematica*, trans. Andrew Motte (1729), rev. and ed. Florian Cajori (Chicago: Encyclopedia Britannica, 1955), 547. See Torrance, *Transformation*, 17. It is however true that Newton did in fact advance speculative hypotheses, as Torrance points out.

31. Torrance, *Transformation*, 18.

32. Newton was actually aware of the problem, for he could not derive absolute space and time (theoretical components crucial for his laws of motion) directly from observation or sense experience. Newton, *Principia Mathematica*, 12. See Torrance, *Transformation*, 22. Einstein noted that "We can see indeed from Newton's formulation of it that the concept of absolute space, which comprised that of absolute rest, made him feel uncomfortable; he realized that there seemed to be nothing in experience corresponding to this last concept." Albert Einstein, *The World As I See It*, trans. Alan Harris (London: John Lane, 1935), 135. See Torrance, *Transformation*, 52.

33. Torrance, *Transformation*, 35. Hume embraced an empiricism from thinkers like Locke with its notion of passive perception and active reason.

34. David Hume, *A Treatise of Human Nature* (London: Longmans, Green & Co., 1909), I.iii.8, 403-4. See Torrance, *Transformation*, 35.

35. See Gunton, *Enlightenment*, 22.

36. David Hume, *An Enquiry Concerning Human Understanding*, ed. L. A. Selby-Biggs (Oxford: Clarendon Press, 1962), VII.2, 77.

37. Torrance, *Transformation*, 36.

38. Torrance, *Transformation*, 36-40.

39. Torrance, *Transformation*, 38. Hence Kant makes his famous statement that "Hitherto it has been assumed that all our knowledge must conform to objects. . . . We must . . . make trial whether we may not have more success in the tasks of metaphysics, if we suppose that objects must conform to our knowledge." Immanuel Kant, *Critique of Pure Reason*, trans. by N. Kemp Smith (London: Macmillan, 1933), 22.

40. Torrance, *Transformation*, 42.

41. Torrance, *Transformation*, 42.

42. Torrance argues that Einstein put an end to Newton's idea that concepts are deduced from observation and Kant's notion that concepts are a priori categories imposed on data by the activity of the mind not just by his criticism of them, but by Einstein's astonishing achievements in developing scientific knowledge of the universe through his theories of relativity. Torrance, *Transformation*, 77.

43. Torrance values the way Michael Polanyi's work on indwelling clarifies the process of scientific inquiry and epistemology. However, Torrance does not build his theology on an epistemology borrowed from natural science and/or empirical philosophy (Einstein or Polanyi). See McGrath's interesting account of Torrance's relation to Polanyi and McGrath's criticism of Colin Weightman's caricature of Torrance as heavily dependent upon Polanyi. Alister McGrath, *T. F. Torrance: An Intellectual Biography* (Edinburgh: T&T Clark, 1999), 228-32.

44. Thomas F. Torrance, "The Place of Michael Polanyi in the Modern Philosophy of Science," *Ethics in Science and Medicine* 7 (1980): 61, republished in Torrance, *Transformation*, 107-73. Also see Torrance, *Mediation*, 13-14.

45. Torrance, *Transformation*, 69.

46. Torrance, "Polanyi," 60.

47. See Thomas Torrance, *Christian Theology and Scientific Culture* (New York: Oxford University Press, 1980), 13.

48. Our implicit knowledge or tacit dimension is affected by the tradition, language, community, and culture we inhabit. Here Torrance concedes not a little to sociology of knowledge, granting that this cultural/linguistic framework can inhibit or further explicit understanding and scientific inquiry.

49. See Torrance, "Polanyi," 60.

50. Visual perception tacitly integrates a subsidiary awareness of marginal elements into an apprehension of the object we see in our focal awareness. Torrance, "Polanyi," 63. Robert K. Martin also sees the way the *Magic Eye* prints help illustrate the integrative activity of the human mind. See his excellent book *The Incarnate Ground of Christian Faith: Toward a Christian Theological Epistemology for the Educational Ministry of the Church* (Lanham, Md.: University Press of America, 1998), 160-64.

51. See Torrance, *Transformation*, 118.

52. See Torrance, *Scientific Theology*, 43.

53. Torrance, "Polanyi," 64.

54. Torrance, "Polanyi," 64, and Torrance, *Scientific Theology*, 43.

55. Torrance, *Transformation*, 119.

56. See Hardy, "Torrance," 81.

57. See Michael Polanyi, *Personal Knowledge* (Chicago: University of Chicago Press, 1958), 13.

58. Torrance, *Transformation*, 80.

59. Torrance, *Transformation*, 123. Also see Torrance, *Scientific Theology*, 133-35.

60. Torrance, "Polanyi," 72.

61. Torrance. *Transformation*, 133-34.

62. Torrance, *Transformation*, 135.

63. Torrance, *Transformation*, viii-xiv.

64. For Torrance's critique of modern critical biblical studies and theology see Thomas F. Torrance, *Space, Time, and Resurrection* (Grand Rapids, Mich.: Eerdmans, 1976), 1-21, 159-93; Thomas F. Torrance, *Preaching Christ Today* (Grand Rapids, Mich.: Eerdmans, 1994), 1-11; and Thomas F. Torrance, "The Historical Jesus: From the Perspective of a Theologian," in *The New Testament Age: Essays in Honor of Bo Reicke*, ed. William C. Weinrich (Macon, Ga.: Mercer University Press, 1984), 2: 511-26.

65. See Torrance, *Preaching Christ*, 5-8.

66. Torrance, *Transformation*, 42.

67. Torrance, *Transformation*, 8.

68. See Torrance, *Mediation*, chapters 1 and 2. We cannot apprehend reality in its interrelations (form intrinsic in being) without a theoretical (theological in this case) element (an appropriate integration of form is knowing which includes a form of life, since knowledge is participatory). For Torrance, the appropriate forms of thought, speech, and life within which we can properly apprehend God's self-revelation are divinely and progressively provided by God within the space-time structures of this world through God's dealings with Israel as reflected in the Old Testament. Thus to sever the Testaments is absolutely disastrous for Christian faith and theology from Torrance's perspective. See Colyer, *How to Read*, chapter 2.

69. Torrance, *Resurrection*, 2-15.

70. Torrance, *Resurrection*, 2-15. Also see Torrance, *Christian Doctrine*, 82, and Torrance, *Scientific Theology*, 83-84.

71. Torrance, *Evangelical Theology*, 45.

72. Torrance, "Polanyi," 164. This is not totally different from natural science, where the scientific community and its tradition also play a major role in the cultivation of the proper mind-set and skills necessary for the student to become a full-fledged scientist. See Alexander Thomson, *Tradition and Authority in Science and Theology* (Edinburgh: Scottish Academic Press, 1987).

73. Torrance, *Evangelical Theology*, 48.

74. See Colyer, *Nature of Doctrine*, chapter 3.

75. See Torrance, *Rationality*, 17.

76. Torrance, *Scientific Theology*, 106.
77. Torrance, *Scientific Theology*, 118.
78. Hardy, "Torrance," 73-75.
79. Hardy, "Torrance," 74.
80. Torrance, *Transformation*, 94.
81. Torrance, *Christian Doctrine*, 89, and Torrance, *Scientific Theology*, 85.
82. Torrance, *Christian Doctrine*, 90.
83. Torrance, *Resurrection*, 11.
84. Torrance, *Resurrection*, 9. Torrance has written many articles and books dealing with hermeneutics. See especially Torrance, *Evangelical Theology*, and the introduction in Torrance, *Resurrection*.
85. Torrance, *Evangelical Theology*, 100-20.
86. Torrance, *Evangelical Theology*, 42.
87. Torrance, *Resurrection*, 12. Also see Torrance, *Evangelical Theology*, 13, 17-19, 46-48, 105-9, 119-20, and 122-24.
88. Torrance, *Resurrection*, 12-13.
89. See Colyer, *How to Read*, chapters 2, 3, and 6.
90. Thomas F. Torrance, "The Integration of Form in Natural and in Theological Science," *Science, Medicine and Man* 1 (1973): 165.
91. Torrance, *Christian Doctrine*, 95.
92. Torrance, *Christian Doctrine*, 95.
93. Torrance, *Evangelical Theology*, 112.
94. Torrance, *Evangelical Theology*, 112.
95. Torrance, *Christian Doctrine*, 1 and 97.
96. Also see Torrance, "Integration," 165.
97. Torrance, "Integration," 165-66, and Torrance, *Scientific Theology*, 152-57.
98. Torrance, *Scientific Theology*, 86.
99. Torrance, "Integration," 165-66.
100. Torrance, *Scientific Theology*, 76.
101. Torrance, *Transformation*, 112-13.
102. Torrance, *Scientific Theology*, 148.
103. Torrance, *Scientific Theology*, 148.
104. Torrance, *Theological Science*, 198.
105. Torrance, *Evangelical Theology*, 154.
106. Torrance, *Evangelical Theology*, 96.
107. Torrance, *Evangelical Theology*, 137.
108. Torrance, *Evangelical Theology*, 138.
109. Ronald Thiemann, *Revelation and Theology* (Notre Dame, Ind.: University of Notre Dame Press, 1985), 40.
110. Torrance, *Rationality*, 198.
111. See Thomas F. Torrance, *The Christian Frame of Mind*, 2d ed. (Colorado Springs, Colo.: Helmers & Howard, 1989), 43-46 and 48-50.
112. Dr. Mark Heim is the first person I know of who has raised this question concerning Torrance's epistemology.
113. Hardy, "Torrance," 86.

114. Hardy, "Torrance," 87.
115. Hardy, "Torrance," 87-88.

Chapter 10

Humanity in an Intelligible Cosmos: Non-Duality in Albert Einstein and Thomas Torrance

by Christopher B. Kaiser

A Twofold Tribute

Albert Einstein was chosen as "Person of the Century" by *Time*, and for those who value the impact of science on human history there could not have been a better choice.[1] Einstein single-handedly rewrote some of the most fundamental principles of physics. By the sheer power of his imagination and the use of some mathematical tools, he created theories that have fundamentally changed our technologies and our lives. And he projected a new and exciting image of the scientist-intellectual for a broader public.

Even as a boy I was awed by the pensive portrait of Einstein that I saw on a magazine cover—I cut out the portrait and placed it on my bedroom wall, where it seemed to watch over me as I collected stamps and rocks or played with my toys. In my teenage years, as I considered various colleges and college majors, my imagination was once again captivated by the semipopular work that Einstein and Leopold Infeld wrote describing the basic ideas of physics.[2] Einstein's vision was the most compelling one I had yet discovered, and from that time on I have disciplined myself to see the world with the eyes of a physicist. Little did I know that Einstein's writings were also being studied by a churchman in Scotland, who would one day be my mentor in theology. Torrance was then disciplining himself to view theological epistemology with the eyes of a physicist.[3]

A discussion of Einstein's ideas plays a prominent role in many of Professor Torrance's lectures and publications.[4] As a result, many scientists, whatever their religious convictions may be, form an immediate bond with this theologian when they sense his high regard for Einstein and his in-depth knowledge of Einstein's writings. If Einstein is the "person of the century" in the judgment of secular media, Torrance's interest is enough to qualify him as "theologian of the century" in the eyes of many science-minded people.

My personal relationship with Professor Torrance began while I was a seminary student looking for a postgraduate program in which I could relate Christian theology to physical science. When I chanced to come across some of Torrance's early works on theology and science, I wrote to him asking about the possibility of doing postgraduate study with him at New College in the University of Edinburgh. He immediately wrote back a very gracious, encouraging letter, and advised me to study the writings of three people who, he said, had deeply influenced his thinking. I might have expected a theologian like Torrance to recommend Anselm or John Calvin or Karl Barth. In my case, however, the recommended writings were those of Michael Polanyi, Walter Elsasser,[5] and Albert Einstein—specifically the epistemological writings of Einstein.[6] I have seen Professor Torrance reach out in similar ways to many scientifically trained people in an effort to stimulate discussion and further genuine understanding between the disciplines. As I shall try to show in this chapter, his outreach is based on a deep belief in the unity of knowledge.

Over the twenty-five years since I completed my studies at Edinburgh, I have come to value more aspects of Torrance's thought than I could absorb or appreciate as a student. I have particularly come to value his understanding of the importance of Albert Einstein for his theology and, specifically, for the integration of science and theology. One of Torrance's favorite ideas is Einstein's notion that we comprehend the universe only at comparatively elementary levels.[7] The miracle is that we comprehend it at all! I feel very much the same way faced with the breadth and profundity of Torrance's own writings. Even after thirty years of study, I only understand them at comparatively elementary levels. Yet they never cease to challenge me and help me reach new insights into the task of theology.

The Problem of Subject-Object Duality in a Technological Society

Why should the writings of a physicist like Einstein be so important for an academic theologian? It is to be expected that a good theologian will be interested in other theologians. It is common for theologians also to sharpen their ideas by reading great philosophers, sociologists, psychologists, and perhaps even popular presentations of scientific topics like evolution or cosmology. But the intense study of the thought of a particular physicist is unusual in our time.

It was not always that way. Scientists and theologians once did commonly read each other in depth—prior to the intense specialization of the late nineteenth century. Eighteenth-century theologians like Samuel Clarke, Cotton Mather, and Jonathan Edwards still regarded the study of natural philosophy (as it was then called) as part of their ongoing work. But today it is often taken for granted that physicists' work has no immediate bearing on the everyday lives of Christians. The unfortunate result is that Christian faith and life are dissociated from the material structure of modern life, most of which has been completely reshaped by the application of physics through creative engineering. Even the most theologically orthodox of us end up being Gnostics with respect to the deployment and experience of technological structures.[8] How could this happen?

We live in a symbiotic relationship with our technologies. A significant proportion of our population is devoted to maintaining and updating them. Some of these people work in basic research; others in design and development. They take promising new ideas and try to develop them into new products and services. Some of these turn out to work better than already existing technologies. They are further developed and marketed. In this way a new world is gradually created—a new world of human construction—a distant echo of the first creation. In fact, our material world has been restructured several times over just in the past century. Electricity, internal combustion, radio, telecommunications, and computers all were invented, developed, and marketed by humans, but each of these technologies in turn has restructured human life in entirely new ways.

As laypeople, we do eventually see the newness. We see it in new appliances, new health care options, and new forms of entertainment. We try to be current in terms that seem important to us. We read the catalogs, watch the sales, and soon we ourselves are participating in the new technologies. They change our lives. Individually and subjectively, we are reborn along with the world we live in. But the creative processes that led to the new technologies are usually beyond our ken. Unless we happen to be among the specialized engineers who worked on the projects (or the historians who document them), they are not of concern to us. We miss out on the actual processes of new creation. Effectively, we are dualists, much like the Gnostics of old. The duality is disguised behind a veneer of pragmatism, but it is there just the same.

It is important to understand the pervasiveness of this deeply seeded duality in order to appreciate the necessity for recovering non-duality and the importance of Professor Torrance's persistent quest for ways to facilitate that recovery.[9] A subject-object duality crops up wherever we interface with current technologies pragmatically, as "users," without much interest in the mathematical theories or the industrial processes out of which those technologies are born. It also comes up in theology, particularly since the advent of revivalism and liberalism, whenever we relate to God in terms of feeling or in pragmatic terms without an adequate grounding in the space-time revelation which made our relationship to God possible in the first place. These dualities between the subjective and objective, or the private and public aspects of modern life are one of the things that attracted Professor Torrance's attention to Einstein.[10] The most important thing about Einstein for Torrance was that he was a champion of non-dualism in General Relativity and also in epistemology.[11]

Torrance's discussions of Einstein range over more than forty years of writing and lecturing,[12] and they deal with many different aspects of Einstein's thought. I will try to point out some significant shifts in emphasis along the way, but the major emphasis has always been on the idea of non-duality.[13] Given the persistence and depth of this interest over the years, this study should help to illuminate some important aspects of Professor Torrance's thinking in general. I will conclude with some questions for further discussion on the related topic of evolutionary epistemology.

General Relativity and Einstein's Epistemology

When Torrance brings Einstein into his theological discussions, he is taking technical arguments in one field and working out implications for other fields. This transfer of ideas is part of a larger goal of realizing an overall unity of knowledge without reductionism of one field to another.[14] In dealing with such cross-disciplinary relationships, there is always the need for balance. If one insists on the absolute purity of one's discipline without reference to other fields, there is the danger of allowing one's thinking to stagnate or to drift. On the other hand, if one imposes ideas from one discipline on another, there is the equal and opposite danger of a-priorism.

Torrance repeatedly warns against these twin dangers: antimetaphysical inductivism, as in logical empiricism or positivism, on the one hand, and metaphysical a-priorism, as in the case of Kantian idealism, on the other.[15]

What Torrance discovered in reading Einstein was that progress in a rigorous discipline like physics requires an element of "free invention" that is quite different from the methodologies of either positivism or idealism. It is necessary for the research physicist to develop a disciplined intuition capable of positing ideas that were not already present in the mind and that could not be read directly out of experimental data.[16] Such free creation does not fit in with either Kantian or positivist epistemologies.

For Kant all empirical knowledge rested on the a priori "forms of perception" (*Anschauungsformen*), such as the forms of space and time.[17] In practice this meant assuming the validity of Euclidean geometry and absolute time as the framework for physics, as was true in the case in Newtonian physics. Any deviation from the Euclidean framework in physics prior to Einstein would have been as hazardous as allowing the earth to move around the sun before the discoveries of Kepler and Galileo.

The significance of the idea of the motion of the earth around the sun (actually around a point near the center of the sun) for our purposes is that Copernicus posited it on strictly theoretical grounds. It was originally a "free invention" in Einstein's sense. The first experimental evidence to support heliocentrism was not forthcoming until Galileo developed the astronomical telescope.[18] The same was true in the case of non-Euclidean geometry. Einstein first posited a new, Riemannian geometry for space and time years before there was any evidence—even before anyone even thought to look for evidence—for non-Euclidean features of the cosmos.

This kind of free theoretical creativity was just what Torrance was looking for—a non-dualistic method with a non-dualistic result, or, more accurately, a non-dualistic scientific theory that gave rise, on reflection, to the articulation of a non-dualistic methodology.[19]

The result of Einstein's investigations (the General Theory of Relativity) was that the structure of the universe could not be assumed a priori to match the flat, foursquare geometry that we work with in everyday life and which was first axiomatized by Euclid in the third century b.c.e. Scientific cosmology can be seen as a refinement of everyday experience, but it is a contingent refinement, not a predictable one.[20] It is contingent both ontologically and epistemically: contingent ontologically in the sense that the geometry of the universe, its space-time metric, depends on its mass-energy content; contingent epistemically in that its geometry has to be determined on the basis of actual measurements, not assumed in advance.[21]

More recently, inflationary cosmology has predicted that the large-scale geometry of our universe may be flat or quasi-Euclidean after all, and, within just the last few years, sophisticated experiments have confirmed the idea of cosmic "flatness." Even if this result holds up (a big "if"), it would not mean that Einstein's basic theory was wrong, however. There are three reasons for this. First of all, whatever its metric turns out to be, the new geometry will apply to space and time together in a single continuum, not to space by itself: space would still not be absolute. Second, the apparent flatness of the universe only shows up on the very large scale; space-time can still be severely warped in the vicinity of high mass-concentrations like stars and galactic nuclei, to say nothing of black holes. Most importantly of all, we know space-time to be flat (if such it is) only contingently: its large-scale flatness had to be discovered by careful observation, and our ideas would have to be revised again if new investigations were to give a different result from earlier probes.

So Einstein gave us an entirely different way of looking at the universe. That was what probably first drew Professor Torrance's attention to Einstein's writings. But contrary to what many of his critics have supposed, Torrance does not attempt to relate General Relativity directly to the doctrine of God or other areas of theology.[22] He is more interested in the method Einstein used in discovering relativity than in the specifics of relativity theory itself. A careful reading will show that Torrance's argument always makes an important shift at this point: a shift from scientific non-duality to epistemological non-duality; from the cosmological non-duality of geometry and physics or, more generally, the ontic non-duality of form and content, to the epistemological non-duality of mathematical theory and the empirical world.[23] Einstein's theory of relativity is essential for modern physics, but his method, Torrance argues, must be important for all areas of human inquiry, including theology.[24]

Torrance on the Mystery of Intelligibility

The question that Torrance focuses on is this: How is it that humans can conceptually grasp structures that go so far beyond their everyday experience and even beyond the reach of scientific instruments available at the time? Einstein formulated this "mystery" of the comprehensibility of the cosmos and brought it to public attention over sixty years ago.[25]

Of course, Torrance realizes that the novelties of the cosmos are practically infinite; consequently humans are unable to understand it in its totality.[26] He never suggests that human theorizing can exhaust reality.[27] But the wonder is that we can understand the universe even dimly once we move beyond the level of ordinary everyday experience.

We have already noted that induction from raw data, for Torrance, is inadequate as an explanation of intelligibility in science. Conceptual structures are needed in order to arrange data or even to know what sorts of data are relevant in the first place. If the inductive method does not account for the comprehensibility of the world, what about the scientist's use of mathematics? Does mathematics give them an inside track of some sort? The problem with this view is that all mathematical tools are developed by humans. In fact, almost all of it is developed without any immediate reference at all to the structures of nature. So why should mathematics be so "effective" (to use Eugene Wigner's phrase)[28] in mapping out the natural world? Do scientists merely impose their formalisms on nature? If so, why does nature resign itself to such an imposition? Why does it allow us to design semiconductors and space probes that actually work?[29]

Here is where Torrance blows the whistle. Time is up! No answer has been forthcoming to one of the great riddles of the modern world, and—this is the key step for Torrance—no answer can be forthcoming as long as subject and object, knower and known, are taken to be separate, unrelated entities.[30] In other words, the failure to answer the question to date is not a license to stop asking it or to write it off as an inexplicable miracle, but rather an indication that a change in assumptions is called for.

Contrary to the direction of Western thought since Descartes, Torrance argues, one must rely on a primordial connection between the human mind and the structures of creation as a starting point in order to pursue scientific research. In fact, scientific work requires the assumption of intelligibility at more than just one level.

Torrance distinguishes these levels of intelligibility in at least two different ways. In his 1970 Harris Lectures, he drew attention to two distinct aspects of the primordial harmony between object and subject: "A double fact evokes our wonder: the openness of the structure of the universe to our rational investigation, and the openness of our knowing to the intelligible nature of the universe. This is what Einstein used to speak of as the religious awe in which he was left by the vast comprehensibility of the universe."[31] The character of the wonder described here depends on one's starting point. If we begin with the fact of human rationality, and a healthy sense of its limits, the wonder is that the universe is accessible to human science—"the openness of the structure of the universe to our rational investigation." On the other hand, if we begin with a sense of the grandeur of the cosmic order, then the wonder is that the human mind is capable of grasping it at all—"the openness of our knowing to the intelligible nature of the universe." Either way, we are faced with the mystery of the intelligibility of the world around us.

Torrance also distinguished levels of rationality in terms of the fundamental beliefs involved. In *Christian Theology and Scientific Culture* (1981), for example, he differentiated between belief in the objective order and harmony of the cosmos, on the one hand, and belief in the possibility of humans understanding that order, on the other: "There could be no science without belief in the inner harmony of the world or without the belief that it is possible to grasp reality with our theoretical constructions. Belief of this kind, Einstein claimed, is and always will remain the fundamental motive for all scientific work."[32] As this crisp quote indicates, two harmonies are presupposed in all scientific work. There is a harmony in the cosmos itself, which is exhibited in its elegant mathematical structure (even in realms of so-called "chaos"); and there is a second harmony between that cosmos, with its mathematical structure, and the feeble efforts of the human mind to grasp the deep structure of the cosmos with its own mathematical tools.

On either of these two readings of the different levels of intelligibility, a remarkable conclusion follows: the possibility of scientific investigation that transcends the bounds of previous experience and prior understanding can be established if (and only if) one makes the assumption of non-duality.[33] For the purposes of later discussion, it may be helpful to translate this conclusion into the language of biology: the human mind is not just adapted to the physical environment in which it evolved; it is preadapted to the larger cosmos.[34] That is, the human intellect is adapted to numerous arenas of nature of which it has had no prior direct experience.

Following Einstein, Torrance refers to this remarkable fact as the mystery of the "comprehensibility" or "intelligibility" of the natural world.[35] The mystery does not prove that God exists, but it does suggest the existence of a transcendent ground of rationality undergirding the processes of both the cosmos and the human mind.[36] At the end of this chapter, I shall return to this point and try to pin it down a little more.

Comparison with Einstein's Views on Intelligibility

Torrance is on solid ground here with the writings of Einstein. Although Einstein never explicitly distinguished two distinct levels of intelligibility the way Torrance does,[37] the basic points recur throughout his epistemological writings. For example, he stated the importance of assuming the rationality of nature itself: "Certain it is that a conviction, akin to religious feeling, of the rationality or intelligibility of the world lies behind all scientific work of a higher order."[38]

The creative scientist must assume and rely on intelligibility from the side of the object. But the scientist must also assume a connection between subject and object. As he reflected on his own scientific work, Einstein concluded that he had always approached his work assuming a primordial connection of some sort between the human mind and nature. He argued that there was no other way to explain how concepts could arise in the scientist's mind that could be applied to the remotest areas of the natural world. In other words, there is no logical bridge between the phenomena and the principles that explain them that could ever take the place of disciplined human intuition.[39]

Even though he was strongly critical of organized religion, Einstein repeatedly pointed to the larger "sphere of religion" to explain the comprehensibility of the natural world to human reason.[40] Using a well-known phrase from Leibniz, he argued for a "pre-established harmony" between the mind and nature that could not be explained in terms of any mechanism, whether logical or natural.[41] He also borrowed a striking phrase from Kant to formulate one of his most cogent statements of the problem: "the eternal mystery of the world is its comprehensibility" (Kant). Einstein then explained Kant's point in his own words: "the world of our sense experiences is comprehensible. The fact that it is comprehensible is a miracle."[42]

Einstein described this idea of a preestablished harmony or comprehensibility as a matter of "belief" or "faith."[43] He spoke of his own firm belief in "a superior mind" that revealed itself in the laws of nature,[44] and he stated the importance of intellectual humility in the face of "reason incarnate" in the world—incarnate yet inaccessible to the human mind in its profoundest depths.[45]

Einstein also realized that this twofold belief in intelligibility was not his own discovery, or even Leibniz's or Kant's. He pointed out that the very founders of modern science were people of profound religious faith. Faith in the intelligibility of the cosmos made the solution of scientific problems seem possible to natural philosophers like Kepler and Newton long before it was an everyday occurrence as it is commonly thought to be today. Einstein also recognized deeper roots for this faith in the Psalms and the Prophets that had inspired early European scientists.[46] However, Einstein consistently rejected any notion of a personal God in the sense of a being who answers individual prayers and judges people according to their actions.[47]

In short, what looks like a simple presupposition in modern science turns out to be a theological truth with deep roots in, if not unique to, the biblical tradition. Einstein was still close enough to his Jewish roots to realize this, and Professor Torrance is conversant enough with Einstein to see the importance of his thought on the matter.

Torrance on Scientific Discovery

The preadaptation or preestablished harmony between the mind and the world is only a necessary condition for scientific discovery. The existence of a sustained tradition of belief in the intelligibility of nature and the possibility of scientific discovery is also (at most) a necessary condition.[48] Even a scientist imbued with faith in the viability of her enterprise must find a way to grasp novel features of a largely unknown universe. Exactly how does the human mind do this? At this point, Torrance goes beyond Einstein's explicit statements and seems to argue for an actual contact of some sort between the mind and the mathematical structures of nature.

Einstein would only speak in rather vague metaphors when addressing the issue. For example, he stated that the scientist has to discern the principles of nature[49] by looking for those general features of the empirical data that can be formulated with precision. The theorist must persist "until principles which he can make the basis of deductive reasoning have revealed themselves to him."[50] Nature itself is rather passive here; the initiative rests with the scientist, and the tools are basically those of pencil and paper, or chalk and board. As a description of Einstein's own creative process, these loose metaphors are suggestive, but they leave the philosophically inclined reader wondering how the mind of the physicist actually discerns anything in nature and how the fundamental principles reveal themselves. It could be argued that Einstein was only referring to the development of hypotheses as inspired guesses (the "hypothetico-deductive method").[51]

It seems to me that Torrance goes beyond the letter of Einstein's statements here. He speaks of the scientist's "penetration into the intelligible order of the universe" or "into the structure inherent in nature."[52] Phrases like these could be read as metaphors like those Einstein used, but I think there is more to it than that. Torrance also claims that we "probe into the depth of being in order to grasp it in its own inherent forms and patterns."[53] This sounds very much like a mental journey of some kind. And, in some of his more recent writings (since the mid-1980s), Torrance even sees a legitimate "Promethean element" in the work of scientists like Einstein: they storm the heavens, as it were, in their quest for truth, and they dare to think of the world as it ought to be rather than just as it is.[54]

But there are also counterbalancing aspects of Torrance's thinking. Sometimes he shifts the emphasis away from the activity of the human mind to the revelatory character of nature itself. In one of his earliest discussions of scientific method, the preface to *Theological Science* (dated 1967), Torrance began with several of the points we have described with appropriate references to Einstein's writings. Then he went on to state that insight into the laws of nature is somehow impressed on the scientist's mind in the process of investigation. The transition from Einstein's point to Torrance's own thought is clearly seen in the following excerpt: "Because there is no logical road to these laws the scientist, in formulating them, must rely on his 'intuition', that is upon the sheer weight or impress of external reality upon his apprehension."[55] The initial emphasis in this quotation is the Einsteinian one on intuition over logic.[56] But the images of "weight" and "impress" attribute more agency to the external world than Einstein's metaphors did.[57]

Perhaps the most extensive discussion of the agency of nature in scientific discovery is found in Torrance's 1970 Harris Lectures. Again the point is made in the context of a discussion of Einstein's wonder about the comprehensibility of the world, but then goes beyond it. Here is one illuminating excerpt: "we are aware of coming under an imperious constraint from beyond which holds out to us the promise of future disclosure and summons us to further heuristic inquiry which it would be irresponsible for us to evade."[58] The natural world clearly plays an active role here. It constrains us. It summons us.[59] It discloses some of its features and lures us with the promise of further disclosures.[60]

If so, another question arises: How does the natural world exercise such initiative in scientific discovery? The most promising clue that I have been able to find in Torrance's published works has to do with the web of interrelationships that exists among objects in nature: "It is in that interrelatedness of objects to one another that we find means of controlling our own subjectivities over against them and of distinguishing what is objectively real from our own subjective projections."[61] If scientists were only concerned with the study of isolated objects, they could never be sure of the correctness of their constructs. But the fact that natural objects exist in dynamic relationships with one another gives them a life of their own. And, as long as scientists focus on those relationships (Torrance also calls them "invariances"),[62] rather than on isolated objects, false notions will gradually be eliminated from our theories.

Scientific Discovery as a Form of Revelation

In attributing an active role to nature in scientific discovery, Torrance is evidently drawing on his understanding of divine revelation in which the Triune God is the subject rather than a passive object of investigation. On occasion, Torrance even uses biblical language about theophany to describe the results of scientific inquiry: "nature manifests itself to us and even discloses to us objective structures that are inherently non-observable but constitute, so to speak, the invariant back-side of reality."[63] In the well-known Exodus account, Moses was not able to see God face to face; so he stood on a rock where he could observe the trail that God left as he passed by, and he recorded the impression for posterity (Exod. 33:17-23). In a similar manner, though scientists cannot grasp the universe in all its depth, they are in a position to recognize the structures that nature discloses to them and to interpret them for the public.

Leaving aside various differences between scientific discovery and divine revelation,[64] the main issue here for Torrance appears to be that of control—who or what is in control of the knowledge relationship? In classical physics and in industrial processes, complete human control is held out as an ideal, even if it is never quite attained.[65] In contrast, Torrance argues that real scientific discovery relies on something that happens in the mind of the scientist before the data can be controlled by either logic or experiment. That is why there can be no logical bridge from the data to the concepts on which a good theory rests. That is also why Einstein described his own ideas as "free inventions." As Torrance states, these inventions arose in Einstein's mind "prior to his reasoning processes and had a free, spontaneous character."[66]

To put it slightly differently, there is an element of musicality, or even playfulness, in the work of creative scientists (as we know there is for artists)—something that cannot be reduced to a method or controlled in any way.[67] This element is quite rational in the sense that it tunes in to the intelligible structures of nature, but it is not strictly logical or inferential.[68] In that respect, scientific discovery is indeed very much like divine revelation. The human mind seems to be preadapted for both. Why this is so remains to be seen.

In all this Torrance assumes the Christian understanding of a personal God. This is the main point with which he takes issue with Einstein.[69] For Torrance, God is not only personal, but also tri-personal and, as for Karl Barth, self-revelation is the key to understanding the Triune nature of God. However, Torrance shares Einstein's criticism of the traditional Western definition of "personality" in terms of self-definition and interventionist manipulation.[70] Much of his theological work is devoted to a critique of this (Boethian) notion of personality and the need to reform it in light of the dynamic, relational character of the Triune God.[71] In fact, Torrance argues that impersonal modes of thought are a legacy of that a-prioristic, mechanical worldview (attributed to Newton) that Einstein sought to replace with relational thinking.[72]

So Torrance agrees with Einstein on the restless, probing, and even Promethean quality of the human mind. However, he balances this emphasis on human action by attributing more of an active role to nature itself in the process of discovery. If Torrance is going beyond Einstein at this point, as I have suggested, he could be said to be engaging in the very sort of "free invention" that Einstein utilized in his scientific work. To insist on logical inference or detailed documentation of each point would be to miss the point. With this freedom in mind, we may ourselves press on in some of the directions Torrance has suggested.

Human Science and Cosmic Light

Having looked at Torrance's analysis of scientific discovery, we may turn our attention back to the remarkable ability of the human mind to comprehend the natural world. Why should some humans have this ability and not others? Why should any humans have the ability to understand nature in depth at all? A non-dualist epistemology must be grounded in a non-dualist ontology. Here Torrance goes even further beyond Einstein, and his theology begins to take the lead.

Torrance holds to the classic Christian belief in the creation of humanity in the divine image. Since biblical times this belief has been understood to imply a unique human ability to understand the works of God insofar as those works are made known.[73] The huge universe in which we have found ourselves is not an alien environment, even though it is largely an unexplored one. Humans are endowed with the ability to investigate and interpret nature as if it were a book written with the finger of God.[74] Furthermore, according to Torrance, the human intellect is illuminated by the uncreated Rationality of God (the Logos) in such a way that it can discern the created rationalities of nature.[75]

If I read him correctly, Torrance is suggesting that humanity plays a role in the universe analogous to that of light, only on a different level. Light orders the material cosmos in the special sense that the invariance of its speed is the basis for the equations governing space, time, and motion that Einstein discovered in 1905.[76] In this special sense, Torrance argues, physical light is a created reflection of the uncreated Light of God.[77] In a similar way, humanity is created in the image of God and plays a unique role in the universe, ordering it epistemically with pure science.[78] So the pre-established harmony between the human mind and the cosmos would seem to have something to do with the fact that both are in tune with divine Light, the Reason or Logos of God.

Classical Christian theology is helpful here in suggesting analogies. But what can all this possibly mean in the context of the modern scientific picture of creation? In the case of light, which for Torrance represents the rationality of the cosmos, the answer is fairly straightforward. Einstein's theories of space, time, and matter have led us to an evolutionary picture of the cosmos. Once the finite age of the universe was accepted (as the "steady-state" model was ruled out by observations) the question of cosmic origins had to be addressed within the framework of physics—relativistic cosmology led to relativistic cosmogony.[79]

Today we work with theories about the Big Bang and the inflation of the early universe in which space, time, and matter took their present form out of an intense burst of energy. When Torrance talks about the creation of light, he is using traditional theological language, but he clearly intends his language to refer to the same space-time development that the cosmologists describe with their theories. The "creation of light" is the ordering of space, time, and matter in the first split second of the Big Bang. This agreement of referent must be sustained even if current cosmological theories need to be revised in some way. There can be no duality here between theology and science. Of course, theologians cannot dictate a theory of cosmic evolution. But they can expect the result to be consistent with the ancient notion of light as a created reflection of the uncreated Light of God.

But what about the creation of that other reflection of God—humanity? Torrance does not work as much with the theory of evolution as he does with physics and cosmology. In fact, he is highly critical of the naturalist fallacy that appears in the writings of many evolutionary scientists. Nonetheless, I think he accepts the theory of biological evolution as a general framework for understanding human origins.[80] So, given the analogy between the role of humanity and that of light, we may assume that when Torrance speaks of humanity being created in the image of God, he refers to the same space-time development that the anthropologists describe with their own theories about human origins.[81] Like that between the idea of the creation of light and scientific cosmology, this agreement of referent is needed even if current theories of evolution are in need of revision in various ways. Theologians cannot dictate a theory of human origins, but they can expect the result to be consistent with the notion of humanity as created in the image of a rational God.

The Mobility of Angels

If Torrance's program of non-dual ontology is to be carried through, it will be necessary to address the thorny issues of evolutionary epistemology. As this is likely to be a major area of interdisciplinary discussion in coming years, it might be appropriate for me to present Professor Torrance with some questions and thoughts of my own that stem from his pioneering work.[82]

At some point in the discussion, we must ask what might have happened in prehistory that could have preadapted the human intellect to understand the deep structures of creation. Of course, as Torrance points out, intelligibility, at both cosmic and human levels, has a transcendent ground that cannot be entirely comprehended by finite minds.[83] Still, like Moses on the rock, we may hope to trace the trail of the Transcendent in creaturely space and time. Just how might divine Light have ordered the human mind (and indirectly human science) in a manner that is as accessible (and as subtle) to human understanding as the way in which cosmic light ordered the space-time structure of the early universe?

It would be a relatively simple (though far from trivial) matter if we were only investigating the adaptation of the human senses to the demands of survival and reproduction in a prehistoric forest environment. We could understand binocular vision, for instance (an attribute of primates in general), as an adaptation to the three-dimensional arrangement of objects like trees and branches and bananas. Consideration of such an environment might even help us understand how binocular vision in humans is preadapted to meet the challenges of travel and sports. But what could possibly be the scientific meaning of Torrance's statement about the human mind being "sympathetically attuned to the intrinsic rationality of the created universe"?[84] Are we right in assuming that this "tuning" (Einstein's "pre-established harmony") is a matter of preadaptation, programmed into the human genotype? If so, what kind of environment could possibly have provided the challenges and fostered the evolutionary selection of early hominids needed for the preadaption of the human mind for probing the realms of microphysics and General Relativity? And what evidence might there be in the prehistoric record of human evolution (as reconstructed by anthropologists) that might indicate human interaction with that environment?

Unfortunately, the problem of finding a scientific correlate to divine creation is complicated in this case by the fact that human cultures have so thoroughly restructured their own environments with their technologies. As a result, it has become extremely difficult for us to differentiate our native abilities from our present, culturally conditioned ones, much less to discern the original connections between our native abilities and our primordial environment. It is as if we all lived in an enclosed, artificially lighted structure and could not figure out how human eyesight had developed in the first place. The primordial environment cannot be projected from the current situation; it must be laboriously reconstructed. Anthropologists are just beginning to do this.[85]

In an effort to articulate new hypotheses, it might be worthwhile to look beyond our own cultural horizons and reconsider some of the ideas of the ancients. Prescientific cultures provided their own accounts of how humanity came into being, and some of their ideas also claimed an instrumental role for the environment in this event. Take, for example, the ancient view of humanity as a microcosm: the human body came from the earth; bodily fluids from water; and the five senses from other elements; but the intellect came from the heavens. Each item in their inventory of human traits came into being from a corresponding feature of the environment as they understood it. For example, according to an ancient Jewish interpretation of Genesis 1, God's Wisdom created each of the five components of the human body from the appropriate environmental element, but he created human reason "from the mobility of angels and from clouds."[86]

As we know, such crude notions of human origins have long since been replaced by more scientific explanations. Or, at least, we have reasonably good explanations for the development of the human body and the five senses (as in the case of binocular vision). But what of the human mind? We are still missing major pieces of the puzzle here. So the microcosm theory might actually be of some heuristic value. In a non-dual ontology, any account of humanity, the microcosm, can only be as complete (or as "thick") as the corresponding description of the macrocosm.

Spiritual forces like angels are no longer part of the scientific worldview, but they were still very real as recently as the era of early modern science,[87] and, from what we can discern from Paleolithic remains, they were very real to the earliest known humans as well.[88] Could it be that the environmental forces that stimulated the development of spiritual gifts among early humans actually preadapted their (our) minds to meeting the challenges of disciplines like mathematics and cosmology?[89]

Of course, the concerted effort of nineteenth-century scientists to disentangle their disciplines from theological strictures eventually led to a ban against any notion of spiritual forces. Angels have generally been regarded as mythic remnants or even psychological projections. But a ban against uncritical assumptions can cut both ways. Any hypothetical environment you may reconstruct that might possibly have preadapted the human mind for probing the laws of microphysics and relativity is likely to look as much like the traditional realm of angels as like the material matrix of food gathering, toolmaking, and mate selection that existed in Paleolithic society.[90] I wish to press Professor Torrance for his thoughts on this subject.

Einstein's writings have made several important contributions to human understanding. They have also confronted us with some fundamental questions about the nature and origin of human intelligence. These are insights and questions with which theologians must grapple. One of the great strengths of Professor Torrance as a theologian is that he has understood this challenge and called for a sustained effort to meet it.

For Professor Torrance, Einstein's main contribution to physics was the integration (or non-duality) of geometry and cosmology in General Relativity. His main contribution to epistemology was the integration of mathematical formalism with the results of empirical investigation and the consequent positing of a preestablished harmony between the human mind and nature. The main question

Einstein's work raises for Torrance is how the particular forms of human intelligence can be adequate for the development of theories that can explain the large-scale structures of the universe. This is Einstein's mystery of the intelligibility of the universe.

Professor Torrance argues that the only way to deal with this mystery is to posit a primordial connection of some kind between the human mind and the extensive structures of the universe. In practice, this connection is based on the mind's ability to make contact with the structures of nature as the latter reveal themselves to human intelligence. Theologically, this uncanny ability is grounded in divine creation: the creation and ordering of space-time through the invariance of the speed of light, and the creation of humanity in the image of God.

Scientifically speaking, the origin of space, time, and light is clearly related to the Big Bang origin of the universe. The emergence of human intelligence is also a space-time process having something to do with biological evolution. Unfortunately, Professor Torrance does not say very much about the evolutionary origin of the primordial connection between the human mind and the structures of the universe. I suggest that something like a theory of the microcosm is needed in order to bridge the gap between human evolution and epistemology here. As human sensory systems are adapted to locomotion and mate selection in the primordial forest, the human intellect must be adapted to a cognitive or spiritual world that underlies the structures of the cosmos.

We are indeed indebted to Thomas F. Torrance for holding up some of Einstein's ideas and pressing the questions in order to stimulate further inquiry.

Notes

1. *Time*, 31 December 1999.

2. Albert Einstein and Leopold Infeld, *The Evolution of Physics: The Growth of Ideas from Early Concepts to Relativity and Quanta* (New York: Simon and Schuster, 1938).

3. While preparing this chapter, I visited Professor Torrance in Edinburgh (10 January 2000) and asked him when he had begun to read Einstein's works seriously. He told me he first read Planck and Einstein as a student at the University of Edinburgh (in the 1930s; the first collection of Einstein's writings came out in 1933; Albert Einstein, *The World As I*

See It (London: John Lane, 1935). But his thinking was particularly stimulated by the reading of F. S. C. Northrop's essay, "Einstein's Conception of Science," in *Albert Einstein: Philosopher-Scientist,* ed. Paul Arthur Schilpp, *Library of Living Philosophers* 7 (LaSalle, Ill.: Open Court, 1949), 385-408, discussed by Torrance, e.g., in T. F. Torrance, *Reality and Scientific Theology*, vol. 1, *Theology and Science at the Frontiers of Knowledge* (Princeton, N.J.: Scottish Academy Press for the Center of Theological Inquiry, 1985 [Lectures 1970]), 131; Thomas F. Torrance, *Transformation and Convergence in the Frame of Knowledge: Explorations in the Interrelations of Scientific and Theological Enterprise,* (Belfast: Christian Journals; Grand Rapids, Mich.: Eerdmans, 1984), 248; Thomas F. Torrance, *Juridical Law and Physical Law: Toward a Realist Foundation for Human Law* (Edinburgh: Scottish Academic Press, 1982). In a later E-mail communication (7 June 2000), Professor Torrance added that he read through all of Einstein's nonmathematical works that he could find (in English) at Princeton while giving a modified version of the 1959 Hewett Lectures (later published as *Theological Science* [London: Oxford University Press, 1969]; see the preface for the locations of the original lectures). He also pointed out that the roots of his rejection of dualistic thinking really go back to Church fathers like Hilary and Athanasius. Alister McGrath comments that Torrance found in the "Einsteinian analogy" a convenient way to illustrate what he already knew from his earlier theological training; Alistair E. McGrath, *T. F. Torrance: An Intellectual Biography* (Edinburgh: T&T Clark, 1999), 187. Even so, the discovery of Einstein's ideas certainly inspired Torrance's endeavor to see parallels in all fields of knowledge; cf. Torrance, *Juridical Law*, 24.

4. By my own count, at least forty-five of Torrance's publications and unpublished lectures discuss Einstein's ideas, not counting the numerous reprints.

5. Professor Torrance particularly recommended that I read Elsasser's *Atom and Organism: A New Approach to Theoretical Biology* (Princeton, N.J.: Princeton University Press, 1966), which had to do with the principle of complementarity and biological systems theory. As a result, I ended up writing my Edinburgh thesis on the ideas of Niels Bohr, particularly the concepts of correspondence and complementarity, their relation to Michael Polanyi's thought, and their possible uses in theology. As it turned out, this was not quite what Torrance had in mind when he recommended Elsasser (cf. Thomas F. Torrance, *God and Rationality* [London: Oxford University Press, 1971], 14-15), and we sometimes found ourselves on opposite sides of the classic Einstein-Bohr debates regarding the validity of quantum mechanics. Yet Professor Torrance values rigorous discussions of science and theology and has always encouraged me in my studies even when they have (temporarily) taken a somewhat different direction than his own.

6. Most of Einstein's methodological essays were written between approximately 1914 and 1953. They are readily available in three English-language collections: Albert Einstein, *The World As I See It* (London: John

Lane, 1935); Albert Einstein, *Out of My Later Years* (New York: Philosophical Library, 1950); Albert Einstein, *Ideas and Opinions* (London: Alvin Redman, 1954).

7. Thomas F. Torrance, *The Christian Frame of Mind* (Edinburgh: Handsel Press, 1985), 145; cf. Torrance, *Scientific Theology*, 52-53, which cites Einstein's "The Religiousness of Science," *The World*, 28; *Ideas and Opinions*, 40.

8. Christopher B. Kaiser, "Holistic Ministry in a Technological Society," *Reformed Review* 41 (spring 1988): 175-88.

9. Torrance uses the term "non-dualist," e.g., in Thomas F. Torrance, *Theology in Reconciliation: Essays towards Evangelical and Catholic Unity in East and West* (London: Geoffrey Chapman, 1975), 74 (italicized), 77; Thomas F. Torrance, *The Ground and Grammar of Theology* (Charlottesville, Virg.: University of Virginia Press; Dublin: Christian Journals, 1980) (lectures 1978-79), 104; Torrance, *Transformation*, 204-6. He also speaks of a "unitary approach" or "unitary thinking"; e.g., Torrance, *Ground and Grammar*, 11; Thomas F. Torrance, *Reality and Evangelical Theology* (Philadelphia: Westminster Press, 1982, The 1981 Payton Lectures), 32; T. F. Torrance, *Christian Theology and Scientific Culture* (Belfast: Christian Journals; New York: Oxford University Press, 1981), 54.

10. Einstein is only just one of many natural philosophers and scientists that Torrance engages in his writing. Others that might fruitfully be studied through Torrance's writings include John Philoponos, James Clerk Maxwell, John Archibald Wheeler, and Ilya Prigogine. Botond Gaál of Debrecen University and Jitse van der Meer of Redeemer College are among those currently working on Torrance's uses of Maxwell.

11. Thomas F. Torrance, "The Integration of Form in Natural and in Theological Science" (Lecture 1972), *Science, Medicine, and Man* 1 (1973), 148, 157, reprinted in Torrance, *Transformation*, 69, 83. It might be argued that relativity theory by itself does not entirely eliminate the disjunction between the objective properties postulated for nature ("primary qualities") and the private perceptions of humans ("secondary qualities"), for example, in our experiences of simultaneity and the transience of time. As Torrance points out, every theory must raise new problems that point to the need for a further refinement; cf. Torrance, *Theological Science*, 296-97.

12. The first occasion on which Torrance discussed Einstein's epistemology in public may have been in the 1959 Hewett Lectures, at least, in the "considerably expanded form" (preface) that was published as Torrance, *Theological Science*; see esp. 110-11, 117-18, 184, 296-97, and compare the brief mention of Einstein's "kinetic model" on page 240 with the discussion of his "kinetic thinking" in the 1962 lecture, entitled "The Influence of Reformed Theology on Theological Method," reprinted in Thomas F. Torrance, *Theology in Reconstruction* (London: SCM; Grand Rapids, Mich.: Eerdmans, 1965), 73.

13. The idea of non-duality ("the unitary character of theological and scientific knowledge") is the first of seven themes that were discussed by W. Jim Neidhardt in the introduction to Torrance, *Christian Frame*, xv-xxxviii.

14. For an impressive effort to unify disparate bodies of knowledge, see, for example, T. F. Torrance, *Space, Time, and Incarnation* (London: Oxford University Press, 1969), 77-90.

15. E.g., Torrance, *Transformation*, 110-11. See also the Northrop article that stimulated Torrance's interest in Einstein's epistemology, Northrop, "Einstein's Conception," 392-96, 407.

16. "The Method of Theoretical Physics" (1933), Einstein, *The World*, 134-35; Einstein, *Ideas and Opinions*, 272-73. The original German phrase is "freie Erfindungen des menschlichen Geistes," *Mein Weltbild* (Amsterdam: Qerido Verlag, 1934), 180-82.

17. Torrance, *Incarnation*, 58.

18. Elsewhere, I call this form of human intelligence "Copernican intelligence"; Christopher B. Kaiser, "How Can a Theological Understanding of Humanity Enrich Artificial Intelligence Work?" *Asbury Theological Journal* 44 (fall 1989): 61-75.

19. Almost all of Torrance's discussions of Einstein discuss this fundamental idea. One of the clearest explanations I have found is in Torrance, *Juridical Law*, 24-25. On Einstein's discovering his method after the fact, see Thomas F. Torrance, "Theological Realism," in *The Philosophical Frontiers of Christian Theology: Essays Presented to D. M. Mackinnon*, ed. Brian Hebblethwaite and Stewart Sutherland (Cambridge: Cambridge University Press, 1982), 182.

20. E.g., Torrance, *Rationality*, 10-11, which cites Einstein's "Physics and Reality" (1936), Einstein, *Later Years*, 59-60.

21. Thomas F. Torrance, "Christian Theology in the Context of Scientific Revolution," *Pluralisme et Oecuménisme en Recherches Théologiques*, Mélanges offerts au R. P. Dockx, O.P., par Y. Congar et al., *Bibliotheca Ephemeridum Theologicarum Lovaniensium*, vol. 43, (Paris-Gembloux: Édition Duculot, 1976); reprinted in Torrance, *Transformation*, 247.

22. In my view, this is where many commentators miss Torrance's point. For example, Colin Weightman appears to confuse Torrance's non-dualistic epistemology with his parallel discussions of unified field theory; Colin Weightman, *Theology in a Polanyian Universe: The Theology of Thomas Torrance* (New York: Peter Lang, 1994), 190; cf. 168, where the author discusses Torrance's epistemological point without any connection to Einstein's field theory. John Polkinghorne mistakenly attributes to Torrance (whom he associates with Pannenberg) the notion that the space-time field functions as a mediator between God and the world; John Polkinghorne, *Reason and Reality: The Relationship between Science and Theology* (Philadelphia: Trinity Press, 1991), 93. In effect, Polkinghorne attributes to Torrance the view of Newton that Torrance emphatically

rejects. Max Jammer's discussion of Torrance is based on Polkinghorne's interpretation on this point; Max Jammer, *Einstein and Religion: Physics and Theology* (Princeton, N.J.: Princeton University Press, 1999), 207-10.

23. This is the main point of the Northrop's article which stimulated Torrance's interest in Einstein; Northrop, "Einstein's Conception," 387-88.

24. E.g., Torrance, *Juridical Law*, 24; Torrance, *Transformation*, xii.

25. "One may say 'the eternal mystery of the world is its comprehensibility,' . . . the world of our sense experiences is comprehensible. The fact that it is comprehensible is a miracle." Einstein, "Physics and Reality" (1936), Einstein, *Later Years*, 61; Einstein, *Ideas and Opinions,* 292. For a more recent statement of the problem, see Paul Davies, *The Mind of God* (New York: Simon & Schuster, 1992), 20, 24, passim.

26. Torrance, *Scientific Theology*, 52, 135; Torrance, *Ground and Grammar*, 4-5, 104-5, usually citing Einstein, *The World*, 28. For Torrance's association of inexhaustibility with Einstein's idea of the "unboundedness" of the cosmos, see Thomas F. Torrance, *Divine and Contingent Order* (Oxford: Oxford University Press, 1981), 53-54; Torrance, *Scientific Culture*, 77. For a good review of the limits of physical cosmology, see John D. Barrow, *Theories of Everything: The Quest for Ultimate Explanation* (Oxford: Clarendon Press, 1991).

27. Hence, the ontic and the noetic are distinct poles within a unitary reality; Torrance, *Juridical Law*, 25. The distinction of the ontic from the noetic is directed against logical empiricism; the non-dual emphasis is directed more against Kant. Torrance draws a parallel to the non-dual distinction between God and the world in Torrance, *Scientific Theology*, 32.

28. Eugene P. Wigner, "The Unreasonable Effectiveness of Mathematics in the Natural Sciences," *Communication in Pure and Applied Mathematics* 13 (February 1960), reprinted in Eugene P. Wigner, *Symmetries and Reflections* (Cambridge, Mass.: MIT Press, 1979), 222-37. Torrance cites Wigner's famous essay in "The Concept of Order in Theology and Science" (lecture 1983), Torrance, *Christian Frame*, 26. The statement of the basic problem derives from Einstein's "Geometry and Experience" (1921), Einstein, *Ideas and Opinions*, 233.

29. The public apologies that are offered when space projects fail are an indication of how quickly we have become accustomed to success in these unbelievable endeavors.

30. Blowing a whistle is not a very sophisticated image to use for a theologian, but it may capture the sense of a "wake up call" that Torrance tries to deliver in his lectures and books. A more biblical image would be blowing the trumpet or the shofar (thanks to my colleague Thomas Boogaart for noting this); cf. William Blake, *Europe* 13:1-5, where Newton himself sounds the trumpet signaling the end of the present world order; cf. Christopher B. Kaiser, *Creational Theology and the History of Physical Science: The Creationist Tradition from Basil to Bohr,* ed. Heiko Oberman, *Studies in the History of Christian Thought* 78 (Leiden: E. J. Brill, 1997), 330.

31. Torrance, *Scientific Theology* (based on 1970 Harris Lectures), 53; cf. 73 on "the "astonishing affinity between the rationality of the subject and that of the object." Reference is made to Einstein's "The Religiousness of Science," *The World*, 28, and "Physics and Reality," Einstein, *Later Years*, 60-61.

32. Thomas F. Torrance, "The Priority of Belief," in Torrance, *Scientific Culture* (preface 1980), 58. In the context of this passage, Torrance traces his own understanding of the fundamental role of beliefs in scientific work through Einstein to Clerk Maxwell; cf. Torrance, *Transformation* (preface 1982), xi-xii. In an E-mail message (22 June 2000), Professor Torrance adds that his study of Maxwell's writings "helped [him] very considerably in [his] understanding and interpretation of Einstein." The 1979 centenary of both Maxwell's death and Einstein's birth appears to have been a significant occasion for Torrance's thinking here; see Torrance, *Contingent Order* (preface 1979), x; Torrance, *Scientific Culture* (lectures 1980), 11; and Thomas F. Torrance, "Christian Faith and Physical Science in the Thought of James Clerk Maxwell" (lecture 1982), in Torrance, *Transformation*, 215. On the Maxwell-Einstein connection, see also Kaiser, *Creational Theology*, 383-84, 388.

33. The actual development of a sustained tradition of scientific research is another matter. Such a development requires not only the comprehensibility of the world but a tradition of investigation based on faith in the possibility of comprehension; cf. Kaiser, *Creational Theology*, 21-27, passim.

34. Ian Tattersall uses the term "exaptation" for "features that originally arose in one context but were later co-opted for use in another"; Ian Tattersall, *Becoming Human: Evolution and Human Uniqueness* (New York: Harcourt Brace, 1998), 108. The ability of the human mind to function on the frontiers of modern science is a good example of this phenomenon. Cf. Willem B. Drees, *Religion, Science, and Naturalism* (Cambridge: Cambridge University Press, 1996), 155-56, on the cognitive ability to do higher mathematics as an example of preadaptation.

35. Torrance, *Scientific Theology*, 77.

36. Torrance, *Scientific Theology*, 53. Hence "a cognate relation obtains between the created rationalities of the human mind and of the natural order"; Thomas F. Torrance, "Christian Theology and Scientific Culture: The Way Ahead," manuscript copy (received January 2000), 8.

37. The closest to a comprehensive twofold statement I can find is Einstein's reference to "the truly religious conviction that this universe of ours is something perfect and susceptible to the rational striving for knowledge"; "Religion and Science: Irreconcilable?" in Einstein, *Ideas and Opinions*, 52.

38. "Scientific Truth" (1929), Einstein, *The World*, 131; Einstein, *Ideas and Opinions*, 262.

39. "Principles of Scientific Research" (1918); "Inaugural Address to the Prussian Academy of Sciences" (1914); "The Method of Theoretical Physics" (1933), Einstein, *The World*, 125-26, 128, 136; Einstein, *Ideas and Opinions*, 221, 226-27, 274. For our purposes, the argument could be generalized: even if such a bridge could be assumed or constructed, one would have to postulate some primordial connection to account for our ability to find that bridge.

40. "Science and Religion II" (1941), Einstein, *Later Years*, 26; Einstein, *Ideas and Opinions*, 46.

41. "Principles of Scientific Research" (1918), Einstein, *The World*, 125-26; Einstein, *Ideas and Opinions*, 226-27.

42. "Physics and Reality" (1936), Einstein, *Later Years*, 61; Einstein, *Ideas and Opinions*, 292. By "world of our sense experiences," Einstein meant primarily the world of empirical scientific discovery; cf. "The Method of Theoretical Physics" (1933), Einstein, *The World*, 133; Einstein, *Ideas and Opinions*, 271. The reference to Kant's notion of comprehensibility (*Verständlichkeit*) implies that the idealist philosopher had a good grasp of the problem of scientific epistemology even if his architectonic systems were dated by their reliance on Newtonian mechanics; cf. Torrance, *Transformation*, 45, and Northrop's article, "Einstein's Conception," 390.

43. E.g., "The Fundaments of Theoretical Physics" (1940); "Message to the Italian Society for the Advancement of Science" (1950), Einstein, *Ideas and Opinions*, 324, 357; "Autobiographical Notes" (1949), Schlipp, *Philosopher-Scientist*, 63.

44. "The Religiousness of Science" (1934 or earlier); "Scientific Truth" (1929), Einstein, *The World*, 28, 131; Einstein, *Ideas and Opinions*, 40, 262.

45. "Science and Religion II" (1941), Einstein, *Later Years*, 29; Einstein, *Ideas and Opinions*, 49. Cf. Einstein's 1952 letter to Beatrice F. of San Francisco: "I am imbued with the consciousness of the insufficiency of the human mind to understand deeply the harmony of the universe which we try to formulate as 'laws of nature.' It is this consciousness and humility I miss in the Freethinker mentality" (letter from Einstein Archive, quoted in Jammer, *Einstein and Religion*, 121-22). Einstein did not explain exactly what he meant here by the limitations of the human mind. Elsewhere he does state that physics deals with only a small part of nature, excluding all its more subtle and complex aspects; Einstein's preface to Max Planck, *Where Is Science Going?* (London: Allen & Unwin, 1933), 11. Presumably he meant those aspects of nature that emerge in human history, which would include the emergence of the very intelligence that physicists rely on in their work. That same year he spoke of "the theorist's hope of grasping the real in all its depth"; "The Method of Theoretical Physics" (1933), Einstein, *The World*, 138; Einstein, *Ideas and Opinions*, 275.

46. "Religion and Science" (1930); "Johannes Kepler"; "Religion and Science: Irreconcilable?" (1948), Einstein, *The World*, 25-27, 141-42; Einstein, *Ideas and Opinions*, 38-40, 52. Here Einstein also cited Spinoza and Schopenhauer's descriptions of Buddhism. See Kaiser, *Creational Theology*, 21-27 on the Judeo-Christian origins of Western belief in the comprehensibility of the world.

47. E.g., Einstein, *The World*, 25, 28; cf. Jammer, *Einstein and Religion*, 47-50, 74-75.

48. Kaiser, *Creational Theology*, 8-9, 133, 399.

49. "Inaugural Address to the Prussian Academy of Sciences" (1914), Einstein, *The World*, 128. The English translation by Alan Harris is: "The scientist has to worm these general principles out of nature." But the original German reads: "Der Forscher muss vielmehr der Natur jene allgemeinen Prinzipe gleichsam ablauschen," *Mein Weltbild*, 171. The metaphor is more like radar picking up a signal than worms digging through earth.

50. "Inaugural Address"(1914), Einstein, *The World*, 128 (here the English is a fair translation of the German).

51. Cf. Einstein's comments on "tentative deduction" in Einstein, *The World*, 180; Einstein, *Ideas and Opinions*, 282. Compare Torrance, *Theological Science*, 239.

52. "Newton, Einstein, and Scientific Theology" (lecture 1971), in Torrance, *Transformation*, 273. Compare Torrance's description of "kinetic" or participatory thinking in theology; Torrance, *Rationality*, 177.

53. "Integration of Form in Natural and in Theological Science" (lecture 1972), reprinted in Torrance, *Transformation*, 78.

54. See Thomas F. Torrance, "Fundamental Issues in Theology and Science" (lecture 1985), in Torrance, *Christian Frame*, 89-90; Thomas F. Torrance, "Realism and Openness in Scientific Inquiry" (lecture 1986), in Torrance, *Christian Frame*, 117; Thomas F. Torrance, "The Transcendental Role of Wisdom in Science" (1990), revised in *Facets of Faith and Science*, vol. 1, ed. Jitse Vander Meer (Lanham, Md.: University Press of America, 1996), 138-39; Thomas F. Torrance "Creation, Contingent World-Order, and Time: A Theologico-Scientific Approach" (lecture 1996), in *Time, Creation, and World-Order*, ed. Mogens Wegener, *Acta Jutlandica* 74 (1999), 213. Torrance borrowed the Promethean image from Einstein's article, "Über den gegenwärtigen Stand der Feld-Theorie," in *Festschrift zum 70. Geburtstag von Prof. Dr. A. Stodola* (Zurich: Orell Füssli Verlag, 1929), 126-67. This article first came to Torrance's attention through reading Cornelius Lanczos, "Rationalism and the Physical World," in *Boston Studies in the Philosophy of Science* 3, ed. Robert S. Cohen and Marx W. Wartofsky (New York: D. Reidel, 1966). When I visited Professor Torrance (10 January 2000), we checked the photocopy of Lanczos's article in his library and found the reference to Einstein's 1929 lecture on p. 185.

55. Torrance, *Theological Science* (preface 1967), 118.

56. In a footnote here, Torrance cites Einstein, *The World*, 23, and Einstein, *Later Years*, 61. The former citation is apparently taken from Northrop's article, "Einstein's Conception," 401. For the English version, it should read Einstein, *The World*, 125-26. This is a further indication of Northrop's influence on Torrance's early thinking about Einstein.

57. Equivalently, Torrance states elsewhere that mathematical structures are formulated "under the pressure of the nature of the universe" (Torrance, *Transformation*, 273), or "under pressure from the relatedness inherent in nature" (Torrance, "Theological Realism," 183), or "under the compulsion of the objective structures of the field" (Torrance, *Juridical Law*, 25).

58. Torrance, *Scientific Theology*, 54.

59. Cf. Torrance, *Ground and Grammar*, 105: "we are aware of coming under an imperious constraint from beyond, which . . . summons us to be open for disclosure from the source of that constraint."

60.Cf. Torrance, *Contingent Order*, 54 on "the astonishing capacity of the universe to reveal itself to us in an ever widening and deepening range of future disclosures."

61. Torrance, *Rationality*, 43.

62. One of Torrance's first uses of the idea of mathematical invariance (borrowed from Einstein) as an indicator of objective reality is in Torrance, *Scientific Theology* (based on 1970 Harris Lectures), 21, 54, 147. Prior to that, instead of invariance Torrance spoke of "the relativity of our knowledge to what is beyond that served to strengthen dogmatic realism"; Torrance, *Theological Science* (preface 1967), 296.

63. Torrance, *Scientific Theology*, 147.

64. In Torrance, *Rationality*, 22, Torrance states that the knowledge of God differs from human comprehension in general in that it relies on the guidance of God's Spirit in the knowing process.

65. For Torrance's Ellul-like critique of technological society, see, e.g., Torrance, *Reconciliation*, 71. It is significant that the ideal of control recurs in post-Newtonian technologies like quantum engineering; cf. Christopher B. Kaiser, "The Laws of Nature and the Nature of God," in *Facets of Faith and Science*, vol. 4, ed. Jitse van der Meer (Lanham, Md.: University Press of America, 1996), 187-89.

66. Torrance, *Scientific Theology*, 77.

67. In Torrance's version of the musical analogy the Logos is the director and the scientist is the listener; see Torrance, *Transformation*, 97-98.

68. Thomas F. Torrance,"The Place of Michael Polanyi in the Modern Philosophy of Science" (lecture 1975), in Torrance, *Transformation*, 111; cf. Thomas F. Torrance, *Belief in Science and in Christian Life: The Relevance of Michael Polanyi's Thought for Christian Faith and Life* (Edinburgh: Handsel Press, 1980), 8; Torrance, *Scientific Culture*, 69. Torrance often discusses this point under the Einsteinian rubric "God does not wear his heart on his sleeve"; e.g., Thomas F. Torrance, "Christian

Theology in the Context of Scientific Change" (1976), in Torrance, *Transformation*, 253; Torrance, *Ground and Grammar*, 119; Thomas F. Torrance, "Einstein and God" (lecture 1997), *CTI Reflections* 1 (1998): 16.

69. Torrance, "Einstein and God," 11-12. Torrance also faults Einstein for neglecting the problem of radical evil and the need for redemption; Torrance, *Ground and Grammar*, 130; Torrance, "Einstein and God," 21-22.

70. Torrance, *Scientific Culture*, 60-61.

71. Some early examples of this critique are in Torrance, *Reconstruction*, 85-86; Torrance, *Theological Science*, 305-7.

72. Torrance, *Scientific Culture*, 60-61. On the question of Newton's own theology, see Kaiser, *Creational Theology*, 242-51. For the same reason, Torrance rejects the common notion that Einstein was a determinist in the Newtonian sense; Torrance, *Contingent Order*, 11-13.

73. Cf. Kaiser, *Creational Theology*, 21-27, passim.

74. Torrance, *Ground and Grammar*, 5. Torrance cites Francis Bacon on humanity as the priest of creation.

75. Torrance, *Ground and Grammar*, 129.

76. Torrance often discusses this point under the Einsteinian rubric "God is deep but not devious" and credits Hermann Weyl with formulating it; e.g., Torrance, *Transformation*, 256; Torrance, *Ground and Grammar*, 128-30; Torrance, "Einstein and God," 19. Torrance's view of light as a constant or invariant requires special treatment in view of the dramatic success of recent experiments designed to control the speed of light. Suffice it to say that Torrance's point has to do with Einstein's comparison of different frames of reference, not with different experimental apparatus, and the payoff is a restatement of the traditional analogy between vision and intellectual understanding. The idea of light as the God's means of ordering space and time has biblical precedent in Genesis 1:1-5.

77. Torrance, *Scientific Culture*, 77. Biblical precedent for the connection between the light of Genesis 1:3-6 and divine light can be found in Psalm 36:9; cf. John 1:1-9; 2 Corinthians 4:6; Genesis Rabbah 3:4.

78. Torrance, *Ground and Grammar*, 3-5; cf. Christopher B. Kaiser, "Humanity as the Exegete of Creation with Reference to the Work of Natural Scientists," *Horizons in Biblical Theology* 14 (December 1992): 112-28.

79. Torrance argues here from the fusion of space and time into a space-time continuum in the equations of relativity theory; Torrance, *Contingent Order*, 80-81. For earlier, post-Newtonian attempts to develop a scientific cosmogony, see Kaiser, *Creational Theology*, 335-49.

80. "The Message of John Paul II to Theologians and Scientists," in *John Paul II on Science and Religion,* ed. Robert John Russell et al. (Vatican City: Vatican Observatory Publications, 1990), 111; Thomas F. Torrance, *The Soul and Person of the Unborn Child* (Edinburgh: Handsel Press, 1999), 10-11.

81. Compare Torrance's claim that "we cannot give an adequate account of the universe in its astonishing structure and harmony without taking conscious mind into account"; Thomas F. Torrance, "Man the Priest of Creation" (acceptance address for the Templeton Prize 1978), reprinted in Torrance, *Ground and Grammar*, 4. I recall Professor Torrance once asking how the development of natural science itself might have been programmed into the expansion of the universe or into the laws governing it (Ancaster, Ontario, August 1992).

82. According to Mariano Artigas, the idea behind evolutionary epistemology is that "our cognitive abilities should be considered as the result of a series of trial-and-error approaches by nature to cope with the problems provoked by adaptation to the environment"; Mariano Artigas, *The Mind of the Universe: Understanding Science and Religion* (Philadelphia: Templeton Foundation Press, 2000), 211. For a good review of recent work in this area, see J. Wentzel van Huyssteen, *The Shaping of Rationality: Toward Interdisciplinarity in Theology and Science* (Grand Rapids, Mich.: Eerdmans, 1999), especially p. 214 on the work of Nicholas Rescher and Paul Davies.

83. Torrance sometimes uses the phrase "contingent intelligibility" in this context; Torrance, *Ground and Grammar*, 104-5; cf. Thomas F. Torrance, "Ultimate Beliefs and the Scientific Revolution," reprinted in Torrance, *Transformation*, 204.

84. Thomas F. Torrance, "Man, Mediator of Order" (lecture 1984), in Torrance, *Christian Frame*, 39, 51; cf. Thomas F. Torrance, "Fundamental Issues in Theology and Science" (lecture 1985), in Torrance, *Christian Frame*, 89.

85. The role of caves and cave art is an example of a challenging primordial environment that is no longer a vital part of modern life. It might be argued that the development of spelunking skills (mental as well as physical) in early hominids contributed to the preadaptation of the human psyche for scientific research. The reader may be able to think of other, even more promising possibilities.

86. Two lines later, Wisdom creates the human spirit from divine spirit and from wind (cf. Gen. 1:2; 2:7); 2 (Slavonic) Enoch 30:8 (manuscript J), the original of which can be dated to the first century c.e. Clouds are often associated with angels in biblical texts; cf. Exod. 14:19; Dan. 7:13; 4 Ezra 13:3; Mark 13:26-27. Angels could also be identified with the stars or with the seven planets; cf. Isa. 14:13-14; Dan. 8:10; Irenaeus, *A.H.* I.5.2 (Valentinus). In other words, there was a close connection in traditional thought between conversing with angels and contemplating the astronomical heavens.

87. See, e.g., Lawrence M. Principe, *The Aspiring Adept: Robert Boyle and His Alchemical Quest* (Princeton, N.J.: Princeton University Press, 1998). Professor Torrance has drawn my attention to his own essay, Thomas F. Torrance, "The Spiritual Relevance of Angels," in *Alive to God: Studies in Spirituality Presented to James Houston*, ed. J. I. Packer and

Loren Wilkinson (Downers Grove, Ill.: InterVarsity Press, 1992), 121-39.

88. Some of the evidence comes from burial practices and cave art. See, e.g., John E. Pfeiffer, *The Creative Explosion: An Enquiry into the Origin of Art and Religion* (New York: Harper & Row, 1982), 102-18, 132-52.

89. Accounts of scientific creativity abound with imagery of mental journeys into unknown worlds. See, for example, Andrew Wiles's description of day-by-day work on Fermat's Last Theorem in Simon Singh, *Fermat's Enigma: The Epic Quest to Solve the World's Greatest Mathematical Problem* (New York: Anchor Books, 1997), 236-37. Comparative studies would be needed to test for cultural biases in these accounts.

90. In *City of God* XI.7, Augustine identified the primordial light of Genesis 1:3 with the heavenly city of angels from which believers are said to be born (Gal. 4:26; 1 Thess. 5:5).

Chapter 11

Natural Science and Christian Faith in the Thought of T. F. Torrance

by P. Mark Achtemeier

T. F. Torrance's contributions to the dialogue between science and religion are magisterial and highly original. Unfortunately, the student who seeks to grasp Torrance's thought in this area faces formidable challenges. The relevant writings are scattered across a significant number of volumes;[1] the prose is dense and touches on a wide range of disciplines, including the history and philosophy of science, the history of doctrine, epistemology, and mathematical logic, in addition to the particular subject matter of both Christian doctrine and the natural sciences; and Torrance's presentations typically assume a familiarity with his own theological work along with a conceptual-level grasp of significant features of modern science.

It is the goal of this chapter to render this corpus more accessible by proposing an outline of the large-scale structure of Torrance's thought and by surveying some of its major themes. We will conclude with some appreciative critical reflections.

Charting the Relationship of Science and Theology

Many modern treatments of the science-and-religion question assume that theology and science stand apart as discrete and segregated disciplines, with the task of the science-and-religion "dialogue" being the construction of bridges between them. Along these lines, Ian

Barbour proposes an influential fourfold typology for relating science and religion, consisting of *conflict*, *independence*, *dialogue*, and *integration*.[2]

Torrance's account of the relation between Christian theology and natural science tends to proceed from an assumption other than the fundamental separateness of the disciplines. Grounded in the narration of a complex, interdependent history in which ideas from the disciplines tend to cross-fertilize with one another, Torrance's work resists neat categorization according to any single typological category. His writing in fact charts both a history and a future prospect of substantive engagement along three broad fronts.

The first is a *formal, methodological account* involving the use that natural science and Christian theology each make of certain formal elements of "scientific" method. Torrance's use of this terminology is potentially misleading, and we will have more to say on what he means by it below. For now suffice to say that while he does not believe theology can or should appropriate its method directly from the natural sciences, he does believe that the formal goals of the two disciplines are sufficiently similar as to enable a mutually beneficial conversation around issues of scientific methodology.

The second front where Torrance charts a substantive engagement between science and theology is in the *material account* each gives of the physical universe. These accounts are naturally quite different. Natural sciences seek to describe the imbedded rationalities and functional interconnections that operate within the universe, considered in itself. Theological accounts approach the task of describing the physical universe through the Christian doctrines of creation, redemption, and incarnation, which is to say, the universe in its orientation toward God and in its function as the arena of God's historical self-disclosure to humankind.

But for all the differences in the natural scientific and theological accounts, the physical universe does nevertheless serve as a common term of reference in each. That common reference establishes a certain kind of mutual accountability between the disciplines and an obligation to work toward reconciling divergent or incompatible claims advanced by the two descriptive enterprises. The urgency of this task comes to light in recent history, as Torrance traces the lineage of distorted and unproductive thinking in modern theology to the lingering effects of now-outmoded natural scientific accounts.

This last observation points to the third front where Torrance finds substantial overlap between natural science and Christian theology, namely in their respective *histories of development*.

Torrance sees these histories as thoroughly intertwined, with intellectual cross-fertilization proceeding—for good and for ill—in both directions between the disciplines.

Torrance's exposition of the historical interplay between the disciplines encompasses both the formal and the material arenas of engagement mentioned above. Indeed, one could plausibly schematize his entire project in theology and science as the presentation of a coordinated history of development of the two disciplines that demonstrates how rigorous fidelity to the formal requirements of proper "scientific" method in each field leads toward convergence and compatibility in their material accounts of the created order. We will proceed now to a more detailed examination of these three areas of engagement.

Formal Methodological Parallels

Torrance characteristically describes theology as a "science." He does *not* mean by this that theology should seek after religious analogues of experimental scientific method. Torrance uses the term "science" in a much broader sense to signify an investigative discipline whose goal is to faithfully expound the intelligible structure of its own particular object. In the case of the natural sciences, thc focus of their investigation is clearly upon features of the natural order. In the case of Christian theology, this focus is upon God's self-disclosure in the history of Israel that culminates in the incarnation, life, death, and resurrection of Jesus of Nazareth.

In seeking faithfully to grasp what is knowable in its specific area of inquiry, a genuine science will develop investigative procedures, analytical tools, and structures of thought that are uniquely suited to its own object. For theological science to simply take over the investigative methods of the natural sciences, then, would make about as much sense as microbiologists adopting a central commitment to telescopes as their primary tools of data collection. Each science requires tools and procedures suited to its own particular focus of investigation.

What theological and natural science do share methodologically is a common commitment to disciplined investigation and a common need for thought structures and habits of mind that mediate a true and undistorted encounter with the reality that constitutes their respective fields of inquiry.[3] Theological and natural science are thus both keenly interested in developing the *mind adequate to its object*—in purifying the active concepts that form the matrix of their encounter with the reality under investigation, and in identifying and eliminating distorting impositions of alien thought patterns that derive from outside sources.

By now it will be apparent that Torrance's account of these common methodological concerns hinges on his critical realist account of human knowing. Torrance's epistemology is *realist* in the sense that it assumes the thought structures of a properly functioning science yield a genuine engagement with an objective reality that is genuinely available to the knower. Thus Torrance assumes that the natural sciences are in touch with a universe that is "*intrinsically* intelligible, because it is endowed with an immanent rationality quite independent of us which is the ground of its comprehensibility to us."[4] In similar fashion, Torrance assumes that theological science mediates apprehension of the God who genuinely has given Himself to be known in the incarnation and the sending of the Holy Spirit. This objective self-disclosure of God is apprehended in the context of "a community of believers living in empirical contact and communion with God, who allow their minds and lives to take shape under the impact of what God reveals of his own nature and truth."[5]

Torrance's epistemology is *critically* realist in that he rejects a simple one-to-one correspondence between the empirical and theoretical components of knowledge. Drawing heavily from Einstein's reflections and from Michael Polanyi's work in epistemology and the philosophy of science, Torrance recognizes that reality-mediating theories such as General Relativity or the Nicene Trinitarian Doctrine are not the product of straightforward inferences or logically determinate paths connecting empirical apprehension to theoretical construct. Such theories are instead the product of creative leaps of cognition, grounded in a stance of openness and personal commitment on the part of the knower. Creative breakthroughs in intellectual apprehension are guided not by any formalizable rules of inference, but by a tacit apprehension of reality's deep structures, grasped intuitively by a mind that has opened itself to be shaped and formed under their influence.[6]

This common interest in purifying active concepts and limiting distorting impositions opens up substantial ground for mutually helpful methodological conversation between the natural and theological sciences. It also brings to light a common set of temptations and distortions that threaten the integrity of each field. Central to Torrance's account of these distortions are *dualisms* of various sorts. Torrance typically employs this term in referring to two different classes of separation that hinder the mind's faithful apprehension of reality.

The first such distortion is *cosmological dualism*, which posits a separation between the reality or essence of something and the empirical sources of our knowledge about it—between substance and appearance. With origins in ancient Greek thought, cosmological dualism assumes that what is really real is an eternal realm of pure, unchanging thought forms, in contrast to the imperfect, changeable, and unreliable realm of concrete appearances. The practical effect of this outlook has been to turn scientific investigation into a top-down exercise that eschews experimental investigation and observation of concrete particulars in favor of a rationalistic approach that seeks to deduce the nature of things from a priori first principles.[7]

In theological science, cosmological dualism has typically asserted itself in an assumed incompatibility between the divine nature and the finite, empirical realm of space and time. For Christian theology, this has historically taken the form of a denial of the reality of the incarnation, driving a wedge between Christian apprehension of the life, death, and resurrection of Jesus of Nazareth, and a genuine knowledge of God. The Nicene *homoousion*, which stands at the center of orthodox Christology, is the Church's emphatic declaration that the fullness of the divine being has become present and knowable within the realm of space and time in the historical, flesh-and-blood reality of Jesus Christ.

The second sort of dualism that threatens the integrity of knowing in both natural and theological science is *epistemological dualism*, which typically posits an unbridgeable gulf between the mind of the knower and the object of knowledge. Such dualism typically asserts that our knowledge is in reality only an imposition of the mind's own thought patterns as a kind of artificial ordering upon the chaotic and undifferentiated manifold of sensory experience. In the realm of the natural sciences, Torrance sees this sort of dualism at work in *instrumentalist* interpretations of science, which assert that scientific theories are best understood as codified descriptions of the interaction between human senses and the behavior of laboratory instruments, without any reliable reference to an underlying reality. Such understandings have proven especially tempting in connection with the submicroscopic investigations of quantum theory, where the reality in question has proven to be extremely elusive and counter-intuitive.

Torrance also associates epistemological dualism with a *technological* approach to science, which assumes that scientific knowing can reliably grasp only those "facts" that are created and controlled by human beings. Torrance sees this dualism lying at the heart of the technological exploitation and abuse of the natural environment, as science replaces its reverent openness to the mysteries of the universe with a dualistic knowledge that becomes "real" only in the context of our manipulation, exploitation, and control.

Within the realm of the theological sciences, epistemological dualism manifests itself in a tendency, especially pervasive in the period since the Enlightenment, for theology to transform itself into anthropology or psychology. In place of an objective knowledge of God grounded in God's own self-disclosure within the concrete structures of space and time, theology assumes as its object of investigation the inward, subjective *experience* of religious believers. This distortion in theological science also manifests itself in a mode analogous to the technological frame of mind, namely, in a *constructivist* approach to theology which assumes that the theologian's task, like a modern artist translating inward subjectivities onto canvas,[8] is to construct symbol systems which serve to project upon the cosmos (via the idea of "god") the aspirations and subjectivities of religious "believers."

All these forms of dualism involve finally the disruption of a genuine relation between the knower and the object of knowledge, and so lead to chaos, fragmentation, and loss of the possibility of consensus within a discipline of inquiry.

Common Material Interests

Both theological and natural science are concerned with the physical universe. Natural science's concern with it as the focus of its investigation is obvious. For theological science the natural order enters the picture as the medium of God's selfdisclosure to us in the history of Israel and in the incarnation. That is to say, God appropriates the physical universe as the created medium of our knowledge of Himself by entering into our time and space as the man Jesus of Nazareth, who is fully (including spatio-temporally!) a human being without thereby ceasing to be God.

In connection with this it is worth noting how Torrance appropriates the term "natural theology" to designate this interest of theology in the natural order as the created medium of God's self-disclosure to humankind in revelation.[9] This usage stands in potentially confusing contrast to more traditional usage, which understands "natural theology" to be the attempt to derive a positive knowledge of God from features of the created order, apart from any reference to revelation. In this section we will review some essential features of Torrance's theological account of creation.

The Nicene Vision of Creation

In the writings of the Greek Church Fathers who lived and worked in the era surrounding the great Trinitarian debates of the Ecumenical Council of Nicaea (a.d. 325), Torrance finds a highly significant effort to think through the implications of Christian faith for our understanding of the created order and God's relation to it. The theologians whom Torrance has principally in mind in this connection are Athanasius of Alexandria (c. a.d. 296-373), Basil of Caesarea (c. a.d. 330-379), Cyril of Alexandria (c. a.d. 370-444) and Gregory of Nazianzus (c. a.d. 300-389). To these theologians fell, as Torrance sees it, the critically important task of rethinking and reappropriating the heritage of classical Greek culture in light of the new insights afforded by developing Christian understandings of God and God's relation to the world.[10] What does it mean to view the world of nature, and our scientific investigation of it, from a Christian perspective? Nicene thinking in this area is the product of extended reflection upon two central affirmations of Christian faith: thc doctrine of God's creation of the world ex nihilo (out of nothing), and the Christian doctrine of the incarnation.

Creation ex nihilo

The first great affirmation of Christian theology which has a decisive bearing on our understanding of God's relation to the world in Torrance's thought is the doctrine of creation ex nihilo: "The Christian doctrine of Creation asserts that God in His transcendent freedom made the universe out of nothing, and that in giving it a reality distinct from His own but dependent on it He endowed the universe with an immanent rationality making it determinate and knowable."[11]

This doctrine is closely linked with the recognition of God's self-sufficiency, and Torrance argues that the doctrine grew out of ancient Israel's reflection on the One whose sovereign power the Israelites had encountered in the events of the Exodus and the nation's subsequent history.[12]

At the heart and center of this doctrine is the affirmation that the universe in its totality is *contingent*: the created order is neither necessary nor self-sustaining, but wholly dependent on God for its origin and continued existence. Torrance uses this term in a rather technical, specialized way and it is worth making sure we are clear what he means by it.

The universe is contingent in the first place with respect to its *existence*. A contingent universe is one that is dependent upon God for its origin and continued existence, and thus the opposite of a universe whose existence is logically necessary or self-sustaining. This means that a contingent universe would not contain anywhere within itself a sufficient explanation for why it should ultimately have come into being, or why it should continue to exist.[13] Its origin and continued existence are the product of God's will and continuing faithfulness, rather than of some necessity contained within itself.

The universe is contingent in the second place with respect to its *order*. That is to say, God's ordering of the cosmos by which it is rendered knowable and predictable—the fundamental laws of physics and biology and chemistry which science seeks to uncover—all of that is a contingent order that doesn't *have* to be the way it is. This order *could* have been quite different—gravitation might have repelled objects rather than attracting them, electrons might have had twice as much mass as they in fact do. Thus a contingent universe should contain within itself no necessary reasons for explaining why it should manifest *this* particular order rather than some other—its order being the product not of an embedded logical necessity but of God's will and intention.[14]

This Christian understanding of the universe as created, rational, and contingent has a number of important consequences. First, the fact that the rational order of the universe is a *created* order means that it has its own relatively independent (though by no means self-sufficient) integrity. It is grounded in God's rationality, but as a creature rather than as an eternally generated extension or emanation from the divine Being.[15] This creaturely integrity rules out any easy and direct movement in thought from knowledge of creation's working to a knowledge of God. Its lack of self-sufficiency means the universe will point away from itself toward *some* transcendent ground beyond itself, but any direct, deductive movement from features of the created order to the nature of God is ruled out because the order of the universe is not a *logically necessary* emanation from the divine nature. Torrance characteristically makes this point by saying there is no *logical bridge* for moving between the created order and God.

Second, Torrance suggests that these insights from the Christian doctrine of creation help explain why modern experimental science experienced its greatest historical flowering in the cultural context of the Christian West.[16] By positing a contingent universe separate from

God, Christian theology desacralizes creation in such a way as to open it up to the investigative probings of experimental science. Among religious cultures that tend to view the natural world as divine in itself, one would expect to find very cautious attitudes toward experimental manipulations of physical reality, these being easily interpreted as a blasphemous violation of sacred spaces.

In a similar vein, such Christian understandings of the contingent universe also help explain why experimental method has been key to scientific advance. If the ordering of the universe is genuinely contingent, then true understanding will require that we *probe* it experimentally in order to see *which one* of the many possible rationalities it does in fact manifest. If the universe reflected a necessary order, by contrast, one would expect natural scientific understandings to be logically derivable from first principles by the application of pure thought. In fact, it was not until this conception of natural science as a mostly philosophical enterprise was overcome that the scientific revolution began to blossom.

A third implication of this Christian thinking about creation is its affirmation of the creation's fundamental openness to God's rule. If the universe depends from moment to moment upon the free grace of God in order to sustain its existence and its orderly operations, this suggests an openness and capacity for novelty in the cosmic process which is reflective of the transcendent freedom of God.

> [God's] creation of the universe out of nothing, . . . far from meaning that the universe is characterized by sheer necessity either in its relation to God or within itself, implies that it is given a contingent freedom of its own, grounded in the transcendent freedom of God and maintained through his free interaction with the universe. It was this doctrine of the freedom of the creation contingent upon the freedom of God which liberated Christian thought from the tyranny of the fate, necessity and determinism which for the pagan mind was clamped down upon creaturely existence by the inexorably cyclic processes of a self-sufficient universe. Just as there is an order in the universe transcendentally grounded in God, so there is a freedom in the universe transcendentally grounded in the freedom of God.[17]

This openness of the created order grounded in God's creation of the world ex nihilo, coupled with the disclosure of God's redemptive purposes in the incarnation, served to establish a view of time and history as a linear rather than cyclical movement. History was now seen as moving somewhere, advancing toward a goal. Instead of persisting eternally in endlessly repeating cycles, history was now seen as unique and nonrepeatable, moving from the origin of creation in God towards its divinely willed consummation. In order to sustain this historical movement, the cosmic process in this view must possess the capacity for emergent novelty, grounded in the gracious and benevolent freedom of God.[18]

The Incarnation

This brings us to the doctrine of the incarnation as the second great pillar of the Nicene Christian understanding of the natural order. This doctrine confesses that God has appeared in human history as a particular man, Jesus of Nazareth. In Torrance's words, it is the faith of the Christian Church "that in Jesus Christ God Himself in His own Being has come into our world and is actively present as personal Agent within our physical and historical existence."[19] This recognition of God's self-manifestation in Jesus is intimately bound up with the Church's witness to Jesus' resurrection from the dead, and the dawning realization that "what Jesus Christ is in his resurrection, he is in himself."[20] In Jesus of Nazareth, "the whole fullness of deity dwells bodily" (Colossians 2:9). This, observes Torrance, is an "utterly staggering" doctrine, "which would be quite unthinkable except on the ground its actual happening has established."[21]

If the doctrine of the incarnation is true, it carries with it profound implications for our understanding of God and God's relation to the world. If the divine presence really has been manifested in a *particular* historical reality—the man Jesus—this calls seriously into question religious attempts to identify the universe in its totality with the divine. The doctrine of the incarnation thus requires us, as with the doctrine of creation ex nihilo, to recognize a certain distance and distinction between God and the world.

On the other hand, if God has entered into material existence, encountering us in the realm of time and space, this leads us to treat physical, earthly reality with a great deal of seriousness as the divinely chosen arena within which God's self-manifestation to humankind takes place.

> The incarnation made it clear that the physical world, far from being alien or foreign to God, was affirmed by God as real even for himself. The submission of the incarnate Son of God to its creaturely limits, conditions, and objectivities, carried with it an obligation to respect the empirical world in an hitherto undreamed-of measure.[22]

This kind of seriousness about physical existence stands in marked contrast to the more common religious tendency to think of the "spiritual" and the "physical" realms (and hence religion and science) as realities which are distinct and separate, having little to do with one another.[23]

It also tends to bring together the empirical and theoretical components of our knowledge of the world. As the incarnation overcomes the dualism that separates our knowledge of God from our apprehension of space-time realities, so it tends to overcome the dualism that separates the intelligible rational structure of the universe ("laws of nature") from concrete physical existence ("nature itself"), recognizing both as creatures whose being is grounded in the one divine *Logos*.

The doctrine of the incarnation, moreover, stands in the closest possible relation to the doctrine of creation, for it asserts that Jesus Christ is the incarnation of the divine Word or *Logos* (which for our purposes we may identify with the divine rationality) by whom and through whom creation comes into being: "All things were made through him, and without him was not anything made that was made" (John 1:3). This *Logos* is, in Torrance's words, the divine reality

> through whom all things, visible and invisible, were created out of nothing, who leaves nothing void of Himself, and who orders and holds the entire universe together by binding it into such a relation to God that it is preserved from breaking up into nothingness or dropping out of existence, while at the same time imparting to it light and rationality.[24]

In Jesus Christ this selfsame *Logos* encounters us within the setting of creaturely existence in time and space.

If the *Logos* is the source and ground of the rational order of the universe, this implies that the incarnation and its attendant miracles are not to be regarded as disruptions of that natural order—a suspension of the "laws of nature," as it were. Rather, says Torrance, the incarnation is "the freely chosen way of God's rational love in the fulfillment of his eternal purpose for the universe."[25] The working presupposition of such a recognition must therefore be a deep and fundamental harmony between God's self-disclosive activity in history culminating in the incarnation, and the rational order of the universe as it is uncovered by science.

This is not to say that science at any given stage of its development will be able to provide rational explanations of God's activity in the world, as though the divine nature stood within the compass of its current theories. But it *is* to say that a science which claims to offer a view of the world *incompatible* with God's activity in creation needs to be regarded with suspicion, as betraying either a false science, or a false theology, or both. The universe stands open to God's purposes.

This essential compatibility, recognized in the incarnation, between God's redemptive purposes and the creaturely structures of space and time, led the Nicene theologians away from what Torrance calls a "receptacle" or "container" concept of space and time toward a more relational and dynamic view.[26] Over against Greek philosophical conceptions of space as a limited or finite container into which material beings "fit," the Christian doctrine of the incarnation asserted that the infinite God who wholly transcends space and time was fully present to us within the confines of that same space and time in the person of Jesus of Nazareth, while at the same time remaining fully Himself. How such a God could be circumscribed within finite space while still remaining infinite was a problem which could not be handled within the framework of traditional Greek metaphysics.

The Nicene alternative conceived of space dynamically, as determined by that which occupies it. Bodies do not fit "in" a statically defined space; rather space itself is the product of an occupying body, the medium which an occupying body opens up, as it were, allowing its relations with other bodies.

> Thus it came about that in seeking to articulate its understanding of God's activity in creation and Incarnation, Patristic theology rejected a notion of space as that which receives and contains material bodies, and developed instead a notion of space as the seat of relations or the place of meeting and activity in the interaction between God and the world. It was brought to its sharpest focus in Jesus Christ as the place where God has made room for Himself in the midst of our human existence and as the place where man on earth and in history may meet and have communion with the heavenly Father . . . [This represented] a *differential and open concept of space* sharply opposed to the Aristotelian idea of space or place as the immobile limit of the containing body.[27]

Space is here seen as the ground of relations among things, rather than as a fixed container.

To sum up, we have seen how the Nicene theologians, proceeding from a starting point in the Christian doctrines of the incarnation and creation ex nihilo, arrived at a view of God and the universe characterized by: (1) a view of God as both transcendent over the cosmos, and immanent within it in the particular historical reality of Jesus of Nazareth; (2) a unified understanding of the universe which sees both the physical-sensible and the rational-intelligible aspects of existence as sharing a common, creaturely nature which is sustained and upheld in ongoing fashion by God's hand; (3) a corresponding de-divinization of all aspects of the universe; (4) an understanding of the natural order as rational and contingent; and (5) an understanding of the natural order as free and open to the purposes of God.

Appropriated positively within a scientific context, this Christian understanding of the natural order contributes to an attitude of modesty and humility with regard to scientific achievement, as researchers come to recognize the unfathomable depths of the divine rationality which stands behind the intelligible structure of the cosmos. This connection with the *Logos* also establishes the possibility of a *material* cooperation between theology and natural science as each pursues investigation of its own distinctive subject matter. This is true because the "logic" of God's intelligible self-disclosure within the space-time structures of creation, and the intelligible order of that creation itself, are *both* grounded in one and the same divine rationality.

This establishes the possibility that analogous structures of thought, reflective of the divine rationality that undergirds the subject of each specialized pursuit, *might* prove fruitful across disciplinary boundaries. As we shall see in our next section, Torrance identifies a number of historical instances in which he believes one can see a fruitful cross-fertilization of this kind taking place between theological and natural-scientific concepts. It is to Torrance's account of the mutually influencing histories of development of Christian theology and natural science that we now turn.

Overlapping Historical Development

The scope of this essay does not permit a comprehensive look at the way Torrance charts historical interactions in the development of Christian theology and natural science. In order to gain a sense of Torrance's project, though, we will look at selected aspects of his treatment of Newtonian and Einsteinian science.

The Newtonian Challenge to Nicene Cosmology

The rise of Newtonian physics yielded a picture of the universe which at a number of junctures was deeply incompatible with Nicene understandings of a cosmos that is contingent, open ended, and responsive to the divine purposes. While the situation in contemporary physics has changed considerably, this is culturally significant even today, since most people's mental image of the universe (including those of theologians!) tends to be thoroughly Newtonian. Torrance charts in some detail the collision between the Newtonian and Nicene worldviews as a key to understanding contemporary trends in theology. There is a relevant distinction to be made in these discussions between Newton's own ideas and those of Newtonianism more generally, for Torrance's critique of the "Newtonian worldview" frequently focuses on trajectories of thought which emerged out of Newton's work, at times in directions which the Cambridge natural philosopher would have neither anticipated nor approved.

Space and Time

We begin with Newton's understanding of space and time. Newton's theory of motion presupposes the existence of an *absolute space and time*, which forms, as Torrance tirelessly observes, a static, universal frame of reference against which the motion of bodies can be described and plotted. Newton on occasion identified this eternal, unchangeable backdrop of absolute space and time with God's mind.

Absolute space in Newtonian physics is structured according to the self-evident and timeless principles of Euclidean geometry.[28] Just as absolute space provides a uniform, Euclidean structure to the Newtonian universe, so absolute time furnishes it with a uniform and universal reference frame according to which events anywhere in the universe may be definitively characterized as occurring simultaneously, before, or after one another. The significance of these seemingly common sense features of Newton's thinking will become apparent when we consider their overthrow in Einstein's physics.

Matter

The contents of universal space-time in Newton's universe are generally conceived in atomistic terms as discrete particles or point-masses. These "corpuscles" are conceived as moving and interacting with one another according to the fixed laws of mechanical motion which Newton and his colleagues had succeeded in bringing to light. This "particles in a box" paradigm lent itself quite readily to mechanistic, reductionistic ways of thinking about the physical universe: If everything we see around us is ultimately composed of moving particles which obey Newton's laws of motion, it stands to reason that all physical phenomena will eventually be explainable on that level. Furthermore, if we could know the motion of all the particles in a closed physical system at any one instant in time, we should in principle be able to predict its unfolding movements for all time to come. The corpuscular view of matter is deeply deterministic, and so in the period following Newton the universe came to be regarded as a vast clockwork *machine*.

Gravitation

The point-masses which made up the clockwork in Newton's universe were acted upon by *forces*, and it was, of course, Newton's great triumph to show how a single, relatively simple description of the gravitational force could be used to account both for the trajectories of everyday falling objects and for the movement of the heavenly bodies.

While Newton provided an astonishingly far-reaching account of gravitational phenomena on one level, on another level he left a great deal unexplained. The mechanism behind the actual operation of the gravitational force, which in Newton's understanding involved instantaneous action-at-a-distance, remained extremely mysterious, not to say suspect, in the eyes of many of his contemporaries. Newton offered several speculations about the mechanisms underlying gravitational attraction over the course of his writings, but for all his theorizing, Newton staunchly resisted the temptation to fix upon any single such hypothesis in the absence of definitive empirical evidence. "Gravity must be caused by an agent acting constantly according to certain laws," he writes, "but whether this agent be material or immaterial I have left to the consideration of my readers."[29]

Scientific Knowledge

Newton's refusal to take a definitive stand on the mechanism of gravitation gives evidence of the thoroughly Baconian[30] understanding of scientific method which undergirds his work. Science, in this view, proceeds strictly by a process of induction from experimental evidence, arriving at a knowledge of causes on the basis of their effects. Speculative "hypotheses" are to be avoided—this is a theme which resounds throughout Newton's writings—in favor of rigorous, experimental investigation. Empirical observation leads to the framing of theories which in turn are confirmed by additional observations.

Theological Implications of the Newtonian Worldview

Torrance draws attention to a number of significant theological implications arising out of this Newtonian worldview. First, Torrance observes that Newton's appeal to absolute time and space as an a priori philosophical backdrop to his theory establishes a rigid (cosmological) dualism between absolute space-time on the one hand and its material contents on the other. This dualism tends to mirror the old Greek distinction between an eternal (or divine) realm of rational form and a material realm of subjective appearances. Theologically this dualism tends to encourage ways of thinking which see the working of the world as an independent mechanism, far removed from the changeless being of God.[31]

The Newtonian understanding of the material contents of the universe as "particles in a box" moving strictly in accordance with deterministic mechanical laws appears to leave little room for God's involvement in it apart from the creation of the cosmic machinery at the very beginning. Newton's dualistic outlook, together with the Baconian understanding of scientific method, in which science is seen as shunning hypotheses and formulating its theories strictly by inductive means on the basis of experimental data, thus tend to drive a wedge between scientific and religious ways of knowing. Science in this view is seen to be empirical and "objective," derived by logical means from the evidence of experience, whereas religion appears to be a far more subjective and tenuous affair, grounded as it is in belief and personal commitment.[32]

The net result of all this is a powerful resonance between Newtonian physics and a deist theological outlook. Deism sees the world as functioning in relatively autonomous, "clockwork" fashion. God need not be involved, indeed *cannot* be involved, in the world in any ongoing sense. The only role left open for the deity in such a view is in the initial creative work which frames the mechanism, establishes the laws and initial conditions, and sets the whole system in motion.

> Deeply embedded in [Newton's] outlook is a deistic relation between God and the creation which goes back not only to the medieval notion of the Unmoved Mover but to the thought of Francis Bacon who in a remarkable Confession of Faith published in 1611 identified "the constant and everlasting laws which we call nature" with those actual laws which "began to be in force when God rested from his work and ceased to create," i.e. laws in which God does not immediately and directly interact with nature. . . . Moreover the massive synthesis of a deistic

> relation between God and the world and a hard epistemological dualism that took place when Newton distinguished between absolute and relative, true and apparent, mathematical and common, conceptions of time, space, place and motion and then clamped down absolute, true and mathematical time and space externally upon relative, apparent, common (or sensible) time and space, had the effect of building deism into the fabric of the new scientific culture and the kind of theology that arose within its constraints.[33]

The radical disjunction in Newton's thought between the philosophical backdrop of absolute, eternal, and unchanging space and time on the one hand, and the dynamic world of objects and appearances on the other, is thus mirrored in an equally radical disjunction between the creator God and the independent, ongoing processes and activities of the created order.

There is one course of thought in a Newtonian universe which reason may follow in order to span the gap that separates the divine watchmaker from the present activity of the clockwork universe. That course involves ascending through the immanent chains of cause and effect, back to that First Cause and Prime Mover who initially set the whole world-machine running.

This chain of reasoning from the creation back to the Creator is what Torrance has described as a "logical bridge" between the world and God. If such a train of thought were possible, says Torrance,

> knowledge of the created world and knowledge of God would be clamped together in such a way that we would derive knowledge of God necessarily and coercively from knowledge of the world, while knowledge of the world even in its natural operations would not be possible without constantly including God among the data. That would mean lapsing back into the old Greek view that the rational forms of the Deity are immanently and materially embodied in the universe.[34]

This type of theological reasoning was in fact very much in evidence in the centuries following Newton's work. The seventeenth and eighteenth centuries witnessed the rise of the "physico-theologies," which sought to derive a knowledge of God from evidences of design in nature.[35] These theologies proved extremely vulnerable to developments in science (Darwin!), and also to naturalistic metaphysics which in its explanations tended to posit inherent, self-organizing properties of matter in place of divine design.

In short, the Newtonian worldview is quite hostile to Nicene understandings of the universe. The contingence and open-endedness of creation in Nicene understanding tends to be swallowed up in the mechanistic determinism and reductionism which are characteristic of the Newtonian outlook. Further, Newton's "container" concept of absolute space and time as the philosophical backdrop of his theories rendered the Christian doctrine of the Incarnation extremely problematic—it is not at all clear how the infinite God, by becoming incarnate, could be enclosed or contained within the static and limited structures of space and time.[36]

Finally, the scientific rationalism and empiricism which stand at the heart of Newton's scientific method tend to drive a wedge between scientific and religious knowledge, much to the detriment of the latter. It is not hard to understand how, in light of all the conflicts between Nicene theology and Newtonian science, the idea has taken hold in our own culture that scientific understanding and religious faith stand opposed to one another, or that religious ideas are slowly being crowded out of the intellectual arena by "rational" scientific advancement.

The Vindication of Nicene Cosmology in the New Science

Space, Time, and Gravitation

Einstein's Special and General Theories of Relativity did away with Newtonian understandings of absolute space and time as a static receptacle. This occurred along two fronts. First, Einstein was able to describe in the context of an experimentally verifiable theory how spatial features like the length of measuring rods and temporal features like the speed at which clocks run are "local" quantities which vary depending on the relative motion of measuring devices and observers. Space and time are not the static, uniform entities Newton thought they were. Einstein further showed how to translate mathematical descriptions of space-time, matter, gravitation, and motion seamlessly between moving reference frames, allowing us no meaningful way to single out one particular reference frame as being "at rest." Thus there is no universal space or time reference frame in Einstein's theory, only particular reference frames tied to the relative motion of particular observers.

Einstein's theory also posits a mutually interacting *relationship* between space-time, now thought of together as a continuous manifold, and matter. Newton's description of the flight of an arrow would involve the gravitational force of the earth acting on the arrow in order to pull it away from a straight flight path toward the ground. Einstein's theory describes gravitation not as a force acting between objects, but as a "curvature," or a change in the geometry, of space and time. So for Einstein, the earth's gravitational field does not exert a force on the arrow to deflect it from its otherwise straight path onto a curved one. Rather, the earth's gravitational field *bends the space* through which the arrow flies, so that it follows a straight path through a curved space whose very geometrical structure guides its motion downward toward the ground.[37] This description sets up a thoroughly relational concept of space and time: the geometrical structure (curvature) of space-time is determined by the motion and distribution of matter within it, matter being what produces the gravitational field. Correspondingly, it is the gravitationally induced curvature of space and time that determines the motion and distribution of the matter.

It is important to note here that Einstein's theory demotes geometry from an absolute, intellectual abstraction to an experimental science. Because the classical Euclidean geometry presented in high-school textbooks holds true only for "uncurved" space, we cannot deduce, on the basis of Euclid's axioms and theorems, the geometrical properties of any given region of space. We do not know in advance whether the three angles of a triangle will sum to 180 degrees, for that is true only of the geometry of uncurved spaces. We have rather to *observe* the properties of a space and the matter within it (always from the perspective of a particular reference frame) in order to ascertain its "curvature" and hence its geometric properties.

Einstein's banishment of the "box" constituted a priori by absolute space and time in Newton's system resonated with the relational concepts of space developed in the Nicene theology, with profound consequences for Christian claims about the incarnation.

> Theologically the most important problem posed by Newton's thought was his association of space and time as an infinite receptacle with Deity, for that had the effect of reinforcing the dualism between space and matter which we have already noted. If God Himself is the infinite Container of all things He can no more become incarnate than a box can become one of the several objects it contains. Thus Newton found himself in sharp conflict with Nicene theology and its famous *homoousion*, and even set himself to defend Arius against Athanasius.[38]

It was in the face of similar problems posed by Greek philosophy that the Nicene theologians, in thinking through questions posed by the incarnation of God in Christ, arrived at their own *relational* view of space and time, a view which conceived space and time not as forming a static container, but as determined in an essential way by their particular contents. Space is thus space *for* something; it is defined by what occupies it. Applied to the incarnation, this means that "Jesus Christ, the man Jesus, is the *place* in this physical world of space and time where God and man meet, and where they have communion with one another."[39]

One would not want to claim here that the relational concepts of space developed in these respective scientific and theological contexts are identical to one another, or that either side of the parallel somehow "proves" the other side. But it *is* the case that in the transition from Newton to Einstein we observe a shift in scientific thought patterns from an outlook which is very difficult to reconcile with basic Christian affirmations to one which is potentially quite congenial. We find here an example of the material convergence in thought forms that Torrance would attribute to their common grounding in the divine rationality.

Matter

Einstein's treatment of matter also differs profoundly from that of Newton. We recall that matter in Newton's universe was thought of in particulate terms, as discrete point-masses acted upon by forces and interacting according to the laws of mechanics. In contrast to this, the foundational conception of matter (actually mass-energy) in Einstein's theory takes the form not of discrete particles but of *fields*. This switch represents a dramatic shift in the mode of thinking used to describe the universe.

Whereas a Newtonian, particle-based description of an object such as the moon would treat it as a discrete point-mass centered at one location in space, a field-based description would construct a kind of infinite mathematical catalog charting the moon's *potential effects* on objects in each point of space over which it exerts an influence. This catalog of potential effects—which scientists call a "field"—is treated as fully real in its own right. Thus the gravitational distortions in the structure of space-time are every bit as "real" and every bit as much the "moon" as what we see shining in the sky when we look up on a clear night.[40] As a catalog of potential effects on other objects, therefore, field descriptions represent a thoroughly *relational* form of thinking.

Scientific Knowledge

In sharp contrast to Newton's self-understanding of scientific method, it became increasingly difficult in the course of Einstein's self-reflection to fit his work into the categories of the old Baconian understanding of inductive scientific method. As Einstein himself puts it, "The supreme task of the physicist is to arrive at those universal elementary laws from which the cosmos can be built up by pure deduction. *There is no logical path to these laws; only intuition, resting on sympathetic understanding of experience, can reach them*."[41]

The core concepts of General Relativity Theory, such as "curved" four-dimensional space-times, are creative intellectual constructs that are deeply disclosive of the nature of things, but inherently unobservable in themselves. These concepts were formulated not as a summary of observation but as intuitive leaps of the scientific imagination.

Einstein's work thus demonstrates well the irreducible constructive and creative dimensions of scientific activity, dimensions which require the cultivation of appropriate habits of mind. Michael Polanyi, to whom Torrance is deeply indebted, has pointed out how various sorts of faith and personal commitment are indispensable for scientists to sustain a program of scientific inquiry.[42] The shape of particular scientific intuitions is also open to influence by the larger thought-world within which the individual scientist operates, suggesting that cultural factors may have a significant effect upon the fruitfulness of scientific work. Scientific intuition shaped by one set of cultural assumptions may turn out to be more fruitful—less productive of dead ends and more adept at generating breakthroughs—than intuition formed in an alternative cultural setting.

This insight opens the way for our recognition of significant interaction between scientific work and larger currents of culture, including philosophy, art, literature, and religion. In short, it becomes a great deal more difficult in the aftermath of Einstein's work to neatly segregate human endeavor into empirical, "objective" domains of science on the one hand, and experiential, "subjective" domains of art, religion, and culture on the other.

Einstein's work also provides insight into the structure of scientific knowledge. Following both Einstein and Polanyi, Torrance champions an understanding of knowledge as layered and stratified in an irreducible hierarchy of ascending complexity—a vision which runs strongly counter to the reductionisms which have sometimes come to characterize the Newtonian scientific tradition.[43]

Torrance argues, as we have seen, that Newtonian physics presents the impression of a rigid, a priori backdrop of absolute space and time being clamped down on the theory from above, giving the impression of a closed, mathematically self-contained structure. In

Einstein's theory, by contrast, the mathematical structure of space and time are integrated into the realm of empirical phenomena, which means that mathematics, instead of forming a closed, limiting superstructure for the theory, now comprises a set of tools which open up our vision to the universe as it presents itself to us. This openness of theoretical structure conveys the impression of a universe that can still surprise us. This recognition that physical theories may not be self-enclosed and self-sufficient suggests further that individual theories may open out at their boundaries into other domains of knowledge.

Torrance describes the emerging picture in these terms:

> This stratification of theoretical structure that has arisen in quantum physics is something that is increasingly being forced on scientific thought under the constraint of the intrinsic rationality of nature, i.e. not only in respect of the relation of sub-atomic to atomic levels, but of physico-chemical to biological levels, and of the biological to the human and social levels of intelligent existence. The universe thus appears as a multi-levelled and multi-variable complex of rational order in which the different levels are hierarchically coordinated with one another. Each level is subject to what Michael Polanyi has called 'the principle of marginal control', in accordance with which the organizational principles of one level govern those of a 'lower' level through its boundary conditions where it is left open or indeterminate, but it is itself controlled in a similar way from the level 'above' it.[44]

Torrance argues that recognition of this hierarchical structuring of physical phenomena helps to overcome the damaging dualisms which have driven a wedge between scientific and humanistic disciplines, for the range of phenomena comprising human culture can indeed be integrated into the rest of the structure as the emergent order at the pinnacle of the hierarchy. The openness of each layer to the one above it, with the uppermost layers pointing beyond themselves to a transcendent ground of rationality beyond the physical universe, comprises a picture which resonates strongly with Nicene understandings of an open-ended, contingent universe which is endowed on a continuing basis with meaning, rationality, and intelligibility as the gifts of a faithful and benevolent God who is the source and origin of all things.

Theological Implications of the New Science

The cumulative effect of these and similar developments is to provide us with a new picture of the universe whose contingency, spontaneity, and open capacity for emergent novelty render the old mechanistic analogies hopelessly obsolete. Torrance humorously describes an international meeting of scientists and theologians that illustrates both the revolutionary effects of the new science, and the lingering culture effects of the older Newtonianism:

> All the scientists reading papers showed by arguments in mathematics, physics, thermodynamics, and the philosophy of science that the era of determinism had come to an end. In contrast, however, we had one Continental theologian who spoke of "the iron determinisms of nature" as though he had not listened to any of the lectures given and was quite unaware of the profound changes going on in the foundations of scientific knowledge.[45]

What is the significance of this change in our picture of reality? Torrance suggests that we find here a vindication of Nicene understandings of the world as *contingent*, i.e., as manifesting types of order which are neither necessary nor self-explanatory.

> It is this astonishing combination of unpredictability and lawfulness, not only in the history of man but in the history of all created reality in its relation to the constancy and freedom of the grace of the Creator, that lies behind the Christian conception of the cosmos as an open-ordered universe. In its correlation with the unlimited freedom and inexhaustibility of the Creator the universe is characterized neither by uncertainty nor by necessity. Far from being closed or predetermined, the universe constitutes an open-textured system in which novel forms of order constantly emerge and yet blend with what has already taken place in invariant consistency and rationality.[46]

It is important again to emphasize that this emerging recognition of contingence in our scientific understanding of the cosmos does not *prove* the dependence of the universe on God, so much as it *correlates* with it. Because God does not function as a cog in the cosmic machinery, there can be no *necessary* connections drawn between the creaturely rationality of the universe and the being of God, even though the universe as a whole is dependent on God as its ultimate ground and points beyond itself in testimony to that dependence. It is precisely because the rationality of the universe is contingent that scientific theories do not require God as a necessary assumption, and this is why scientists consequently are often tempted to treat the world as self-explanatory and self-contained![47]

If our emerging recognition of contingence in the natural order does not *require* a theological interpretation as a matter of logical necessity, this emergence manifests at the very least a striking congruence with those understandings of the universe in its relation to God that have grown out of Christian reflection on the incarnation and the creation of the cosmos ex nihilo. Such congruence is precisely what one would expect to find in a universe whose rationality was grounded in the selfsame Logos that has been given for our apprehension in the incarnation. It also suggests the benefits of cross-disciplinary interaction, as practitioners of the natural and theological sciences share with one another the structures of thought and habits of mind that have proven especially fruitful in their own areas of inquiry.

Torrance's Achievement

Torrance's achievement in the science-religion dialogue is enormously promising in its ability to bring natural and theological science into fruitful dialogue. The shame is that his work has not received more attention than it has to date. Any survey of the positive achievements of his program would have to include the following.

First, Torrance brings natural science and historically orthodox Christianity into fruitful engagement with one another in a way that preserves the integrity of both fields. This is especially significant because the landscape of proposals for interrelating the two disciplines is littered with demands that one or the other modify or discard fundamental assumptions in order to enter into dialogue with the other. Extreme examples of this type of maneuver on the religious side would include the insistence of "creation scientists" that the Book of Genesis be treated as a scientific textbook with which natural scientific accounts need to be harmonized.[48] On the side of the natural sciences one could cite the equally vehement insistence by scientific materialists that substantive dialogue must necessarily involve the abandonment of all transcendent reference in religion in favor of a reductionism that grounds religious belief in brain physiology, psychology, and evolutionary adaptation.[49]

Even modest proposals for cross-disciplinary dialogue regularly call for substantial modification to the tradition of classic Christian orthodoxy. Leading voices in the science and religion dialogue commonly advocate the modification of classical Christian understandings of creation and providence by concepts deriving from A. N. Whitehead's process metaphysics.[50] In such a context, Torrance's vigorous championing of classical Nicene doctrine as the foundation for fruitful engagement with the natural sciences is a bold and highly significant contribution.

Torrance's program is also significant for the positive incentives given to the science-and-religion dialogue. Beyond the common generalized appeals for reconciliation between the disciplines on grounds of intellectual consistence, Torrance's nuanced exposition of their epistemological and material common interests provides a framework for mutually beneficial conversation around the shared commitment to purify concepts and open up the investigative mind to ever more precise fidelity to its particular object of investigation.

Finally, it is among the more remarkable features of Torrance's work that it would appear to yield historically testable predictions regarding the relations between natural science and Christian faith. If Torrance's theological account of the contingently rational universe is correct, it follows that science ought to find itself up against boundary situations in the course of its advance where the universe points beyond itself for sufficient explanation of its own being. These are strong predictions whose material plausibility appears to have increased in recent decades,[51] despite their standing in opposition to some current speculations about the future course of scientific development.[52]

Torrance's affirmation that the contingent, creaturely rationality of the material universe is grounded in the same divine rationality that is self-disclosed in the revelatory events to which Christian faith attends creates concrete expectations for the history of science. In particular it suggests that habits of mind formed by Christian faith would lend themselves to fruitful scientific investigation of the rational structures embedded in the natural world. Torrance can claim significant historical confirmation of this expectation in the fact that the tradition of experimental science has taken root and blossomed precisely in the cultural soil of the Christian West. This correlation provides suggestive grounds for more particular study in the history of science, some of which Torrance himself undertakes.[53] It will be fascinating to see whether future developments in scientific understanding show a tendency to confirm this hypothesis.

Assuming as a given the scope and significance of Torrance's achievement, we turn now to a few aspects of his work that may be problematic or require further development. In the first position on this list is the status of some of his historical claims.

Torrance narrates a sweeping intellectual history of the mutually influencing development of scientific and theological ideas in the West. While his account of the character of scientific knowing in both theology and the natural sciences gives a plausible account of their potential interactions, his particular historical claims for cross-fertilization between the disciplines are in certain instances difficult to evaluate. As an example, consider his discussion of Reformation-era christological debates in chapter 2 of *Space, Time, and Incarnation.* Torrance there claims that the debate between Reformed and Lutheran theologians over the mode of Christ's presence in the Eucharist can be understand as a contest between receptacle and relational understandings of space and time. To oversimplify a bit, Torrance sees a receptacle view underlying the Lutheran position. This leads to daunting problems in explaining how the infinite divine nature could become "enclosed" as it were in finite and limited spaces like the human body of Christ and the Eucharist elements.

> [T]he receptacle had to be enlarged in order to make it receive the divine nature within its dimensions, and so it was held that the Son of God communicated to the humanity of Christ an infinite capacity enabling it to be filled with the divine fullness. In regard to the real presence in the Eucharist this took the form of the ubiquity of the body of Christ.[54]

Torrance suggests that the Reformed position, by contrast, operated with a relational concept of space much closer to that of the Nicene fathers, in which space is treated not as a static, finite container, but in dynamic terms, so that the human body of Christ and the Eucharistic elements can be seen as the space-time locations in which God "makes room" for Himself to be wholly available and present to us, without sacrificing the divine transcendence over space and time.[55]

This analysis is suggestive, but its status as a historical claim is open to question. Torrance does not cite, nor is this author aware of, any historical evidence to suggest that the original participants ever thought of this debate as a quarrel between rival means of conceptualizing space. Torrance's argument could perhaps stand credibly as an ex post facto logical analysis serving the *constructive* task of re-framing the debate in new terms, perhaps in order to assist with ecumenical efforts aimed at overcoming the original impasse. The precise status Torrance intends for some of the claims emerging from his historical narrative has a tendency to remain rather obscure, however.

Torrance's exposition of the implications of scientific development is likewise open to question at certain points. An example here would be his claim, put forward in chapter 2 of *Divine and Contin-*

gent Order, that Einstein's theory of relativity serves to undermine the deterministic picture of the universe that grew up out of Newton's work. Torrance rightly associates determinism very closely with Newton's understanding of matter as composed of discrete particles acting in accord with the classical laws of motion. In Einstein's reconception of the universe as a continuous space-time manifold described relationally in terms of field concepts, Torrance sees the demise of the rigid, causally self-enclosed determinism that was so characteristic of the Newtonian universe.

The problem with this is that Einstein's theory remains, strictly speaking, a deterministic theory. If by determinism we mean that a physical system which assumes at some point[56] a particular physical configuration *A* will evolve by fixed and unchanging laws toward a unique and rigidly determined successor configuration *B*, then the general theory of relativity is a deterministic theory. Torrance is right of course that the theory does away with the particulate descriptions of Newtonian mechanics. But the configuration of the relational, space-time manifold of Einstein's theory evolves in rigidly defined patterns set by fixed and unchanging laws no less than did the moving, gravitating point-masses that populated Newton's theory.

Torrance's claims here could perhaps be retrieved as a *psychological* argument. The presence in Newton's theory of the static background of universal space and time structured according to thc eternal laws of Euclidean geometry lends itself to very particular understandings of the relation of mathematics to reality. In particular, such a picture suggests a determinative understanding in which "eternal" mathematical truth stands in a kind of sovereign relationship to the cosmos, in such a way that the cosmos's possibilities seem rigidly delineated, enclosed by the limits of the equations themselves. Mathematical abstractions thus appear to exercise a kind of veto power over the possibilities of being.

In contrast, Einstein's picture of a universe in which the static framework of universal space and time has been replaced by a dynamically evolving space-time manifold whose geometrical configuration must be empirically determined, presents us with a very different set of subjective impressions. Einstein's theory is much more congenial to an understanding of mathematics as the servant rather than the master of the universe's empirical possibilities. Mathematics in Einstein's schema has the "feel" of a cognitive tool that provides entry into the mysteries of a universe that is deep and open, in stark contrast to the Newtonian cosmos that is determined and enclosed by a rigid framework of eternal mathematical structures clamped down upon it "from above."

This objection does not fatally compromise Torrance's overall claims—the picture of the universe that modern science develops is *genuinely* nondeterministic and open when quantum mechanics, chaos theory, and developments in mathematical logic such as Gödel's theorem are added to the mix. But one could wish for some clarification regarding the status of the claims Torrance wants to make for relativity theory.

A final area of critical concern lies in the amount of weight carried in Torrance's program by his realist epistemology. Torrance holds up, as the anchor of the methodological common ground shared by both theological and natural science, the conforming of our thought to the objective givenness of the real which presses itself upon us. The following description of the "classical frame of mind" is typical:

> Thus there became entrenched a way of knowing in which people were determined to think as the facts compelled them to think, or to think strictly in accordance with the nature and activity of the given reality. This was not arbitrary, speculative thinking, but thinking bound to its chosen field . . . thinking that acknowledges only the authority of its object and will not submit to any kind of external authority. This is rigorously objective thinking which will take nothing for granted in its determination to be real but which operates by allowing the object being investigated to disclose itself in its own state and light, by penetrating into its inner connections, and by establishing knowledge in terms of principles and laws which it derives from those inner connections.[57]

This strong emphasis on the open stance of the knower before the objective pressure of external reality stands in apparent tension with other aspects of Torrance's epistemological account, most notably his emphasis (following Polanyi) on the role of creative intuition and imaginative leaps of intellect in producing genuine scientific advance. This tension is not irreconcilable, but it is potentially misleading. One could easily get the impression from passages like the one cited above that scientific knowledge was the result of a merely passive stance of receptivity on the part of the knower.

More serious is the tension that exists between Torrance's stress on epistemological objectivity and the character of recent scientific findings in the field of quantum mechanics. It has become clear in recent research that the universe changes in real and astounding ways when quantum systems are subjected to observation. These changes are more than just perturbations introduced by our measuring instruments, and they involve much more than a simple change in the status of our knowledge. Observation of quantum systems elicits a profound change in a system from a state of potentiality, whose various possibilities are real entities open to manipulation, to a single concrete actuality. This "collapse of the state vector" in quantum reality from potentiality to actuality that occurs with measurement exerts real physical effects, effects that under certain circumstances are instantaneously detectable at substantial distances from the location where the measurement actually takes place.[58]

The upshot of all this is that mind or observation or *something* connected with measurement appears to be profoundly connected in constitutive and wholly counterintuitive ways with the very fabric of reality. There is at present no philosophical or epistemological consensus concerning the implications or proper interpretation of these findings, but at the very least such developments pose a question mark over Torrance's picture of mind conforming itself to the pressure of an objective, external reality that "presses in" upon the knower. The quantum mechanical universe appears to be one in which the mind of the knower "presses back" upon reality in quite startling fashion.

Torrance's realism need not be fatally compromised by this—the objective reality that presses in upon the knower could well be one in which mind and universe are causally intertwined in odd ways that we are only beginning to understand—but at the very least it will require careful attentiveness to present developments in order to maintain the credibility of Torrance's position.

At the end of the day one could argue that this vulnerability of Torrance's position to new directions in scientific development ought to count as a strength rather than a weakness of Torrance's program, because it shows just how deeply engaged is his work with the concrete particulars of contemporary science. It is the hope of this author that the present volume will help to bring a new and richly deserved level of attention to Torrance's far-reaching contributions to the emerging dialogue between theological and natural science.

Notes

1. A basic list would include: T. F. Torrance, *Theological Science* (London: Oxford University Press, 1969); T. F. Torrance, *Space, Time, and Incarnation* (London: Oxford University Press, 1969); T. F. Torrance, *God and Rationality* (London: Oxford University Press, 1971); T. F. Torrance, *Space, Time, and Resurrection* (Edinburgh: Handsel Press, 1976); T. F. Torrance, *The Ground and Grammar of Theology* (Charlottesville : University of Virginia Press, 1980); T. F. Torrance, *Christian Theology and Scientific Culture* (New York: Oxford University Press, 1981); T. F. Torrance, *Divine and Contingent Order* (New York: Oxford University Press, 1981); T. F. Torrance, *Transformation and Convergence in the Frame of Knowledge: Explorations in the Interrelations of Scientific and Theological Enterprise* (Grand Rapids, Mich.: Eerdmans, 1984); T. F. Torrance, *Reality and Scientific Theology* (Edinburgh: Scottish Academic Press, 1985); T. F. Torrance, *The Christian Frame of Mind* (Colorado Springs, Colo.: Helmers & Howard, 1989).

2. See Ian Barbour, *Religion in an Age of Science: The Gifford Lectures, 1989-1991,* vol. 1 (San Francisco: Harper San Francisco, 1990), chapter 1.

3. Torrance presents a comprehensive, comparative investigation of scientific methodology in theological and natural science in Torrance, *Theological Science.*

4. Torrance, *Scientific Theology*, 3.

5. Torrance, *Scientific Theology*, 83.

6. See Michael Polanyi, *Personal Knowledge: Towards a Post-Critical Philosophy* (Chicago: University of Chicago Press, 1958).

7. A hint of this tendency in recent times is discernible in suggestions by cosmologist Stephen Hawking that there may turn out to be only one possible rational form for a complete and consistent grand unified Theory of Everything, which as such would be rationally deducible as a matter of logical necessity. See Stephen Hawking, *A Brief History of Time: From the Big Bang to Black Holes* (New York: Bantam Books, 1988), 174.

8. Torrance argues explicitly that this "modern" conception of the artist's task is corrupted by the same sort of dualism. See Torrance, *Scientific Theology*, chapter 4.

9. See, for example, his discussion in chapter 2 of *Scientific Theology*.

10. A detailed treatment of Athanasius's theology in relation to Hellenistic culture can be found in Torrance's article, "Athanasius: A Study in the Foundations of Classical Theology," chapter 5 in T. F. Torrance, *Theology in Reconciliation: Essays towards Evangelical and Catholic Unity in East and West* (Grand Rapids, Mich.: Eerdmans, 1975). More

generalized discussions of Nicene theology in this connection can also be found in Torrance, *Ground and Grammar*, chapter 3; Torrance, *Christian Frame*, chapter 1; and Torrance, *Incarnation*, chapter 1.

11. Torrance, *Incarnation*, 59.

12. Torrance, *Contingent Order*, 33.

13. "[A]s created out of nothing the universe has no self-subsistence and no ultimate stability of its own, but . . . is nevertheless endowed with an authentic reality and integrity of its own which must be respected. . . . [T]he orderly universe is not self-sufficient or ultimately self-explaining but is given a rationality and reliability in its orderliness which depend on and reflect God's own eternal rationality and reliability." Torrance, *Contingent Order*, vii-viii. Cf. also Torrance, *Transformation*, 335.

14. Torrance, *Ground and Grammar*, vii.

15. Torrance, *Ground and Grammar*, 55-56.

16. See Torrance, *Ground and Grammar*, 56f. Also Stanley L. Jaki, *The Road of Science and the Ways to God* (Chicago: University of Chicago Press, 1978); Eugene M. Klaaren, *Religious Origins of Modern Science: Belief in Creation in Seventeenth-Century Thought* (Grand Rapids, Mich: Baker Book House, 1977); Eric L. Mascall, *Christian Theology and Natural Science: Some Questions on Their Relations* (London: Longmans, Green, 1956). A succinct critique of such historical arguments may be found in John Hedley Brooke, *Science and Religion: Some Historical Perspectives* (Cambridge: Cambridge University Press, 1991), 42-51.

17. Torrance, *Ground and Grammar*, 4. Torrance's thought on this point is indebted to Stanley L. Jaki's writings, in particular *Science and Creation: From Eternal Cycles to an Oscillating Universe* (Edinburgh: Scottish Academic Press, 1974), and Jaki, *Road of Science*.

18. Torrance, *Contingent Order*, 69.

19. Torrance, *Contingent Order*, 52.

20. Torrance, *Resurrection*, 60.

21. Torrance, *Contingent Order*, 134.

22. Torrance, *Contingent Order*, 33.

23. Torrance, *Transformation*, 337.

24. Torrance, *Incarnation*, 14.

25. Torrance, *Contingent Order*, 24.

26. Torrance, *Incarnation*, 1-21; T. F. Torrance, "The Relation of the Incarnation to Space in Nicene Theology," in *The Ecumenical World of Orthodox Civilization*, ed. Andrew Blaine, *Russia and Orthodoxy Series*, vol. 3*: Essays in Honor of George Florovsky* (Paris: Mouton, 1973); T. F. Torrance, "The Greek Conception of Space in the Background of Early Christian Theology," *Ekklesia kai Theologia* 11 (1992): 245-294.

27. Torrance, *Incarnation*, 24-25.

28. There was actually some disagreement between Newton and his scientific peers over the epistemological status of geometry, with Newton arguing, over against the likes of Galileo and Descartes, that geometry had its foundations in the practical art of measuring—"mechanical practice" is

Newton's term—rather than in self-evident principles of reason. Newton's own views here seem not to have been picked up to any significant degree by the later "Newtonian" tradition of science. For a discussion of Newton's position, see Michael J. Buckley, "The Newtonian Settlement and the Origins of Atheism," in *Physics, Philosophy and Theology: A Common Quest for Understanding*, ed. R. J. Russell, W. R. Stoeger, and G. V. Coyne (Vatican City: Vatican Observatory, 1988), 84ff.

29. Newton, in the third of four letters to Richard Bentley (1692-1693); in *Newton's Philosophy of Nature: Selections from his Writings*, ed. H. S. Thayer (New York: Hafner., 1953), 172; quoted in Brooke, *Science and Religion*, 145.

30. This term derives from the name of Sir Francis Bacon, an early proponent of empiricist philosophy, who lived from 1561-1626.

31. Torrance, *Reconciliation*, 268-69. See also Torrance, *Transformation*, 204-6.

32. Torrance, *Scientific Culture*, 44ff.

33. Torrance, 43-44. See also Torrance, *Ground and Grammar*, 22ff.

34. Torrance, *Contingent Order*, 34.

35. Prominent examples of this genre would include William Derham, *Physico Theology: A Demonstration of the Being and Attributes of God from His Works of Creation* (London: W. Innys, 1714); William Paley, *Natural Theology; or, Evidences of the existence and attributes of the Deity, collected from appearances of Nature* (London: R. Faulder, 1802); and the *Bridgewater Treatises*, a series which opened in 1836 with the publication of Thomas Chalmers's *On the power, wisdom and goodness of God as manifested in the adaptation of external nature, to the moral and intellectual constitution of man* (Philadelphia: Carey, Lea, and Blanchard, 1833).

36. Torrance, *Incarnation*, 39.

37. We have simplified this example a bit—Einstein's theory actually describes gravitation as a curvature of space and time together. Because time is involved in the description, the theory can account for the fact that arrows flying at different speeds are seen to trace different arcs.

38. Torrance, *Incarnation*, 39-40.

39. Torrance, *Incarnation*, 128.

40. Actually the space-time curvature at any given location is a product of the way all the mass in the universe is distributed. We are here artificially treating the moon as if it were an isolated body for ease of explanation.

41. Albert Einstein, *The World As I See It* (New York: Covici Friede, 1934), 22 (emphasis mine).

42. See Michael Polanyi, *Science, Faith, and Society* (London: Oxford University Press, 1946); Polanyi, *Personal Knowledge*; Michael Polanyi, *Knowing and Being* (Chicago: University of Chicago Press, 1969).

43. Einstein and Polanyi actually tend to approach the subject rather differently from each other. Einstein's chief interest seems to be in the different conceptual layers which form the total approach of a particular discipline to its object of study, whereas Polanyi's emphasis tends to be in a hierarchical ordering of entire disciplines in relation to each other. Torrance alludes to these differences in *Space, Time, and Resurrection*, 188ff.

44. Torrance, *Contingent Order*, 102.

45. Torrance, *Ground and Grammar*, 19.

46. Torrance, *Contingent Order*, 69.

47. "This [theological interpretation of the universe] has been and no doubt will continue to be a source of friction between the theological and the natural reason, for the natural reason, rightly recognizing the autonomous (or at least semi-autonomous) status of empirical reality, constantly strives to find necessary reasons for the natural constitution of things in the universe as though it were after all a self-sufficient and a self-explanatory system—yet the very rigour of scientific method, so often demonstrated in our own times, halts that imperious drive of autonomous reason in recognition of the limits of natural science and in increasing respect for the capacity of the natural world to disclose itself to scientific enquiry in quite unexpected ways." Torrance, *Contingent Order*, 70.

48. See, for instance, Henry M. Morris, ed., *Scientific Creationism* (El Cajon, Calif.: Master Books, 1985).

49. See, for example, Willem Drees, *Religion, Science, and Naturalism* (Cambridge: Cambridge University Press, 1996), or E. O. Wilson, *Consilience: The Unity of Knowledge* (New York: Alfred A. Knopf, 1998).

50. Whitehead's influence is frequently introduced into theology by way of the process theology of Charles Hartshorne, John Cobb, and others. For prominent examples of this influence in the science-religion dialogue, see Barbour, *Age of Science*; also Arthur Peacocke, *Theology for a Scientific Age: Being and Becoming—Natural, Divine, and Human* (Minneapolis: Fortress Press, 1993).

51. See Michael J. Behe, *Darwin's Black Box: The Bio-Chemical Challenge to Evolution* (New York: Free Press, 1996); John Barrow and Frank Tipler, *The Anthropic Cosmological Principle* (Oxford: Oxford University Press, 1986); Dean L. Overman, *A Case Against Accident and Self-Organization* (New York: Rowman & Littlefield, 1997).

52. Cf. for example Stephen Hawking's prediction that the grand unified "theory of everything" that modern physicists are striving to uncover will turn out to possess a character of logical self-evidence that will make it look more like necessity than contingence. Hawking, *Brief History*, 174.

53. See, for example, his discussion of the influence of Christian faith upon the scientific work of Michael Farraday and James Clerk Maxwell in chapter 6 of Torrance, *Transformation*.

54. Torrance, *Incarnation*, 36.

55. Torrance, *Incarnation*, 31.

56. In relativity theory, speaking about the universe at some such "point" in time would assume the choice of a particular reference frame from which the temporal scheme would be constructed.

57. Torrance, *Scientific Theology*, 13-14.

58. For a readable introduction to these and other quantum mechanical phenomena, see chapter 2, "The Mysteries of Quantum Physics," in Roger Penrose, *The Large, the Small, and the Human Mind* (Cambridge: Cambridge University Press, 1997).

Chapter 12

Thomas Torrance Responds

by Thomas F. Torrance

It is most kind of Elmer Colyer to have compiled this collection concerned with my theological *oeuvre* over the years. Some of the authors have been former students of mine from whom I have myself learned not a little. One is a brother, and others are friends and colleagues who have sought to serve the cause of theological research and teaching on different sides of the Atlantic.

We are all very grateful to Karl Barth for what he has done under God to clarify for us in our times the biblical foundations of Christian theology, and the powerful way in which he has expounded the truth of the Gospel for our generation. Barth is the most biblically informed and the most biblical theologian in modern times. That is evident even in the countless biblical citations and expositions in the *Church Dogmatics*.

Some of us are also deeply indebted to scientists who under God have helped to clarify for us an understanding of the space-time world in which the Creator Word became incarnate, and within which we are committed to preach the Gospel of his saving love to all people until Christ Jesus comes again, and makes all things new. Then we shall no longer know the truth in dim or partial ways, but shall see Christ face to face, and know him as we are known by him.

David Torrance

I am glad that David has been asked by Professor Elmer Colyer to make a contribution to this volume about his brother, for it was in the midst of our parents' missionary activity that our own faith in the

Lord Jesus Christ and his Gospel developed. For us to believe in Jesus Christ as Lord and Savior, our daily reading and study of the Holy Scriptures and active service in the Gospel meant that ours was very definitely a biblical family imbued with missionary zeal.

That has been my concern throughout my life: devotion to the teaching of the Holy Scriptures and their message of the saving Love of God incarnate in Jesus. Concern for the propagation of the biblical message in China has remained with me, even when it was evidently not God's will that I should be a "foreign missionary," for I have remained a missionary at heart, and have regarded my theological work as a form of missionary activity. Since retiring I have three times been back in China, if only to encourage those who preach the Gospel and spread the biblical message in the face of great difficulties.

As David reports, when I came back from my first visit I wrote private letters to a number of friends and leaders in Bible Society activity on both sides of the Atlantic, and to several people in the Far East, to say that China now needs Bibles and pastors above all else. This met with a very fine response, so that I had the privilege of initiating activity that led to the foundation of the Amity Printing Press in Nanjing. Dr. John Erickson then of the American Bible Society in New York warmly supported me, and the final step was taken when Dr. Choi, the Korean head of the United Bible Societies in Kowloon to whom I had written, paid an urgent personal visit to see Bishop Ting in Nanjing, who had previously rejected such an idea, and gained his warm agreement.

Since then many millions and millions of Bibles have been printed and continue to be printed on an eight-acre site outside Nanjing where a modern printing facility has been established, and are steadily being distributed throughout China, for which I daily thank the Lord and ask his continued blessing upon the dissemination of the Word throughout China. I am sure that my dear father in heaven knows that in this way his form of missionary activity continues throughout China, and that one of his sons has had a part in it.

Now I must not write more about my biblical and missionary concern, but about my brother David, the youngest of the Torrance family. Like my brother James, David studied philosophy and theology in the University of Edinburgh, and then sat at the feet of Karl Barth in Basel. There he had the privilege, not only of attending Barth's lectures and seminars, but of participating in the small group of students which Barth selected each year for personal and informal teaching and discussion in his own home. In that way David gained an intimate and profound understanding of Barth's theology which left a decisive imprint on his mind and theological commitment. My other brother, James, and I, also, had that privilege.

It was at the feet of the master theologian and in discussion face to face with him that David's understanding and appreciation of Barth's profoundly biblical and evangelical theology was gained. It had the effect of giving him a deep personal insight into Barth's mind which never left him, and has informed his reading of the massive volumes of Barth's *Church Dogmatics*, his study of the Holy Scriptures, and affected his preaching of the Gospel and pastoral ministry throughout his life. It also had the effect of enabling him to gain an unusually perceptive grasp of the *Institutes* and *Commentaries* of John Calvin on the New Testament, as I realized when he joined me in checking and editing the fresh translations of Calvin's *New Testament Commentaries* which I had organized.

A special missionary concern of David, deepened by his studies under Karl Barth, has long been the witness of Christians to the Jewish people, and the witness of the Jews to the world. That was also the concern of cousins of ours, Dr. David Torrance, known as the Galilee Doctor, and his son, Dr. Herbert Torrance, in the Scottish Hospital at Tiberias, which my father used to visit when he could when returning to Scotland on furlough or on his journey back to China. My brother David's deep interest became very apparent to others when he initiated and edited the book *The Witness of the Jews to God*, which was "concerned with ways and means whereby the Church could exercise her responsibility to the Jews more effectively, as well as learn to share in Israel's mission to the world."[1]

Although like David, James and I both spent some years in the pastoral ministry and in the armed forces during the war, David has devoted his whole life to preaching and teaching the Gospel to men, women, and children in several parishes in Scotland. Like our father he has always been a missionary, and as such took an active part in several evangelistic campaigns in Scotland, sharing also in those conducted in Scotland by Dr. Billy Graham. It is as such that David has kindly written this biographical account of me as a minister of the Gospel, pastor, and evangelical theologian. He shares with me and my brother James a passionate commitment to Christ which informs our ministry of the Gospel whether in a parish, a college, or a university.

David has written that our father and mother were dedicated missionaries of the Gospel in Sichuan, China, at first with the China Inland Mission, and then with the American Bible Society. As David remarks, father's transfer to service with the Bible Society gave him more scope and freedom for his considerable energy and missionary zeal. In Chengdu he took over the premises of the American Bible Society which had been established by an American Scot, but after several years he found his work had grown so much that he had to find rather larger quarters for the Bible Depot and for the colporteurs and preachers he trained and engaged in his expanding missionary activity in that region of western Sichuan between Chengdu, the capital of Sichuan, and the Minshan mountain range. I am glad that my brother has written about this as he has, for it was in the midst of that ongoing activity of the Bible Society that the Torrance family lived, and grew up in daily passionate devotion to the Lord Jesus Christ and the spread of the Good News of God's saving love.

Alasdair Heron

Alasdair Heron was a student and then a former colleague of mine in New College, Edinburgh. He was indeed one of the very ablest students I have had. He gained such a profound and acute understanding of Reformed and patristic theology that I hoped he would be my successor in the chair of Christian dogmatics. Readers of his contribution to this volume will understand why I thought and still think of him so highly.

As I read and learn from him in what he has written in this book I recall that I used to learn from him already when still a student in the seminars and discussions we had in Edinburgh. He has sent me back to my essay on "The Distinctive Character of the Reformed Tradition," the Donnell Lecture I delivered in Dubuque in 1988 and contributed to the festschrift for Ray Anderson, another former student of mine, in 1990. At one point, where he refers to a disagreement between us over "the tendency towards a Nestorian view of Christ that keeps on cropping in Calvinist theology," from which I used to exempt Calvin himself, I must really agree with him that "it is hard to let Calvin off the hook at this point."

Alasdair Heron is certainly right in pointing out that I "share with my brother James a pronounced distaste for certain aspects of Puritan Calvinism combined with the conviction that a radical and destructive shift occurred in the theological and pastoral perspective between Calvin and the Calvinists." Yes, it was certainly the imposition of a rigidly logicalized system of belief upon Reformed theology that gave rise to many of the problems that have afflicted Scottish Church life and theology. The change came about with the disastrous place given to the priority of God's eternal decree over the doctrines of the Trinity and the Incarnation.

Unfortunately that way of thinking, due not to Calvin but largely to Theodore Beza, was given wide currency in England and Scotland through the writings of Perkins concerning "the order of the causes of salvation and damnation." It devalued the centrality of the Incarnation, and cut behind the basic message of the Gospel about unconditional grace. Thus it had the effect of damaging the evangelical message of what was called the Gospel offer to sinners, and of taking joy out of public worship. Again and again what became more important was subscription to a system of belief rather than joyful commitment to Jesus Christ as the Lord and Savior of sinners. It also had the effect of giving rise to deep splits in the Church, as the history of the Church life in Scotland shows.

With regard to what Professor Heron says of my independence over against Barth, he points to a "higher understanding of the priesthood of Christ, and with it order, ministry, sacraments, and liturgy." I recall at least one occasion when I raised with Barth the question of the heavenly priesthood of Christ to which he seemed to have given little attention, but which I claimed to be essential for our understanding of the ascended Christ and of his Body the Church. When I referred to the teaching in the Epistle to the Hebrews about the heavenly priesthood of Christ, which Calvin had stressed, Barth agreed that he should have included that in his teaching about the risen and ascended Christ, and about the life and ministry of the Church in its union with Christ.

With that in mind I contributed to the volume entitled *Calvin's Books: Festschrift for Peter De Klerk*, 1997, a discussion of the prayers which Calvin included in his *Commentary on the Book of Malachi,* which John Knox used at the Reformation in Scotland. In those prayers Calvin referred not only to the heavenly priesthood of the ascended Christ, and the royal priesthood of the Church as the Body of Christ, but to the fact that God has chosen *some* people to stand before him in a priestly capacity, and chosen *some* to be priests before himself, in which Calvin evidently included himself. It was in this direction that Scottish Theology developed under the influence of William Milligan of Aberdeen and the Scottish Church Society, which John Heron, Alasdair Heron's father, supported, as he tells us in his essay.

Markus Barth, however, was not at all pleased with my views expressed in my contribution on "The Paschal Mystery of the Eucharist" to the dialogue between Reformed and Roman Catholic theologians about the Eucharist that was held in 1974 at

Woudschouten-Zeist in Holland. It was published in 1975 as chapter 3 of *Theology and Reconciliation*, and in French in the journal *Istina* in the same year. I had no negative reaction from Barth himself about that. On the other hand, it stimulated Markus Barth to give further attention to the sacrificial dimension of the atoning work of Christ, and in a small paperback book published in Edinburgh he even rendered the familiar words of St. John in the prologue to the Fourth Gospel, "The Word became flesh," as "The Word became sacrificial flesh."

With regard to the doctrine of the Trinity I am certainly indebted to John Calvin and to Gregory of Nazianzus, "The Theologian," a title which Melanchthon gave to Calvin for he seemed to be a Nazianzus redivivus. And of course I was immensely influenced by Karl Barth on the Trinity, but differed somewhat from him in *Christian Dogmatics* I.1 where he tended to follow the thinking and terminology of Basil on the mode of existence or being of the three Persons of the Trinity, rather than the teaching of Athanasius, Epiphanius, or Cyril of Alexandria.

On the other hand, Barth's use of the Augustinian conception of the *communio quaedam consubstantialis* in the same half volume of the *Church Dogmatics* left a signficant and enduring imprint on my mind, for it helped me to clarify what I called the inner or material logic of Christian theology, which I sought to develop in a more Athanasian way. When Barth asked me as a student in Basel what I would like to work on for my doctoral dissertation, I referred to the *communio quaedam consubstantialis* which he had cited from Augustine's *De Trinitate* in his chapter on "The Eternal Spirit," in *Church Dogmatics* I.l, and said that I would like to make use of that as a central concept in working out the inner logic and "scientific structure of Christian theology" with special attention to the doctrine of Grace.

To my chagrin, Barth said that he thought I was too young for that! When he learned of my interest in Greek patristic theology, he suggested that I might consider writing on the theology of grace in the second-century Greek Fathers, to which I agreed. Eventually, however, that was cut down to an examination of the teaching of the Apostolic Fathers, with special reference to their doctrine of Grace. When Alasdair Heron discussed with me what he might work on for his doctorate, he opted for a study of Didimus the Blind, which has filled a big gap in patristic theology.

Andrew Purves

Andrew Purves and his wife both studied in New College, Edinburgh, and attended my lectures on Christian dogmatics and seminars on patristic texts which are reflected in this essay expounding the doctrine of Christ, with special attention to the relation in being and act between the incarnate Son and the Father. In it he expounds the crucial significance of the ontological and soteriological heart of Nicene theology expressed by the *homoousion* formulated by the Ancient Church at the Council of Nicaea in the face of dualist ways of thinking that threatened to undermine the faith of the Church by calling in question the relation in being and act between Jesus and God, the incarnate Son and the Father, that lay at the very heart of the Gospel. That still remains the crucial issue in the Church's understanding of the faith which it must think out anew and recover in every generation.

What Andrew Purves has written about this, and the illuminating way in which he has spelled out the implications of the *homoousion* for our understanding of the incarnation of the eternal Son of God in space and time, and the light it throws upon the creation as well as redemption, is quite superb. I am pleased that he has taken and developed the epistemological and scientific stress I have tried to lay upon rigorous scientific thinking of rcalities according to their nature, *kata physin*, which I have learned from my patristic investigations and find supported by modern scientific method.

Hence I appreciate the relevance of his critical reflections, and their appropriateness for an in-depth understanding and clarification of the epistemological issues involved in a strict examination and appropriate theological account of the central doctrines of the faith such as the great Greek Fathers gave us in their formulation of the Nicene and Chalcedonian concepts of the *homoousion* and the hypostatic union between the divine and the human natures in Jesus Christ as the incarnate Son of God. At the same time he takes up the idea that empirical as well as theoretical factors are involved in any rigorous understanding and formulation of Christian truth, which is at the same time deeply personal in relevance and character. There is here a kind of "scientific theological fideism," he claims, but one that results from the nature of God's revealing and saving act in Jesus Christ.

While taking these epistemological and critical issues into account, Professor Purves has discussed one of the most critical issues which many Roman Catholic and evangelical Christians seem to neglect or even deliberately avoid. I refer to the inner connection between the incarnation and the atonement, and in particular, to the redemptive assumption of our fallen humanity in Christ, and thus to the relation between the sinless incarnate life of Jesus and his vicarious death on the Cross when, as St. Paul startlingly expressed it, Christ "was made sin for us," yet of course without sin. This means that the atonement is to be understood not simply in terms of what happened at the Cross, but in terms of the whole incarnate life of the Lord Jesus from his birth of the Virgin Mary to his death on the Cross, which was sin-bearing and redemptive. Thus the atonement is to be understood as having taken place within the inner depths of the incarnate life of Jesus Christ, and not just as an external judicial transaction in his death on the Cross.

This leads Andrew Purves to lay soteriological stress upon what my brother James and I have called "the vicarious humanity of Christ," and to draw out its implications for our understanding of Jesus himself, and of his twofold ministry, in which, as Athanasius taught, he is to be regarded as "ministering the things of God to man and the things of man to God." That cannot but affect our understanding of the hypostatic union between God and man in Christ and of the Church's worship and liturgical life, and its ministry of the Gospel to the world.

Another point to which I must refer is Andrew Purves's account of the doctrine of our *union with Christ*, which Calvin called a "real and substantial union" with him in his human nature. While that was given an essential place in the Reformation theology of the Church of Scotland beautifully expressed in the *Scots Confession*, and several sixteenth-century catechisms, it was given scanty place in subsequent Scottish theology due to the Westminster Confession of Faith, with its exiguous attention to the Trinity, and the Puritan form of Calvinism that characterized it. When that was given currency in the larger and shorter catechisms, the Reformation emphasis on union and communion with Christ scarcely survived, although it was rescued from time to time by Christ-centered churchmen and theologians. Andrew Purves is such a Christ-centered theologian who has sought to restore the evangelical doctrine of union with Christ in our day, as he has done in this essay with attention given to the teaching of St. Paul in Galatians 2:20.

Moreover, Andrew Purves and his friend Mark Achtemeier have recently published an important study book entitled *Union with Christ: A Declaration for the Church*, which they have kindly dedicated to me. In it they seek to restore belief today in the union of believers with Christ and in their communion with him which constitute their very existence and life as Christians. Union with Christ is the evangelical source of the continuing life of the Church; and communion with Christ lies at the heart of all Eucharistic fellowship between believers, and is the source of their life and mission in the world as the body of Christ.

Gary W. Deddo

I believe that in any doctrine of the Holy Spirit we must take seriously and keep steadily in mind the teaching of the Lord Jesus to his disciples recorded by St. John. When he the Spirit of truth is come, Jesus told them, he will not be visible in the way that Jesus himself was visible in his incarnate reality, *nor will he speak of himself*, but will direct the disciples to Jesus himself, glorify him, bring to their remembrance what he had taught them, and lead them into all truth. By his very nature *the Holy Spirit hides and effaces himself, and directs all our attention to Christ as the Lord and Savior.*

After the crucifixion, resurrection, and ascension of Jesus Christ, the Holy Spirit was poured out upon the Church in a once and for all unique way, and the disciples were sent out empowered by the Spirit to proclaim Christ Jesus as the Savior and Lord of all humankind, who will come again in fulfilment of his saving purpose in the consummation of all things. That is why the focus of attention in the New Testament Revelation is upon the grace of the Lord Jesus Christ in union and communion with whom we have access to God the Father and enjoy his love. Thus again and again in the Epistles reference is made explicitly of the Father and the Son, without direct reference to the Spirit. Gary Deddo cites from me: "There is not a separate activity of the Holy Spirit in revelation or salvation in addition to or independent of the activity of Christ, for what he does is to empower and actualise the words and works of Christ in our midst as the words and works of the Father."[2]

This does not mean, however, that there is no place for a definite doctrine of the Holy Spirit, as Dr. Deddo shows, but that teaching about the Spirit is given in Trinitarian relation to the doctrines of the Father and the Son, for the Holy Spirit is the intensely active presence of God himself among us in and through Jesus Christ. And so Gary Deddo, in writing about the Holy Spirit in my theology, points out that my pneumatology, in conformity with the actuality of Revelation, is Christocentric and incarnational, and that a proper Christology does not make pneumatology less central. And in the face of a critique of my doctrine of the Spirit he shows that often the Person and work of the Spirit remain implicit in my treatment of other doctrines. He rightly adds that "this corresponds to the actual nature of the subject-matter. It reflects the ineffable and self-effacing nature of the Spirit whose ministry is to shed light on everything else rather than to be the spotlight himself. Consequently the working of the Spirit cannot and need not always be explicitly referenced."

Yes, it is the case that I have not devoted a special work to the doctrine of the Holy Spirit, as I have of the Father and the Son, although in my lecture courses in Christian dogmatics I have given specific attention to the doctrine of the Spirit, as I did in my Auburn Lectures in 1938-1939. In particular, with reference to the letters of Athanasius to Serapion on the Holy Spirit, I have expounded the all-important conception of the *homoousion* of the Holy Spirit. It was in the light of this truth about the Holy Spirit who, no less than the Son, is *homoousios* with the Father, that the full doctrine of the Holy Trinity was understood and formulated. And that, in turn, led to my account of the onto-relational understanding of the three Persons of the Holy Trinity in their mutual coinherent or perichoretic relations between the Father, the Son, and the Holy Spirit.

In face of the criticism that my view of the work of the Spirit "does not show a proper independence of the other Trinitarian Persons and so fails to exhibit the equality of the Deity," Dr. Deddo very rightly points out that if I am right about the coinherent nature of the working of the Triune God then one should not expect the Spirit to have some kind of autonomous working. That is indeed the danger point where serious problems arise in many charismatic movements, when an emphasis on the Holy Spirit incompatible with the coinherent nature of the activity of the Triune God can become unbiblical and heretical.

In face of misunderstandings of this kind I have often turned to the great Alexandrian theologians and sought to think out with their help a way of resolving if possible the debated question of the "procession of the Holy Spirit." And so I show that if we think through an understanding of the perichoretic relations between the three divine Persons it is possible to restate the doctrine of the procession of the Spirit homoousially and consubstantially from God the Father in a way that cuts behind and sets aside the problems that divided the Church in East and West over the *filioque* clause the West added to the Creed. That is what I argued in the *Trinitarian Faith* (and later in *The Christian Doctrine of God, One Being Three Persons*).

It was with that in mind that I proposed a dialogue between the Eastern Orthodox Church and the Reformed Churches, and suggested that we should operate not from a basis in the teaching of Basil and Gregory Nyssen, but on the impeccably orthodox axis of Athanasius, Epiphanius, and Cyril of Alexandria, and thus indeed of Gregory of Nazianzus. When they agreed and we entered into dialogue first with the Greek Orthodox Church and then with all the twenty-four Orthodox Churches, we reached an agreement on the doctrine of the Holy Trinity which Dr. Deddo succinctly describes. I am grateful that he has done this, for evangelical theologies have as a rule not yet given these crucial issues between East and West sufficient attention. Apart from any thing else it would help them to take a more biblical and positive understanding of the mission of the Gospel.

What about the so-called "how question"? In my contribution to the festschrift for James Packer, *Alive to God: Studies in Spirituality*, "The Spiritual Relevance of Angels," I showed that angels, of which the Bible speaks in the Old as well as the New Testament, have a ministry on the boundaries of space and time, directing attention to acts of God in space and time which cannot be understood or construed in terms of the kind of logico-causal connections and explanations that obtain in space and time with which we have to do, for example, in natural science. That is also how we are to understand the acts of the Holy Spirit such as in the Virgin Birth of Jesus or in the Resurrection of Jesus, which while being real acts of God in space and time, are not to be understood or construed in terms of the kind of logico-causal relations or connections of our space-time world.

Thus the presence and operation of angels in salvation-history indicate that God's gracious interventions and saving acts are not to be put down to chance or necessity or explained in terms of the kind of logico-causal nexus that obtains between intramundane events in our finite and fallen world, but only by reference to the Holy Spirit and the inexplicable power of the immediate presence and operation of God himself. That is why any notions of "irresistible Grace," to which Dr. Deddo refers, can have no place in biblical, evangelical, or Reformed theology.

One final point. I would like to recall again the way in which Jesus spoke of the Holy Spirit as "the Spirit of truth." That is something I had in mind in my essay published in *God and Rationality*, entitled "The Epistemological Relevance of the Holy Spirit" which I penned in honor of Professor C. G. Berkhower of Amsterdam. In it I wrote: "The Holy Spirit is not cognoscible in himself, but it is in the Spirit that we are confronted with the ultimate being and presence of God. . . . He does not show us himself, but shows us the

Face of the Father in the Face of the Son, and shows us the heart of the Son in the heart of the Father. By his very mode of being as Spirit he hides himself from us, so that we do not know him directly in his own hypostasis, and in his mode of activity as transparent Light he effaces himself that the one Triune God may shine through him to us."[3] I had hoped that others would engage with this question about the epistemological relevance of the Spirit— and take it further: but no one as far as I know has really done so! Perhaps after reading this book and Dr. Deddo's contribution to it, some other theologians will do so!

Colin Gunton

I am grateful for this contribution of Professor Colin Gunton, who is undoubtedly one of the leading theologians in Britain, and who has built up what is, I believe, the strongest theological faculty in Britain, to which I often recommend students. He is also noted as an authority on the doctrine of the Holy Trinity. As he reports in this essay he was one whom I invited to join an international discussion on the Trinitarian teaching of the great Roman Catholic and Jesuit theologian Karl Rahner in the hope of reaching an ecumenical consensus on the Trinity.

I was then president of the International Academy of Religious Sciences, a Dominican foundation in Brussels, which took its rise at the end of the Second Vatican Council. Its first president was Professor Gerard Phillips of Leuven who had written the final draft of the *Lumen Gentium* of the Second Vatican Council, but after he died two years later I was asked to succeed him as president of the academy.

Since then I have been instrumental in bringing about the discussions between the Reformed Churches and the Orthodox Churches which had reached an agreement several years earlier on the doctrine of the Trinity. We took as the basis for our discussions not the Cappadocian theology of Basil and his brother Gregory Nyssen, but that of the great Alexandrian theology of Athanasius, Epiphanius, and Cyril of Alexandria, which our Orthodox brethren agreed to be impeccably Orthodox. The Greek Orthodox participants did not want John Zizioulas to join them, for they disagreed with him rather radically in spite of some of his very fine theological works. In due course I published an account of these discussions and the agreement we reached in two volumes entitled *Theological Dialogue between*

Orthodox and Reformed Churches, in 1985 and 1993.

Following the successful dialogue and agreement we reached between the Orthodox and Reformed theologians, I had hoped that we might make some progress toward theological agreement with Roman Catholic theologians. I proposed that we should study the thinking of Karl Rahner, who, following Karl Barth, had rejected a dualist approach that operated with a distinction between the One God and the Triune God, such as that advocated by Bernard Lonergan in his two works entitled *Deo Uno*, and *De Deo Trino*, published in Rome by the Pontifical Gregorian University in 1964.

In spite of Rahner's disagreement with that dualistic approach to the doctrine of God, I did not ask him to join us in our discussions, although he was also a member of the International Academy of Religious Sciences, so that we would have freedom to discuss his position set out in his brilliant little book, *The Trinity*, published in English in 1970. Our discussions about his understanding of the Trinity were set out in my book, *Trinitarian Perspectives: Toward Doctrinal Agreement*, published in Edinburgh in 1994, in which were included chapters on the Trinitarian teaching of Calvin and Gregory of Nazianzus, and a report on the "Agreed Statement by Reformed and Orthodox on the Doctrine of the Holy Trinity."

I have written about this here as I sense that Professor Gunton's disagreement with me here and there in his essay reflects the different approach he has to Greek patristic theology due in part to his friend John Zizioulas (whom I once brought to lecture at New College in Edinburgh), whereas mine is closer to that of the Greek Orthodox theologians in the University of Athens who disagree with him quite radically.

Perhaps the first point I might make in clarifying what Colin Gunton says about my theology is to question the contrast he draws between me and Barth over our emphases on revelation and the *homoousion*. For both of us the doctrine of the *homoousion* underscores commitment to God's self-revelation in the incarnation. I am certainly no less committed to revelation than Barth, and hold that a proper understanding of the *homoousion* reinforces our view of the reality of the incarnate self-revelation of God in space and time.

Gunton's faulty contrast at this point is reflected in what he says about my spelling out of the three levels in our theological understanding of God's *self*-revelation in the Gospel and of our acceptance of the *homoousion* both as an exegetical and clarificatory expression of the evangelical witness to Christ in the New Testament and then as an interpretative frame with which to give the Church a more exact understanding of the truth of the incarnate relation between God and man in Jesus Christ. I had spoken of that in the academy's celebration in 1981 of the sixteenth centennial of the formal authorization of the Nicene Creed at Council of Constantinopolitan in a.d. 381 (see *The Incarnation: Ecumenical Studies in the Nicene Constantinopolitan Creed*, 1981). In the book to which Colin Gunton refers, *The Christian Doctrine of God: One Being Three Persons*, I tried to spell out our evangelical and theological understanding of God's self-revelation in Christ in the Gospel in terms of three interpretative steps taken in a disciplined movement of thought from the biblical witness about Christ to a doctrine of the Holy Trinity.

I do not believe that my proposal to speak of those interpretative steps in terms of "scientific" levels of thought is distorting—but of course it depends on how one understands "scientific" used in this way! Barth and I differed somewhat in our understanding of science and Christian theology, and my use of scientific concepts in this way. It was about that, incidentally, that I had my last discussion with Barth before he died, in which we were concerned about the misunderstanding of several eminent theologians in Germany about Barth's firm belief in the *bodily* resurrection of Christ.

There are several points in Gunton's essay to which I would offer a rejoinder or correction.

1. In relation to what Gunton says about economic subordination of the Son, that is, I believe, properly to be understood of the incarnate Son, but may not be read back into the eternal Godhead unless one operates with the altogether dubious idea that the Father is the "cause" of the being of the Son, as both Basil and Gregory Nyssen held, a notion which Gregory of Nazianzus rightly rejected in line with the teaching of Athanasius.

2. The idea that the notion of "*perichoresis*" is derived primarily from "the economy" rather reflects the error that attributes it to Gregory of Nazianzus. He used the verb *perichorein* to elucidate the relation between the human and divine natures in Christ, *not* to the three Persons of the Trinity. The term and concept of *perichoresis* applied to the Holy Trinity is first found in the *De Sancta Trinitate* of Pseudo-Cyril, from which it was appropriated, without acknowledgment, by John of Damascus in his *De Fide Orthodoxa*, who gave it currency.

3. I object to the way Dr. Gunton misinterprets what I have written about the precise theological usage of *ousia* not simply as what it is in respect of its internal reality, while *hypostasis* refers to 'being' not just in its independent subsistence but in its *objective otherness*. I cited in a footnote a reference to Prestige's remark that for him, "*ousia* denotes being in its 'inward reference,' while

hypostasis denotes being in its 'outward reference,'" which I took to make the same point about the *objective otherness* of the divine Persons to one another. However, Gunton fastens on Prestige's use of the term "inward" to misconstrue what I have said about the objective relations. I certainly do not! Incidentally is he not aware of the influence of Gregory of Nazianzus's conception of relation on Augustine?

4. Gunton asks whether the Eastern Fathers were read too much through western eyes. That is often true, as when the teaching of Athanasius has been attacked by scholars in the West, as in Belgium and Oxford, because it conflicts with Augustinian ideas. I wonder whether Gunton is aware of the teaching of Grillmeier and others in this respect, and of the attempt to make out that Athanasius was an Apollinarian; or of the brilliant and massive work of Professor G. D. Dragas, *St. Athanasius Contra Apollinarem*, refuting that idea. I am delighted with Gunton's reference to my essay published in *Theology and Reconciliation*, "The Mind of Christ in Worship: The Problem of Apollinarianism in the Liturgy," of which there is no trace in the writings of Athanasius, to whom we cannot but attribute the two books *Contra Apollinarem*.

5. One of the ideas that I have found distressing is the use of causality (*aitia*) by Basil and his brother Gregory to speak of the relations of the Persons in the Holy Trinity in terms of a chain of causality, spelled out particularly by Gregory Nyssen, and which is compounded by the Greek stance on the *filioque* clause. Professor Gunton gives little attention to the way in which I have sought to clarify the issues involved, in putting forward a way of understanding the relation of the Son and the Spirit to the Father which I believe cuts behind the sad division between the East and the West over what was added to the Nicene-Constantinopolitan Creed. It was and is a grave mistake to import *aitia*, or causality, into our understanding of Triune relations in God. That has a disastrous effect of distinguishing between God the Father as uncaused or underived Deity, and the Son and the Spirit as caused or derived Deities, a heretical notion found sometimes in English theology. Colin Gunton thankfully does not countenance that idea. My attempt to put the *filioque* question in a different way and on a deeper basis, in *The Trinitarian Faith: The Evangelical Theology of the Ancient Catholic Church*, and in *The Christian Doctrine of God: One Being Tree Persons*, has found not a little support in the West as in the East. I would have valued Colin Gunton's reaction to this.

I have singled out a number of critical points at issue between Colin Gunton and myself on the Christian doctrine of God, but I want now to thank him very warmly for his profound and perceptive contribution to our understanding of the doctrine of the Holy Trinity today.

George Hunsinger

I am very grateful to Dr. George Hunsinger for his essay and delighted with his appreciation of what I have written about the sacraments of baptism and the Eucharist. They are matters over which I have had not a little discussion with churchmen and theologians in Europe, and sometimes in the United States and Canada, from whom I have learned not a little. What we have inherited from our Reformation origins has had to be rethought and reexpressed in face of the massive theology of Karl Barth, and also the tradition and teaching of our Roman Catholic and Orthodox brethren.

In both parts of his essay Professor Hunsinger has laid his finger upon the all-important truth of *participatio Christi,* and of our union and communion with Christ upon which John Calvin laid such great stress in his teaching about baptism and the Lord's Supper. About both of these I had personal discussions with Karl Barth and his sons Markus and Christoph. On the issue of union with Christ I persuaded Barth to give fuller attention to the teaching of the Reformers. He responded with a lengthy account in the *Church Dogmatics* of the teaching of Luther about union with Christ, but I felt that he did not give the attention he should have given to the teaching of John Calvin, for whom union and communion with Christ, as Hunsinger emphasizes, was so very important.

When it came to the doctrine of Baptism in volume 4, *The Doctrine of Reconciliation*, Karl Barth was caught between the different views of his two sons, Christoph and Markus, and he deferred to the view of Christoph in one chapter and to those of Markus in another!

With regard to baptism I am pleased that George Hunsinger thinks that I have tried to bring Calvin and Barth together in a new synthesis, of which he approves. I had hoped to contribute an essay, "A Neglected Aspect of Baptism" to the festschrift for Barth in 1956, but when my contribution arrived too late to be included in the volume being edited by Ernst Wolff, entitled *Antwort*, he offered to include it in *Evangelische Theologie* for that year of which he was the editor. It was entitled: "Ein vernachlässigter Geschichtspunkt der Tauflehre" [A Neglected Aspect of Baptism].

In it I put forward for Barth's consideration a number of points about baptism and infant baptism with reference to teaching in the New Testament and several early Fathers of the Church. But, unfortunately, I got no "comeback" from him, probably because of the rather "Baptist" notions of his son Markus! However, he gave me a signed copy of *Antwort*, which I cherish. Perhaps I might note here that the address entitled "The Paschal Mystery of Christ in the Eucharist," from which George Hunsinger cites later on in his essay, rather upset dear Markus Barth, but brought no comment from his father!

In the Church of Scotland I was asked by the General Assembly to convene a commission on baptism for a number of years, 1953-1962, in the course of which I learned a great deal about baptism in relation to our union and communion with Christ in the fine way in which Professor Hunsinger has written here. One of the main issues which we were forced to face and think out was that of the relation of baptism, understood as a sacrament of our participation in and of union with Christ, to *faith*, not just because of the teaching of British Baptists, but because of the semi-Pelagianism that seemed to have become rather rife in all our Churches on both sides of the Atlantic.

Then in 1966, at the request of the General Assembly of the Church of Scotland, I prepared a pamphlet entitled *The Doctrine of Baptism*, in which after speaking of baptism as the sacrament of union with Christ which initiates us into communion with him, I wrote this about "Baptism and Faith," which echoes what George Hunsinger has written here taken from the chapter "The One Baptism Common to Christ and His Church" in *Theology in Reconciliation*. "Baptism is not a sacrament of what we do but of what God *has done* for us in Jesus Christ, in whom he *has bound* us to himself, before ever we could respond to him."[4]

At the request of our General Assembly I reemphasized that in my pamphlet stressing the evangelical truth that in being baptized into Christ we are united with Christ in his faithfulness and obedience to the Father. In baptism as an act done in the name of the Savior upon us, it is not upon our faith or our own faithfulness that we rely, but upon Christ alone and upon his faithfulness. Therefore Baptism directs us to the solid and unshakeable foundation on which we are summoned to build our faith in genuine freedom and personal decision for Christ; for it is God's own great act in Christ which not only creates and inspires our faith, but undergirds and upholds it, and encloses it within his own faithfulness.

Dr. George Hunsinger has very rightly pointed here to the importance I have laid upon *the vicarious humanity of Christ*, for it is in Christ's assumption of our humanity in his own Person as lived out in his birth, life, death, and resurrection that our saving union and communion with him and our sanctification have taken place. Dr. Hunsinger goes on to show the relevance of this truth to what I called "The Paschal Mystery of Christ in the Eucharist," for it is of crucial significance in a proper doctrine of the Lord's Supper, and in it of the Priesthood of Christ. It is the vicarious humanity of the Lord Jesus Christ, the priesthood of the incarnate Son of God, that is the key to the understanding of the Eucharist.

That is why I wrote the chapter entitled "The Mind of Christ in Worship: The Problem of Apollinarianism in the Liturgy" (published as chapter 4 in *Theology in Reconciliation*). In wrestling with that question I found that in many respects the dividing issue was some form of the Apollinarian heresy, the failure to take seriously the place of the *human mind* of the Lord Jesus Christ in our worship. It is when we discern the crucial importance of this in the celebration of the Eucharist that, as in the early Alexandrian liturgy, we pray "through Jesus Christ our Lord, *by* whom and *with* whom and *in* whom" in the unity of the Holy Spirit, in offering thanksgiving and worship to the Father. And so I prepared for our use in the General Assembly in Scotland an edition of "Form and Order for the Celebration of the Lord's Supper, or Holy Communion," which I used when I was moderator of the kirk, with the all-significant words in the Eucharistic prayer: "through Jesus Christ our Lord, by whom and with whom, in the unity of the Holy Spirit." Because of the long reaction in Scotland against patristic and Anglican use of the term "Eucharist" to speak of the celebration of Holy Communion, it became an old tradition among our Scottish divines, such as Thomas Boston of Ettrick, to speak of sermons at the celebration of the Lord's Supper as "Action Sermons," forgetting that the *Actio Gratiarum* was simply the Latin for εὐχαριστία, Eucharistic thanksgiving!

I could not be more pleased with the spiritual insight and the sensitive way in which George Hunsinger has written about the celebration of the Lord's Supper and the Eucharistic Sacrifice. He has raised no questions for me, for I cannot but say "amen" and "amen," as I read his pages. Thank you, George, with all my heart. I would love to have the privilege of worshiping the heavenly Father with him when he officiates at the celebration of the Holy Supper, and engage with him in Eucharistic worship which on earth and in time echoes through the priestly Spirit the heavenly intercession of the Lord Jesus risen from the cross and ascended as the Lamb of God. Let me now cite two verses from the wonderful Communion Hymn by William Bright.

And now, O Father, mindful of the love
That bought us, once for all,
on Calvary's Tree,
And having with us in him that
pleads above,
We here present, we here spread
forth to thee
That only offering perfect
in thine eyes,
The one true, pure immortal
sacrifice.

Look, Father, look on his
anointed face,
And only look on us as
found in him;
Look not on our misusing
of thy grace,
Our prayer so languid, and
our faith so dim:
For lo! between our sins, and
their reward,
We set the Passion of thy Son
our Lord.

Ray Anderson

I first met Ray Anderson at Fuller Theological Seminary in Pasadena, California and got to know him when he came to Edinburgh to work on his doctorate. Like my father, he was, if I remember correctly, brought up on a farm, and brought to his study of theology an open-air freshness of mind that was not lost in his academic life and thinking. I got to know him also when I was delivering the Payton Lectures on *Reality of Evangelical Theology: The Realism of Christian Revelation*, and then when he came to Edinburgh to work on his doctorate. I was very impressed with the unusual way in which he combined remarkable insight into human life and thought with a Christ-centered theology. Particularly characteristic of his theological outlook, influenced then by the writings of Dietrich Bonhoeffer, was his linking of divine transcendence and personal otherness, and his ability to discern the practical and pastoral relevance of profound truths. In due course he published a remarkable volume helpful not only for scholars, but also for pastors and students preparing for the ministry, entitled *Theological Foundations for Ministry: Selected Readings for a Theology of the Church in Ministry* (Edinburgh: T & T Clark, 1979).

I realize, as Ray Anderson writes, that students of mine in Edinburgh often found it difficult to relate the kind of disciplined academic theology they heard from the rostrum in my lecture room with the actual ministry of the Gospel to which they felt called and for which they were being prepared. I always made a point of praying before and after each lecture, for I was aware of trying to talk about the truths of the Gospel in the reality of the Lord's presence, and in the awareness of my inadequacy to speak of them in a way worthy of them.

Actually I myself learned more about those truths in my own pastoral ministry than through reading books. Again and again as I wrote a lecture or delivered it, I said to myself that is something that I learned in Alyth or Aberdeen, and remembered the situation when that truth of the Gospel really came home to me when I was engaged on a pastoral visit, and read a passage of the Bible and prayed with people in their homes. I used to recall Calvin's injunction about speaking of the Gospel *domatim et privatim*, face to face with people personally in their own homes. It was when the truth of the Gospel struck home to me like that, that I really understood it and its relevance to people in their everyday life.

In thanking Professor Ray Anderson for what he has kindly contributed to this volume, I would like to single out several things in particular to which he refers. The first point is the *vicarious humanity* of Christ to which Anderson refers in the way in which revelation and reconciliation operate together in the saving acts of God: "Simultaneous with that act of self-revelation, not sequential to it, a corresponding movement from below to above constitutes an act of reconciliation by which humanity is vicariously represented in the personal life, death, and resurrection of Jesus Christ." That truth has always been a source of strength to me in my understanding of the Gospel and attempts to speak to others about it, for in and through all my stumbling words and acts, I rely on the crucified and risen Lord Jesus himself who is present fulfilling his own ministry, undergirding mine in his name from below and above. I believe that trusting in and teaching about the vicarious humanity of Christ is of supreme importance both in our own theological understanding of the saving truth of the Gospel and for our ministry of it pastorally to others, not least of course in our celebration of the Lord's Supper or our understanding of the Paschal Mystery of the Eucharist. It is when we partake of the body and blood of Christ in Holy Communion that the

Gospel of Christ's vicarious life and work strikes deeply into our souls, and gives us grace to minister it to others.

The second point is the truth of *unconditional grace*. It is here that I often find the Gospel of salvation by grace alone to be so difficult for people to understand and believe. In preaching and speaking about it to good people in their homes I have sometimes found the sharpest reaction, for it is unconditional grace that cuts so deeply into our life, and unconditional grace which strangely upsets so many evangelical Christians, as I have found in their reaction to my book, *The Mediation of Christ*. It is sometimes the case that would-be evangelical Christians shy away from the sheer truth of salvation by grace alone, and yet it is there, as I have so often found in my pastoral ministry and theological writing, that people feel so "liberated," as they say. That is something that Ray Anderson knows well in his teaching and preaching about the grace of the Lord Jesus—it cuts deeply into the very quick of the soul and frees it from deep seated bondage to the self. It is when people think of salvation through what Christ Jesus has done for us not only on the Cross but also through the whole of his incarnate life from his birth of the Virgin Mary to his bodily resurrection from the grave, that they can really understand the deep truth of the vicarious humanity of Christ and his unconditional grace.

The third point has to do with Ray Anderson's questions to me at the end of his essay: "I wonder if Torrance would agree with me that the vicarious humanity of Christ has as much to do with contemporary ethical issues as it does with the more classical issues of epistemology and soteriology? Torrance has recently affirmed the practice of ordaining women for pastoral ministry in the church based on the 'new humanity of Christ.' Would he be equally affirming of the inclusion of gay Christians in the church, if not also for ordination? And if not, why not?"

In all questions of this kind I try to be guided by what we learn in the Holy Scripture. Both in the Old and in the New Testament Scriptures homosexual behavior of men and of women is clearly condemned, but in his unlimited divine love the Lord Jesus Christ died for them and as well as for all others that they may be saved. And he calls all people irrespective of who they are, including homosexuals, to repent and believe in him, and through his Holy Spirit he unites them to himself in the Church which is his body.

The current use of the term "gay" for homosexual people seems to indicate a rather ambivalent view of homosexual people. Once when our Lord referred to "eunuchs" he said that while some people have been made eunuchs by men, there are eunuchs who have been so from birth. Are we to think of homosexuals in the same way? I think that there is little doubt about the fact that most so-called homosexuals have become that way during puberty, and many of them have been changed through belief in Christ. But what of those who have been so from birth? If there are such, there should be no objection to their inclusion in the Church if like other members they believe in Jesus Christ as their Savior and Lord, and do not engage in homosexual practices. The trouble today is that the use of the term "gay" to refer to homosexuals can easily become a cover for practicing homosexual people, male and female alike.

I have, however, a basic scientific question for those who claim that their homosexuality is due to their genes. Why is it that their genes have shaped their bodies and sexual organs for heterosexual activity, when they claim genetic grounds for their homosexual activity? The widespread prevalence of so-called "gay" people in modern society seems to me often to be due not really to their genes but to sin. Hence while showing them great kindness and sympathy, we must invite them to repent like all other sinners and believe in Jesus Christ as their Savior and Lord.

Kurt Richardson

In 1997 I had a memorable meeting with Professor Kurt Anders Richardson of Gordon-Conwell Theological Seminary when he and Professor George Dragas of the Greek Orthodox School of Theology in Brookline, Massachusetts, invited me to give a lecture. Then I "met him" again in a different way when in 1999 he kindly wrote a foreword to my book *Reality and Evangelical Theology*, when he gave the book a subtitle, "The *Realism* of Christian Revelation," and entitled his Foreword "Wonder over the Intelligibility of God." In it he cited a statement of mine to the effect that "understanding and interpretation of the Scriptures does not focus myopically . . . upon the words and statements themselves, but *through* them on the truths and realities they indicate beyond themselves."[5]

That is the point of his essay here which is not only about revelation and Scripture, but about mystical apprehension of divine knowledge. I find the word "mystical" rather strange, for I have very rarely spoken of mysticism or of mystical knowledge. But I interpret that here to refer to the kind of "intuitive" nonlogical knowing that arises under the constraint of reality upon the mind, which, Einstein claimed, characterized that of Clerk Maxwell, as well as himself, who did not work with a logical bridge between ideas and reality. That would certainly be true of my apprehension of divine knowledge in interpreting Holy Scripture. And so Dr. Richardson writes: "Torrance means a kind of intuition that is occasioned by the unique relational knowing of God by the creature." I would add that this relational knowing of God and our being reconciled to him belong together.

It is because I understand God's self-revealing to us through his Holy Spirit mediated to us in the Scriptures inspired by the Holy Spirit, and our knowing of him in this intuitive nonlogical way, that I cannot understand divine inspiration in terms of "propositions." That would be a rationalistic conception of divine inspiration to which many would-be evangelical fundamentalists seem unfortunately to be addicted. What Kurt Richardson is emphasizing by his use of the word "mystical" here is, I believe, that as the Truth of God retains his own essential mystery in his self-revelation, we must respect that mystery in our understanding and interpretation of Holy Scripture given to us through the inspiration of his Holy Spirit. That is what he calls the mystical dimension of my scientific theological method.

I would add here one other point: the emphasis by the Lord Jesus upon "hearing" the Word of God. What we are basically concerned with in our response to divine revelation is what (as Dr. Richardson points out) I have long called "audits," that is with *hearing* (ἀκοή) requiring on our part *obedience* (ὑπακοή) for its spiritual understanding (in which revelation and reconciliation go together) rather than concepts or propositions calling for logical attention. This is in line with Kurt Richardson's understanding of the use I make of the patristic distinction between apophatic (which he calls "mystical") and kataphatic theology, although of course the apophatic is not to be separated from the kataphatic, and the apophatic refers to what is inexpressible and unspecifiable.

I am also delighted that Kurt Richardson refers to my point that the "real text" with which we are concerned in biblical interpretation is the "*humanity* of Jesus Christ since we only hear the Word of God when we hear him in the words of inspired scripture." This is also why I feel that some "propositional" notion of the inspiration and interpretation of the Holy Scriptures is very far off the mark. He also refers to what I have written about St. Paul's statement in 1 Corinthians 13:12: "Now we see through a glass, darkly; but then face to face: now we know in part; but then I shall know even as also I am known." That means that in the resurrection or in heaven we will have no need of Bibles, for we shall see and know Christ face to face.

Dr. Richardson also draws attention to my reference to the

teaching in the Epistle to the Hebrews 9:19f., that even the book of the covenant was sprinkled with the blood of atonement. Dr. Richardson interprets that as "where the atoning act of sacrifice cleanses the text of Scripture as well as the people who hear the word of reconciliation." That tells us that even the Bible comes under the cleansing of the atoning blood of Christ.

Then he goes on to add: "Torrance is indicating that Scripture is to the Word of God what the flesh of Christ is to the flesh of all humanity, something on the order of the second *homoousion* of the Chalcedonian formula. Borrowing an analogy from Luther, the Word of God in the Bible is heard only through the redemptive reading that corresponds to the *theologia crucis* over against a *theologia gloriae*." I understand and appreciate the point being made in that statement, but I would *not* agree with his words "something on the order of the second *homoousion* of the Chalcedonian formula"!! He probably did not mean it as it sounds to me! But I like that he adds "carrying the paradigm of *the theologia crucis* still further, for the Bible is to be heard for what it is, the Word of God, it must be heard within the experience of God's saving action in Christ. Scripture is part of the unity of divine action in revelation and reconciliation, in 'self-impartation' and 'atoning propitiation' (cf. Eph. 2:12-22)."

Returning again to what he calls my "mystical" apprehension of Revelation, he points to "the communion of the redeemed with the Redeemer and therefore in participation with God in his own Triune life. In this communion the created knower is raised up through the statements of Scripture to a knowledge of God that grasps the Trinitarian whole (Father, Son, and Holy Spirit) which has been revealed by Christ." Then he rightly says "Torrance derives this mystical apprehension (the true *theologia* of Christian knowledge) from the Greek fathers' methodology, especially Athanasius." Then, again rightly, he links this up with my use of Polanyi's "tacit knowing" in which we come to know more than we can actually tell at the time, and with what Polanyi describes as "indwelling."

He refers to my idea that Polanyi should significantly use here language found in the Fourth Gospel, where Jesus speaks of the mutual indwelling between himself and his disciples, their indwelling in his Word and his dwelling in them through the Spirit, enabling them to enter into the more intimate knowledge of his mind as the revelation of the Father, and so to be led forward into the truth. And he adds: "it is in this way that there takes shape in our minds the primary concepts which are directly and intuitively connected with the basic complex of Christian experience and which we need for scientific theological activity." That is cited from *Divine Meaning*, but he could have cited a similar point which I made in *The Christian Doctrine of God: One Being Three Persons*, where I indicate how through an exegetical indwelling in the New Testament Scriptures we take our basic steps in a doctrine of the Holy Trinity, which is also the proper way to develop a scientific account of the formulation of the doctrine of the Holy Trinity. Dr. Richardson refers here, however, to what I called "The Integration of Form in Natural and Theological Science" with reference to *Transformation and Convergence in the Frame of Knowledge*.

What interests me in what Dr. Richardson writes here is that he discerns something of the way in which I seek to develop a "scientific theology," and one in which, he writes, that what I finally seem to be after is "a *mystical realism* of reading Scripture in communion with God by the Spirit who inspired the Scripture." This is not allegorical or "eisegetical" interpretation but one "that must seek to lay bare the internal hermeneutic already embedded within the Scriptures." And so he ends his account of this way of mystical and scientific theological thinking with a section on "The Convergence of Dogmatic and Mystical Theology" in which he brings together lessons I have learned from Einstein and Clerk Maxwell, and even Kurt Gödel's famous theorem "of the impossibility of any system containing a principle of self-completion."

"In this way," Richardson points out, "the ongoing task of theology becomes the progressive clarification of understanding, the uncovering of hitherto unrecognized relations between the knowledge of God and of created reality, and most importantly, the transcendent knowledge in relation to the living, personal God himself. This, finally, affords Torrance the occasion to introduce the full extent of his thinking about theological knowledge as it is apprehended at its uppermost levels in human experience."

Then Richardson cites from my book *Reality and Scientific Theology*: "That is to say dogmatic theology may be axiomatised in a consistent and meaningful way only if at decisive points it is correlated with *mystical theology*, for it is in mystical theology that the boundary conditions of our dogmatic formalization are kept open toward the transcendent and unlimited Rationality and Freedom of the living God. Dogmatic theology of this kind is informed by open concepts that are both worthy of the nature of God and empirically relevant to the world he has made."[6]

At last Professor Richardson discovers several of my very rare references to "mystical" theology! He adds that my introduction of this relationship of mystical theology to dogmatic theology "is only surprising when we either do not see its relationship to everything else he has proposed or if we neglect to see how so much of what he has been claiming about knowledge of the divine through Jesus Christ and the Scripture already manifested this dimension." He then notes my references to what Polanyi spoke of as "the tacit dimension," which I regard with him as "the inarticulate grasp of reality . . . upon which all rational knowledge and all scientific inquiry rely."

I wonder if Professor Kurt Richardson realizes then, that I am *not* concerned at all with what textbooks on mysticism or mystical theology are concerned, and that what I am concerned to emphasize in these references to the "mystical" is much the same point made by St. Anselm when he spoke of God as infinitely greater than we can ever conceive or express. And stated otherwise, echoing Job, that there are holy moments in his knowing of him and speaking of him and worshiping him, when a theologian can only clap his hand on his mouth, for what God is or who God is, is quite inexpressible.

That is a situation when in our interpretation of God's self-revelation in the Holy Scriptures, and in our worship of him in and through the Lord Jesus Christ, we only can fall down on our knees in adoration, thanksgiving, and praise, for God is infinitely and inexpressibly more wonderful than we can ever think or grasp. Is that not what the New Testament Scriptures tell us about when we know and worship God ineffably *in the Spirit*? That is *not* what the usual text-books speak of as "mystical theology"! Let me remind him of my words in his citation from *Reality and Scientific Theology*, now putting in italics what I would have him consider: "it is in mystical theology that the *boundary conditions* of our dogmatic formalization are kept *open* toward the *transcendent and unlimited Rationality and Freedom* of the living God."[7]

I thank Professor Richardson very warmly for his perceptive, appreciative, and helpful discussion of what I have written. I wish I had gotten to know him much earlier in my life for I find in him a kindred spirit and know that I would have benefitted much from personal discussion with him.

At the end of his essay, Professor Richardson, as he has been asked, offers several reflections upon my approach to Scripture, to which I respond briefly. But is he not asking me to pass beyond the boundary not only of what is expressible but of what is quite inexpressible?

1. His first point has to do with what he calls "the nature of mystical experience," something which not everyone enjoys, but about which there are numerous mystical schools and methods of mystical reflection. But here Dr. Richardson seems to presuppose the very notion of mysticism or the mystical which I set aside. What I am

concerned with in theology is *humility before God*, not with some special or esoteric way of thinking!

2. His second point is that Scripture's inspiration could bear a more exalted role in my account. Here he seems to confuse Scripture's inspiration with some theory of inspiration, one, for example, with reference to what he calls "the Western mystical tradition," or some Eastern esteem for the sacredness of the text which goes hand in hand with Eastern approaches to mystical reading!! Again this is really to miss the intention of my thinking about theological science and seems to presuppose the kind of approach which I have to set aside!

3. His third point is that "the inspired Scripture and its disciplined exegesis must be allowed to critique or at least reinforce more than it does in Torrance's perspective. Torrance has not yet shown how this might be done." I would not dream of trying to interpret Holy Scripture under the guidance of some preconceived hermeneutical theory or method! Dr. Richardson suggests, however, that I may have helped to pave the way for a new openness in this regard. That indicates that he glimpses why I referred to "mystical theology," where our theology is and must be *open-ended* in its speech about God.

4. Dr. Richardson thinks that I should be more cautious on the use of "mystical theology" since I seem to be uncritical of the tradition. The fact is that I do not work with any so-called mystical tradition. Nor do I operate with some mystical theology, but simply endeavor or try to show that at certain crucial and decisive points where humility in thinking, or, if you like, some form of apophatic thinking, is in place.

5. This final statement that Professor Richardson makes appears to indicate that the first four points need not have been raised, as they really bypass what I have had in mind! But perhaps I should never have referred those few times, and in the last chapter of *Reality and Scientific Theology,* to "mystical thinking" or to "mystical theology." For if they have misled such a very fine and able theologian as Professor Kurt Anders Richardson, they should have, and could have, been omitted, without damage to the argument.

Elmer M. Colyer

Professor Colyer has headed his account of my scientific theological method with a citation from my book *Theological Science* (1969):

"Theology is the unique science devoted to knowledge of God, differing from other sciences by the uniqueness of its object which can be appreciated only on its own terms and within the actual situation it has created in our existence in making itself known."[8] That citation rightly heads his essay in this book, "A Scientific Theological Method," of which I approve, though there are some statements here and there where I would have written differently. Here, however, I will address myself only to several points which he has raised.

The first point concerns my notion of scientific method where I am sometimes criticized for building my theology on natural science or philosophy of science. Here let me say that, unlike most of my critics, I have been heavily influenced by early Christian theologians and thinkers of the Church like Athanasius, Cyril, and John Philoponos of Alexandria, about what they called positive or "dogmatic science" (*dogmatike episteme*), as much as I have learned from Clerk Maxwell, Albert Einstein, and Michael Polanyi in modern times.

In any rigorous scientific inquiry, they held, you seek to let the nature of the field or of the object, as it is progressively disclosed through interrogation, control how you know it, how you think about it, and how you formulate knowledge of it strictly in accordance with its nature (*kata physin*) and reality (*kat'aletheian*). That was the scientific method used by the great Alexandrian theologians, and by John Philoponos, theologian and physicist in sixth-century Alexandria. In Christian theology it yielded the theological understanding of Athanasius and Cyril about the contingent nature of the created order. Applied by Philoponos to physics, in criticism of Aristotle, it yielded his remarkable theories of light and of impetus, and relational ideas of space and time, in which he anticipated Clerk Maxwell, and in some respects even Einstein.

Perhaps my critics might study carefully the scientific method of those great theologians and scientists (and do it in Greek!), before they start trying to interpret my scientific method in accordance with their own rather positivist ideas, or accusing me of what they call "foundationalism." While I have learned my scientific method from these great Greek thinkers and theologians (and not just from people like Karl Barth), I have tried to set it out in terms which people in modern times might understand.

A scientific theology must always be determined by the unique nature of its "Object," the Lord God as he reveals himself to us. That takes place as we know him in accordance with his revealed nature, and in our worship of him. In any faithful knowing and worshiping of God as he has made himself known, the modality of the reason in the human inquirer changes in appropriate accordance with the nature of God as he becomes revealed to us. Perhaps I may invite my readers to read the address I gave in April 1992 at Princeton, about this, published in *Preaching Christ Today* (Eerdmans, 1994).

My use of the term intuition in Christian theology is basically the same as that of Einstein in science, for example, in his address on "Principles of Scientific Research," when he showed that there is no logico-causal path to the laws of nature, no logical bridge between phenomena and their theoretical principles, but only intuition resting on sympathetic understanding of experience. That was the kind of epistemic intuition or belief on which Clerk Maxwell relied, as Einstein pointed out, in making the greatest change in the axiomatic substructure of physics, and on which Einstein himself relied in the development of relativity theory. As I understand it, this relates to what Polanyi spoke of as the kind of tacit conviction reached through "indwelling." Let me express it in another way: intuition relates to an ultimate belief, like *order*, which we sense but cannot prove yet which we have to assume in all orderly scientific thinking and activity.

Nothing could be further from the truth or even more bizarre than Ronald Thiemann's rhetoric in which he claims that I use the term "intuition" "to signify the indubitability and incorrigibility of this *causally imposed knowledge*,"[9] and when he accuses me of what he calls "foundationalism"!! That would be equivalent to saying that Clerk Maxwell and Einstein were "foundationalists" operating with logico-causally derived conceptions in their understanding and development of continuous dynamic fields, which is what they explicitly rejected.

I appreciate much that Daniel Hardy has written of my realist theology and its relation to realist science, but I find one or two of his criticisms rather surprising. Let me refer, for example, to what he has written that "we might be driven to the conclusion that Torrance was too much concerned with a logical account of structures, with a 'Christ-idea' by which the full relatedness of God and mankind is established."[10] That seems to indicate that he too has been infected by Thiemann's misguided rhetoric about so-called "foundationalism." He knows my thought better than to countenance any suggestion that I would ever be concerned with a logical or causal bridge between ideas or concepts and reality in theology or in science. He holds firmly with me in the realization that there are ultimate beliefs in science, as in Christian theology, for which there are no alternatives, which are not logically or causally demonstrable, but without which there would be no real theological or scientific knowledge.

Chris Kaiser

I am thrilled with the essay by Chris Kaiser. I first met him when he came to attend a course of lectures I was giving at Yale. When he introduced himself to me he said something to the effect that I was the first theologian he had heard whom he as a scientist could really appreciate. He told me that he had studied physics at Harvard and taken a doctorate in astrophysics in Colorado, where he had become a Christian. Then he had decided to study theology at Gordon Conwell Seminary, conveniently situated near his parental home in Massachusetts. He asked me whether he could study with me in Edinburgh toward a doctorate in theology. He followed this inquiry up with a letter to which I sent him a definite "yes."

I was delighted to have him as a physicist and astrophysicist in New College, where he came the following year. There he wrote a brilliant doctoral dissertation, and then to my delight he stayed in Edinburgh for several years and taught in my department, where he assisted me also in my seminar classes in patristic texts—if I remember correctly, they were texts of Athanasius on the Holy Spirit and of Hilary on the Trinity. In Edinburgh he was a great help to me in my struggles to get to grips with natural science, not least with my grappling with relativity theory, and quantum theory in its Copenhagen and Tübingen forms.

We differed somewhat in his support for Niels Bohr and the Copenhagen form of quantum theory, for I was suspicious of the Kantian presuppositions it seemed to involve, and was more inclined to favor Einstein's more realist conception of the intelligible relations in quantum theory. I learned a great deal from Chris Kaiser not only in science where he was the master, but also in Christian theology, and the epistemological connection between theology and science with which we were both very deeply concerned.

To my chagrin we were not able to keep him in Edinburgh, but I recommended him to Western Theological Seminary in Michigan where he has given brilliant and distinguished service for many years. I could not have wished for a more thoughtful and understanding contribution to this volume of essays about my understanding of the relations between Christian theology and natural science than he has given. I am most grateful to him.

I am particularly pleased that Chris Kaiser chose to write this essay on Einstein because of my long and deep interest in his unparalleled scientific achievement and that he allowed what I understood of it to bear on my theological thinking and writing. I have hung in my study a line portrait of Einstein, given me in Princeton, looking across to the desk where I work, but I also have in my study portraits of Michael Polanyi and James Clerk Maxwell, from whom I have learned so much.

It was later in my academic life that I studied in earnest the work of James Clerk Maxwell, and was delighted to learn that Einstein had a portrait of him hanging in his study in the Institute for Advanced Study in Princeton. Clerk Maxwell was a devout evangelical Christian, an elder in Corsock Parish Church in Dumfriesshire to which he used to return from London and Cambridge, not least during the communion seasons when he visited the parishioners committed to his care as an elder of the Kirk. Einstein held that Clerk Maxwell had brought about the greatest change in the axiomatic substructure of physics, for after him scientists conceived physical reality as represented by continuous fields, not mechanically explicable.

It was when I steeped my thinking in the work of Clerk Maxwell, and his belief in a divinely established harmony between the world God has created and the human mind, that I found myself taking an even deeper interest in Einstein, and was able to grasp and appreciate rather more fully his unparalleled achievement, and its implications for our thinking out real intelligible relations in Christian theology. It is about this that Chris Kaiser has written, and in fresh ways which help me to understand more of the mystery of intelligibility in the conceptual interrelations between Christian theology and natural science.

I would like to confine my reaction to Professor Kaiser's essay to two issues.

First. I am very grateful to his explanation and support for my stand on what he calls the recovery of "non-duality," that is, in my opposition to all forms of dualism in theological, cosmological, and epistemological thinking which have infected Christian thought from its early encounter with Hellenic and gnostic forms of dualism to fresh forms of dualist thinking arising under the impact of Cartesian, Kantian, and pragmatic philosophies as well as romantic forms of religion. Forms of such a duality still pervade our thinking in philosophy, science, and religion alike, and are particularly damaging in epistemology and methodology. In science it was Clerk Maxwell who led the way in calling for *holistic* thinking and method, especially in his great work, *A Treatise on Electricity and Magnetism*, which yielded such spectacular results that have now transformed science under the genius of Einstein, the champion of realist intelligible relations and non-duality in relativity theory and epistemology.

Professor Kaiser shows that I have tried to carry that way of thinking into the epistemology and methodology of Christian theology. The idea which he has singled out for special attention is "the mystery of intelligibility," and the primordial connection between the human mind and the structures of creation, that is, to the intelligible nature of the created universe and the transcendent ground of its rational order (which Einstein spoke of as the ultimate "Why") in relation to which we organize and formulate our knowledge in science and theology alike.

Professor Kaiser rightly stresses here the point I make that there is *no logical bridge between ideas and reality*, and therefore no logical bridge between data and the concepts on which a good theory rests, no logical road to the discovery of the laws of nature. That is why the scientist, in formulating them, must rely on what Einstein referred to as "intuition," that is, an intuition arising under the constraint or impress of the rationality of the created order upon the scientist's mind. I am particularly grateful to Chris Kaiser, a scientist as well as a theologian, for the illuminating way in which he has expressed and explained this.

Second. Professor Kaiser refers to a statement of mine to the effect that the human mind is "sympathetically attuned to the intrinsic rationality of the universe," and asks whether this "tuning" (Einstein's preestablished harmony, adopted from Leibniz, and reaffirmed by Clerk Maxwell) is a matter of preadaptation, programmed into the human genotype, and whether I think of this as in some way the result of evolutionary selection of early hominids needed for the preadaptation of the human mind for probing the realms of microphysics and general relativity. I do not think of that in any evolutionary way, but I agree that some measure of *information* must come into the picture, which calls for our attention to "information theory."

Here let me refer to the utterly astonishing way in which John Philoponos in the sixth century put forward twin theories of light and impetus which anticipated Clerk Maxwell by more than a thousand years. How was that? In line with the Christian doctrine of the creation of the universe out of nothing and its contingent rational order he put forward the theory that light was created by the Word of God and endowed with its force. He then went on to develop relational conceptions of space and time which anticipated Einstein as well. That is to say, he took his basic queue from *information* derived from the Word of God. That is a startling indication of the impact of Christian theology on scientific discovery, which is what happened when Clerk Maxwell put forward his theories of light and impetus in the continuous dynamic field.

John Philoponos and James Clerk Maxwell, and indeed Einstein, realized in their different ways that there is and must be a fundamental harmony between the laws of the mind and the laws of nature, an inherent relation between how we think and how nature behaves independently of our minds. Einstein held that in physical science we "tap into the mind of God," and "think the thoughts of God after him." That is to say that *information* from beyond ourselves is needed in the understanding of the behavior of physical light and its dynamic role in the universe.

John Philoponos and Clerk Maxwell in particular point us in seeking understanding of the universe toward some *metasource* of knowledge or *metaorder* to guide our research and develop appropriate scientific theory—that is, to knowledge we cannot gain through the inquiries of natural science alone. I have in mind here what the physicist Paul Davies in his book *The Cosmic Blueprint* has spoken of as some kind of "metaplan." Where, for example, does the information content of the human genome come from? That must surely be related to the transcendent source and ultimate ground of rational order with which we are concerned in the formation of all physical laws, for which physical laws themselves cannot account—which Einstein spoke of as the supreme "Why," or the ultimate ground or justification of physical law. It does not and cannot be produced by accident or through random self-organization in natural processes, for the information is of such an intelligible complex nature that it must have an intelligent source.

There is and must be an ultimate intelligent ground, a regulative ground and controlling source of information, something over and above our genetic composition which bears upon the nature and life of every human being from the very moment of conception, from the very beginning of his/her existence in the womb of the mother. Is this not the creative source of which the Bible speaks as the Word of God by whom all things were made, and in whom was life and the light of human being? Let me emphasize: natural processes by themselves cannot explain or generate order—what is needed is an intelligible input beyond them, from the Creator.

Mark Achtemeier

I am very grateful to Mark Achtemeier for his superb essay about what I have written over the years on natural science and the

Christian faith, and for its clarity in presenting some of the major issues with which I have wrestled in a constructive and very readable way. He has been very faithful in his presentation of what I have called theological science in its relation to and difference from natural science, with shrewd attention to the deep epistemological issues involved. Again and again he has clarified and sometimes simplified what I have written, in ways for which I am deeply grateful, and from which I have learned not a little.

What a joy it would have been to have had him for several years in my department in New College, Edinburgh, along with Christopher Kaiser! We have never met, but I knew of him as the son of Professors Paul and Elizabeth Achtemeier who were fellow students with my brother David in Basel when they sat at the feet of the great Karl Barth. I want to thank him also very warmly in joining with Andrew Purves in dedicating to me their fine, timely book, entitled *Union in Christ: A Declaration for the Church.*

I am particularly pleased with the attention which Professor Achtemeier has given to the basic significance and importance of the Nicene theology in Christian thought, not least its teaching about creation and incarnation. He has discerned and explained their bearing throughout the centuries upon the thinking and teaching of the Church when its vision of the creation and its contingent rational order rejected dualist modes of thought in theological and natural science alike, and had to face up to the challenges and new insights that kept on arising from the developments of natural science.

Throughout, Professor Achtemeier has put his finger again and again on the fundamental and decisive issues which have been and still are of such paramount significance in the theology-science dialogue, and clarified them when my own account appeared somewhat rather difficult. I have in mind here the thoughtful and helpful way he has clarified the implications of Nicene theology and its cosmology for Newtonian and Einsteinian accounts of space and time, and not least his support for my "Einsteinian" insistence that there is no logical bridge between concepts and reality and therefore no logical path toward the establishment of physical law or in the development and exposition of primary theological truths.

Toward the end of his essay Professor Achtemeier raises critical questions about the way in which I have deployed the difference between a relational and a receptacle concept of space in discussing and defending the Calvinist position about the "real presence" against the Lutheran position over how one is to understand the nature of the "real presence" of Christ at the Eucharist or the Lord's Supper. I accept gratefully what he has written about this, although I would wish to stand by what I have written, while taking into account his call for a more cautious approach to this problem. It is one, however, which I have put to the test again and again in dialogue with Lutheran and Roman Catholic theologians about the nature of the "real presence."

Throughout Professor Achtemeier has given a faithful, perceptive, and supportive account of my view of the relations between theology and science, for which I thank him very warmly. There is another side to these relations, however, which I consider very important, namely the *positive* contributions which Christian theology has made to empirico-theoretical science. I have in mind here particularly James Clerk Maxwell, the devout evangelical Christian whose work I got to know later in my life, which has since made an enormous impact on my attempts to understand the relations between theology and science.

I was astonished in 1982 when I found that neither Edinburgh University where Clerk Maxwell had studied under the teaching of Sir William Hamilton, professor of metaphysics, nor the Royal Society of Edinburgh of which he was their most distinguished fellow, were doing anything very significant about commemorating Clerk Maxwell's supreme achievement in science! And so I published with the Scottish Academic Press in Edinburgh (in an independent form for the first time) his epoch-making essay, *A Dynamical Theory of the Electromagnetic Field*, presented to the Royal Society in London on 27 October 1864.

In my edition in 1982, I republished an appreciation of Clerk Maxwell by Albert Einstein, with a list of the mathematical symbols, in vector form, which Clerk Maxwell used in formulating his famous partial differential equations, through which, as Einstein claimed, Clerk Maxwell had transformed the rational structure of science. In my introduction I gave an account of the steps which Clerk Maxwell had taken in moving away from Newtonian conceptions to his epoch-making dynamical theory. He was to follow that up in due course with his two volumes entitled *A Treatise on Electricity and Magnetism*, 1873, on the foundation of which, along with Isaac Newton's *Principia Mathematica*, modern science now rests. I have referred to Clerk Maxwell both because my study of his work has deepened and transformed my understanding of the relations between Christian theology and science, and because it shows decisively how good theology has and can in very important ways influence heuristically the actual development of science.

That brings me back to the original impact of Nicene thought upon science in *positive* ways. The bearing of science on theology is not just a one-way relation, for there is a not inconsiderable cognitive relation between theological science and natural science due not least to the impact of the Christian doctrine of creation ex nihilo upon scientific understanding of the contingent rational order of the universe. Clerk Maxwell is an outstanding example of a scientist whose Christian beliefs influenced his relational concepts of space and time which he first developed under the impact of his theological and philosophical thinking in Edinburgh, and his reading of "the older divines." In Edinburgh he went to Edinburgh Academy for his schooling, after which he attended the lectures of Sir William Hamilton in the Old College who stressed the importance of *relation* (and even of "relativity"!) which Clerk Maxwell was later to carry over in his formulation of the dynamical field and relational concepts of space and time. And that in turn was eventually to influence Einstein in his Special Theory of Relativity.

Yet long before Clerk Maxwell the astonishing John Philoponos at Alexandria in the sixth century, under the impact of the Nicene theology of Athanasius and Cyril, put forward theories of impetus and light and even relational notions of space and time in his critique of Aristotelian science! When that dynamical way of thinking affected his use of basic theological terms such as nature (φύσις) and truth or reality (ἀλήθεια), he was sadly anathematized by the Aristotelian establishment in Byzantium, which had the effect of retarding the development of science for more than a thousand years. It is through studying the theology and science of John Philoponos, together with that of James Clerk Maxwell, that I have come to realize how deep the positive cognitive relation between Christian theology and natural science has been and can still be in heuristic ways.

I believe firmly that today we have reached a stage in the development of natural science at which rigorous theological science can through dialogue with natural science enable it to take heuristic steps at the very boundary between being and nonbeing where quantum theory seems to have taken it, the zero point beyond which it cannot go, but where the undeniable rationality of the universe disclosed to science will not lie down. Far from dwindling away into nothing or meaninglessness, the contingent nature of the universe demands a range of rationality beyond the limits of what can be conceptualized and explained in explicit terms in order to sustain its inner consistency and meaning. That is the crucial point to which our science has now carried us, particularly in quantum theory, where we have to do with what the great John Archibald Wheeler of Princeton has spoken of as "meaning physics" at the frontiers of knowledge. In quantum theory we penetrate to the basic constituents of matter, electrons, quarks, gluons, and bosons, where we reach the ultimate border between being and nonbeing or the very boundary of being in its creation out of nothing.

Immediately upon trying to cross that boundary through an extension of normal scientific conceptualization or extrapolation of physical law, we are utterly baffled, and yet it is on that very boundary that we are dealing with the all-important initial conditions of nature. Although at that point we have to reckon with an elusive dynamic state of affairs which cannot be subsumed under formal law, we refuse to believe that the circle of intelligibility has been broken, but commit ourselves to the search for what John Wheeler has called "the regulating principle," some "law without law," or "law beyond law," that gives order and meaning to what would otherwise appear quite lawless. Hence we find ourselves caught up in an intense struggle for the hidden meaning integrating the foundations of physical knowledge, for the rationality and objectivity of those foundations are at stake. It is surely at that crucial juncture, the search for "law without law," that Christian theology points to man (that is of course to man and woman) created in the image of God, to humanity, in Francis Bacon's words, as "the priest of creation."

That is to say, it is humanity's task under God, as scientist and theologian, to point natural science at the frontiers of knowledge, where being borders on nonbeing, to the ultimate source of *meaning*, in the Creator of the Universe himself, the Source of its rational order, whose creative Word became incarnate in space and time—in the Lord Jesus Christ. In other words, it is in the interaction of theological science and natural science that what John Wheeler called the regulating principle, law without law, or law beyond law, is to be found in the service of "meaning physics."

That is, I believe, the kind of service which theological science may under God render to natural science today. They are both concerned, and ought to be, not just with methodological relations between them, but with a significant conceptual interface between them. I believe that rigorously pursued Christian theology and natural science can contribute positively to one another, and that the reciprocal impact between them is much more profound and heuristically important than is usually realized by theologians and scientists. That is partly why I like to think of Christian theology pursued in this way not just as "theological science," but as "scientific theology."

Notes

1. David W. Torrance, *The Witness of the Jews to God* (Edinburgh: Handsel Press, 1982), viii.

2. Thomas F. Torrance, *The Christian Doctrine of God, One Being Three Persons* (Edinburgh: T&T Clark, 1996), 196.

3. Thomas F. Torrance, *God and Rationality* (London: Oxford University Press, 1971), 167.

4. Thomas F. Torrance, *Theology in Reconciliation: Essays towards Evangelical and Catholic Unity in East and West* (Grand Rapids, Mich.: Eerdmans, 1975), 104.

5. Thomas F. Torrance, *Reality and Evangelical Theology: The Realism of Christian Revelation* (Downers Grove, Ill.: InterVarsity Press, 1992), xix, 64.

6. Thomas F. Torrance, *Reality and Scientific Theology* (Edinburgh: Scottish Academic Press, 1985), 93.

7. Torrance, *Scienitific Theology*, 93.

8. Thomas F. Torrance, *Theological Science* (London: Oxford University Press, 1969), 281.

9. Ronald Thiemann, *Revelation and Theology* (Notre Dame, Ind.: University of Notre Dame Press, 1985), 40.

10. Daniel Hardy, "Thomas F. Torrance," in *The Modern Theologians: An Introduction to Christian Theology in the Twentieth Century*, ed. David Ford (Oxford: Basil Blackwell, 1989), 1:87.

Thomas F. Torrance's Major Publications

A Selected Bibliography

This selected bibliography is arranged chronologically under each category and includes almost all of Torrance's books published since 1965 and his most significant articles since 1970. The most complete bibliography of Thomas F. Torrance's publications is in Alister E. McGrath, *T. F. Torrance: An Intellectual Biography* (Edinburgh: T&T Clark, 1999), 249-96. I have also included the significant secondary literature published to date.

Books

Theology in Reconstruction. London: SCM Press, 1965. Reprint, Eugene, Oreg.: Wipf & Stock, 1997.

Space, Time, and Incarnation. London: Oxford University Press, 1969. Reprint, Edinburgh: T&T Clark, 1997.

Theological Science. London: Oxford University Press, 1969. Reprint, Edinburgh: T&T Clark, 1996.

God and Rationality. London: Oxford University Press, 1971. Reprint, Eugene, Oreg.: Wipf & Stock, 1997.

Theology in Reconciliation: Essays towards Evangelical and Catholic Unity in East and West. London: Geoffrey Chapman, 1975. Reprint, Eugene, Oreg.: Wipf & Stock, 1997.

Space, Time, and Resurrection. Edinburgh: Handsel Press, 1976.

Christian Theology and Scientific Culture. New York: Oxford University Press, 1980.

The Ground and Grammar of Theology. Charlottesville, University of Virginia Press, 1980.

Divine and Contingent Order. New York: Oxford University Press, 1981. Reprint, Edinburgh: T&T Clark, 1998.

Juridical Law and Physical Law: Toward a Realist Foundation for Human Law. Edinburgh: Scottish Academic Press, 1982.

Reality and Evangelical Theology. Philadelphia: Westminster Press, 1982.

Transformation and Convergence in the Frame of Knowledge: Explorations in the Interrelations of Scientific and Theological Enterprise. Grand Rapids, Mich.: Eerdmans, 1984.

Reality and Scientific Theology. Edinburgh: Scottish Academic Press, 1985.

The Hermeneutics of John Calvin. Edinburgh: Scottish Academic Press, 1988.

The Trinitarian Faith: The Evangelical Theology of the Ancient Catholic Church. Edinburgh: T&T Clark, 1988.

The Christian Frame of Mind: Reason, Order, and Openness in Theology and Natural Science. Colorado Springs, Colo.: Helmers & Howard, 1989. New and enlarged edition.

Karl Barth: Biblical and Evangelical Theologian. Edinburgh: T&T Clark, 1990.

The Mediation of Christ: Evangelical Theology and Scientific Culture. Edinburgh: T&T Clark, 1992. New enlarged edition.

Preaching Christ Today: The Gospel and Scientific Thinking. Grand Rapids, Mich.: Eerdmans, 1994.

Divine Meaning: Studies in Patristic Hermeneutics. Edinburgh: T&T Clark, 1995.

The Uniqueness of Divine Revelation and the Authority of the Scriptures. Edinburgh: Rutherford House, 1995.

The Christian Doctrine of God: One Being Three Persons. Edinburgh: T&T Clark, 1996.

Articles

"The Place of Word and Truth in Theological Inquiry according to St. Anselm." In *Studia medievalia et mariologica: P. Carolo Balic OFM septuagesimum explenti annum dicata*, ed. R. Zavalloni, 131-60. Rome: Editrice Antonianum, 1971.

"The Framework of Belief." In *Belief in Science and in Christian Life*, ed. Thomas F. Torrance, 1-27. Edinburgh: Handsel Press, 1980.

"The Place of Michael Polanyi in the Modern Philosophy of Science." *Ethics in Science and Medicine* 7 (1980): 57-95.

"Ultimate Beliefs and the Scientific Revolution." *Cross Currents* 30

(1980): 129-49.

"Theological Realism." In *The Philosophical Frontiers of Christian Theology: Essays Presented to D. M. MacKinnon*, ed. B. Hebblethwaite and S. Sutherland, 169-96 Cambridge: Cambridge University Press, 1982.

"The Deposit of Faith." *Scottish Journal of Theology* 36 (1983): 1-28.

"The Substance of the Faith: A Clarification of the Concept in the Church of Scotland." *Scottish Journal of Theology* 36 (1983): 327-38.

"The Historical Jesus: From the Perspective of a Theologian." In *The New Testament Age: Essays in Honor of Bo Reicke*, ed. William C. Weinrich, 2:511-26. Macon, Ga.: Mercer University Press, 1984.

"A Pilgrimage in the School of Faith—An Interview with T. F. Torrance," by John I. Hesselink. *Reformed Review* 38, no. 1 (1984): 49-64.

"Karl Barth and the Latin Heresy." *Scottish Journal of Theology* 39 (1986): 461-82.

"Karl Barth and Patristic Theology." In *Theology beyond Christendom: Essays on the Centenary of the Birth of Karl Barth*, ed. John Thomson, 215-39. Allison Park, Penn.: Pickwick Publications, 1986.

"The Legacy of Karl Barth (1886-1986)." *Scottish Journal of Theology* 39 (1986): 289-308.

"My Interaction with Karl Barth." In *How Karl Barth Changed My Mind*, ed. Donald K. McKim, 52-64. Grand Rapids, Mich: Eerdmans, 1986.

"The Reconciliation of Mind." *TSF Bulletin* 10, no. 3 (1987): 4-7.

"The Goodness and Dignity of Man in the Christian Tradition." *Modern Theology* 4 (1988): 309-22.

"Interview with Professor Thomas F. Torrance." In *Different Gospels*, edited by Dr. Andrew Walker, 42-54. London: Hodder & Stoughton, 1988.

"The Soul and Person in Theological Perspective." In *Religion, Reason and the Self: Essays in Honour of Hywel D. Lewis*, ed. Stewart R. Sutherland and T. A. Roberts, 103-18. Cardiff: University of Wales Press, 1989.

"The Christian Apprehension of God the Father." In *Speaking the Christian God: The Holy Trinity and the Challenge of Feminism*, ed. Alvin F. Kimel, Jr., 120-43. Grand Rapids, Mich.: Eerdmans, 1992.

"Incarnation and Atonement: Theosis and Henosis in the Light of Modern Scientific Rejection of Dualism." *Society of Ordained*

Scientists, no. 7, Edgware, Middlesex (spring 1992): 8-20.
"The Atonement: The Singularity of Christ and the Finality of the Cross: The Atonement and the Moral Order." In *Universalism and the Doctrine of Hell*, ed. Nigel M. de S. Cameron, 225-56. Exeter: Paternoster Press, 1992; Grand Rapids, Mich.: Baker Book House, 1993.
"Ultimate and Penultimate Beliefs in Science." In *Facets of Faith and Science,* vol. 1: *Historiography and Modes of Interaction*, ed. Jitse van der Meer, 151-76. Lanham, Md.: University Press of America; New York: Pascal Center for Advanced Studies in Faith and Science, 1996.
"Einstein and God." *Reflections* 1 (spring 1998): 2-15.

Secondary Works: A Selection

Books

E. L. Mascall. *Theology and the Gospel of Christ*. London: SPCK, 1977, 46-50.
Ronald F. Thiemann. *Revelation and Theology: The Gospel as Narrated Promise.* Notre Dame, Ind.: University of Notre Dame Press, 1985, 32-43.
Christian D. Kettler. *The Vicarious Humanity of Christ and the Reality of Salvation*. New York: University Press of America, 1991, 121-55.
Alan G. Marley. *T. F. Torrance: The Rejection of Dualism*. Edinburgh: Handsel Press, 1992.
Colin Weightman. *Theology in a Polanyian Universe: The Theology of Thomas Torrance*. New York: Peter Lang, 1994.
Roland Spjuth. *Creation, Contingency, and Divine Presence in the Theologies of Thomas F. Torrance and Eberhard Jungel*. In Studia Theologica Lundensia Series. Lund, Sweden: Lund University Press, 1995.
John Douglas Morrison. *Knowledge of the Self-Revealing God in the Thought of Thomas Forsyth Torrance*, vol. 2, *Issues in Systematic Theology*. New York: Peter Lang, 1997.
Robert K. Martin. *The Incarnate Ground of Christian Faith: Toward a Christian Theological Epistemology for the Educational Ministry of the Church*. Lanham, Md.: University Press of America, 1998.
Alister E. McGrath. *T. F. Torrance: An Intellectual Biography*. Edinburgh: T&T Clark, 1999.

Elmer M. Colyer. *How to Read T. F. Torrance: Understanding His Trinitarian and Scientific Theology*. Downers Grove, Ill.: InterVarsity Press, 2001.

———*The Nature of Doctrine in T. F. Torrance's Theology*. Eugene, Oreg.: Wipf & Stock, 2001.

Articles

Thomas A. Langford. "T. F. Torrance's Theological Science: A Reaction." *Scottish Journal of Theology* 25 (1972): 155-70.

Bryan J. Gray. "Towards Better Ways of Reading the Bible." *Scottish Journal of Theology* 33, no. 4 (1980): 301-15.

Robert J. Palma. "Thomas F. Torrance's Reformed Theology." *Reformed Review* 38, no. 1 (August 1984): 2-46.

Frank D. Schubert. "Thomas F. Torrance: The Case for a Theological Science." *Encounter* 45, no. 2 (spring 1984): 123-37.

Edward O. De Barry. "Review Article." *Saint Luke's Journal of Theology* 27, no. 3 (1984): 209-13.

Frederick W. Norris. "Mathematics, Physics, and Religion: A Need for Candor and Rigor." *Scottish Journal of Theology* 37, no. 4 (1984): 457-70.

Walter R. Thorson. "Scientific Objectivity and the Listening Attitude." In *Objective Knowledge: A Christian Perspective*, ed. Paul Helm, 59-83. Leicester, England: InterVarsity Press, 1987.

Walter Jim Neidhardt. "Thomas F. Torrance's Integration of Judeo-Christian Theology and Natural Science: Some Key Themes." *Perspectives on Science and Christian Faith* 41, no. 2 (1989): 87-98.

Daniel W. Hardy. "Thomas F. Torrance." In *The Modern Theologians: An Introduction*, ed. David Ford, 1:71-91. Oxford: Basil Blackwell, 1989.

C. Baxter Kruger. "The Doctrine of the Knowledge of God in the Theology of T. F. Torrance: Sharing in the Son's Communion with the Father in the Spirit." *Scottish Journal of Theology* 43, no. 3 (1990): 366-89.

Richard A. Muller. "The Barth Legacy: New Athanasius or Origen Redivivus? A Response to T. F. Torrance." *Thomist* 54 (1990): 673-704.

David F. Siemens, Jr. "Two Problems with Torrance (reply to W. J. Neidhardt. *Perspectives on Science and Christian Faith* 43, no.

1 (1991): 112-13.

Kang Phee Seng. "The Epistemological Significance of *Homoousion* in the Theology of Thomas F. Torrance." *Scottish Journal of Theology* 45, no. 3 (1992): 341-66.

Stephen D. Wigley. "Karl Barth on St. Anselm: The Influence of Anselm's Theological Scheme on T. F. Torrance and Eberhard Jungel." *Scottish Journal of Theology* 46, no. 1 (1993): 79-97.

P. Mark Achtemeier, "The Truth of Tradition: Critical Realism in the Thought of Alasdair MacIntyre and T. F. Torrance." *Scottish Journal of Theology* 47, no. 3 (1996): 355-74.

John D. Morrison. "Thomas Forsyth Torrance's Critique of Evangelical (Protestant) Orthodoxy." *Evangelical Quarterly* 67, no. 1 (1995): 53-69.

Elmer M. Colyer. "Thomas F. Torrance." In *A New Handbook of Christian Theologians*, ed. Donald W. Musser and Joseph L. Price, 460-68. Nashville, Tenn.: Abingdon Press, 1996.

John D. Morrison. "Heidegger, Correspondence, Truth, and the Realist Theology of T. F. Torrance." *Evangelical Quarterly* 69 (1997): 139-55.

Paul D. Molnar. "God's Self-Communication in Christ: A Comparison of Thomas F. Torrance and Karl Rahner." *Scottish Journal of Theology* 50, no. 3 (1997): 288-320.

Name Index

Subject Index

About the Contributors

P. Mark Achtemeier is associate professor of systematic theology at the University of Dubuque Theological Seminary.

Ray S. Anderson is professor of theology and ministry at Fuller Theological Seminary.

Elmer M. Colyer is professor of historical theology and Stanley Professor of Wesley Studies at the University of Dubuque Theological Seminary.

Gary W. Deddo is associate editor at InterVarsity Press.

Colin Gunton is professor of Christian doctrine at King's College, University of London.

Alasdair Heron is professor of Reformed theology at the University of Erlangen-Nuremberg.

George Hunsinger is Hazel Thompson McCord Professor of Systematic Theology at Princeton Theological Seminary.

Christopher B. Kaiser is professor of historical and systematic theology at Western Theological Seminary.

Andrew Purves is Hugh Thomson Kerr Professor of Pastoral Theology at Pittsburgh Theological Seminary.

Kurt Anders Richardson is associate professor of theology and ethics at Gordon-Conwell Theological Seminary.

David W. Torrance is a retired minister of the Church of Scotland.

Thomas F. Torrance is professor emeritus of Christian dogmatics at the University of Edinburgh.